SALVAGE WORK

Salvage Work

U.S. and Caribbean Literatures
amid the Debris of Legal Personhood

ANGELA NAIMOU

Fordham University Press

NEW YORK   2015

Fordham University Press has no responsibility for the persistence or accuracy of URLs for external or third-party Internet websites referred to in this publication and does not guarantee that any content on such websites is, or will remain, accurate or appropriate.

Fordham University Press also publishes its books in a variety of electronic formats. Some content that appears in print may not be available in electronic books.

Visit us online at www.fordhampress.com

Library of Congress Cataloging-in-Publication Data

Naimou, Angela.
  Salvage Work : U.S. and Caribbean Literatures amid the Debris of Legal Personhood / Angela Naimou. — First edition.
     pages cm
  Includes bibliographical references and index.
  ISBN 978-0-8232-6476-6 (hardback)
  1. American literature—History and criticism. 2. Caribbean literature—History and criticism. 3. Self in literature. 4. Law and literature. 5. Citizenship in literature. 6. Human rights in literature. 7. Juristic persons—Moral and ethical aspects. I. Title.
PS169.S425N35 2015
810.9'353—dc23

2014045374

Printed in the United States of America

17 16 15   5 4 3 2 1

First edition

A book in the American Literatures Initiative (ALI), a collaborative publishing project of NYU Press, Fordham University Press, Rutgers University Press, Temple University Press, and the University of Virginia Press. The Initiative is supported by The Andrew W. Mellon Foundation. For more information, please visit www.americanliteratures.org.

To my families, and in memory of my grandmother,
Lucy Katrina Meram

Contents

Acknowledgments   ix

Introduction: Contemporary Literature and the Legal Person   1

PART ONE   **Legal Debris**

1   The Free, the Slave, and the Disappeared: States and Sites
of Exceptional Personhood in Francisco Goldman's
The Ordinary Seaman   47

2   Sugar's Legacies: Romance, Revolution, and Wageless Life
in the Fiction of Edwidge Danticat and Rosario Ferré   92

PART TWO   **Salvage Aesthetics**

3   Fugitive Personhood: Reimagining Sanctuary in Gayl Jones's
Song for Anninho and *Mosquito*   141

4   Masking Fanon   183

Epilogue: The Ends of Legal Personhood   205

Notes   219

Works Cited   261

Index   285

Acknowledgments

This project began as a question about statelessness. With the launching of the global war on terror, the invasions of Afghanistan and Iraq, and the politics of migration and surveillance of Southeast Asian and Middle Eastern communities (including my own), I wanted to make sense of how old and newly invented legal identities could be assigned to authorize, propel, redirect, delimit, and disallow conditions of statelessness. That these identities were highly conventional legal fictions was clear to me in the range of legal categories that defined my family and other Iraqi Americans as well as in the asylum claims I helped my father complete for friends and relatives. It was in reading literary fiction, which grapples in imaginative and provocative ways with these legal fictions, that personhood more fully emerged for me as a complex and crucial product of the law's defining powers: legal personhood shaped how people were allowed to live their lives and how they may imagine themselves as persons.

I am grateful to have had so many friends and colleagues whose conversations and readings are registered in this book. Cornell University's vibrant intellectual life shaped my thinking in too many ways to track. Lisa Patti, Cristina Dahl, and Ana Rojas generously discussed my research, as did the members of a writing group organized by Mary Pat Brady. Meghan Freeman's friendship and her astute comments at various stages of this project have been energizing and nourishing. I learned a lot from all of my teachers there, most especially Mary Pat Brady, Molly Hite, Kate McCullough, Natalie Melas, Nicole Waligora-Davis, Hortense Spillers, and Paul Sawyer. I am also grateful for the Cornell Forum for

Justice and Peace and the fellow students and professors who participated in it.

When Lee Morrissey, as chair of the English Department at Clemson University, introduced me to the campus by recounting its history as the site of three former slave plantations, I could not have known how much I would love my job. This book has been much improved by the collegiality, friendship, and critical engagement of students and colleagues at Clemson. Thanks to graduate students Zachary Snow for early research assistance, Sumood Almaowashi for conversation, and Chloe Whitaker for crucial assistance in preparing the manuscript for publication. This project developed in response to the intellectual energies of my Clemson colleagues, including Susanna Ashton, Michael LeMahieu, Brian McGrath, Lee Morrissey, and Rhondda Thomas. In addition to the readers in the junior faculty writing group and to the many colleagues in the department who make it such a terrific place to work, a special thanks is due to colleagues who shared invaluable comments on parts of the manuscript: Michael LeMahieu, Dominic Mastroianni, Elizabeth Rivlin, and Brian McGrath. Cameron Bushnell and Kimberly Manganelli read sections more than once and in the best spirit of academic generosity and friendship. A very big thanks to young Alice Laura Rivlin LeMahieu, who rescued me from a printing disaster just as the manuscript was about to be sent off (and I was about to go into labor).

A research fellowship at Wesleyan University's Center for the Humanities in Spring 2012 on affect and civic life showed me what is possible when colleagues from across the humanities and social sciences share work, conversation, and meals. I'm especially grateful for Jill Morawski's leadership and discussions with J. Kēhaulani Kauanui. A graduate fellowship in 2005–6 at the Society for Humanities at Cornell on the theme of culture and conflict, under the direction of Brett DeBary, supported the start of this project; thanks to all the participants for their work and comments. An Idol-South Award from Clemson's English department in 2012 funded my travel to the Howard Gotlieb special collection on Gayl Jones at Boston University. A version of chapter 4 was originally published in a special issue on Human Rights and Cultural Forms in *College Literature*, guest edited by Ali Moore, Elizabeth Swanson Goldberg, and Greg Mullins. That chapter was significantly improved by their comments and by feedback from an anonymous reviewer. A portion of chapter 2 was published in *Callaloo*.

I am indebted to the two anonymous readers of this manuscript for their incisive, generous, and insightful comments and suggestions: they, along with the Fordham University Press Editorial Board, helped me shape the arc of the book and sharpen its engagements. It was the late Helen Tartar's editorial vision that encouraged me, as it did so many other—and better—academics, to be a part of a broader conversation about art, ethics, and theory. It is a measure of Tom Lay's editorial gifts that he continues working, with grace and insightfulness, to bring this and other books into the world. Thanks to Yisa Fermin at Creative Time and photographer Jason Wyche for providing cover art from Kara Walker's *A Subtlety*, 2014. Thanks to Tim Roberts and the copy editor, Sheila Berg, for a smooth production process.

I am grateful to my family, the stories they shared and the ones they preferred to leave unsaid. To my mother and father: a world of love and thanks. To my sister and brothers and to my dear nephews: my unabiding love. To my grandmothers and extended families: my gratitude for having grown up with you. David Sweeney Coombs has been my best and most discerning reader, enriching this book and lightening my burdens. Without his humor, generosity, and love, so much more than this book would not have been possible. To Davey Naimou Coombs: you show me every day that the world is wondrous, full of life and love and delight. Nothing could mean more to me than the time we have together.

Introduction: Contemporary Literature and the Legal Person

The husk of skin first becomes an imaginary essence. It stands in for the racial substance of inferiority; and then the imagined quality, the metaphysical state, becomes the unchangeable legal status.
—COLIN DAYAN, *THE LAW IS A WHITE DOG*

I am unsure if it is possible to salvage an existence from a handful of words: the supposed murder of a negro girl.
—SAIDIYA HARTMAN, *LOSE YOUR MOTHER*

Ruins! Everything's just in ruins! And I couldn't just produce ruins.
—KARA WALKER, ART21 EXCLUSIVE

"Haunted Atlantic," Narrative Failure

To understand contemporary literary responses to global capitalism and the forms of legal personhood it has generated in the Americas, one must look to the Atlantic and to the persons it has wrought. There, working slowly over centuries and across vast oceanic and sovereign spaces, the spirits of law held millions of humans flickering between being persons and being money. This unstable transformation of human beings into legal slaves depended upon the power of law to create its own object of recognition—the legal fiction of the person—as an individual entity entitled to legal rights and duties.[1] Law transformed its invented person into many kinds of persons, into proliferating hierarchies of legal personalities inscribed in slave, penal, maritime, colonial, and civil law. Throughout the Americas, law ascribed racial meaning to its persons. It seized hold of philosophies that debated the presumed boundaries between person, thing, animal, and human self only to reinforce those boundaries and invent new ones.[2] Taxonomies proliferated along the axes of presumed rationality and autonomy, and the legal fiction of personhood ascribed the animate and inanimate to various conditions of enslavement and liberty, dependence and self-possession, legal death and civic life. Persons are invented by law through a power "both legal and magical," as Colin Dayan demonstrates in her study of how persons are made or unmade by court decisions and legislative acts that arise from reason as much as from ritual and irrationality, turning human into slave, ghost into person, or the biologically alive into the legally dead.[3] The legal racial slave is one such invention. As an unstable category that transforms self into "both self and property," the legal racial slave is a figure disavowed in contemporary jurisprudence and the perpetual subject of uncertain recovery and loss in the archive of Atlantic slavery.[4] Flickering between absence and presence, the figure of the legal racial slave both haunts the archives of slavery and materializes as the debris of legal personhood in twenty-first-century life.

The archive of Atlantic slavery has emerged in recent decades as a site for thinking about the limits of recuperating this figure of the legal racial slave through historical and literary narrative. As Stephen Best notes, "a logic and ethic of recovery" has shaped written histories of slavery since at least the 1970s, when historians scoured the archive for primary sources left by slaves and former slaves.[5] By contrast, the more recent "archival turn" in thinking about Atlantic slavery has been organized around the loss of faith in the adequacy of any such project. The value of the archive becomes its ability to signify the impossibility of recovery. Drawn from conceptions of the archive by Michel Foucault and Jacques Derrida, along with psychoanalytic theories of trauma and deferred action, recent studies turn the archive of slavery into its negative image: it becomes "a space of absence," a repository of silences, or a ghostlike flickering between erasure and inscription.[6] To the extent that the archive is a record of the enslaved, it is a record of the violent erasure of its own contents.

Such conceptions of the archive inform an ethic and logic that aim not to recover the stories of the dead so much as to dwell upon their discursive disappearance in archives of loss, economies of theft, sites of haunting, and laws of false equivalence. Saidiya Hartman's essay "Venus in Two Acts" (2008) encapsulates the dilemma of this archival turn by reflecting on a story she did not or could not tell in a memoir published that same year.[7] The story is that of a slave girl called Venus by the crew on board the slaver *Recovery*, whose only record of existence comes from her brief mention in two 1792 indictments of the ship's captain for her murder and for the malicious torture and murder of another female slave. Recognizing this legal archive as "inseparable from the play of power that murdered Venus and her shipmate and exonerated the captain,"

Hartman writes of the impossibility of bringing the girl to narrative life: "The necessity of recounting Venus's death is overshadowed by the inevitable failure of any attempt to represent her."[8] She cannot find a narrative mode—be it "tragedies," "romances," "shrieks that find their way into speech and song"—fit to the task of representing Venus outside the legal personality that incapacitates her representation in court.[9] This failure is inevitable but potentially productive: "The history of black counter-historical projects is one of failure," Hartman suggests, "precisely because these accounts have never been able to install themselves as history, but rather are insurgent, disruptive narratives that are marginalized and derailed before they ever gain a footing."[10] Ultimately, the story of Venus can only be told as one of these narratives, paradoxically "insurgent" and "disruptive" in the performance of its own failure to represent its subject. It is a failure that presents itself as critique of conventional historiography and as spectral eruption of eighteenth-century slave dead in twenty-first-century life.

Archival absence generates these counterhistories, and Hartman's relation to them, as "personal." They are personal both in the power of the legal slave past to engender ongoing conditions of African American life and in "the pain experienced in [her] encounter with the scraps of the archives"—in her relation to the archive as a weapon wielded against her sense of self and in the histories that mark her bodily person as raced and sexed by the law.[11] What can such stories of slave commodification and its afterlives tell us beyond the pain of loss created by encounters with the archive of slavery? What can they do but "dramatize the production of nothing—empty rooms, and silence, and lives reduced to waste"?[12] Hartman figures the archive as so much textual scrap, not to stitch the scraps together, but to let them hang as tattered threads to frame the space and sound and human value of nothing. Or, if the metaphor of scraps evokes the archive as the rich man's table, then its scraps do not promise nourishment so much as guarantee the pain of its endless deferral: "the loss of stories sharpens the hunger for them."[13]

Hartman's narrative failure surfaces most explicitly in encounters with the drowned captives who enter the legal archive only as conundrums for the law back on land. Captives who did not survive the ocean crossing become especially provocative figures for imagining the extralegal personalities of the enslaved—for speculating on the thoughts of the captive who is weighted with chains and thrown into the sea alive, or who jumps overboard, or who refuses food and is diagnosed with melancholy, or who openly revolts, or who is dumped (once the slave trade is legally abolished by the British in 1807) so that a ship would not be

discovered with its illicit cargo. To imagine the psychic life of these captives is to reflect not merely on archival absence but also on the power
of legal personhood to fracture or submerge the psychic life of human
beings. Legal personhood also generates new cultural forms of relation
through its power to fracture and submerge human life, as elaborated in
Édouard Glissant's theory of the poetics of relation and Kamau Brathwaite's assertion that, in Caribbean cultures, "the unity is submarine." In
the paradigm of the haunted Atlantic, such unity lies not only in ocean
currents, seafloor tectonics, and the drifting remains of the sea dead but
also in the instability of circum-Atlantic forms of legal personhood that
produced such slave deaths at sea and that continue to propel the under-
currents of contemporary life.[14]

Perhaps no other case dramatized the absence generated by the insta-
bilities of legal slave personhood more publicly than that of the *Zong*.
Informing recent encounters with the archive of the Atlantic slave trade,
including Hartman's own, the *Zong* mass killings were widely publicized
in England through court trials and took place roughly a decade before
the two captive girls would be killed on board the *Recovery*. In 1781, after
several months of navigational errors, missightings, and leaking water
barrels threatened food and water supplies for the long voyage from the
slave fort of Anomabu to Jamaica, the captain of the slave ship *Zong* is
said to have ordered, on three separate occasions, a total of between 132
and 150 slaves to be collected on deck. Alive, chained, and begging to
stay on board despite the certain prospect of dying from dehydration
and starvation, the slaves were dumped into the "dark waters west of
Jamaica."[15] Those killed at sea became the contested subjects not of murder but of a maritime insurance policy. When the group of Liverpool
merchants (Gregson) who shared ownership of the ship and its cargo
filed an insurance claim for the value of lost cargo, the policy underwriter
(Gilbert) refused the claim.[16] The Gregson group sued the underwriter in
court and won, prompting the underwriter to appeal for a retrial hearing, *Gregson v. Gilbert*, in 1783.

What to British abolitionists should have been a legal indictment
for the murder of the unnamed Africans killed at sea was to the owners a legitimate insurance claim and to the insurance underwriter a
fraudulent one.[17] The British courts framed the case as an argument over
whether the manner of the slave killings fell under the insurance policy
as a recoverable loss: not a murder charge, but insurance fraud.[18] Yet the
distinction between murder and insured loss of property turned out to
be an unsettled question for both the defense and the plaintiff. While
the owners' legal team succeeded in getting Chief Justice Lord Mansfield

to introduce the case narrowly as an action on insurance policy, the lawyers for the underwriter took the abolitionist Granville Sharp's cues and defined the case more broadly as an insurance fraud perpetrated by the more atrocious crime of mass killing—"a Crime of the Deepest and blackest Dye" that, when determined by the court to fall legally within an insurance policy, "shocks Humanity." "Were the compensation to stand," the legal team concluded, "it would be such an intent of Fraud and Oppression upon those Persons least capable of Protection."[19] In its display of righteous indignation at the Africans' legally incapacitated personhood, the underwriter's legal team figures the captives as objects of exchange and endless substitution: a ruling for compensating the owners would not be an unjust financial loss to the underwriter but "a Fraud and Oppression" on the Africans as deserving subjects of human rights, a class of persons stripped of rights and in need of protection by the very law that structures their insurability as cargo in the first place.

Whereas the captives' legal status as property shadows the insurers' attempts to transform them into murder victims, their legal status as persons haunts the case built by the owners' legal team. To convince the court that the *Zong*'s mass killings were a necessary result of "perils of the seas" and thus a legitimate insurance claim, the owners' legal team had to redefine "peril" beyond its usual scope of exceptionally rough seas, pirate attack, or slave revolt to allow for the captain and crew's acts of admitted negligence and error. "In an indictment for murder," the team for the owners argues, "it is not necessary to prove each particular circumstance. Here it sufficiently appears that the loss was primarily caused by the perils of the seas."[20] The legal team opposed to a retrial thus invokes the one term—"murder"—that they had strained to avoid by turning to analogy, which establishes a structural similarity about the sufficiency of evidence. But the proximity of the words referencing unforeseeable risk and murder undermines the rhetorical effort to distance them by analogy. The link between maritime insurance and murder is made and disavowed: the flickering between money and person haunts every word.

Gregson v. Gilbert shows how maritime insurance law enables contradictory forms of loss that reveal enduring bonds between finance capital and the legal person. The fictions of capital and personhood are entwined within these competing meanings of "loss": the ship's loss of provisions at sea; the loss of cargo that was either covered by the underwriter or not; the loss of Africans lawfully killed, not murdered; the loss of their names; and the loss of any knowledge of their story except through the records and testimony of those in the business of trading and insuring slaves. The *Zong*'s logbook was lost or destroyed before the case ever came to court, a loss supplemented (or magnified) by affidavits, court transcripts, and commentaries by the parties involved and by black and white British abolitionists.[21] These losses return us to the questions of the archive.

The slave ship, the floor of the Atlantic, the slave market, the colony, and the plantation: in writings on the Black Atlantic, these sites become recurring metonyms of exceptional forms of loss generated by the law's incomplete denial of the enslaved as full "natural persons," or human beings. These sites—what Salamishah Tillet evocatively calls the "sites of slavery" and Achille Mbembe describes as "the repressed topographies of cruelty"—produce a loss that generates and legalizes the others: the log-books of captives with no names but made equivalent to an exact finan-cial value, victims of killings not counted as murdered, narratives they never wrote, testimony they would never be called upon to give.[22] By now it is a commonplace to say that the history of legal racial slavery belies the promise of liberal political philosophy and challenges its premise of abstract legal personhood as the sign of formal equality for every person under the law. After all, the captive and enslaved were recognized and included in the law as human and as persons of a certain kind, as part of the taxonomies (shifting, unstable, and incoherent though they are) that construct and order the meanings of personhood.

Absences in the legal archive—the names, testimonies, bodies, vic-tims, and survivors that comprise its obliterated core—emerge, para-doxically, as the presence of law's defining powers over the person. As Black Atlantic and African American scholarship shows us, it is not the absence of law but rather its presence as a productive force that invents forms of legal injury and categories of degraded legal person-hood such as the legal slave. Legal personhood is always there—in the logbooks and ledgers, at the plantations, on board the ship, or along the ocean floor, in an abyss that makes "one vast beginning, but a beginning whose time is marked" by "these balls and chains gone green."[23] Legal personhood is always there and yet, like the par-ticular category "legal slave," it is the outline of a subject that cannot be stabilized, that does not cohere, that is made up of heterogeneous fragments of juridical thought, case law, legislation, stories, and the particularity of scenes in which the slave must be named, its body identified and made to inhabit the law.

The archival turn in studies of Atlantic slavery highlights the absences that official national histories both depend upon and conceal, as part of the "forgetting" Ernst Renan argued was necessary to cultivate a shared national memory out of an originary brutality.[24] It is important work that nonetheless prompts us to ask, with Best, "What are the risks of conceptualizing the archive of slavery as a space of absence and of imagining slave culture as always already lost?"[25] When the archive is presumed to hold only the expressive traces of absence that evoke but cannot represent the devalued, nonfunctional, lost, dead, or degraded—when the archive of Atlantic slavery illuminates only what cannot exist outside of it as the repository of death, unfathomable depth, and negation—the critic gets caught in what Best calls a double bind. Under this "double bind," "critical truths of the slave past are assumed to be hidden in unalloyed traces of it (preferably those left by the slaves themselves)," even as "the project of recovering those traces involves us in the pursuit of degraded fragments in an impoverished archive."[26] Fred Moten makes a similar point in his response to the Afro-pessimist embrace of blackness as a position of noncommunicability and mode of nothingness when he insists "that Afro-pessimism and black optimism are not but nothing other than one another."[27] Redirecting Best's question from one of historiography and the visual archive to one of contemporary literature and the law, this book considers the risks and possibilities in conceptualizing the archive of circum-Atlantic slavery as a productive site of ruin for the contemporary U.S. and Caribbean aesthetic imagination.

The sites, legacies, and debris of legal racial slavery remain in the twenty-first century. *Salvage Work* draws from and responds to scholarship on representations of slavery in twentieth- and twenty-first-century literature and art.[28] Attentive to particular historical contexts while moving across disciplinary lines and state borders, this book also reevaluates the significance of the legal racial slave figure for contemporary studies of human rights; citizenship; labor, migration, and refugee policies; postcoloniality; and decolonial thought. The category of the legal slave reveals the very system of legal personhood to be among the hemisphere's "imperial debris," what Ann Laura Stoler describes in another context as "*the uneven temporal sedimentations* in which imperial formations leave their marks."[29] As the imperial formations of legal personhood shape the "psychic and material space in which people live," they also shape the terms and logic of the law that defines those very people as such.[30] The category of the legal racial slave emerges as imperial and postimperial, national debris, a fractured legal identity, scattered and not always apparent, but shaping the spaces in which the legal person dwells.

Salvage Work contends that the legal racial slave emerges as a category of personhood in the Americas whose fragments, while degraded, participate in shaping the conditions of contemporary life. Such debris continues in its particular national and historical contexts to do the work of law—to establish, as Caleb Smith puts it, a "set of possible selves."[31] The book brings into view the legal debris of circum-Atlantic slavery, debris that gets reworked into new figurations across state powers and within particular legal identities of race, gender, labor, and nationality. Moving across literary and legal histories of the Americas, *Salvage Work* explores how the legal racial slave animates the literary imagination of personhood even when representations of slavery or figurations of blackness do not seem to be the primary subject matter. A core argument of this book is that the legal personality of the slave finds its extraordinarily varied afterlives in contemporary legal identities no longer explicitly defined by race and in literary texts that may not qualify as neo–slave narratives or as historical fictions concerned with depicting a slave past. The chapters that follow explore literary texts to track the links between the legal slave and other legal identities that would appear to be unrelated.

Precisely because the figure of the legal racial slave does not appear prominently at the level of character or genre, it is the most important for elucidating the apparently disparate textual, cultural, and racial dynamics at work across literary storyworlds depicting late twentieth- and early twenty-first-century life. Appearing as a haunting figure rather than an acting character, the legal slave becomes an assemblage of legal fragments that work their own modes of "slow violence" on the storyworld and on narrative form.[32] The literary texts explored in this book, for instance, rework the formal and generic conventions that shape notions of personhood and that have become hallmarks of the immigrant novel (chapter 1), the romance genre of anticolonial narratives (chapter 2), the narrative trope of the "talking book" (chapter 3), and the bildungsroman (chapter 4).[33]

Salvage Work explores literary texts that imaginatively track the debris of legal personhood as it gets disassembled and assembled by law into a variety of masks, and as those masks are fitted on their subjects— whether like a protective skin or an instrument of torture, or, true to the history of legal personhood, something that proves more difficult to define upon closer scrutiny. Such literary texts develop an aesthetics of salvage that reckon with the law's defining powers over personhood in the Americas and the often-spectral afterlives of legal cultures. This debris of legal personhood may be found amid the physical debris of collapsed economies and in recent theories on the economic and juridical status of human lives as wasted, disposable, bare, or dead in law.

Where there is ruin, there has always been its salvaging. This book elaborates a critical aesthetic practice and a mode of reading that begins by declaring legal personhood in ruins. Highlighting the interplay between ruination and the literary and social imagination, Stoler observes, "Stories congeal around imperial debris, as do critiques. So do disqualified knowledge and subjugated histories decoupled from the processes of which they were a part."[34] Salvage is neither a full nor a failed recuperation; it is not a miracle of reanimation or resurrection; it is not part of the economy of recycling. It is not an inherently liberatory act and may be an exploitative one, as Jeannine DeLombard and Nicole Waligora-Davis show in their readings of the legal slippage between refugees, slaves, pirates, and salvors in Herman Melville's *Benito Cereno*.[35] Legal, archaeological, corporate, scientific, industrial, and financial modes of salvage may depend on and produce forms of political and social violence just as easily as have an ethical or ameliorative aim. In contrast, the aesthetics of salvage examined in this book reflect a critical and creative practice that animates every encounter with the ruined, junked, and trashed: What is to be done with it? What is being valued, what is being purposed, and who is at work?[36] They are questions that may quite literally delimit the condition of artistic possibility, as the title to Kara Walker's massive 2014 site-specific sculptural art installation in Brooklyn, New York, makes clear:

> At the behest of Creative Time Kara E. Walker has confected: A Subtlety, or the Marvelous Sugar Baby, an Homage to the unpaid and overworked Artisans who have refined our Sweet tastes from the cane fields to the Kitchens of the New World on the Occasion of the demolition of the Domino Sugar Refining Plant.[37]

A temporary public art project commissioned in the shadow of the site's destruction as part of the Brooklyn waterfront's residential and commercial development, Walker's *A Subtlety* is paradoxically authorized, enabled, and constrained by the neoliberal time it also counters. Its conditions of possibility sit uneasily with its critical commentary on the racist economic and legal regimes that have powered the sugarcane industry in the Americas for centuries (and that continue to bind the lives of Haitian cane cutters at the San Pedro de Macorís *bateys* in the Dominican Republic and inmates at Louisiana's Angola State Penitentiary in the United States). The salvage aesthetics of *A Subtlety*, alongside the narrative fiction of Edwidge Danticat and Rosario Ferré, are explored further in chapter 2 as feminist responses to the use of romance as a mode for representing anticolonial revolution and sugar's other legacies. While the contemporary salvage aesthetics with which this book is concerned are quite varied and actively work against a singular, rigid aesthetic template, they share with Walker's *A Subtley* an attunement to the unresolvable tensions and ethical complexity at the core of any practice that identifies what has been junked—or, in the case of past lives, what has been left unburied—and seeks to repurpose, redirect, and revalue it anew.[38] To invoke the language of haunting, salvage aesthetics stages the "active yet unseen" presence of the past and, as Jenny Sharpe says of Afro-Caribbean fiction, "makes the ghosts of slavery speak."[39] Through close, contextual readings, *Salvage Work* shows how a salvage aesthetics both calls into question and refashions the objects and subjects of history, creating literary and visual assemblages of historical fragments figuratively pulled from the wreck of the present. The book explores what it means to salvage from a "shipwreck of fragments" when those fragments are imagined specifically as the wreckage of legal personhood.[40]

Refashioning the objects of legal history into visually experimental poetry, M. NourbeSe Philip's *Zong!* (2008) creates its particular salvage aesthetics in response to the *Zong* case and in its performative desire to give voice to the ghosts of slavery. Published the same year as Hartman's essay and memoir, *Zong!* draws from the archival turn in studies of Atlantic slavery in its use of *Gregson v. Gilbert* as a "word store" for the poems, which confound the meaning and rhetoric of rationality in the case. Letters float and drift; multiple languages are formed out of the English text as it gets pulled asunder and pulled apart visually on the page. *Zong!* is a brilliant eulogy shorn of eloquence; a refusal to let the dead speak except through those broken pieces of language pulled and reworked from the same document that testifies to their silencing. In an essay that follows the poetry, Philip recounts her shifting relation to the legal case of the *Zong* as she works to establish the poetics that structure poetry made from the words, letters, and "imperfect anagrams" found in the legal report.[41] She writes, "I come—albeit slowly—to the understanding that *Zong!* is hauntological; it is a work of haunting, a wake of sorts, where the spectres of the undead make themselves present." The essay stages her own struggle to explain her relation as lawyer-turned-poet to the case as legal text: she imagines herself as both "censor" and "conjurer," like the law in its purpose to "proscribe and prescribe," to decide "what is or is not," and to create, assign, and destroy categories of legal personhood.[42] Philip imagines herself as a thief or smuggler, a fugitive breaking and entering into the legal text, and as a medium for an ancestral persona, whom she calls Setaey Adamu Boateng. As a poetic medium, Philip's voice sounds out the voices, against the conventions of narrative, of the now ancestral African dead—those who survived to be sold and those killed, all of whom were denied a voice at sea and in court.

The poetics of *Zong!* is a poetics of salvage: it is the work of revaluing and repurposing the legal text that Philip undertakes in this encounter with the law. Where Hartman implies that "salvage" is interchangeable with "resurrection" and "salvation" (with which it shares the meaning of "saving"), salvage requires the acceptance and incorporation of existing loss, ruin, and injury into the fragments that are nonetheless generative of something more than absence. But the uncertainty in the potential to save what cannot be wholly recovered—the feeling that Hartman is "unsure if it is possible to salvage," as quoted in the epigraph above—does allow for the possibility of a form of salvage work that is as concerned with how the salvaged object or subject is valued as it is committed to the ethical and imaginative effects on the present. Out of the ruins of "a handful of words" lies the potential for a partial recovery, a revaluing and repurposing of "an existence" that remains unknowable. The etymology of the word *existence* refers to the ability "to stand outside" one's own life, to be aware of oneself as a living being.[43] It is this possibility, fraught with the burden of the dead and their history, that seems to elude the excavator, at least explicitly: as a partial recovery effort, salvage is a possibility that verges on the inconceivable. Such a recovery from the archive by assembling its fragments into narrative would seem to risk, among other things, repeating the discursive and historical violence that constitutes the archive of slavery.

And yet to make the legal slave the singular subject and object of recovery—or to lament the impossibility of recuperation—also risks ignoring how the figure of the slave, generated in common law and statutory law, has been used to shape a variety of legal categories of laboring and of fugitive personhood, long after the apparent abolition of slavery. It is to consider the category of the legal slave as the cover of inaccessibility that seals away from the present the humanity of those captured under it. It is to treat the figure of the legal slave as absolutely exceptional and confined to a past slave system rather than a legal category—itself made out of earlier laws and conceptions of sovereignty, norms, and economies across multiple legal systems—that continues to animate, in partial ways, categories of personhood that continue to be marked as exceptions to ideal abstract personhood. Such a position cannot account for how this exceptional legal identity pervades the legal imagination, or why it remains such a powerful but unstable figure in the contemporary literary imagination.

Failing to "recuperate," "resurrect," make speak, or humanize the dead but aware of the limitations of merely performing the narrative failure that archival absence generates, Hartman translates the archival violence of the slave trade into an unfinished history of black injury:

> If this story of Venus has any value at all it is in illuminating the way in which our age is tethered to hers. A relation which others

might describe as a kind of melancholia, but which I prefer to describe in terms of the afterlife of property, by which I mean the detritus of lives with which we have yet to attend, a past that has yet to be done, and the ongoing state of emergency in which black life remains in peril.[44]

The failed recovery of Venus redirects value and redefines loss so that the story is not unrecoverable but "unfinished," showing us that the archive is less like a tomb and more like a metonym for the afterlife; in this case, the afterlife of the legal slave personality as property. Hartman thus shifts from racial melancholia or failed mourning to failed death, suggesting that the artificial life of legal constructs never fully end but rather move into other categories and classify other bodies. The racial slave past may animate conditions of black life long after the hemispheric founding of blackness in racial slavery and the binding of black life to property.[45]

But what does it mean to describe the productive force of the law as one that takes lives and makes of them waste, debris, or "disintegrated material," to pull from another meaning of detritus? The ambiguity of the term "detritus" suggests a more complicated possible reading of such lives bound by the violence of law. Etymologically, the Latin *detritus* means a "rubbing away"; in physical geography, the term once referred to the "wearing away or down by detrition, disintegration, decomposition," but it has come to refer to the stuff produced by such friction, as "the matter" produced by the wearing away of surfaces such as gravel, sand, or clay, or other material "eroded and washed away by aqueous agency."[46] Referring to both the act of eroding and the product of that erosion, the sliding meanings of *detritus* highlight the tensions between accumulation and erasure, waste and the grating work of slow time.

The "afterlife of property" is an enduring effect of the commodification and economic valuation of black life, in which otherworldliness—the haunting of an unfinished past, the spirit without a resting place, a presence wrongly taken for dead—merges with the materiality of human bodies consigned to waste. The afterlife of property remains in the debris of legal personhood, as Best and Hartman suggest when they ask, "What is the slave—property, commodity, or disposable life?"[47] This merging evokes the abuse voiced to black Martinicans by the personified land they cultivated in Aimé Césaire's *Cahier d'un retour au pays natal*, where "this land screamed for centuries that we are bestial brutes; that the human pulse stops at the gates of the slave compound; that we are walking compost," even as the colony claimed the authority of divine law.[48] The debris of racial legal personhood is spatialized into the shantytown and nearby oil refinery that share the name "Texaco" in Patrick Chamoiseau's Martinique or into the Dungle of Michelle Cliff's Jamaica.[49] It is in John Edgar Wideman's Homewood section of Pittsburgh and the overseas war zones it describes, where African Americans are consigned to clean up city trash in one place and the "war mess [of] dead people" in the other.[50] It is in the abandonment of an entire crew in Francisco Goldman's stalled maritime novel, deserted by shipowners as unwanted human cargo inside a broken ship. And, mingling profanity of a certain kind with sacredness of a certain kind, the debris of legal personhood returns to the sea as the sewage from resort hotels that Jamaica Kincaid imagines floating in the same waters where Africans were dumped during the slave trade.[51] "Compost," "mess," "sewage": such depictions of the "detritus of lives" in literature resonate with a major current in social theory that considers the devaluation of human life in contemporary economic and political theories and practices, from the "disposable people" captured by modern slavery and illicit human trafficking to the production of "human waste or wasted humans" as an "inevitable outcome of modernization" on a global scale.[52] The following chapters examine the aesthetics of salvage in contemporary literature as provocative responses to the legal, political, and economic forms of violence that would consign enormous swaths of the world's population to the dustbin of the present.[53]

American Salvage

Salvage Work reads American literature in its geographies of apparent colonial, imperial, and neoliberal exception in order to consider how the debris of legal personhood inhabits, underwrites, and incorporates itself within and beyond the sites of the Black Atlantic. These sites are as diverse as a ghost ship in Brooklyn Harbor and its nearby spaces of exception (chapter 1); the once-central sugar mills in Léogâne, Haiti, and fictional Guamaní, Puerto Rico (chapter 2); a destroyed sanctuary in colonial Brazil and the refugee routes along the legally constructed and militarized U.S.-Mexico borderland (chapter 3); and the circum-Atlantic tracks through prisons, cities, colonies, and postcolonies (chapter 4). In the tendency of law to personify itself and its objects of concern, what is the site and what is the person might not be stabilized. Economic ruins shadow the ruin of persons, as detailed in Goldman's *The Ordinary Seaman* (1997), in which international seafarers and cargo ships shuttle between animate persons and property in law: the seafarer, whose legal status is entirely dependent on employers' documentation, comes to resemble abandoned cargo even as the ship takes on legal life as a vessel that "acts and speaks" and could make "herself" the object of suit.[54] Confined to the exceptional space of a stateless cargo ship, the abandoned crew members slip between the legal identities of multiple sovereign powers—between seafarers, undocumented economic migrants, refugees, de facto stateless persons, slaves, pirates, and *los desaparecidos*, those forcibly disappeared by twentieth-century dictatorships in Latin America.

These sites and the husks of legal personhood scattered there serve as difficult ground for salvaging, revaluing, and redirecting the purpose of those ruins. Consider the loss of those who were "disappeared" by the American states Argentina, Chile, Brazil, Uruguay, Peru, Colombia, and Mexico and by paramilitary forces in Haiti, El Salvador, Guatemala, and elsewhere. They populate that space between sovereign power and the system of legal personhood it may promulgate or annul. The many thousands tortured, killed, thrown into secret mass graves, dumped into the ocean, or belatedly returned on family doorsteps as mutilated corpses are victims of the sovereign power that reserves the right to categorize persons within and outside "legal channels, such as a trial."[55] Jean Franco and others have argued that these wars and paramilitary operations depended on taxonomies of personhood and a state impetus for economic modernization: within this system, the state classified indigenous peoples as a class of persons racially resistant to modernization and thus enemies of development; in Argentina and elsewhere, the category "subversives" was established to target a wide swath of dissidents and activists committed to social justice as well as victims chosen for incidental reasons. The loved ones of the disappeared suffered what Franco calls a "triple deprivation—of a body, of mourning, and of a burial."[56] Present only as the uncertain dead, the disappeared are thrown into a space of limbo in personal and public memory, heightening the terror of what one writer calls a punishment "even more cruel than public assassination" because of the uncertainty it inflicts on families, friends, and neighbors.[57]

Goldman's novel contrasts this condition of limbo with the empowering strategy of corporate persons, and the individuals hiding behind the corporate person, to disappear from the purview of the state and thus evade its laws. The two men who buy the ship invent a corporate person as the ship's owner: when the venture fails, the men vanish from legal sight by hiding behind the corporate mask even as the Central American crewmen are made, in their abandonment, unrecognizable to legal protection. The owners' disappearing act is made possible by the same system of legal recognition that confines the crew to spaces of detention, illegality, and interment.

Tropes of human detritus and exceptional legal personhood highlight the need for modes of salvaging personhood in literature and culture. The Caribbean, shaped ineluctably by its literary invocations as archipelagoes fractured, haunted, consumed, wasted, or ruined, generates especially complex philosophies and aesthetics of salvage. Derek Walcott figures the Antilles as a "broken vase," the "cracked heirlooms" of Asian and African diasporas for which Caribbean poetics becomes the art of "restoration" and "remaking": a wholeness that cannot be assumed but must be pieced together after the fall. The "white scars" formed by the glue testify to that violent break and to an effort to remake the vase into a new object of imperfection, one that nonetheless emulates its original form. Like the metaphor of the crafted vase, the performance of the epic *Ramleela* by the descendants of indentured cane cutters in Trinidad form, for Walcott, the "fragments of epic memory," figured by the "gigantic effigy" of a Hindu god made of sugarcane and burned by the end of the performance.[58] The vase and the cane effigy become figures of imperfect restoration, the products of salvaged Antillean history as incomplete conservation and half-remembered rehearsals, a history of breaks and "white scars" emulating an original wholeness.

While the plantation "does not contain all that is planted" in Caribbean cultures, as Brathwaite notes in his critique of the plantation model and its dominance in academic discourse on the Caribbean, it nonetheless has been crucial to Caribbean cultural theories and aesthetics of salvage.[59] Glissant's poetics of relation provides a distinct alternative to Walcott's image of the broken vase, but one that again participates in the artistic vision of salvaging from among the ruins of Atlantic slavery and the plantation. It is from the trope of the sugar plantation that a Caribbean poetics and its social as well as aesthetic modes of relation emerge: out of Glissant's image of the plantation as a "closed place" comes the "open word"; from the collapse of the rigid plantation system blossoms a "creative *marronage*," what Glissant also calls "the passion of memory," which paradoxically returns to the plantation and, having transformed it into metaphor, seeks flight beyond its boundaries.[60]

Reenvisioning creative *marronage* not as escape but as return to the site of ruin, Michelle Cliff figures ruination as a decolonial process. "Ruination" evokes an uncontrolled form of salvage that relies on organic tropes of ecological reversion, in which lands cleared for human cultivation become overrun by the vegetal layers of a changing ecology made possible by the disappearance of plantation labor. Cliff's trope on land that is "ruinate" underscores an overtaking, repurposing, and revaluing of the site of the sugar plantation, powered by empire and slavery, in an era of neoliberal globalization. She notes in her 1991 essay "Caliban's Daughter," "When a landscape becomes ruinate, carefully designed aisles of cane are envined, strangled, the order of empire is replaced by the chaotic forest."[61] For Cliff, the ruinate land prepares the way for figuring a kind of slow undoing of the models of personhood—especially around gender, sexuality, race, and labor—shaped by empire. Ruinate land and ruinate personhood converge by the end of Cliff's 1996 novel, *No Telephone to Heaven*: speaking of her heroine Clare Savage's violent death on the ruinate, ancestral lands she has worked to recultivate as part of a nationalist guerrilla movement against the old order of the sugarcane and the new order of the neocolonial state, Cliff observes, "The forest will grow from her."[62]

If historical *marronage* was an escape from the slave plantation economy—and thus the legal taxonomy of personhood that ensured the very existence and operation of that plantation—then creative *marronage* may be understood also as a process for the imaginative salvaging of the postslavery debris of legal personhood. *Salvage Work* reads cultural *marronage* as a response to the enduring effects of the plantation economy on conceptions and practices of legal personhood. Such creative *marronage* as a challenge to contemporary categories of legal personhood finds expression in the narrational tactics of Gayl Jones's novel *Mosquito* and book-length poem, *Song for Anninho,* discussed in chapter 3 as elaborating a poetics of sanctuary that draws not only from the Underground Railroad but also from immigration and asylum conflicts along the U.S.-Mexico border. The figure of the fugitive slave is seen as an early figure of the unauthorized refugee and demands a rethinking of contemporary asylum, refugee, and immigration debates across categories of race, age, sex, and nationality.

It is the person in need of refuge—especially stateless persons, internally displaced persons, and unauthorized refugees—who has been depicted in scholarship on globalization and human rights as populations of waste or detritus. Such writings highlight both the spectacular and the occluded violence inflicted on vulnerable populations by state sovereignty no less than by the presumably nonterritorial sovereignty of the market. With, for example, the "wasted lives" of Zygmunt Bauman's refugees and immigrants—whom he describes as inhabiting new forms of ghettos and for whom the "surrounding society has no economic or political use"—the trope of waste not only binds the living to uselessness and consigns them to zones of disposal but also transforms them, unsurprisingly, into the material refuse of the dead.[63] The dead become not what gives life its completeness but that which, "with disastrous results for the living," is merely "eliminated."[64] Biological existence becomes captured by the law that excludes it, assigning no value and consigning life to the trash heap.

Contemporary literature has both drawn from and responded to this discourse of waste, registering how biopolitical systems devalue human life while also experimenting with narrative tactics to actively speak against that devaluation. Rob Nixon's study of the capacity of writing to address the "slow violence" of environmental catastrophes "that are low in instant spectacle but high in long-term effects," for example, extends and complicates the discourse of human populations as disposable.[65] Nixon explores how the global poor and the racially marginalized, whose neighborhoods and bodies are often most vulnerable to environmental toxins, might challenge the rhetorical collapse between waste and life by using a wide range of narrative fiction and nonfiction as part of their environmentalism.

Evoking the link between environmental toxins and the precarity of humans consigned to the status of waste, Elizabeth Deloughrey shifts attention back to the world's oceans, what she names "heavy waters," in reference to the toxic dumping of heavy metals into the Atlantic, and which dissolve into the same waters where African slaves were drowned during the middle passage, and where Haitian refugees have drowned or have been interdicted, held at Guantánamo, and forcibly returned to Haiti by the U.S. Coast Guard.[66] The interdiction agreement violates international law and the Law of the Sea guidelines for intercepting refugees. It participates in a long history of U.S. policy and practices to harass and refuse refugees and migrants deemed undesirable because their very presence in search of economic or political refuge challenged particular domestic or foreign policies, as the discussion of Central American migration briefly in chapter 1 and more fully in chapter 3 of this book makes clear.[67]

Deloughrey reads Kamau Brathwaite's poem "Salvages" as an attempt "to recover the drowning and wasted bodies of Haitian refugees"—one that the poem ultimately breaks from when it becomes clear that the Coast Guard cutter, Salvages, is not at all "trying to save, or salvage, the refugees."[68] Pointing to the poem's break from the romantic anticolonial narratives of overcoming outlined by David Scott (to which I respond in chapter 2), Deloughrey points out that we as readers discover that there is, after all, no salvation for the Haitian refugees. While Nixon and Deloughrey look to writers who seek to decry the conflation of poor and marginalized populations with material waste, however, the trope risks becoming reinforced: as if to say that the wasting of lives is unjust but, again and again, proven to be an inevitable, even ordinary, operation.[69] The life wasted is the life devalued to the point of no value, the life that is metaphorically dead: and the shift from metaphor to biological reality becomes a small one.

Extending Caribbean theories of salvage as a critical practice in theory, art, and political philosophy, *Salvage Work* responds to the rhetoric of human life as wasted, bare, and dead that has become so influential in American studies, postcolonial theory, and critical black studies. The book advances readings of contemporary literary texts that elaborate not what Sibylle Fischer calls "an aesthetics of 'bare life'" but rather an aesthetics of salvage, one that searches amid the legal debris of the person in the effort to rethink a poetics and ethics of personhood.[70] It draws on but also departs from the discourse of "wasted lives," which highlights the process by which sovereign power values and devalues human life in service to economic goals but also slips into the death-bound theories of personhood discussed later in this introduction.

Salvage Work asks how a concern with "the detritus of lives" leads to literary narrative tactics that repeatedly figure legal personhood as debris or in ruins, even as that ruination enables the aesthetic operations of salvage within narrative. This salvage work responds to discussions of the historical imagination in contemporary literature of the Americas, in which catastrophic violence, whether cataclysmic or slow-moving, seems to consign human lives to the status of just so much neoliberal debris. Drawing on the strong currents of an aesthetics of salvage in U.S. and Caribbean literature, this book elaborates a mode of reading and literary narrative tactics akin to the work of pulling from the ruins that which may be revalued and repurposed without erasing the marks of its ruination.[71] Mindful of the slow violence and heavy waters that tell any story of legal personhood, *Salvage Work* identifies this salvage work as a response to the trashing of human life.

In contrast to the rhetoric of a postracial present or of disposable populations as the inevitable if tragic by-product of global modernity, this book traces the links between the history of legal racial slavery, political economy, and contemporary legal personhood in ways that move across, beyond, and beneath the Atlantic. The figure of the legal black slave casts its shadows both behind and ahead of itself—on, for instance, the forced labor of indigenous and white slaves, peons, indentured servants, Southeast Asian "coolie" laborers, impressed seafarers and those working in conditions of effective "sovereignlessness" under flags of convenience, victims of human trafficking and illicit enslavement, targets of antiprostitution campaigns, unauthorized economic refugees, the felon and ex-felon, and the underemployed free wage laborer consigned to "wageless life."[72] In short, the figure of the legal slave continues to be enormously productive of contemporary forms of legal personhood: it haunts the archive and contemporary black life but also moves across and beyond those sites, to other categories of personhood deemed at once exceptional and junked, washed away, wasted, cast out, disposable, or ruined.[73]

Masks of Personhood

The person is a figure shaped by conditions of life and death, of biological existence and social recognition, legal status and cultural representation. A figure whose plasticity, artificiality, and instability is often obscured by its apparent naturalness as a synonym for any human being, the legal person—as a subject of certain rights and duties recognized before the law—is the originary legal fiction and the foundation of modern politics. The status of human beings as "natural persons" cannot explain the unstable and exclusionary taxonomies of personhood in English legal history.[74] Drawn from the Latin *persona*, which refers to the mask worn by classical actors on stage to amplify the voice, the person evokes a much longer history as a paradoxical figure of concealment and disclosure, in which the mask stands in for the human as one whose voice may be heard before the law. Individual political rights depend on giving the abstract figure of the person a human face and voice, and on giving the person its own story of individual development, one that culminates in the full incorporation of the person into civic life. The language of liberal democratic rights and international human rights paradoxically creates the gap between person and human in order to disavow it: legal "person" and "human being" are invoked as if one and the same, when they are not equivalent or interchangeable so much as they are the tenor and vehicle of a metaphor masquerading as a performative speech act. The declaration of "We the People" in the U.S. Constitution famously fractions and fractures this gap between human and person when it counts "free Persons" and (white) indentured servants as a "whole number," excludes "Indians not taxed," and converts "all other Persons," namely, the enslaved, into "three fifths" of a person.[75] So, too, does the 1948 Universal Declaration for Human Rights (UDHR) generate and disavow this gap between human and person by referencing the human in its title only to detail the rights of persons in the body of the document: as Joseph R. Slaughter observes of the UDHR, "the term 'person' became a kind of mask for the human, a rhetorical feint for not naming the human itself as a question."[76] The figure of the person in modern human rights discourse cannot be entirely freed from the imperial and national frameworks that invented it, and chapter 4 of this book explores how the masks of personhood comprise the material traces of colonial, imperial, and national histories of labor, gender, race, and migration.

The root meaning of *persona* as a mask highlights legal personhood as a fabrication made in positive law: it is a self-denying fiction—a kind of lie that presents itself, unlike literary fiction, as merely a reflection of ontological truth—despite its purpose to make one recognizable to law in particular ways.[77] The literary texts I examine reimagine the masks as composed of the legal debris of colonial, slave, civic, and international law. A legal mask of personhood—when understood as an assemblage of current but also seemingly defunct legal fragments—helps to bring into view how the person, as a legal fiction, complicate the pervasive tropes of human waste and social death in current discussions of neoliberalism.

For legal theorist John T. Noonan, "Masks are a variety of fiction. At the points of a legal system where it is too much to recognize that a human being exists, a mask is employed. The intolerable strain is relieved."[78] My discussion of the masks of personhood is indebted to this reading of masks but also departs from its terminology. Criticizing a legal process that relies on "masks" to conceal the human participants in the legal process, including judge, lawyers, jury, plaintiff, and defendant, Noonan argues against a way of teaching and practicing law that privileges rules over justice, love, and respect for human beings.[79] He refers to "masks" as operating modes within the legal process rather than as static objects of concealment: "masks" are the "magical ways by which persons are removed from the legal process" and "ways of classifying individual human beings so that their humanity is hidden and disavowed."[80] "Mask" also refers to the product of such operating modes, as "a legal construct suppressing the humanity of a participant in the process."[81] The critical task, for Noonan, is "to remove the masks" and thereby "to distinguish between them and the person," where "person" means "particular flesh and blood and consciousness."[82] Noonan insists on referring to human beings as persons—and for good reason, as his project is to upend the entire structure of legal theory by calling for the legal process to serve the dignity of human beings rather than the other way around. The literary texts explored in this book demonstrate the capacity for literature and art to explore the enormous significance of the legal fiction—the mask—of personhood in generating law and the "flesh and blood and consciousness" on which law has worked its magic.

That law has determined categories of personhood according to its racialized and gendered meanings of "flesh" and "blood"—as U.S. law continues to do in its logic of blood quantum for the definition of "native Hawaiian"—suggests that the masks are themselves comprised of "flesh" and "blood." J. Kēhaulani Kauanui's study of this logic of blood quantum points to the important consequences that legal status has on the politics of sovereignty and conceptions of identity.[83] Law and aesthetics are systems of value and judgment. Legal opinions and literary narrative are modes of world-making. This book examines legal processes and literary practices as they generate and respond to the core fictions of legal personhood.

Exploring literary responses to legal personhood by African American, U.S. Latino, and Caribbean writers, *Salvage Work* calls into question both liberal narratives of personhood (which affirm civic and human rights law as imperfect but structurally adequate and progressive) and theories of biopolitics and law that rely on tropes of waste and death to conceptualize how the political captures human life. Liberal political philosophies inform a startling range of current reform projects in the U.S. context, particularly the conservative fetal personhood and the progressive nonhuman animal rights movements, two movements I consider in the epilogue. The push to expand the boundaries of legal personhood depends on the same assumptions about legal personhood that has led civil rights and human rights projects into difficult waters.[84] This book asks how legal identities proliferate and fracture precisely at those moments when legal personhood is proclaimed to be colorless, when the law claims to hear the voices of all persons equally and the market is hailed as a free system open to anyone with entrepreneurial grit. It questions the assumptions of contemporary neoliberal and democratic citizenship across national and imperial contexts: the post–civil rights United States, in which ostensible legal race neutrality generates staggering racial effects; the contexts of U.S. imperial exception, which paradoxically split citizenship from coloniality and reconcile them into a distinctly attenuated form of legal citizenship, as with Puerto Rico; and the Haitian context, in which citizenship is given one color in the name of forging an authentic national political identity that reads blackness not as skin color but as a political category of belonging (in contrast to the repressive 2013 Constitutional Court decision in the Dominican Republic to revoke the citizenship of all Dominicans born after 1929 to parents of Haitian descent, or to parents not of Dominican ancestry, effectively excluding blackness from Dominican citizenship and making it the political category of statelessness).[85] Responding both to liberal narratives of citizenship and to theories of biopolitics, which examine the politicization of life only to the extent that it affirms the sovereign power to kill, this book also asks how contemporary literary texts give narrative shape to the legal forms of life that traverse the interstices between the ideal citizen and bare life.

The masks of the legal slave in the Americas and their partial abolition pose some of the clearest challenges to the political assumptions of reform projects that equate full civic incorporation with legal citizenship. One such challenge has been understood as lying outside the purview of the law. In this view, the paradox of a free republic founded on legal slavery and its vestiges largely have been resolved as a legal matter following the civil rights legislation of the 1960s, but the "ascriptive and affective" racial injury remains, giving rise to the post–civil rights paradox of "African Americans' formal possession of full legal citizenship and their inherited burden of 'civic estrangement.'"[86] Tillet's readings of late twentieth-century African American writing and art centered on the "sites of slavery" examine such efforts to resolve the dilemma of an incomplete civic incorporation in the realm of the affective and political imagination. Drawing on psychoanalytic theories of injury, failed mourning, and racial melancholia, Tillet describes contemporary experiences of African American citizenship as "'a melancholic bind between incorporation and rejection' for people of color since the nation's beginning."[87] This racial melancholia motivates an imaginative return to the antebellum past and generates a new democratic aesthetic precisely because, Tillet argues, post–civil rights African American art and writing no longer need to make claims for legal civic equality: "shuttling between the pessimism of civic estrangement and the privilege of African American legal citizenship," a major current in African American cultural production is to redefine national belonging and democracy outside of law and through a "critical patriotism."[88] While the imaginative turn to sites of slavery works to refigure the affective relationship of African American citizens to the state, such a turn is not necessarily a turn away from the law: as the chapters in this book demonstrate, such a turn to the slave past in U.S. and Caribbean literature also explores the traces of the legal slave personality that still operate in the present, preventing any kind of full civic incorporation through legal citizenship and revealing the precarity of legal identities. Legal identities may be assigned in highly racial ways, shaped by the ghosts of chattel slavery, even when the legal category is not explicitly a racial one: the felon at Angola Penitentiary in Louisiana inherits the legal burden left by the U.S. slave system, and the onetime chattel slave plantation, now a prison farm plantation, remains as a literal site of slavery.

The literary texts examined in *Salvage Work* complicate the topographies and temporalities of slavery and its relation to contemporary meanings of legal personhood. Rather than depict *the* legal slave personality, as if it were singular and ahistorical, these literary narratives range across multiple figurations of the slave as they respond to conventional histories told about slavery within and across North America, Central America, and the greater Caribbean. They undermine economic accounts of the slave as the captive counterpart to the free wage labor of the citizen (chapters 1 and 2), and they complicate national histories that center on the Haitian slave as masculine revolutionary hero or—as in the myth of *la gran familia puertorriqueña* in twentieth-century Puerto Rican letters—that subordinate the mixed-race descendants of slaves as feminized and sexualized creatures to nationalist patriarchs through the genres of romance as much as through colonial antiprostitution laws targeting mixed-race Puerto Rican women (chapter 2). They also perform, through experiments with narrative structure, the agonistic struggle to link radical movements of the African diaspora against slavery and colonialism to the possibilities and failures of radically decolonial futures (chapters 3 and 4). Whereas Sharon Cameron looks to literary representations of "impersonality," to "suspend, eclipse, and even destroy the idea of the person as such," Jones and Wideman set out to challenge the idea of the person as such by reimagining its figuration, its shape, its history.[89] These literary texts incorporate into their narratives the legal traces of the racial slave imagined as fractured into parts, combined with other fragments of the masks of legal personhood, and, in this way, still inhabiting the present: in the free Haitian citizen condemned to "wageless life" or exile, in the free wage laborers made exceptional and effectively stateless, in the political asylum seeker or the "economic refugee," in the citizen of a postcolony, or in the "enemy combatant" of the "war on terror," who may be indefinitely detained, tortured, drone-killed, even made to live by force feeding, but who may not be heard by civil law.[90]

As the chapters that follow demonstrate, an aesthetics of salvage reveals and critiques—rather than reaffirms—the legal scavenging of personhood. Such literary salvage work contends with the often-spectral afterlives of legal cultures and provides alternative visions for the ethics and poetics of personhood. Salvaging retains the historicity of junked objects and ostensibly junked legal categories by giving them new value and new functions without removing the traces of their ruination: it is less the economy of newness promised by recycling and more the aesthetics of collage or junk art.

Conventionally, the masks of personhood function as if they were skin, encasing the human body with meanings—not rights—that sometimes cannot be shed, meanings that simultaneously conceal, seal, and give shape to the human being and to differential rights. The racial constructs from European colonial systems operate as a second skin in one's consciousness and within legal systems as mutually exclusive, imprisoning, and distortive: as Fanon observes of the colonial relation in Martinique, the "white man is sealed in his whiteness. The black man in his blackness."[91] That "corporations are people" (or more precisely, legal persons) sounds startling only when personhood has been so tightly fitted onto the figure of the human in Western law that we mistake the mask for the skin and the skin for the psychic personality of human beings.[92] That, moreover, corporations gained personhood rights in U.S. law as a result of an interpretation of the equal protection clause under the Fourteenth Amendment in the Supreme Court case *Santa Clara v. Southern Pacific* (1886) suggests that corporate persons are not clearly distinct from "natural persons" but highlight the conventionality and changeability of human personhood, as if personhood (and the rights it presumes) were inalienable from the human being, or as if the Civil War had been fought to free the corporations.

Where colonial and slave histories read blackness as negation, the law forges the legal racial slave personality as a mask with no hole from which to speak. It is as if the legal slave mask inverts the assumed purpose of persona as a mask that amplifies the voice of its wearer: for the legal slave, the metaphor of personhood as a mask has its material counterpart not in the masks of civic drama but in instruments of torture—the muzzle or the bit, those slave masks that kept the tongue "held down by iron" and that "put a wildness" in the eye "where before there wasn't any," as Toni Morrison writes.[93] The silencing mask of the legal racial slave, especially as it became conflated with blackness, is thus forged in a "negative relation" to that most idealized form of abstract personhood in liberal legal thought, that of the full citizen in positive law.[94]

What does abolition produce when it destroys the slave mask, forged, as it is, unevenly and with an assemblage of materials but always as an instrument of violence? Why return to the figure of the legal racial slave to think about the relation of human life to personhood as legal status at a time when the racial slave no longer has any standing as a legal personality anywhere in the world, and when the vestiges of the slave system throughout the Americas are not affirmed, at least officially, by law?[95]

Any one category of legal persons, any one mask of personhood, is forged out of the scavenged legal histories of many others: they are not pure categories but unstable composites, not the fantasy of order promised by taxonomies but the disorderly transformations made in countless courts and legislative decisions in any one state. The enduring power of the legal slave mask, one mask among many, lies in what it shares with and reveals of the variety of legal identities in the Americas. It is an especially formative and complex legal identity to which a wide range of writers, artists, and intellectuals since the late twentieth century have returned. After abolition, the fragments of the legal slave mask serve as legal material for the assemblages of other masks of legal personhood. In the United States, for example, the slave system was formally but incompletely destroyed in at least two ways: first, the constitutional amendment that abolished slavery also established categories of exceptional personhood that could legally be forced to work; second, abolition did not prevent court rulings and legislation from scavenging earlier laws and legal precedents to invent and manage other legal personalities. These acts of legal scavenging respond to major political-economic changes—in the United States, this includes abolition and its aftermath, reconstruction and postreconstruction, segregation and racial terror, periods of immigration and anti-immigration fervor, wartime states of exception, civil rights expansion, neoliberalism, and the so-called war on terrorism. The aesthetics of salvage explored in this book works to track and reveal such legal scavenging as well as the legal genealogies it produces.[96]

While all the literary texts examined here highlight the conventionality and economic imperatives that have shaped the masks of personhood, it is Jones's *Mosquito* and *Song for Anninho*, as well as Wideman's *Fanon*, that also experiment with narrational tactics to reconceptualize those masks as an assemblage of fragments and of voices that cannot be reduced to instruments of legal will. Wideman's novel is a provocative experiment, styled as an extended case of writer's block, on how to construct the masks of the legal human personality in ways that challenge conventional models of personality development. As I explain in chapter 4, this novel about a writer's failed attempt to write a novel about Fanon uses a variety of narrative tactics to draw from, but ultimately refuse to remain within, waste- and death-bound theories of personhood. Refiguring the masks of personhood as an assemblage of fragments in the post–civil rights neoliberal present becomes among the novel's most provocative challenges to liberal and neoliberal ideologies of development. The narrator, John, highlights his attempts to move beyond the models of psychological human personality development so central to international human rights discourse and to the historical Fanon's anti-colonial thought. The novel distinguishes the masks of legal personhood from Fanon's trope of the (white) mask as a psychological disavowal of one's (black) skin, where masks disguise and distort the development of the human personality beneath them and where a truly liberatory future would be free of masks altogether. The masks of personhood, when depicted as an assemblage of legal debris, repurpose the political legacy of Fanon to challenge neoliberal logics of legal personhood. Wideman's narration brings together the trope of prosopopoeia, of giving voice to the dead through another figure, with Frantz Fanon's trope of the mask as it explains the distortions of the human personality by colonialism. Wideman's mask of legal personhood thus draws from Fanon's trope of the mask but complicates it by refusing the normative human personality development that serves as Fanon's premise.

The law may define and assign the masks of personhood in ways that are indefinite and even internally inconsistent. Neither fully visible nor invisible, neither included nor excluded, "neither citizen nor alien," those human beings who do not fit easily within the categories of legal personhood become explicit problems for liberal political and legal conceptions of the person and, thus, of the nation.[97] Citizenship and the national identity it constitutes is disrupted and re-formed, made strangely familiar and familiarly strange in those who, whether in court or in their writing, "conspicuously fail to conform" to the personhood they are assigned in official narratives of the nation.

"Legal Being" and the Limits of Death-Bound Paradigms

"Legal being," observes Priscilla Wald in her study of nineteenth-century and early twentieth-century U.S. Supreme Court cases and literary texts, "determines social being, and identity is experienced as essence."[98] These categories of identity constructed by law become social subjects and the object of legal regulation. In spite of the real political urgency to construct exceptional categories of legal personhood for the subjects of U.S. empire, these new legal identities proved difficult to stabilize and revealed the instability and incompleteness of the very concept of legal personhood. From Indian Removal to the Insular Cases, which sought to define the relationship of the United States to its overseas territorial possessions (including Puerto Rico, as I discuss in chapter 2), legal personhood both constituted and disrupted official narratives of national identity. The decision to define the territory of Puerto Rico as "foreign in a domestic sense" and "domestic in a foreign sense"[99]—or as an "unincorporated territory" of the United States—shows how contradictory and ambiguous definitions of the relation of sovereignty to human beings define the forms of life that get recognized as legal identities. Such legal masks are ill-fitting, forged unevenly, incompletely, and indeterminately in ways that reveal their construction to be a failed attempt to shape the contours of the human through and through. Under scrutiny, these masks reveal the cracks and plasters that belie the coherence and naturalness of even that consummate category of the citizen.

If the autonomous, individual, rational subject of political rights is a founding and central subject in the modern political imagination, it must be as a phantasmatic figure that has never known flesh, a ghost from the moment of its conception, and a cover for the unstable taxonomies generated by legal personhood.[100] In "Beyond Human Rights," Giorgio Agamben calls for the abandonment of the traditional subject of politics in order to build a new political philosophy around the subject—the "one and only figure of the refugee"—that brings "the originary fiction of sovereignty to crisis."[101] The refugee not only breaks "the identity between the human and the citizen and that between nativity and nationality" but also, in doing so, reveals the gap between the human and the person in all its categories.[102] Sovereignty names its enemies and subjects of political expulsion, subjects not born into rights but proleptically transformed into their death masks. But the rights-bearing subject is recentered as quickly as it is displaced in Agamben's account: "Only in a world in which the spaces of states have been thus perforated and topologically deformed and in which the citizen has been able to recognize the refugee that he or she is—only in such a world is the political survival of humankind today thinkable."[103] Redefined by its seemingly negative image, the citizen is revealed to be, itself, in need of refuge.

Drawing explicitly from Agamben's theories of bare life and the state of exception, Waligora-Davis extends this thinking on the refugee to the historic condition of African American citizens. Demonstrating how "the law's historic alienation of black bodies" has transformed black Americans into "domestic refugees" and prompted a long literary and cultural history of pleas for sanctuary, she examines moments in U.S. history when the categorical distinctions between refugees, stateless persons, and race have collapsed around the figure of the African American citizen and shaped the conditions of its emergence.[104] This figure of the "black American refugee" captures the tensions of black U.S. citizenship as a condition disclosed by "the suspension of law and time animating a racial state of exception."[105] It also cannot be understood without accounting for U.S. imperial formations and its figuring of aliens and refugees globally. The alien seeking refuge in U.S. immigration law under the 1924 Johnson-Reed Act, which was officially enforced until 1965, entered into a system of restrictive immigration that legally, if sometimes tacitly, racialized categories of nationality and national origin. As Mae Ngai recounts, this system of restrictive immigration produced the now so-called illegal alien as "a *new legal and political subject*."[106] Unauthorized refugees, like all unauthorized aliens, become criminal and thus fugitive in ways that collapse into race even when this collapse may be not legal but a metaphor for the de facto conditions of internal exile, as Waligora-Davis reflects in commentary on the public discourse that named black residents of the Gulf Coast "refugees" in the 2005 aftermath of Hurricane Katrina, where differential forms of legal, economic, and political violence converged on African Americans. African American citizenship and immigrant naturalization are shaped out of this history, in which race and statelessness seem to endlessly collapse into each other. These categories also emerge out of one another, forged out of a complex language of categorization that borrows from colonial, imperial, and national formations—a point underscored by Imani Perry in her reading of the resonance between terms such as "illegal," "criminal," "foreign," or "domestic" and the pathologizing of black families in U.S. public discourse.[107] The refugee, as one who flees to the law or sovereign for protection, finds its mirror image in the fugitive, as one who flees from the law or master: the unauthorized refugee, as effectively stateless and as fugitive, is subjected to—and made into fugitive subjects by—the punitive structures of the liberal legal framework. The liberal legal framework becomes visible not as imperfectly bending toward justice but as structurally bent toward the unjust.

Philosophies of biopolitics, or how forms of life have become the main stakes and the primary subjects of politics, offer some of the most trenchant critiques of liberal political philosophy and its model of the contract between the sovereign and the individual granted personhood. These theories tend to focus on the limit zones of personhood because such limit zones bring into view the sovereign violence that necessarily constitutes the person, thus throwing into question the entire project of expanding the legal recognition of rights foundational to liberal thought. Yet these death-bound theories eclipse the forms of living crucial to the contemporary literary and social imagination.

Theories of biopolitics use metaphors of nakedness to account for the living body that, to paraphrase Agamben, may be killed but not murdered: the subject is "stripped" of rights and reduced to "bare" life, or *nuda vita*.[108] Personhood lies not in human flesh, political rights do not inhere in the skin: in the tradition of Western political thought, having nothing but one's skin confirms one's status outside the civic order, as a "naked savage."[109] The law vests one in personhood as if it were a covering over of mere biological existence, a mask or a piece of cloth, endowing the living with a legal personality and particular forms of civic and economic life. Naked, the human is bare and in a civil condition akin to death; but dressed, the human becomes a legal person. Hannah Arendt's famous challenge to the supposed sacredness of secular human rights still proves insightful:

> The survivors of the extermination camps, the inmates of concentration and internment camps, and even the comparatively happy stateless people could see . . . that the abstract nakedness of being nothing but human was their greatest danger.[110]

Before Agamben called on the figure of the refugee, he put this form of naked life, the "bare life" of *homo sacer*, at the very origins of the political and at the very center of his philosophical inquiry, which translates bareness into another kind of death.

This death-bound theory of personhood eclipses the taxonomic logics and contingencies that have shaped the histories of legal personhood across states, with the effect of reducing these thanatropic theories of personhood to a set of binaries that, I argue, limit the capacity to track the enormous variety of legal personhood in ruins. While death-bound theories of personhood bring into view the sovereign violence that necessarily constitutes the person, everything else threatens to fall out of view. Consider Agamben's reading of *homo sacer* as a form of bare life, the exemplary figure of modern biopolitics and thus the paradigmatic condition of our era.[111] In a paradoxical convergence of political death with biological life, the condition of *homo sacer* comes into view at the threshold of the political order; but rather than mark a horizon, a boundary, or an entryway that can be crossed, the "threshold" transforms itself into a "zone of indistinction" between "law and nature, outside and inside, violence and law," and so on.[112] The dependence on the rhetorical structure of the threshold—borrowed partly from the spatial metaphor of a doorway—shapes Agamben's theory of personhood, in which the human is always and anywhere caught within a structure formed by the "materialization" and spatialization of the "state of exception."[113] Threshold marks a "limit" but shows the limit to be where the boundary between life and death, inclusion and exclusion, collapses, at once marking an absolute limit and a zone whose limits are both permeable and fungible.[114] Each of us is caught within the threshold. Whereas Foucault may imply that there is no position outside of knowledge/power, Agamben affirms that there is no position—even in death—outside the indistinct zone of the threshold. In an oft-quoted passage, he proposes:

> If the essence of the [Nazi concentration] camp consists in the materialization of the state of exception and in the subsequent creation of a space in which bare life and the juridical rule enter into a threshold of indistinction, then we must admit that we find ourselves virtually in the presence of a camp every time such a structure is created, independent of the kinds of crime that are committed there and whatever its denomination and specific topography.[115]

In *Homo Sacer*, the citizen, who assumes "all the rights and expectations that we customarily attribute to human existence," finds himself bereft of those rights and expectations: everywhere and every time the state of exception is materialized, "we" as citizens "find ourselves virtually in the presence of a camp."[116] Agamben rightly warns against a politics that invests the meaning of humanness with rights, expectations, and forms of belonging: for the political is the threshold between language and biology, and the originary structure of sovereignty is revealed in the condition of bare life.[117] In this heavy reliance on the threshold, however, Agamben slips repeatedly from thinking of the threshold as a horizontal borderland to thinking of threshold as a vertical limit. *Threshold* becomes a recurring word that, as one critic notes, "invariably signifies a passage that cannot be completed, a distinction that can be neither maintained nor eliminated."[118] As a metaphor, it is a lower limit below which nothing perceptible occurs. This lower limit effectively doubles as an upper one: bare life occupies the threshold that meets the lower limit for biological life, and bare life occupies the maximum threshold of sovereign power on the body.

Bare life becomes the lower and upper threshold of modern political life: the minimum existence barely distinguished from death is also what makes the extreme limit of modern politics visible. Biologically, anything less than bare life means death; but also, anything less extreme than bare life is not as important to Agamben's thought. The result is that the structure of modern sovereignty and biopolitics only becomes visible on the "horizon," or at the "limit zone" of "the most extreme misfortunes": the comatose patient in a hospital room, the VP (*Versuchspersonen*) treated as a living dead and thus consigned to medical experimentation, the "Musselman" in the Nazi concentration camps. Such threshold cases serve as paradigms through which his study of classical

Western metaphysics is made to matter, literally: the threshold limit has been shuttled from the horizon to the centers of our political existence, our biological, material bodies. What begins as a deconstructive move ends by positing a new norm, the threshold of the state of exception, which produces the threshold of bare life. Whatever moves below this extremity (now revealed to be the center) can, in this model, no longer be thought. In this way, bare life marks a limit to thought: it questions "every theory of the contractual origin of state power and, along with it, every attempt to ground political communities in something like a 'belonging,' whether it be founded on popular, national, religious, or any other identity."[119] The threshold becomes a needed response to the end of the Cold War, when the "very threshold of the political order itself" must be called into question in order to respond to the "bloody mystification of a new planetary order."[120] It is this "urgency of catastrophe" that brings him to question the sacredness of life.

In Agamben's story of sovereignty from the origins of Western politics to the global catastrophe of the post–Cold War era, *homo sacer* is "the protagonist" that reveals "every attempt to found political liberties in the rights of the citizen" to be "in vain."[121] Echoed in his later figure of the refugee, *homo sacer* serves as antihero to the figure of the citizen we presumably thought we knew (and thought we were). Visually, *homo sacer* becomes the photographic negative—or, to follow the trope of nakedness, the image produced by the body scan devices now ubiquitous at airport security points. The point is this: in its negative or naked image, the citizen is still the main concern of the story, and this presumption distorts the relations of sovereign power to human life as they have played out in European and U.S. colonies and in slave systems.

How does a theory of biopolitics change when it is not the rights of the citizen but the alienation of the slave or the colonized subject that is at the center of one's analysis? Achille Mbembe responds to the traditional focus on the citizen by presenting a theory of necropolitics, in which multiple forms of sovereignty, including nonstate sovereign actors, take as their explicit goal the instrumentalization and destruction of human life at a massive scale. Mbembe revises Foucault's notion of biopower and Agamben's biopolitics when he observes that "any historical account of the rise of modern terror needs to address slavery, which could be considered one of the first instances of biopolitical experimentation."[122] Under slavery and colonialism, traditional notions of state sovereignty fall away and reveal death to be a more active operation, and possibly the main goal, of sovereign power. To understand how contemporary state and nonstate actors produce "*death-worlds*," Mbembe convincingly argues for the need to redefine sovereignty and the biopolitical.[123] His necropolitics extends biopolitical thought into multiple forms of sovereignty and its disaggregation of populations into categories of injury, death, and predation under slavery, in the colony, and through the contemporary "war machine." While Mbembe redefines the meanings of sacrifice, terror, and freedom in the context of how sovereign power structures forms of labor and work, debt, and commodification, Warren Montag proposes what he calls "necro-economics" as a way to understand more fully the process of necropolitics as it relates to liberal economic thought, and as a way of thinking about sovereignty and humanity beyond dualisms such as that of the political and the economic. He reads Adam Smith's economic theory of the free market in *Wealth of Nations* as a necro-economics, drawing from Mbembe's reading of slavery and colonialism to arrive at the centrality of the free wage laborer, Smith's "workman":

> Thus alongside the figure of Homo Sacer, the one who may be killed with impunity, is another figure, one whose death is no doubt less spectacular than the first and is the object of no memorial or commemoration: he who with impunity may be allowed to die, slowly or quickly, in the name of the rationality and equilibrium of the market.[124]

The "workman" as a form of bare life anticipates the conditions of laboring personhood in neoliberal theory, and Montag asks us to think seriously about how the economic joins the political and the legal. What does not change in this model, however, is the language of life stripped and made to undergo a living death that becomes virtually or literally indistinct from biological death. Such accounts of biopolitics do not account for the generative impulse of the law to disassemble and reconstitute legal identities during major political-economic shifts and the crisis they cause to the process of individuation and to the meanings of the individual.

For Mbembe and others theorizing biopolitics not with the Nazi camp but with the topographies of slavery in mind, the slave economy is sometimes occluded by its stunning physical and social violence. Despite the presence of significant histories of the slave system as an economic and modern capitalist system, biopolitical theories of slavery perhaps suggest a greater indebtedness to Orlando Patterson's comparative sociological history *Slavery and Social Death* (1982), even as critics rightly point to Patterson's serious shortcomings in treating "social death" as the defining feature of racial slavery in the Americas and cultural pathology as the defining feature of much of contemporary black life.[125] For

Patterson, the legal slave of any society is recognized as a person before the law but nonetheless undergoes a "natal alienation" and, borrowing from the anthropologist Claude Meillassoux, "social death," in which the legal slave person—"marked by an original, indelible defect which weighs endlessly upon his destiny"—is excluded from not only his or her cultural history but also any participation in the social life of the slave society.[126] Drawing on the language of the "defect," Patterson shifts thinking about slavery's persistent effects in the present from the law to the sociological discussion of black pathologies, which I briefly consider in chapter 4.[127]

Extending the criticism that "social death" eclipses the sociality and "political activity of the weak" as they actually existed within slave systems, Colin Dayan challenges Patterson's concept of social death not for its presumption of cultural absence and natal alienation but for its silence on the differential logic of legal personhood.[128] While Patterson notes the slave as a legal person, he nonetheless "remains silent about the disabling inherent in the legal action that invents a personality only to enslave, reduce, and exclude it. . . . Patterson's insistence that slaves in every legal code are treated as persons in law urges us to ask: When and in what way were slaves allowed to be persons? When resurrected as legal personalities, what can they do, what are their possibilities for recognition?"[129]

What lies between the ideal citizen and bare life is an enormous range of particular legal identities. This differential logic of legal personhood generates meanings of sovereignty and national culture through law and finds its particular formulations encoded in a state's founding legal documents. In the cases of the United States and Haiti, the declarations of slavery abolition in state constitutions capture the contradictory effects of differential legal personhood in distinct ways. Legislators, prison abolitionists, and historians of convict labor in the United States have called attention to the line of continuity established between the slave and the prisoner in the Thirteenth Amendment, which writes slavery into the U.S. Constitution at the moment of its abolition: "Neither slavery nor involuntary servitude, except as a punishment for crime whereof the party shall have been duly convicted, shall exist within the United States, or any place subject to their jurisdiction."[130] There, the slave and the unfree laborer cease to exist at the same moment that slavery and involuntary servitude are now constitutionally declared to live on in the person of the convict and the felon. The declared break between slavery and blackness gives cover to—and, without the slaveholders' power to punish, necessitates—the links now forged by the Constitution between the ex-slave or free black person and the penal system. Earlier competing models of prison reform in New York and Pennsylvania were organized around narratives of rebirth that, as Caleb Smith argues, following Dayan, were predicated on the civil death of the convict who previously laid claim to citizenship, or civic life: the prison, with its regimes of forced labor, solitude, and "arbitrary and discretionary violence," took the convict and "buried him alive in a solitary cell. But it also promised him a glorious return to citizenship and humanity. It mortified the body, but it also claimed to renovate the soul."[131] Dayan reads this form of civil death in the northern states in relation to what the Thirteenth Amendment enabled the post-Reconstruction southern states to do in reinforcing racial forms of legal personhood: to reharness and terrorize persons categorized as black (unstable as it was) or otherwise below the threshold of whiteness (unstable as it was) through the convict lease system, in which prisons sold the labor of convicts to private companies; the chain gang, in which convicts were made to labor for the state; and the prison farm, in which convicts were made to live and labor on plantations in the Deep South. When private companies requested to rent convicts that the state did not yet have, police power responded with rashes of new arrests; when convicts were killed or died, nobody lost the money that once endowed the slave with economic value. Whether captive in Mississippi's infamous Parchman Farm, rebuilding Atlanta, constructing university campuses, or figured as fugitive and outlaw, the legal black personality became the enemy and criminal around which police power emerged. The black cultural tradition in the several decades after slavery thus took shape "from inside a story that denies its existence": it continually indexes "its negative relationship with the law," at once disavowed and constituted by the fictions of legal personhood.[132]

The criminalized legal person arising from the figure of the legal black slave in turn prompts other legal personae not delimited by race. Paradoxically invented by negation but captured within the ordering impulses of taxonomy, the legal black slave personality in turn generates the creation of other legal personalities beyond racial categories. Founding national documents and their revisions register these generative—and transformative—moments as much as any legal decision or piece of legislation. The language of exception in the Thirteenth Amendment, for example, inscribes the convertibility of personhood in an economy of civil death, so that former slaves get transformed into criminals, and convicts become not souls to be reborn but slaves of the state, to be bought and sold between public institutions and private companies by law. The precedent-setting case of *Ruffin v. The Commonwealth* (1871) invokes the medieval fiction of civil death in defining the legal personality of the convict.[133] Its most frequently quoted passage affirms that the convicted person "is for the time being the slave of the State. He is *civiliter mortuus*; and his estate, if he has any, is administered like that of a dead man." As with the slave codes and later cases invoking the Thirteenth Amendment—including the 1897 Supreme Court case *Robertson v. Baldwin*, discussed in chapter 1, which union seafarers dubbed "Dred Scott II"—*Ruffin v. Commonwealth* carves out of personhood its own ostensibly exceptional category, that of a living dead man whose legal nonexistence enables the law to compel him to labor and to live without the right to live. The case invokes the language that death-bound theories of personhood inadvertently reaffirm, a language of rights "stripped" from the body, in which nakedness thus signifies a condition of civil or biological death. The Court opinion personifies "the law in its humanity" as one who may strip the convict of the clothes (or rights) lent to him by the law and dress the prison authority in clothes of legal authority: the convict has "forfeited his liberty" and lost "all his personal rights." If he commits "an offence not amounting to a felony . . . the superintendent is vested by law with authority, to punish him by stripes, or the iron mask, or the gag, or the dungeon." An offense deemed felonious would give a convict the "privilege" of a trial, not the right to it. Rather than follow the court opinion in naturalizing the stripping or vesting of legal rights, what we see is again the generative force of the masks of personhood. Between the iron mask and the "privilege" of a trial by jury lies not one but two persons formed by law as its exceptions, one biologically alive but a "dead man" in law, the other a person enlarged by the power of the law itself to define crime and inflict punishment.[134]

The destruction of the legal slave—which was itself constructed in a pernicious act of juridical scavenging, produced out of the haphazard and instrumental use of earlier Roman, canon, medieval European, colonial, and national laws and customs as precedence—gave legal life in the United States to the convict-lease system and other "badges and incidents of that institution" that the Thirteenth Amendment ostensibly was intended to stamp out.[135] Mindful of Hartman's observation that *"the recognition of the slave as person depended upon the calculation of interest and injury,"* Dayan traces the genealogy of slavery in relation to civil death and civic expulsion without, I suggest, becoming bound to the limitations of social death theories I describe above.[136] Tracing how legal personhood works not only to protect or enlarge individual rights but also to inflict injury through civil death, slavery, or imprisonment, Dayan assembles the sequence of legal fictions that lead to the category of civil death, of the individual who "though possessing *natural life* has lost all *civil rights*" but has retained the personhood required for receiving civil punishment.[137] The slave and the felon are categories of "negative personhood," constructed out of "a negative relation to law."[138] Negative personhood is not an absence of personhood or the failure of law to recognize personhood; rather, it is a form of personhood paradoxically constructed in the law as that which is negated or incapacitated by the law. These conditions echo contemporary attenuated forms of statelessness: whereas citizenship is the legal bond between a state and an individual, statelessness is the shape of the bond's absence. Without the legal recognition of a state, today's stateless persons effectively become "nonpersons, legal ghosts."[139]

Tracking the genealogy of the law by tracing the movements of its ghosts, the afterlives of its constructions or creatures, Dayan reminds us that the felon shares with the slave a form of civil death, dependent on the notion of tainted blood, that continues to structure the U.S. prison system as a space permitted by law to also be outside it. When the felon is understood as a "slave of the state" who is dead in law, and when the courts determine that they should defer to prison authorities on the administering of the rights and duties of prisoners, as with policies on solitary confinement or punishments for crimes and infractions allegedly committed while incarcerated, what gets created is legal limbo or a legal sinkhole, an anomalous space into which the convicted person falls.[140] As Dayan notes, "The medieval fiction of civil death lives on in the present. The felon rendered dead in law is no anachronism but a continuing effect of dehumanizing practices of punishment." The mythologies and fictions that underpin the invention of legal personalities lead Dayan to question the spirit or spiritedness of the law in ways that draw on death-bound theories of personhood and wasted life while importantly refusing their finality: there is an ambiguity in the spirit of the law and its interplay between life and death, human and animal, person and thing, substance and ghostliness. The zombie in Haitian thought is an especially generative figure of the living dead; its ambiguity between life and death, freedom and captivity, and spirit and form keep Dayan's theory of personhood from being irresolutely death-bound.[141] Where Dayan finds ambiguity and complex, changeable, and mixed forms of being, more absolute theorists of personhood find only death and waste.

Abolition proves incomplete and unbound by race even when a state constitution is not amended, as in the U.S. context, but radically invented and reinvented, in more than one way, by more than one actor, throughout the antislavery revolution and in its aftermath. Such is the case with

Haiti and the 1801 and 1805 Constitutions that emerged during and after the Haitian Revolution. Sibylle Fischer brilliantly argues that the radical antislavery of the Haitian Revolution and its disavowal by modern political discourse since the nineteenth century foreclose the possibility of fully reckoning with the potential of the radical challenge to slavery and to the scientific-turned-legal taxonomies of race.[142] The Haitian Constitutions at once invoke and disavow the abolition of slavery through their attempts to define the citizen in relation to political economy. Consider the Constitution of 1801 in Saint-Domingue, drafted in the midst of the revolution under the military leadership of Toussaint Louverture, and which invoked "the absence of laws" as justification for its declarations, which stopped short of independence from France. Rather, the 1801 Constitution ordered the slave to disappear and made the French citizen appear in its place: "There cannot exist slaves on this territory, servitude is therein forever abolished. All men are born, live and die free and French."[143] It names free citizenship as civic responsibility for "cultivators," however, in what amounts to forced plantation labor: "The colony being essentially agricultural cannot suffer the least disruption in the works of its cultivation," and "cultivators [are thus] indispensible to the reestablishment and to the growth of agriculture."[144] In the struggle to create a form of free personhood as yet "unthinkable" within European epistemologies yet under French sovereignty, Louverture struggles to find a language—to speak not of slaves but of cultivators.[145]

The 1805 Imperial Constitution of Haiti written under Jean-Jacques Dessalines declares Haiti radically free "from all other powers of the universe" and its people citizens and "brothers," for whom "equality in the eye of the Law is indisputably recognized" and "the same for all, whether it punishes or protects."[146] Whereas Louverture's 1801 Constitution sets forth a race-neutral politics, in which the only mention of race is that "all men, regardless of color, are eligible to all employment," the radical antislavery language of Dessalines's 1805 Constitution makes blackness *the* political category of citizenship.[147] But, in the more radical promise of declaring an antislavery sovereign state power, the latter constitution is still not free from the economic imperatives of the plantation colonial structure. Citizenship, as tied to blackness and to absolute loyalty to the state and its laws, also remains bound to the market: "Agriculture shall be honored and protected as the first, the most noble, and the most useful among the trades," to be followed by "Commerce," which "neither needs nor admits fetters."[148] This free market ideology of a certain kind will come to structure the legal identities of the nation through the neoliberal era. Unchained and unrestrained, the plantation system renews the economic dispossession of Haiti's laboring class both within Haiti and outside it, those with uncertain legal status who seek work as cane cutters and sugar mill workers in the Dominican Republic and nearby Caribbean states, the United States, and Brazil.

As the 1805 Haitian Constitution and the Thirteenth Amendment of the U.S. Constitution show in their distinct ways, the importance of the racially demarcated legal slave in the Americas and its incomplete abolition cannot be understood solely in relation to a presumably stable blackness, whether historically or in contemporary life, as if blackness has ever been a natural or closed subjectivity. The legal slave, for all its particular historical variations in jurisprudence as its fragments appear and disappear across imperial, colonial, and state legal systems over centuries in the Americas, starkly highlights what liberal models of recognition conceal: the problem of rights is not the narrow exclusions of liberal politics, in which some are recognized as full persons and others less so, but that political dispossession, qualified forms of exclusion, economic imperatives, and phantom taxonomies inhere within the very category of the legal person itself.

It is legal personhood and its extraordinary powers—its infinite malleability, its capacity for metamorphosis, its spontaneous generation of new categories, its taxonomic drive, particular contingencies, and variable practice—that enable the archive of legal slavery to become visible in the workings of law in the twenty-first century, both within and beyond categories of blackness and across and beyond the Black Atlantic, African American, African diaspora, Caribbean, Latina/o studies, and critical theories of civil, labor, refugee, and human rights. The history of the legal slave personality animates a range of recent literary and cultural texts that also respond to the crises of legal personhood that come with the rise of neoliberalism even as civil rights are imagined to be moving ever closer to their fullest and most progressive expression. "The tangled mess that is the modern usage of neoliberalism," observes one scholar of political economy, "may tell us something about the tangled mess of neoliberalism itself."[149] I won't claim to untangle the threads here, then, so much as to bring into view one aspect of this mess: its project of redefining personhood in law, a project that involves retasking the state to change the relation of individuals to politics and economics. The figure of the individual so crucial to neoliberal doctrine is the figure of the legal person. And here we have again the problem of an imagined single subject in political-economic thought, where the liberal individual is enlarged and revamped into the neoliberal individual person. In neoliberal theory, the asymmetry of power between individuals is not recognized as being structured in the law.[150] The neoliberal state protects strong individual property rights and individual responsibility for one's own well-being—but what emerges as possibly the ideal legal person under neoliberalism is a person whose property rights are enlarged and whose responsibility is stunningly limited, and that is the corporation, a financial person with no physical body to punish.[151] The economic insecurity of populations, so essential to the market, gets recast as evidence of the defective human personality of individuals rather than of economic-political-legal transformations under neoliberalism. As Margaret Thatcher famously retorted to those who would look to "society" for protection and security, "And who is society? There is no such thing! There are individual men and women and there are families and no government can do anything except through people and people look to themselves first."[152] Society having been disappeared, the state and the individual undergo a transformed relation through the market: "Economics are the method; the object is to change the heart and soul."[153] Where Frantz Fanon dreamed of a "new man" who would transcend the distortions of colonialism and nationalism in the human personality, here Thatcher dreams of an individual whose heart and soul would be changed by neoliberal economics—changed into what is not quite clear.

As I suggest in the chapters that follow, literature highlights the legal person as a paradoxical and unstable construction, one that promises individuals equality before the law even as it has historically generated complex and differential legal taxonomies. Such literary texts narrate the challenges of telling unrecoverable stories, so that their play with narrative form and structure shows an aesthetic of salvage as a narrative process, a practice that must also be improvised in response to what is found and how it might be salvaged. Here, the ruins are figured as the remains of economic collapse as well as the ruins of legal personhood, with its legally defunct categories (legal slave, enemy alien) that persist and perpetuate current legal identities (felon, enemy combatant). To alter William Faulkner's famous line, the legal past is never dead: it's not even past.[154] Always undead, the legal past is also never merely itself—not past and not fully present: defunct, sometimes vestigial, sometimes merely latent, the legal past may be invoked as law and jurisprudence bring into being categories of legal personhood that are not absolutely new so much as transformations and alterations of what once was. Thus, as mentioned above, the enemy alien morphs into the enemy combatant; the Dominican citizen born of Haitian parentage becomes stateless; or the indigenous Guatemalan becomes utterly alienated from the state, forced either to serve as its agent of terror or become the enemy upon which state terror is unleashed.

Salvage Work tracks the instability of legal personhood as its figures edge or fall into the category of the criminal and the stateless. The convicted criminal, like the fugitive and the stateless person, embodies the haunting figure of the legal black slave. As the successor to the legal slave, the prisoner is the figure of the criminal that shadows the conditions of fugitivity and criminality that are the concern of this book. Chapter 1 reads the abandoned Central American crewmen in Goldman's *The Ordinary Seaman* in relation to the case of imprisoned merchant seamen in *Robertson v. Baldwin* before turning to consider the interrelated histories of three New York sites: the salvage archaeology and liberal discourse of national belonging used to commemorate the African Burial Ground in lower Manhattan, the history of Ellis Island as immigrant gateway and detention center, and the prison labor used for decades to bury the unclaimed and anonymous dead at the potter's field in Hart Island. The shadow of the convicted criminal looms over the potential criminality of the abandoned crew members in Goldman's novel, and it shapes the figurative economic imprisonment of Danticat's characters at a sugar mill in neoliberalized Haiti and the antiprostitution laws that help animate the competition over the deed to a sugar mill in Ferré's novella in chapter 2. Chapter 3 reads Jones's *Song for Anninho* and *Mosquito* as responding to death-bound theories by redefining sanctuary as a vital and open practice rather than a bounded space—a literary experiment that also demands a rethinking of giving sanctuary to certain kinds of legal persons. The chapter thus moves between historical narratives of sanctuary through early church sanctuary laws, the Underground Railroad in the United States and the earlier Maroon communities in colonial Brazil, the historical Sanctuary movement begun in the 1980s (when unauthorized Central American refugees were welcomed by U.S. movement organizers in violation of immigration law), and the Zapatista movement (which promises new visions of what sovereignty could mean in the Americas). In chapter 4, the figure of the prisoner erupts in Wideman's narration in *Fanon* through dialogues with his incarcerated brother Robert as he serves a life sentence; it haunts public memory in the face of Emmett Till, whose extralegal lynching was affirmed by a U.S. court that refused to convict the fifteen-year-old boy's white murderers; and it haunts the decolonial future that Fanon hoped for and that has yet to arrive. In other words, this book does not focus on prison literature so much as it explores literature of the conditions of fugitivity and incarceration generated by legal personhood. For the characters and storyworlds examined in the chapters that follow, the prison is always there, even or especially when they aren't in it.

Nonetheless, when the literary texts discussed in this book narrate carceral, fugitive, or statelesss forms of life, they do so in ways that undermine the rhetoric of bare life that organizes critical scholarship on rights and rightlessness. Take, for example, the death-bound reading that informs Waligora-Davis's theorizing of sanctuary not as a safe space for African Americans but as a space of peril: "Sanctuaries are Hannah Arendt's camps. They are Giorgio Agamben's state of exception." They are "spaces of interment in the fullest sense: places realizing forms of social and—tragically—sometimes literal death."[155] In this view, the ostensibly safe space becomes not a refuge from legal and informal racial violence against African Americans, whose own state has marked them for death, but a space of death. Jones's *Mosquito* provides a direct response to this reading of sanctuaries by reconceptualizing sanctuary as not a space at all but instead a decolonial and liberatory process, a movement that does not stop but that narrates lines of flight, of *marronage*, through narrational digressions that become textual counterparts to the Underground Railroad and "not the mainstream" fictional sanctuary movement's evasion of U.S. Customs and the Border Patrol.[156] In *Mosquito* and *Song for Anninho*, Jones's poetics of sanctuary refuses to depict sanctuary as a bounded, safe, and protective destination: she highlights the limits of finding refuge in law through the reclassification of one's legal status or of making pleas for a sanctuary space of temporary reprieve from law even as she refuses to confirm a death-bound imagination of personhood.

Salvage Work draws together studies of nineteenth-century literature, slavery, and legal culture and studies of twentieth- and twenty-first-century African American, Latina/o, and Caribbean literature, culture, race, ethnicity, and migration. Informed by theories of personhood that arise at the intersections of literature, law, critical race theory, and history, *Salvage Work* explores texts that variously perform but also refuse to remain within the feedback loop of failed narratives and archival hauntings.[160] Such theories rely, in varying degrees, on death-bound theories of personhood even as they try to resist collapsing all distinctions into a politics of death. Where Agamben seeks to extend and replicate the threshold paradigm in his theory of sovereign violence, revealing "naked life" where we assumed there were persons, for example, Dayan is better attuned to the haunting force of the law as a complex assemblage of legal, economic, political, and cultural thought about personhood that produces violent effects even when such effects would fall below the "threshold" of recognition, outside the limit cases of bare life. Her work provocatively attends to how legal thought and court law perpetually salvages from among its own ruins, retaining spectral or apparently obsolete traces of earlier medieval European laws as they migrate into Caribbean slave codes, antebellum U.S. legal reasoning, and legal rulings on the modern prison that revitalize conditions of civil death in the "making and unmaking of persons" in the twenty-first century.[158] As my readings demonstrate, contemporary literature figures nineteenth-century taxonomies of legal personhood as animating taxonomies of legal and criminalized persons since the late twentieth century. They also highlight questions of how economic roles get defined in legal identities too often presumed to be merely political or merely economic, as in the case of the legal distinction between an economic alien and a political refugee.[159]

Revealing the inability of current theories of both legal liberalism and death-bound personhood to address the history of the person as a juridical as well as an aesthetic figure, *Salvage Work* explores the literary labors of pulling from the ruin—or the toxic waste—of legal history. It turns to contemporary narrative fiction that gathers together the fragments of legal personhood as they cohere around race, labor, sex, migration, and citizenship status, and as they develop, morph, pass out of, or remain spectrally within the public record. These literary texts pointedly do not make it their primary goal to humanize victims by "giving a human face" to tragedy.[160] These texts do not recuperate the humanness of devalued forms of life. Nor do they displace the ethical onto the theologically inspired relation of one to an other. Rather, they point up the discursive and physical violence generated by the fiction of legal personhood itself, with its capacity for malleability and metamorphosis, translation, and adaptation across categories, legal systems, and sovereign power.

What lies beneath the masks of personhood, then, for so-called natural persons—how to conceptualize, experience, or recuperate the meanings of human beings that have been individuated through what Foucault calls "governmentality"—is not the primary subject of this book. The "natural person" in positive law, much like the inalienability of human rights, is fictive and "conventional" in the multiple meanings of the word, despite the pervasive conflation of person with human in contemporary theory and public discourse. These texts experiment with narrative forms that point up the fictiveness of the law in its taxonomic drive to construct categories of personhood that are then recognized as exceptions to the normative legal personality of the abstract legal person. Ultimately, as I hope this book demonstrates, contemporary narrative fiction offers provocative ways of thinking anew the politics and poetics of person-hood. It asks us to consider what it means that the masks of person-hood do not disguise true personhood but reveal it—when we consider Wideman's aphorism, "Masks do not disguise truth. Masks are true."[161] Whereas liberal recuperation would seek to remove the masks of oppres-sion and find the face of the natural person beneath, and death-bound theories of personhood would prize off the mask to find the figure of death always already constituted by sovereignty, I contend that we must look to the masks of personhood itself, as they get made and remade, assembled and reassembled. Legal masks are already formed from ruin and debris: they are the product of legal scavenging and the material for future assemblages of legal personhood. And the recognition that this is so is the first step toward a political imagination that does not mistake the mask for flesh, and that neither merely entrusts the human being to the protection of liberal progress nor names her or him as inevitably lost to the apocalyptic deathworlds of the biopolitical. In this sense, *Salvage Work* draws on tropes of ruin and waste, but it does so while insisting that to end there—as does so much recent public and intellectual discus-sion—is to stop where we should begin.

PART ONE

Legal Debris

1 / The Free, the Slave, and the Disappeared: States and Sites of Exceptional Personhood in Francisco Goldman's *The Ordinary Seaman*

For thousands of today's international seafarers life at sea is modern slavery and their workplace is a slave ship.
—INTERNATIONAL COMMISSION ON SHIPPING REPORT,
SHIPS, SLAVES, AND COMPETITION

The cover of Francisco Goldman's *The Ordinary Seaman* (1997) features the image of a massive cargo ship as it looms above three minuscule human figures in silhouette. From the photographer Sebastião Salgado's *Workers: An Archaeology of the Industrial Age,* the image is one of a series of photographs that document the ship-breaking industry, which, Salgado informs us, has waned over the course of the 1980s due to the rising costs of demolition.[1] Hailed by Gabriel García Márquez as "the photography of humanity," *Workers* is vast: it includes three hundred fifty large duotone photographs of laborers from twenty-six countries in an effort to construct a global vision of manual labor at the cusp of its visual and material disappearance. Shot between 1986 and 1992 at the shores of Chittagong, Bangladesh, the ship-breaking series focuses on the sandy deathbed of ships run aground to be disassembled. Massive mooring chains descend from the cargo ship's nostrils and across the image, toward the camera's location, as if the viewer were gazing up at a giant, rusted beast restrained. Salgado describes this scavenging in the way that whale hunters might describe their kill: "Everything from that huge animal lying on the beach has a use. Iron and steel will be melted down and given new roles as utensils. The entire ship will be turned into what it once carried: machines, knives and forks, hoes, shovels, screws, things, bits, pieces."[2] The raw materials of this animal undergo the miracle of transformation, evidence of an economy perfectly without waste because the waste itself is valued for its ability to be reshaped into something unrecognizable from its previous form, the vessel turned into the things it once carried.

What about the laborers tasked with scavenging among these ruins? It is only some time after the eye moves over the foregrounded image of the massive ship and chains that it discerns the silhouettes of three human figures standing idly by the shore, the reason for their presence not yet clear.[3] Ship breakers themselves are treated as disposable laborers whose labor's worth has further declined: many shipowners now sink their ships because it is cheaper than breaking it down and recycling its parts. In photographing the scavenging of ship breakers, the romanticized salvaging of *Workers* is on display. The ship breakers' disposability is visually evoked even as the images risk reproducing rather than questioning the economic devaluation of industrial workers: "Just as a cat will pounce on a slowly moving piece of string only when it is about to disappear from sight," writes Julian Stallabrass, "so there is a powerful aesthetic urge to grasp the fugitive at the moment of its extinction."[4] In his "ambition to provide a universal image of a disappearing working world," Salgado risks edging into the thoroughly critiqued but also enduring geopolitical "salvage paradigm" in anthropology and ethnography, what James Clifford names as "a desire to rescue something 'authentic' out of destructive historical changes."[5] Salgado frames the images as a visual elegy to the industrial era, "a farewell to a world of manual labor that is slowly disappearing and a tribute to those men and women who still work as they have for centuries . . . provid[ing] the central axis of the world."[6] These photos aim to contain the contradictions of the present in transition, of a past persisting into the present even as the present is generating a future incompatible with that past: "part of the immediate shock of Salgado's work is simply to present contemporary scenes which should have long been banished from the perfectible neoliberal state."[7] A variant of "imperialist nostalgia," in which ethnographers seek to rescue through scholarship that which they are complicit in destroying, Salgado's work feeds neoliberal narratives of market progress by portraying the timeless physical strength and dignity of manual laborers around the world even as it prepares us for the coming of the new global economy. In what now sounds like a relic of the nineties economic bubble, the editors of *Wired* exhibit this unbridled millennial enthusiasm for corporate technoculture. "When we talk about the new economy," they write in a 1998 issue, "we're talking about a world in which people work with their brains instead of their hands. A world in which communications technology creates global competition. . . . A world at least as different from what came before it as the industrial age was from its agricultural predecessor. A world so different its emergence can only be described as a revolution."[8] Salgado oddly joins his tribute to workers with a post-1970s celebratory discourse on neoliberal globalization as an economic revolution in which manual labor becomes vestigial to the new, high-tech global economic body—or even disappears (despite the many hands in mines, sweatshops, and free trade zones that manufacture technological commodities in the "digital age").[9] For both Salgado and the cyber-revolutionaries of the 1990s, the workers vaguely remain as visual traces while their material and manual labor undergoes erasure.

The Ordinary Seaman interferes with all the talk of clean futures and global flows by pointedly *not* moving: by turning off the engine, so to speak, and slowing one economic venture to a standstill.[10] The story revolves around the changing fortunes of a scheme to salvage a cargo ship, and it ends with the shipowners abandoning their vessel and the hired crew on board, who cannot legally leave the ship but who cannot stay on board either. The newly formed motley crew arrives at Brooklyn Harbor to find that they have been hired to repair and inhabit this ghost ship—a "phantom ship," "a ghost ship stone silent," "a dead ship, a mass of inert iron provocatively shaped like a ship," what the experienced ship waiter Bernardo calls a "broken eggshell," the floating remains of potentiality, in need of electricity, unseaworthy, and unhomely.[11] The secret shipowners are depicted as bumbling middle-class U.S. entrepreneurs who come into some money: unbeknownst to the crew, the owners have conspired to buy the burnt-out ship in the name of a dummy corporation invented for this purpose, get the vessel tugged to the cheapest berth in Brooklyn Harbor, hire a repair crew of cheap migrant laborers under false pretenses, insure it for more than its worth, and then sell it or sink it for the insurance money. As their plans falter, the owners allow the ship's registry to lapse and do not complete the necessary papers for the men they hire, leaving the ship and the men to freefall into statelessness and illegality. By the end of the novel, the Central Americans who paid to leave their countries and work legally in the United States are transformed into undocumented migrants without any enforceable rights; the shipowners are left with a failed investment but retain their anonymity under cover of the corporation; and the ship itself, its Panamanian registry expired, is hotwired by the crew just long enough to run it aground, leaving the ship—unlike the vessel of Salgado's photograph—in a state that is not even worth its weight in scrap.

In the slow unraveling of this entrepreneurial venture, the ship never sails more than a few inches. Elias, one of the secret shipowners, assumes the linear temporality of the anthropological salvage paradigm, in which progressive societies must rescue the more primitive and thus vanishing ones, and the neoliberal optimism in free market futures. In a comical fit of imperialist nostalgia, Elias names the dummy corporation that buys the ship Achuar Corporation, after an Amerindian tribe he encounters on his adventures in the Amazon. Such neoliberal imperialist nostalgia is persistently unraveled in *The Ordinary Seaman*, whose verb tenses alternate between past and future anterior, the recounting of what was once the future. During the months of slow abandonment, one crewman— nineteen-year-old Esteban, a Sandinista veteran who fought in a special counterinsurgency unit of the Batallón de Lucha Irregular (BLI) against Contra fighters during the war in Nicaragua—reflects on the stagnant temporality of the venture. Bringing together the left revolutionary rhetoric of the Sandinistas and the free market ideology of the ship venture to bear on his present condition, he thinks: "They were always telling you that the war was over the future, no? But it was really always about the present, a world spiked and shadowed with the portents that looked ahead to the next second, minute, hour, day, and no further. And now the future is here and, hijueputa, look at it: a ship that doesn't move" (177). This sense of the future as a failed salvage operation, pulled into the time of the past and harnessed in a state of suspension, is reinforced by passages in the future anterior tense focalized through John the Ship Visitor, who eventually finds the abandoned crew and whose job it is to advocate for the health, safety, and rights of international seafarers. John's narration shifts frequently to the future anterior tense, in which the future again is shuttled into the past as that which "will have happened." His belated and ultimately ineffectual effort to rescue the abandoned crew as well as their lost wages rehearses his previous (and likely future) efforts with abandoned or abused crews. For John, the future of the *Urus* is that which will have happened to past crews on other ships. The future of the *Urus* is its past, and the rehearsal of that past leads, as if inevitably, to disappearance and death.

This chapter on *The Ordinary Seaman* considers how competing modes of salvage operate to manipulate or to reveal the states of exceptional personhood in the neoliberal era. It traces exceptional states of personhood as they are formed at particular sites of exception, from the broken cargo ship in Brooklyn Harbor to the sites of anonymous burial and immigrant detention. Building on trenchant readings of the novel by April Shemak, Kirsten Silva Gruesz, and Ana Patricia Rodríguez, the first section of the chapter examines the novel's depiction of refuge and enslavement before focusing on the little-known U.S. maritime labor case *Robertson v. Baldwin*, which I argue exemplifies the very slippages between exceptional labor identities that the novel explores. The abandoned crewmen are not merely victims of anti-immigration policies:

they are also figures formed out of the slow accumulation of legal logics used to authorize unfree laboring persons in societies that posit the free wage laborer as the normative and ideal legal subject. Importantly, the punitive exceptionality of the legally unfree laborer finds its counterpart not in the ideal free wage laborer but rather in the liberating exceptionality of the ship and the corporate person. One category of exceptional personhood ratifies the other within the maritime site of exception, and it is the ship as exception to the usual sovereign and legal order that has been instrumental to the circum-Atlantic slave trade and European colonialism no less than to the business of contemporary cruise lines and commercial shipping. The seafarer of Goldman's novel emerges as exceptional in the legal impossibility of redress for the crew's loss of labor and human rights and in the historical rendering of seafarers within U.S. law that animates the novel's depiction of the crew members, who resemble sailors, victims of human trafficking, enslaved persons, migrants, and stateless refugees but who are ultimately criminalized as undocumented economic migrants or so-called illegal aliens.

The next section of the chapter considers how the shipowners' attempted economic salvage of the *Urus* provides the novel with the opportunity to trace the tangled relationship between histories of global economic trade and the mask of sovereignty that enables the anonymity of the maritime corporate person—resulting in an economic system supported by state mechanisms that paradoxically enable maritime corporate personhood (and sovereign states themselves) to evade state law. This section tracks the figure of the ship as a generative site of exceptional forms of maritime sovereignty and corporate ownership, forms such as the modern open registries system, which originated as a way for ships to evade British law abolishing the slave trade.

The final section of the chapter examines how competing modes of salvage shape the meanings of exceptional sites and exceptional categories of laboring and corporate personhood. It tracks one plot line in the novel, the disappearance and death of the ship waiter Bernardo, in order to examine New York not merely as the core of the financial economic booms of the 1980s and 1990s but also and relatedly as the city of immigrant detention and abandonment, invisible labor, and anonymous burial. Reading how competing modes of salvage inform the representations of three related New York sites of exception—Hart Island, the African Burial Ground, and Ellis Island—this chapter contrasts neoliberal economic and liberal political modes of salvage with the aesthetics of salvage as an artistic practice and a mode of reading that responds to the histories of legal personhood. Against the neoliberal imperialist nostalgia of the novel's shipowners and mindful of the limits of memorializing New York's slave past as part of a national myth of benign immigrant origins, the novel invites a critical mode of reading that traces the persistence of the legal slave personality as it continues to shape the states of exceptional personhood.

Ordinary Labors

The effects of neoliberal and neocolonial practices on laborers haunt the storyworld of the novel, as a world of transnational human migrations, postindustrial decline, and U.S.-supported conflicts—including the Reagan administration's "war on drugs," which included its covert funding of Contra fighters in Nicaragua using money from crack cocaine imports to U.S. inner cities, the wars in Guatemala and El Salvador, and the 1989 invasion of Panama that reasserted U.S. control over the Panama Canal. Inspired by a 1982 newspaper account of a Central American crew abandoned on the Brooklyn waterfront by anonymous shipowners, the ship—registered as a Panamanian vessel—becomes one nexus of these wars, the criminalization of Latino migration, and the Reaganite embrace of neoliberal entrepreneurship. Goldman sets the story in the sunset months of 1989, amid the neoliberal economic boom on Wall Street and the decline of industrial port jobs and anticipation of the Cold War's end. The Cold War operates like white noise throughout the novel, with occasional references to the invasion of Panama and through the flashbacks and thoughts of the young veteran Esteban, confined to the *Urus* even as the Sandinista regime was on the cusp of collapsing.[12]

Esteban, the eponymous "ordinary seaman" of Goldman's novel, arrives at a dilapidated section of Brooklyn Harbor to find that the cargo ship in which he and fourteen other men (some from Nicaragua, others from Honduras, and one from Guatemala) will live and work for months is little more than an iron hulk, unseaworthy and in bad disrepair. Grimly surveying his surroundings—"abandoned, wrecked shells of old warehouses, office, and shipping terminals," the "stumps of collapsed piers," a "defunct" grain elevator and the "rubble" of the old grain terminal—Esteban focuses his attention on one terminal, "its blue paint eroded by age and salt," that "looked like a giant circus tent, sky showing through its broken slates, faded lettering in English, French, and Arabic over its broad doorways: 'Wienstock Spice Co.'" (29). The lettering on this terminal, whose collapsed structure suggests the once-festive exoticism of the spice trade as well as its transience, functions as a trace of the assemblage of colonial histories that comprise the men's present condition in Brooklyn Harbor. In reading this trace, Esteban repurposes what is otherwise a junked remainder of a past economy. He revalues the sign so that it offers a clue to the crew's present condition: reading the junked remainders of economic history amounts to a practice of reading that resembles the process of salvaging, of revaluing and repurposing the marks of their history. Those marks hold the potential for a mode of reading that historicizes the present, and to read for those marks is to attempt to recover and make meaning of what has not been lost so much as devalued or considered defunct. As Esteban and the other men eventually discover, the harbor's ruins have silently registered the shifts and the continuities in the legal personhood of laborers—especially the citizens, sailors, migrants, and unauthorized refugees that have passed through, or been detained, there.

Esteban is the first to escape the ship and establish a life in the surrounding Latino neighborhood as an undocumented and unauthorized refugee. Highlighting the refuge sought most immediately from the economic venture of the *Urus,* Esteban identifies himself as "a refugee from a ship" (266). Some of the men eventually follow him; several are deported; and one, the old ship waiter Bernardo who first understood the futility of their salvage work on the ship, vanishes. In narrating a story of failed economic salvage, *The Ordinary Seaman* reveals the traces of economic, legal, and political histories that constitute the conditions of possibility for the laboring person in the neoliberal present. In this way, the novel incorporates often-hidden or seemingly minor labor histories of the Americas, such as the faded lettering of the Wienstock Spice Company in English, French, and Arabic: its repetition in three languages, which were brought together through a once-powerful colonial spice trade, is under partial erasure by the weathering of time but persists nonetheless, albeit in a state of abandonment and wreckage in Brooklyn Harbor. The sign is an obvious reflection of the present and future state of the *Urus,* a cargo ship that, as the men soon learn, is as thoroughly wrecked (and will be just as fully abandoned) as the shells of the once-vibrant, pre-container-shipping maritime commerce now lining the harbor with the material history of its ruination. The reference also evokes the centrality of the cargo ship to the spice trade, whose significance to the economic and political histories of the Americas is demonstrated by its dominance of the world economic market, its expansion of colonial trade routes by European empires to the Americas, and its role in developing port cities into sites of enormous economic power and labor dispossession, as happened with New York City. The history of the cargo ship and the spice trade have been thoroughly entangled, one powered by the other, in ways that persist, even if they persist as ruins.

Haunting *The Ordinary Seaman*'s Central American crew are these histories and their traces in contemporary immigration discourse on the economic migrant and the political refugee. The novel's title refers to a legal status and a question, since the crewmen's legal status as "ordinary seaman" depends on the paperwork that the owners never fill out—what J. L. Austin would describe as an infelicity, the failure of a performative speech act.[13] The ordinary seamen in the novel, it turns out, have no definite legal identity. Their indefinite affinities with the slave, wage laborer, economic migrant, unauthorized refugee, or alien challenge the prevailing binary categorization of laboring persons into free and unfree status. The category "ordinary seaman" becomes one point in the lines of emergence and descent for a conventionally exceptional category of legal labor identity: in this and other ways, it is linked to the category of the legal slave.

What the fifteen crewmen encounter in the form of a burnt-out, unseaworthy contemporary containership is the revenant of the ship at the height of its imaginative, economic, and military powers in the hemisphere—the specter of a slaver. The crew members are suspended between multiple categories of legal personhood: they have become something like slaves without literally being enslaved, they have become something like seamen without ever setting sail or receiving the work papers that would declare them as such, and they are something like stateless persons without formally losing their citizenship from their respective Central American states. The ship operates as an effectively stateless and spectral vessel in the seas of global capital, concealing its owners and suspending the crew's legal personalities in a condition of limbo, as the men's status undergoes a "slippage from salaried [seamen] to slaves—from steerage of the *carguero* to unwanted and abandoned human cargo."[14] The border system—what Mary Pat Brady names an "abjection machine"—proliferates as sovereign jurisdictions overlap in the space of the ship in Brooklyn Harbor and as legal categories reveal their indistinctness.[15]

In search of economic and psychic refuge from the devastations of the Central American wars, the crewmen's presence effectively casts the ship into the role of a broken-down refugee boat and the men as refugees. Shemak argues that the crew's position evokes the category "refugee seamen," established after World War II in the United Nations Convention Relating to the Status of Refugees and the Agreement Relating to Refugee Seamen: this category itself may be read as a kind of exception from the general category of the refugee in that "refugee seamen" identifies a class of refugees defined by their occupation. In this way, this category of personhood contradicts "the cleavage between the economic and political distinctions used in determining refugee status."[16] When the crew members' promised refuge becomes the site of their captivity, Esteban's description of himself as "a refugee from a ship" underscores the complexity of their condition as political-economic refugees who are subject to criminalization by the state as "illegal aliens." As the secret coowner Elias frequently reminds them in the early period of their captivity, the men are unauthorized aliens on U.S. territory; unspoken is the understanding that, as unauthorized persons, they are refugees who in seeking refuge would be recognized instead as fugitives of the law (indeed, "refugee" and "fugitive" share more than an etymological link in the Latin *fugĕre,* meaning to flee). The men at once exist outside the law and are defined by that very outsideness: they are made into refugees who cannot flee and fugitives that have themselves committed no legal crime.

Nineteenth-century legal interpretations of the enslaved person and the merchant mariner oddly come to haunt twentieth- and twenty-first-century legal interpretations of the undocumented laborer or "illegal alien." Whereas the legal personhood of the slave entailed an "instrumental alternation between person and thing," the legal personhood of the sailor has alternated between recognized legal identities (citizen, seaman) and legal identities that have ostensibly been abolished (slave, indentured laborer, victim of human trafficking).[17] The crewmen ultimately fall outside the framework of recognized legal personhood as free wage, rights-bearing laborers, in part because existing legal institutions provide no recourse.

When John the Ship Visitor eventually finds the abandoned crew, he fails to make the men recognizable in law except as unauthorized aliens subject to deportation. Called "the Ship Visitor" in the novel, John's title underscores the informality of his role as labor advocate (as if he were just visiting). John fails to recover pay for the crewmen and to bring charges against the shipowners—a failure made inevitable by past U.S. legal cultures, which delimited the nineteenth-century categories of the enslaved person and of the merchant mariner in particular as they continue to animate the process by which certain categories of the laboring person effectively exclude (whether formally or informally) individuals from making any legal claim to civil and human rights. The Ship Visitor's failure can be seen most obviously in the contexts of uneven U.S. immigration and asylum policy as well as the lack of national and international legal protections for maritime and immigrant laborers.[18]

In a departure from the narrative conventions of the immigrant novel, *The Ordinary Seaman* does not dramatize a high-risk border crossing or culminate in the passage through Ellis Island and the trials and pleasures of acculturation or assimiliation. Instead, Goldman's novel inscribes itself in the traditions of the maritime novel and of nineteenth-century accounts of legal personhood at sea, especially Herman Melville's 1855 novella, *Benito Cereno,* which itself draws on U.S. legal cases over the classification of Africans in revolt on slave ships and over the spoils of maritime salvage, and the 1897 U.S. Supreme Court case *Robertson v. Baldwin,* which upheld criminal punishment for merchant mariners who challenged their contracted labor status. The case served as a belated echo of earlier debates over the legal personhood of seamen as exceptional to the rule in U.S. labor law that free wage laborers cannot be criminally punished by their employer or forced to perform work, even if under contract. These texts grapple with the ambiguous legal status of laboring persons as something akin to mariners, slaves, prisoners, and refugees.

Melville exploits the fundamental ambiguity and politics of salvage in *Benito Cereno,* whose marine salvage plot explores the juridical limits of slavery and the politics of black fugitivity. Salvage is more than a metaphor of recuperation: as a legal term, *salvage* refers to the authorized acquisition by a *salvor* (one who salvages, one who saves) of property that has been relinquished by its current owner, whether due to death, incapacity, impending peril, or abandonment. A salvage operation refers to the rescue of an imperiled seafaring vessel and its contents by a salvor entitled to the salvaged property as reward. In the effort to distinguish salvage from simple theft, the claimant must prove altruistic intent— that "the service performed by claimant must have been of benefit to the property involved in the rescue" rather than performed with the expectation of acquiring such property.[19]

The potential ambiguity between liberation and exploitation, rescue and entrapment, personhood and property, thus makes legal maritime salvage a strange sort of salvation. Salvage rights have the potential to redefine the limits and conditions of legal personhood for both the salvor and—when the property in question is human—to the salvaged cargo. State-sanctioned salvage depends on the legal fiction of personhood in its qualified categories of inclusion and exclusion—especially of fugitivity (of being outside the law and yet inscribed within the space of the law) and property (of being a person who may be alienated into property to the benefit of the owner and/or the state). Such unstable fictions are constructed and buttressed by racial paradigms, cultural and historical contingency, the juridical reading of personhood, and legal precedent. The anomalous zone of marine salvage—at once outside of and inscribed by sovereign laws—displays the politics of racialized personhood and the legal alienability of human rights with stunning force for both masters and captives, captains and crew.

Melville's story revolves around the *San Dominick*, a slaver whose African captives wrest control of the vessel from its crew even as they must perform their black captivity in front of Amasa Delano, captain of the *Bachelor's Delight*, whose own interest involves control of the ship and its human cargo as due reward for salvaging it. The novella's concluding section appends the criminal proceedings against the insurrection and Benito's translated court depositions. Jeannine Marie DeLombard turns to the conflict between the two ship captains—the American Amasa Delano and the Spaniard Benito Cereno—in order to show how the conflict over Delano's salvage rights claims exposes a crucial paradox of the legal and literary discourse of personhood:

> Contracts and testimony pile up within and between [the historical] Delano's *Narrative* and Melville's *Benito Cereno*, but instead of corroborating the legal personhood of their agents, these amassed textual assertions of civil agency cumulatively deauthorize text and author alike. Far from affirming autonomous selfhood, legal and extralegal acts of testifying and contract making document its absence. Together these seafaring tales suggest that, rather than anchoring the subject in the bedrock of accumulated precedent, the seismic accretion of legal and literary texts unmoor their putative agents, casting them, Pip-like, adrift in a sea of legal personlessness.[20]

The law that should affirm free personhood negates it; the testimony that should affix legal identities to laboring bodies sets it adrift; and the logic of precedent that should anchor the subject in a tradition of rights unmoors him. DeLombard evokes here the effects of what Waligora-Davis has called the politics of recognition in legal cases involving insurrections on slave ships, cases that turned on whether the Africans who revolted were rightly identified as pirates, mutineers, fugitive property (slaves), or human beings illegally kidnapped and trafficked.[21]

The politics of salvage measures human and civil rights by calibrating legal personhood to economic categories of dehumanized labor and human property. As an exceptional legal space, the cargo ship at the center of Goldman's novel, the *Urus*, becomes a space of sanctuary that enables such a calibration of legal to economic categories of personhood and that echoes the ship in Melville's *Benito Cereno* as a putative space of sanctuary.[22] Building on scholarship by Eric Sundquist and others,

Waligora-Davis reveals *Benito Cereno* to be a complex meditation on the racialized vision that adjudicates the legal personality denied to the black body. The *San Dominick* emerges as a site of refuge in line with the "cultural work of asylums" as "sites for managing unmanageable populations."[23] The slaver in Melville's novella, the *San Dominick*, is figured as a sanctuary—that is, "an anomic legal state predicated on the rupture of blackness from legal personality that is achieved by denying the humanity of the black body. . . . Sanctuaries are spaces that mirror the violence that constitute them."[24] Melville's range of national and international sources—including the Fugitive Slave Act of 1850, the Haitian Revolution (1791–1804), the slave insurrections on the Spanish *Tryal* (1805) and *Amistad* (1839) and their resulting court trials, and the 1817 travel narrative of the historical Amasa Delano, in which Delano argues for his salvage rights to the *Tryal*—tell the history of slave revolution as inextricable from the politics of salvage both on land and at sea.[25] The Fugitive Slave Act of 1850—or the majority decision in the *Tryal*—becomes a mandate to U.S. authorities and civilians to kidnap black persons by state sanction and call it the recovery of property. In its legal meanings, maritime salvage, like the capture parties for runaway slaves, resembles a scavenging expedition: one simply takes what's usable or valued during a moment of disorder and claims it as his own.

The concept of scavenging provides a way to think about the often-spectral afterlives of defunct legal cultures. The laws and jurisprudence on legal personhood—on what I will focus on as the legal sanction of slavery and its afterlives in legal cases regarding racialized labor—provide stunning examples of how nominally defunct laws remain operational and potentially repeatable in everyday social life and in the more technical use of legal precedent. They are instances of laws made by scavenging earlier legislation and court decisions. Over the course of Goldman's novel, these tropes of salvage forge a genealogy of legal personhood within a nexus of legal subject positions that historically have revealed the fundamental incoherence of the law and confounded the U.S. national imaginary. The men's presence on the ship changes their relationship to the law, to national states, and to the history of race, labor, and migration. As at once migrants, slaves, sailors, and refugees, the main characters of the novel are, to borrow from C. L. R. James, "mariners, renegades, and castaways" in a world whose time is marked by a social awareness that what is behind also lies beyond it: a postindustrial, postcolonial, postrevolutionary, neocolonial, and neoliberal time in the closing decade of the twentieth century.

Robertson v. Baldwin highlights a long tradition of regarding the sailor as a quintessentially stateless laboring person who, paradoxically, required the full coercive power of the state in order to perform work. The sailor figure, in the nineteenth century and especially under the flag-of-convenience system since the twentieth century, experiences the double bind of being at once bound to and excluded from the nation. Historically, the Anglo and European merchant sailor figure lived and labored outside national territory but under the constraints and demands of sovereign nations. Their labor was needed to build empires and world markets, but the work branded them (sometimes literally) as wanderers, as men of the "Shining Empire" who, at heart, were of no earthbound nation.

As effectively stateless but subjected to their vessel's sovereign flag, sailors were often laborers left with little or no legal recourse against their employers. Near the end of the nineteenth century, when U.S. sailors were organizing to form a union, they successfully pushed for new legislation aimed at weakening the oppressive practices of forced labor and "crimping" while strengthening the rights of sailors.[26] The spirit of this new legislation was tested in 1895, when four merchant mariners attempted to quit the American vessel *Arago* on reaching domestic port in Oregon. The mariners were arrested, jailed without bail, and forcibly taken on board the ship before it was to sail to Chile.[27] Still they refused to perform their duties on board. They were arrested and charged with refusing to work in accordance with a federal statute concerning merchant seamen; the mariners sued, claiming they were unlawfully imprisoned and that the federal statute violated the provision of the Thirteenth Amendment to the U.S. Constitution, which prohibited "involuntary servitude," except—significantly—as punishment for someone convicted of a crime.

The U.S. Supreme Court soon deliberated the case. Could the seamen legally be punished as criminals for breaking their labor contract with the "master," and, in addition, be made to fulfill the terms of the contract against their will? The majority opinion was yes: sailors may be governed by coercion if they seek to default on their labor contracts, and such coercion did not violate the Thirteenth Amendment. Seamen, as an "exceptional class of men," were a class of laboring persons whose character deficiencies rendered them incapable of enjoying the rights and responsibilities of other free laboring persons. The specialized nature of their labor also made them indispensable to both private commerce and national security. Finally, the Court ruled, sailors have been coerced into labor on pain of punishment since "time immemorial."

Robertson exposes the contradictions of the labor contract entered into by sailors, who are at once recognized as possessing skills deemed economically and politically necessary and yet lacking in the full intelligence needed to enjoy liberty. The majority opinion noted seamen's nationality and national duty as U.S. merchant seamen, comparing seamen to soldiers whose legal bond with the nation, called citizenship, was rightly constrained or truncated in the name of protecting national sovereignty. The Court's decision further reveals the legacy of slavery and its belated afterlives in the logic of incarcerating labor and in the troubled distinction between slavery and legal and illegal forms of involuntary servitude. Legally recognized or identified by the labor they performed rather than by rights deserved on the grounds of being citizens, seamen were one of many groups in a legal limbo between statelessness and national belonging.

It was precisely because seamen had long served as figures that were by definition outside the national land, either in its service or as its potential menace, that they were still considered "exceptional" and therefore not subject in the same way to the national prohibition of indentured servitude. Indeed, these sailors were U.S. citizens whose mode of labor was deemed exceptionally crucial to the political sovereignty and economic power of the nation. Judges deployed a range of contradictory arguments explaining the merchant seamen's exceptional nature: like soldiers, their labor was recognized as indispensable to the national economy and thus to "national security" while also being defined as outside of the national body politic, characteristically unsuited to political participation in the state and located in the extraterritorial space of international waters. They were recognized as necessary to the state as U.S. citizens but for a kind of labor that necessarily curtailed the labor rights that normally would be afforded to U.S. citizens.

Sailors have a long history of social exclusion and exceptional legal status that depended on the identification of their bodies, first through the markings of the working class that often led to a seaman's initial impressment and then through the markings of seafaring experience that made him perpetually vulnerable to subsequent impressment. In his history of the eighteenth-century Anglo-American maritime world, Marcus Rediker writes that "crimps" and impressment gangs needed only to scout around taverns to immediately see and hear what the eighteenth-century sailor could not hide; the thick, grayish skin, tattoos, injuries, and distinctive pidgin languages of the seas would mark his flesh and voice.[28] Often begun through forced labor, the seaman's life became captive to a circular logic that held his body, marked by maritime labor, as evidence of his identity as fit only for the sea and thus as a man whose legal personhood was limited to this exceptional category of his labor status.

Excluded by the Supreme Court decision from the protections of the Thirteenth Amendment, the sailors at issue in *Robertson v. Baldwin* became legally subjected to labor coercion as a form of "protection of seamen against . . . the consequences of their own ignorance and improvidence." Seamen were thus defined by the Court in terms that earlier helped to define "Africans" and "Indians" through the law, recognized as adult wards, childish, and with limited intelligence and in need of protection from their own immaturity. Seamen were not considered persons possessing self-control and agency. The majority opinion commends, for example, the wisdom of employers in keeping seamen's salaries for them, as they would otherwise spend unwisely. Because they were wards and irresponsible for themselves, they also needed to be disciplined and could not be relied on to understand the proper terms of the labor contract, including criminal punishment for breaking it. Using the language of racial categorization but disavowing its applicability to the situation, judges deemed the seaman to be constitutionally inferior in intelligence; a "ward" in need of national protection and national discipline when (as children do) they impetuously abandon their work; deficient and degraded except in their specialized labor; and yet *not* the intended benefactors of the Thirteenth Amendment because it was meant to stop racialized indentured servitude of the "Mexican 'peonage'" and the "Chinese coolie" trade.

While the majority opinion distinguished between the sailor and the slave and other forms of racialized labor prohibited by the Thirteenth Amendment, the result of the judges' distinctions was to assign the sailor to the same racialized and contradictory status of indentured laborers through "other and less offensive names," as the dissenting judge John Marshall Harlan put it.[29] The racial logic of the majority opinion is on full display in the strained reading of the Thirteenth Amendment, even as the implicit racialization of white seamen in *Robertson v. Baldwin* may have contributed to the persistence of the legal endorsement of coerced labor, more than seventy-five years after the Indiana State Supreme Court ruled in *The Case of Mary Clark, A Woman of Color* (1821) that workers must be allowed to break a labor contract, regardless of whether they previously entered into it voluntarily, as a right that distinguished free labor from an indentured servitude no better than enslavement.[30] As the legal labor historian Robert J. Steinfeld has argued, *The Case of Mary Clark* signaled a departure from common law doctrines, which previously saw no contradiction between free personhood and coerced labor (i.e., between the right of free persons to enter into labor contracts and the right of employers to coerce labor from those same free persons, should they default on the labor contracts). Steinfeld has challenged the common historical narrative of labor law, which posits a long history of laborers whose legal freedom was fully secured by the sixteenth century, after which workers would continue to make progressive gains in labor rights. Rather, Steinfeld argues, most forms of labor entailed a legal obligation to work or be subject to legal coercion to fulfill the terms of a contract until at least the eighteenth century. Under the regime of racialized slavery, common law doctrine presumed the freedom of all white workers to enter into contracts (if not to break them), thus distinguishing the coerced labor of a free white laborer from the coerced labor of legally enslaved persons.

Outraged by the majority decision, the young Sailors' Union of the Pacific made the link between contract labor, indentured servitude, and slavery explicit by invoking the specter of slavery as it presided over the union between the interests of the private shipping industry and the state to keep American sailors in a form of involuntary servitude.[31] Referring to sailors as "bondsmen," union members refused to partake in Fourth of July celebrations after what they dubbed "Dred Scott II." "The spectacle of a slave worshipping his chains," declared union members, "would be less ludicrous than that of the American seamen celebrating Independence Day."[32]

The *Robertson* case presented an unresolvable contradiction to the Court, which wrestled over how to include this racialized labor class within the nation while simultaneously excluding it from the nation. The Supreme Court justices also argued for conflicted narratives of the nation, at a time of strident racism, nativism, and immigration and just months before the rapid intensification of U.S. colonialism with the Spanish-American War. The majority opinion rests on racialized economic and political structures foundational to the republic and to postbellum U.S. ideas of personhood and labor. And though it is an obscure case largely unknown outside maritime law, it anticipates the continuing series of unresolvable problems encountered by the official attempt to define and clearly distinguish not only between the alien and the national but also between free and coerced labor.

The debate over the meanings and limits of free labor in *Robertson v. Baldwin* is also a struggle over the desire to establish precedent and the burden that the law inherits from what has preceded it. The majority opinion in the case repeatedly cited the precedence of maritime traditions and earlier decisions in labor law to prove that the Thirteenth Amendment's prohibition of slavery and indentured servitude of free persons should not apply to sailors. As part of its justification, the majority opinion looked outside of U.S. law, to maritime law—the body of ancient and medieval Western practices regarding the social order of seafaring—and noted, for instance, the fifteenth-century maritime practice of branding the faces of sailors who abandon their ship at port with the initials of their places of birth. The temporal logic of legal precedence enacts the scavenging work of law. Precedence affirms and produces authority instead of evaluating its enabling conditions, and it cloaks the process of producing authority instead of exposing it to scrutiny. This use of precedence has far-reaching consequences for legal personhood, whether the precedent is a formal legal one or whether it is an appeal to conventional practice—what the majority judges in this case referred to as "usage"—even when U.S. law would undermine the practice. Consider, for instance, the Court's conclusion in the *Robertson* case that because earlier practice punished sailors who deserted or took absence without leave, a practice "which was in force in this country for more than sixty years before the Thirteenth Amendment was adopted, and similar legislation abroad from time immemorial, it cannot be open to doubt that the provision against involuntary servitude was never intended to apply to their contracts."

The irony of citing legislation on seamen that preceded the Thirteenth Amendment in order to exclude seamen from the Thirteenth Amendment was not lost on the sole dissenting opinion. Justice Harlan saw in this case the resurrection of the ghosts of legal subjection:

> Under this view of the constitution, we may now look for advertisements, not for runaway servants as in the days of slavery, but for runaway seamen. . . . [W]e can but be reminded of the past, when it is adjudged to be consistent with the law of the land for freemen, who happen to be seamen, to be held in custody, that they may be forced to go aboard private vessels, and render personal services against their will.

Like the legal personhood of the U.S. prisoner, the merchant mariner embodies a continuity between civil death (*attainder*), the legal slave, and "being judged a criminal." Such categories of legal personhood, as Dayan notes, have "made explicit the [chiasmic] doubling, back and forth transaction between prisoner and the ghosts of slaves past. Moreover, once the connection had been made, Southern slavery, now extinct, could resurface under other names not only in the South but in the North."[33] The ruling in *Robertson v. Baldwin* gave new, if narrowly applied, life to that which the Thirteenth Amendment sought to prohibit because of legislation that existed before the Thirteenth Amendment. The case itself is an exception to Steinfeld's main argument that free labor became common law doctrine by the mid-nineteenth century, and Steinfeld cites the case to illustrate, as the reviewer Jonathan A. Bush puts it, "the persistence of traditionalist notions of coerced labor."[34] Bush aptly paraphrases Justice Harlan's dissent as a rejection of the logic of precedence in this case, in which precedence represents not authority but the burden of an unwanted inheritance: "Who cares about inherited common law structures? We are Americans, new men, created and, in the Reconstruction Amendments, recreated as a nation under the sheltering wing of new emancipatory ideas. We can do better."[35] Hearing an echo in Justice Harlan's dissent and Steinfeld's critical account of the invention of free labor, Bush concludes, "It is this fundamental American vision that continues to animate the work of Steinfeld and others."[36] And yet what Harlan's dissent equally suggests is the impossibility of escaping the logic of precedence and the inheritance of earlier legal logics that support forms of coerced labor. Moreover, the case of *Robertson v. Baldwin*, along with Goldman's novel, demonstrate that such exceptional forms of legal personhood for coerced laborers have proven as fundamental to the legacies of personhood in the Americas as have been national projects for expanding labor rights and freedoms.

Cases such as *Robertson v. Baldwin* reinforce the exceptionality of labor identities by scavenging earlier versions and fragments of law in order to fashion newly usable legal identities for certain kinds of laborers: in this way, they reanimate the specter of otherwise obsolete legal punishment, including the branding of flesh. As if inevitable, any legal recourse that the Ship Visitor attempts for the men fails: Esteban's repeated statement that he is a refugee from a ship to the other Latinos who grant him hospitality in Brooklyn cannot fit into the conventions of refugee and asylum narratives; despite their good faith in working through legal channels to arrive in New York, the crewmen's lack of papers signed by their employers effectively criminalizes them; and, as the Ship Visitor explains, any legal charge against the employers for Bernardo's injury would require at least Mark's and Elias's full names, unknown to the crewmen.[37] John the Ship Visitor cannot contend with the haunting traces of forced labor that animate contemporary U.S. law; nor can he contend with the category of the undocumented migrant that obscures the long, ongoing history of U.S. intervention in Central America, Mexico, and the Caribbean. He is led to the *Urus* belatedly, after Esteban has begun his new life on land and Bernardo has disappeared. Aside from giving the men sweaters and supplies to endure the onset of winter and taking a few of them to a lawyer for a preliminary consultation, his only help is to notify the crew that there will be no legal recourse for their sufferings and that the most they can expect is deportation to their home countries. Pínpoyo, a crewman who becomes addicted to sniffing paint solvent fumes over the course of their abandonment, is the only one who challenges the Ship Visitor's "integrity" and efforts:

> Pínpoyo, stumbling forward with his blanket still wrapped around him despite the new clothes, blocks his way in front of the gangway. He's raving about gringo hijos de puta stealing his pay and calling the Ship Visitor a liar and a bunch of other babosadas. . . . [T]he Ship Visitor looks around at the crew with a baffled expression, while Pínpoyo goes on raving. But then El Barbie steps forward and firmly pulls Pínpoyo out of the Ship Visitor's path and throws him down on the deck, and Pínpoyo lies there as if he's dead, though of course there's nothing the matter with him except for paint solvent fumes. The Ship Visitor, with an embarrassed smile[,] . . . stands there blushing, with an almost apologetic smile, until they're done [applauding him], and then he thanks them, waves good-bye, and goes down the ladder to his van. (350–51)

The narration portrays this moment with heavy irony, as Pínpoyo plays the role of the fool whose truth goes unrecognized by its listeners, much like the taunts of "los blacks" on the pier who nightly proclaimed the men "fucked" soon after their arrival at Brooklyn Harbor. Ultimately, John the Ship Visitor's labor is limited to that of the storyteller, and of the poet, who translates the ultimate futility of his job as seafarers' advocate into stories that fuel his erotic relationship with his cosmopolitan girlfriend, the aptly named Ariadne. The Ship Visitor likens the pier, emptied of the ship and of the men who had run it aground in a final act of defiance, to "love without lovers," comparing lovers to "all the ships that have ever berthed there and all the ships that ever will, and all the faraway ports those ships have come from and are headed to, and all the hidden lives on those ships" (381). Left without any legal recourse to advocate for the men's visibility as legal laboring persons before the law, the Ship Visitor transforms the crew's hidden experience aboard the *Urus* into his personal object of poetic salvage—something he cannot do until the men and the ship already have, in multiple senses of the word, disappeared from view.

Ruinous Vessels

If, as Joseph Slaughter suggests, international human rights law modeled human personhood on the corporation (rather than the reverse), then it is also true that U.S. law preceding the UN Declaration of Human

Rights modeled corporate personhood on the expanded rights of human personhood after the Civil War. The Fourteenth Amendment, whose broadened definition of citizenship overturned *Dred Scott v. Sandford*, was invoked to recognize the legal rights of personhood for corporations while allowing those corporations to escape the corporeal responsibilities and threats of the embodied human person, such as incarceration, physical punishment, and biological death. The legal fiction of corporate persons—an impersonal, inhuman personhood—allows a kind of human rights to extend to abstract bodies without the trappings of corporeality. In the case of the *Urus*, it is left to the undocumented humans to embody the corporeal effects of the corporation's disembodiment. Corporate personhood in Goldman's novel is specifically anchored to the status of cargo ships as determined by legal systems that precede the postbellum U.S. constitutional amendments and whose modern forms originate in the British abolition of the slave trade.

The system of international shipping registries enables the shipowners of *The Ordinary Seaman* to act within an exceptional legal space that reconfigures the link between corporate personhood and state sovereignty, and it is this exceptional space that produces the "retractable personhood" that the contemporary sailor might share with the legal racial slave.[38] Goldman's cargo ship emerges as a site of accumulated exceptionality—loaded up with the cargo of histories of maritime exception, as it were—that grants shipowners anonymity from the law. Where the abandoned crew in the novel suffers from its legal unrecognizability, the owners are freed by a legal anonymity that shields them from being recognized as criminal actors.

The broken cargo vessel at the center of the novel's plot—set in a dilapidated port harbor once vital to the future of New York City—is figured as a remnant of cargo shipping's historical significance, as among the earliest and most vital means of world trade leading to the development of the planet's oldest "world cities" both before and after European world hegemony.[39] Hailed as "engine of commerce, the machine of empire," the cargo ship announced the terror of colonial modernity in the Americas; an instrument of war, violent conquest, racialized slavery, and wealth extraction, the cargo ship also served as a floating prison for its human cargo and its seafarers.[40] In response to the rapid expansion of circum-Atlantic systems in international capitalist economies and racialized slavery during the eighteenth and nineteenth centuries, the ship also becomes (as maritime labor history and Black Atlantic scholarship have shown) a chronotope of radical black cosmopolitanisms as well as anti-slavery and democratic traditions among seafarers in a long tradition of multiethnic, multinational, and multilingual crews, some of which abandoned statist systems of merchant maritime commerce, the navy, and even buccaneering in favor of a piracy against all nations.

The cargo ship's transoceanic history of conquest, slavery, and empire inspires both terror and romance of all kinds, even as it also shadows the contemporary workings of maritime commerce with ships flagged by foreign states under systems of open registries. The maritime labor historians Peter Linebaugh and Marcus Rediker have helped to renew scholarly interest in the history of the cargo ship and its dynamic relations of labor, culture, capital, and sovereignty: especially from the seventeenth through the nineteenth centuries, the ship is revealed to be at once a singularly productive space for these relations and a social laboratory that anticipates the future of territories and waterways around the globe. In its apparently anachronistic and yet insistently contemporary figuration within the novel, the *Urus* is a signal example of what Foucault calls a heterotopia. Calling into question the operations of labor, time, capital, and sovereignty, the ship produces an exceptional space and an imaginatively and historically articulating one, an extraterrestrial vehicle whose vital social work is to join together different temporalities and geographies. Foucault's "heterotopia par excellence," like Gilroy's "chronotope," is a paradoxical maritime otherworld that is bounded, yet open; a microcosm whose movement creates global encounters, as at once "the greatest instrument of economic development" and "the greatest reservoir of imagination."[41] Foucault ends his essay on heterotopia with the ship and a prediction: "In civilizations without ships the dreams dry up, espionage takes the place of adventure, and the police that of the corsairs."[42] With this perhaps ironic flourish that shifts power from sea routes to dry land, Foucault oddly signals the onset of sinister Cold War surveillance and information warfare by loading the ship with the heavy imaginative cargo of a European colonialism, rich with dreaming. Gilroy instead locates the ship as the time-space articulator that invites us to "rethink modernity via the history of the black Atlantic and the African diaspora into the western hemisphere."[43] For both writers, the ship also is an exceptionally rich symbolic-material space whose power lies in its taken-for-granted mobility and its dominance in a time before our own. Clearly, the ship participates in the rich spectrum of meanings for European and American imaginaries, be it the dreams and nightmares of the Jolly Roger or the middle passage. At once confining and mobile, the large ship was a signifying and material driving force of world markets and contemporary globalization, even as it has become erroneously figured as a past or leisurely form of transoceanic mobility. The Western ship evokes the world beyond the state as well as the world as its purview:

outside of land and country, the ship's liquid realm defines the limits of terra and territory even as it overrides such limits.

Like the slave ship in *Benito Cereno*, the *Urus* is depicted as masking its own catastrophic history from full view even as the ship reveals itself as that secret history's haunting remains. In a nod to Melville's *San Dominick*, the name of the *Urus* is only an echo of a previous identity now disavowed: the men read "*Urus* painted high up on the prow against a dark smear covering up what must have been its previous name; *Urus, Panama City* on the stern. But there were no lights onboard; everything looked painted with shadows" (20–21). The crew's job, and the phantom owners' plan, is to conceal the marks of the ship's disabling history— to erase its genealogy, former incarnations, and visible scars in order to deny its death and make it live again. This work is formidable: to erase the palimpsestic layers of paint, smears, and shadows that might tell the history of the ship, the men must conceal evidence of fire damage, apply fresh paint over what the old reveals, and otherwise repair or mask the injuries that have turned the ship into junk.[44]

The ship's owners, Elias and Mark, view the ship as a blank (albeit oxidized) slate, insensible to its own history, to be remade into their desired image by naming and staging the ship as new, with fresh coats of paint and a repair crew. Initially, the ship was for Mark "the iron-and-rust manifestation of a dream finally made real" (294–95). Mark imagines them as two new masculine heroes who will rescue the ship, which is figured as a woman abused and neglected by her previous man: "A dead ship, dumped by an owner too impatient and cheap and unimaginative and law-abiding to know how to make her seaworthy again; a ship that was only acting dead, just waiting for someone to come along, recognize her true worth, and rescue her from scrap" (295). A failed experiment in reanimation, the ship's repairs by the crew resemble little more than the dressing up of a corpse: "The new cables and wiring have been threaded up and down the ship's length like a whole new set of veins in an old body. But the ship still has no self-generating electrical power" (95). Tellingly, the one thing holding the ship back from its full repair is the "circuit breaker" badly damaged in the fire that had destroyed the ship before Mark and Elias came along. The Frankensteinian ambition of creation through reanimation, and the delusions that one can make an utterly new (or newly recycled) creation that can be fully possessed and free from any history but that of its creation, from any genealogy but that of itself as origin, soon becomes apparent. Dr. Frankenstein's monster is, after all, never new so much as a composite figure of the undead, the product of anonymous human scraps salvaged and electrified into animation.

Key to the owners' fantasy of salvaging the *Urus* is the international system of open registries, also called "flags of convenience" because there is no genuine link between the nationality of the shipowners and that of the ship. Flags of convenience provide Mark and Elias with two crucial advantages: first, they are free to turn themselves into "phantom owners," able to appear and disappear from legal view as it benefits them; and second, they are able to grant the newly named *Urus* a new nationality, effectively erasing its histories under other nationalities from its new legal status as a Panamanian ship.[45] Touted by one advocate of the strong British maritime state in the early eighteenth century as "the Sovereign of the Aquatic Globe, giving despotic laws to all the meaner Fry, that live upon that Shining Empire," the seafaring merchant ship has carried since at least the sixteenth century an unstable double status as both a sovereign of the maritime commercial world unto itself and an extension of the sovereign state it represents by way of the flag under which it sails, subject to its laws and jurisdiction.[46] The relationship between a cargo ship, capital, and state power has become all the more flexible and strategic under the modern system of open registries established in the early twentieth century, in which certain states offer to register a ship as being under their sovereign jurisdiction in exchange for a fee.

Panama created the first open registry in the world in the years following 1916, gradually changing its registry laws to allow for and attract the entwined U.S. interests in shipping and military power (it was the U.S. Shipping Board, a governmental body charged with preventing the reflagging of U.S. ships, that in fact directed the mass reflagging of U.S. ships under Panama).[47] As a young U.S. neocolony whose strategic location on the isthmus guaranteed ultimate U.S. control over the Panama Canal, Panama flagged commercial ships that were also subject to the needs of the U.S. Merchant Marines during war and "states of emergency." Throughout the 1920s, U.S. shipowners gained international economic advantage and evaded national laws (including Prohibition laws) by flagging in Panama. The United Fruit Company and others quickly dropped European registries to fly the Panamanian flag; soon the United Fruit Company would create the Honduran registry, with guidance from the U.S. government, to keep its bananas moving cheaply and reliably from Central America to northern consumers.[48]

The Liberian registry was established in the wake of World War II, when newly implemented international human rights regimes and U.S. development programs for Third World countries formed part of a concerted effort to achieve U.S. global dominance. Like Panama, the Liberian registry also granted the reflagging of U.S. ships, revealing the dual status of ships as economic vessels that always convey political state power, whether latently or explicitly and whether it is the state represented by the flag it flies or one hiding behind it, or both. Former U.S. secretary of state and businessman Edward Stettinius Jr. created the Liberian Maritime Code and registry in 1947, initially as an even cheaper and better-managed alternative to the Panamanian registry (especially for Standard Oil), further strengthening the ability of "U.S. political and financial interests to manipulate national and transnational economic codes."[49] The Liberian Maritime Code and the Liberian registry initially operated within the liberal developmentalist framework of Cold War military, economic, political, and ideological policies vis-à-vis the Third World: Liberia would "develop" through a racialized colonial maritime education. Flagged ships—what Stettinius called "liberty ships"—would be run by European officers but "manned by native Liberian boys, who would receive in the neighborhood of a dollar a day."[50] Stettinius's vision for Liberia simply follows from the country's colonial history, a history that haunts the novel's sites of exception, salvage, and disappearance.

The colony of Liberia was among the earliest U.S. plans for the figurative or literal return to Africa by free people of color and the formerly enslaved, who would colonize the small area on the western coast of Africa in the early nineteenth century and declare Liberia an independent republic in 1847. Financed by the U.S. government and popularized by a growing number of white colonization societies, the colony served as the white population's dream of salvaging the United States from its multiracial condition, specifically, from the consequences of the growing population of free people of color. An 1817 congressional committee report concluded that while U.S. colonies were "formed with great ease" by white settlers, with "the colonization of the free people of color, it seemed obviously necessary to take a different course.—Their distinct character and relative condition, render an entire separation from our own states and territories indispensable. And this separation must be such as to admit of an indefinite continuance."[51]

Other U.S. schemes for establishing racialized colonies quickly failed, as did Haiti's attempt to attract people from the United States. While some people of African descent favored the colonization projects, their opinions did not matter to the effort coordinated by the government and white colonization societies determined to expel them from U.S. land and contiguous territories through the project of empire, which in the case of Liberia yielded to the United States not only a small but significant "sanctuary" for its residents of African descent but also a colonial foothold in West Africa that ceded its economic dependence to the newly reconfigured U.S. "homeland" rather than identify with the indigenous subjects whose land the Americo-Liberians colonized. As the 1817 congressional report observes of "Africa":

> It is the country which, in the order of Providence, seems to have been appropriated to that distinct family of mankind. And while it presents the fittest asylum for the free people of color, it opens a wide field for the improvements in civilization, morals and religion, which the humane and enlightened memorialists have conceived it possible, in process of time, to spread over that great continent.[52]

Liberia's ambiguous status as exile colony and a U.S. neocolony would go on to dramatically shape Liberia's economy, politics, and complex legacy of racialized personhood to the twenty-first century. Shemak tracks the vanishing circuit between capital, sovereignty, and human rights in Liberia during Charles Taylor's infamous dictatorship from 1997 to 2003, when Taylor used funds from the registry, operated all the while by U.S. companies, to buy the weapons that would lead to the murder of hundreds of thousands of Liberians and provoke an international refugee crisis that pushed Liberians onto those very decrepit Liberian-flagged ships in search of asylum.[53] The Liberian flag of convenience (FOC) continues to be known as among the most liberal of all open registries; but, despite occasional efforts to improve and enforce standards on board, all flags of convenience are limited by their economic raison de être and by the only precariously national, extraterrestrial ship at sea.

These open registries offer advantages without much risk: they generally "do not require citizenship of shipowners or operators, levy no or minimal taxes, allow ships to be worked by non-nationals, and have neither the will nor capability to impose domestic or international regulations on registered ships."[54] They promise shipowners an impossible labyrinth that masks them from international law and the national requirements of major maritime states, like the United States, whose laws seek to uphold environmental, safety, and labor standards on the ships that fly their flag.

Goldman's novel takes that labyrinth as its premise. Created as fronts for the entrepreneurial venture that Elias sets up, the *Urus* and the Achuar Corporation participate in the masquerade of open registries, to be played out as part of the operations of contemporary capitalism, which relies on interdependent legal channels and gaps between national laws that are never made explicit in order to maximize the ownership's flexibility, often at the expense of workers' rights.[55] The names *Urus* and *Achuar* become unstable signs within the narrative plot, thinly covering over what is finally revealed to be unidentifiable/anonymous—a stateless vessel without owners and a corporation without any identifiable individuals responsible for its operation.[56] Under the flags of convenience, a shipowner like Achuar Corporation may be based in the United States, register a ship in Panama, and assemble a multinational crew. The ship flies under a flag that identifies the ship as under Panamanian sovereign jurisdiction, but the flag is purchased with the understanding that Panama will maintain such jurisdiction in name only, through the appearance of the flag and state bureaucratic documents central to the definition of the formal economy. In this way power is wielded by the captain or shipowners (in this novel, they are one and the same), who are shielded from sovereign law: the man in charge is given free rein to rule the ship. In other words, the economic transaction of registering a ship under a flag of convenience is a transaction that takes place within the formal economy but whose value as a transaction comes from the formal cover it provides for a shipowner to operate within the range of informal economic acts, from hiring undocumented workers to withholding wages to using violence as a means to control the labor force. The cover of sovereignty continues to be mobile, flexible, sold, and contingent on the purchaser's desires: as Elias and Mark realize that their enterprise is doomed and the ship will never be seaworthy, they allow its Panamanian registration to lapse, and the *Urus* itself becomes a stateless no-place place housing a crew rendered alien on board as well as on land. Flags of convenience depend on the freedoms of a certain kind of position outside the bounds of any state—a certain statelessness—that allows shipowners to choose a ship's state identity. While the flagged cargo ship quintessentially points up the legal fiction of sovereign territory and its relation to capital, the modern systems of open registries sharpen the fiction into a complex masquerade in which seafarers and shipowners are marked (or unmarked) by anonymity—seafarers are out of sight and out of law (made vulnerable), and FOC shipowners are made textually invisible, legally concealed, and thus freed from responsibility.

FOC registries thus promise a sovereignty of paper and cloth: its flags are textual and textile signs of a sovereign power valued precisely for its weakness, its almost empty formality. Nineteenth- and twentieth-century international treaties and laws have ensured the old maritime practice that every ship "shall have a nationality" and that states have had the power to grant a ship nationality as it would grant citizenship to a legal person: as

Amasa Delano recognizes in *Benito Cereno*, the absence of a flag signals extreme danger or opportunity on the high seas—a ship that has been overtaken or a ship that is open for the taking, or both.[57] Registering ships also has been used tactically by merchant and naval ships for centuries; for example, British citizens flagged ships with Spain to evade the Spanish trade monopoly with the West Indies, and in the nineteenth century slave-trading ships owned by citizens whose countries had made international agreements abolishing the slave trade were registered elsewhere "to avoid detection."[58] But it was not until the creation of the first open registries in the early twentieth century that the practice announced a decisive shift in international shipping. The invention of open registries coincided with strengthened U.S. maritime laws for U.S. citizens and U.S. political dominance over the seas. Between 1915 and 1922, U.S. laws such as the Seamen's Act of 1915 and the Jones Act of 1920 formalized the legal rights of sailors, strengthening the U.S. Merchant Marine and introducing protective measures for its mariners.[59] Alongside this strengthening of its shipping laws, the U.S. state actively worked to set up shields that would protect U.S. shipowners from those laws while increasing U.S. economic and military power around the globe. Significantly, the only crime with which Mark and Elias could be charged is their violation of the 1920 Jones Act, which provides for a sailor or sailor's representative to sue an employer for injuries or death caused by negligence but which depends on obtaining the deposition of a disappeared man and the names of the owners. With Bernardo dead, the crew scattered and unaware of Bernardo's fate (they're told that he made it safely back home to Nicaragua), and the owners hidden under the cover of the Achuar Corporation, the Jones Act hangs in the air for the Ship Visitor as just another defeat.

The thriving open registries of Panama, Honduras, and Liberia offer a sovereignty of paper and cloth that masked and served yet another sovereign state, one whose strong military and economic powers were concealed by the masquerade of strong Panamanian, Honduran, and Liberian sovereignty. The registries—"intermediaries in the flow of capital to Western power"—need not be located in, or even operated by, the states whose sovereignty they are selling.[60] The Panamanian registry (currently the world's largest), for instance, is headquartered in New York City; the Liberian registry (the world's second largest) is currently operated by Liberian International Ship and Corporate Registry (LISCR) in Virginia; and the Marshall Islands (the world's third largest registry) is also run out of Virginia, by the same company that ran the Liberian Registry until 2000, originally Stettinius Associates-Liberia, Inc. and now International Registries, Inc.

Significantly, Goldman notes in his acknowledgments that the historical ship on which he bases the *Urus* was flagged in Liberia. Perhaps fittingly, given shipowners' common practice of changing ship names and ship registries, even in mid-voyage, in search of ever more advantageous contracts, Goldman renames the ship the *Urus* and reflags it as Panamanian. The choice of a Panamanian registry explicitly links the *Urus* to the hemispheric histories that its new owners seek to disavow. Providing the spatiotemporal, economic, and emotive conditions of possibility for the novel's plot, the Panamanian flag of convenience establishes the venture as transnational while calling up the historical relationship between Panama and global capital, from the colonial designs on an isthmanian passageway to the dominance of the United States in establishing Panama as a state, constructing the canal, and maintaining effective influence over the government and the canal zone. As Gruesz notes, *The Ordinary Seaman* seizes hold of "the history of domination and intervention . . . [which] has made Panama the dead center of US hemispheric hegemony."[61] Indeed, the FOC system serves as a hidden history of U.S. empire and its participation in structuring the contemporary world system.

Flags of convenience reveal longer histories of the maritime world as a zone of lawlessness circumscribed by the law, of invisible spaces in which labor, environmental, and safety laws, no less than national and international politics, flicker between absence and presence. Open registries operate at a global scale by trading in what Pheng Cheah has called "spectral nationality," and it is their spectrality, the flickering between presence and absence, that enable open registries to simultaneously flag well over half of the world's shipping fleet in deadweight tonnage, raise stunningly high state revenues for small countries, and yet be invisible, cloaking shipowners and ships in the legal sanction of absentee sovereignty. The shipowners, the corporation-based states, and those in charge of the FOC state rely on the very strategies of disappearance and concealment to safeguard profit and political power that leave crews and other workers perilously invisible, their legal personality ignored or undetected in the flickering absence-presence of spectral law.

Against the general invisibility of the maritime economics of FOC ships, an old cargo ship purchased by the International Transport Workers Federation (ITF) was transformed into a floating exhibit that sailed around the world for nearly two years, bringing the ITF campaign against FOC ships to port cities and inviting the public on board. The *Global Mariner* traversed what Allan Sekula elsewhere calls a "forgotten space" falsely relegated to an economic past: "It is all the more profound that this ship should seek to represent the workings of empire at a time when the global economy is assumed to be entirely virtual in its connectedness, magically independent of the slow maritime movement of heavy things."[62] Before it was sunk in 2000, the *Global Mariner* "was a *metaship*, representing and figuring within itself, within the exhibition that was its only cargo, all the other invisible, ignored, and silent ships of the world."[63]

Flags of convenience further enable the spectrality of ships—but with persistent material remains subject to future uses. They allow ships to operate even as they resemble a material, floating ruin, an object of potential salvage with "their ambiguous status as already existing but transformed object and context."[64] In his commentary on the ITF exhibit of the *Global Mariner,* Sekula echoes the tropes of salvage, reuse, and disappearance that animate Goldman's *Urus* and its prehistory, which I discuss below. Sekula traces the history of the vessel as a working cargo ship named the *Lady Rebecca*:

> *The Lady Rebecca . . . had gone through five names, a series of superimposed reinscriptions of bow and stern, each prior name an increasingly obscure trace beneath the bright white paint announcing a new identity. One of the stranger stories of this common practice: in mid-passage a captain receives a telex noting that the ship has been sold and must be renamed. The captain politely asks the new name and is told to send a crewman over the side—risky business when under way—to paint out every other letter of the old name. What would Mallarmé make of this? The concrete poetry of the contemporary maritime world, the nominative magic worked out between the telex machine and the paint locker. . . . Whose ship? Which ship? A palimpsest of disguises and deceits, a deliberate muddying of the waters.*
>
> Nearing the end of its/her working life, the ship formerly known as the *Lady Rebecca* entered a state of dangerous decrepitude, owned by a Hong Kong shipping company, flagged, I believe, to Panama, crewed by Filipinos, and finally—at the literal end of her ropes—moored at offshore anchorage in the bustling port of Pusan, on the southeast coast of Korea, waiting. For what? A shady buyer willing to squeeze out the last bit of profit from the laborious and plodding and dangerous journeys of an aging vessel, a death ship in the making. Or, the owner makes the final blunt decision. . . . Send "her" to the gently sloping beaching of India, to be run ashore at high tide by a skeleton crew . . . to be broken by the sledges and

cutting torches of vast crews of gaunt laborers[,] . . . the last toiling
victims in the cycle of oceanic exploitation.[65]

Sekula's account uncannily echoes the history and anticipated futures
for "death ships" such as the *Urus:* to be sold again to sail, a living-dead
vessel; or to be scrapped and recycled into some economic afterlife after
being dismantled at the sort of ship graveyard Salgado photographs in
Workers. Unlike the *Urus,* the ship formerly known as the *Lady Rebecca*
experiences a "miraculous" turn: it is rescued by the ITF, who reflag the
ship in Britain, name it the *Global Mariner,* and operate it with a motley
crew that sets out for eighty-three port cities and numerous union soli-
darity and anticorporate globalization protests.[66]

The ITF's *Global Mariner* exhibit launched soon after the 1997 publication of *The Ordinary Seaman,* but it replays the novel's key tropes of
salvage, death, and disappearance. Goldman's novel eventually reveals
the prehistory of the *Urus,* whose previous name was the "Seal Queen,
port of registry Monrovia" (275), as a story of serial maritime salvage
and disappearance. In a narration that chiastically echoes the plight
of the *Urus* for the reader as if, in the future anterior tense employed
at key moments by the narration, it "will have been" a foreshadowing
of the ship's fate, the *Seal Queen,* "dark and without power," had been
"stranded" outside St. John Harbor, New Brunswick, with its crew still
onboard.[67] The history of the *Seal Queen* haunts the ship under its new
name and anticipates the death and evacuation of its crew. The ship
waiter Bernardo, who indirectly alerts John the Ship Visitor to the crew's
plight, is himself disappeared by the time the seafarers' advocate finds
the ship. Bernardo suffers a bad oil burn on his leg from cooking for the
crew in deplorable conditions. Captain Elias claims to treat the burn on
site, but the leg eventually becomes infected. The first mate, Mark, drives
Bernardo to an emergency waiting room and abandons him there, his
name not recorded anywhere and his body ignored by the hospital staff
until after he is dead, to be buried anonymously at the city's potter's field,
an allusion in the novel to Hart Island. Belatedly foreshadowing Bernardo's disappearance and the men's abandonment and injury on board
the *Urus,* two seamen on the *Seal Queen* had been badly burned by an
engine plant fire that broke out during a storm; with one dead engineer,
the crew had to wait for the blizzard to calm before rescue helicopters
could evacuate them (275). When Elias tracks down the ship's operator
and arrives at the St. John shipyard, he sees that workers "had already
begun removing everything of salable value from the ship," which was
not even worth demolishing for scrap. The story of the *Urus,* in this

sense, had happened before it began: the ship, in its naming and renaming, becomes newly christened by the entrepreneurial spirit while being
haunted by the trace of its old names. It is given the makeover of a name
even as its dismemberment had already begun.

The novel's description of the unseaworthy ship being towed from
New Brunswick to New York (where it would come to be the *Urus*) captures the perversity of forming new ventures from the funeral of previous ones. Suggesting a marriage with a corpse, "the tug's wake foam[s]
back toward the ship like a luminous, lacy bridal train trailed all the way
from New York," as Elias presides over the union with tales of profitable
shipping fraud for his friends (298). Just before Elias finally, unmistak-
ably jumps ship (so to speak), he himself paints over the name *Urus* and
its home port, Panama City, with a can of gray paint. He announces to
the crew that the owners have found a buyer for the ship: "in another day
or two, caballeros, this will all be over" (344). But there was no buyer.
The ship had been dropped from the Panamanian registry because of
the owners' failure to pay its fees and taxes and allow an inspection. The
crew will never see Elias again, and they will spend their final few weeks
on board a stateless ship, its name concealed by the color of overcast sky
as the *Urus* is unceremoniously left to its own ruin.

While the novel's trope of failed salvage finds its expression in the
future anterior tense, as that which will have happened, it is further
qualified by the prospect that what will have happened might also happen again. The effect is one in which the future is experienced as the
past even as that past may continue to recycle itself indefinitely into the
future. In Goldman's acknowledgments, written as a narrative account
of how he came to write the novel, Goldman suggests that the *Urus* and
its story also might come to happen again, even after the abandoned
crew manage to power the ship just long enough to run it aground and
abandon it themselves. He relates his initial discovery of the November
1982 *New York Daily News* story on abandoned sailors.[68] Living in New
York City, he immediately drove to the harbor to find the ship evacuated
but for one man who claimed to be a crewman but who offered to sell
the ship to Goldman and a friend, posing as interested buyers. Goldman
believes he had met the owner, who promptly disappeared.

> The "phantom owners" of that ship escaped legal prosecution, but
> they were banned by the Liberian Registry from ever again register-
> ing under that flag of convenience. Amazingly, the ship, once seized
> and auctioned off as scrap to a machinery company in Brooklyn,
> was repurchased by those hapless owners; sometime later they were

caught trying to work the same scam, with the same ship, in Staten Island; and then again in the Caribbean. (Perhaps the *Urus* is on her way to a similar destiny.) (385)

In the naming compulsion that drives such repetition, capitalism operates on the belief—reaffirmed by legal channels—that naming makes anything new and that histories thus are to be erased through language rather than perpetuated as haunting traces.[69] The ship is a palimpsest of "disguises and deceits," its names a perpetually changing series of newly erased and newly painted letters: the vessel is a disavowed chronotope, a space whose historical time is denied in its performance of the present as all that matters. Even as the heights of colonial and industrial international commerce are revealed by dilapidated signs written over Brooklyn Harbor and its collapsed terminals, such as with Wienstock Spice Company, the ship, long after it appears to be wrecked, continues to embody yet another venture under another name, as if it were not condemned to a disavowed and perpetual salvage.

Anonymous Death in New York and Its Islands

The disappearance of the old ship waiter Bernardo anticipates the crew's failure to recover their wages or to be recognized as rights-bearing laboring persons under U.S. or Panamanian law. Indefinitely detained on board the Panamanian-flagged vessel, without the proper papers to step onto U.S. territory, and dependent on the captain and first mate (who secretly own the ship and who eventually abandon the men) for food and any word on future prospects, the crewmen are left to speculate a future in which their own bodies become, like the ship, the objects of someone else's economic salvage. Seeing beyond the "hundreds of cans of antirust solvents, primers, and paints" on board (58), Bernardo is the first to call the whole venture a sham: "The muchachos didn't know what a true ship, a true capitan, was like and acted as if they had no choice but to believe that when the ship was fixed, she'd sail" (58). As their abandonment gradually becomes clear to the crew, Jose Mateo, the ship cook and the only other experienced crew member onboard, flatly relates to Bernardo the common fate for abandoned crews: they must wait, "stuck on a ship forever while all the legal pendejadas get resolved, [before] auctioning the ship off for scrap to pay everybody off, melt[ing] a ship like this down to make razor blades, beer cans, refrigerators" (183). Bernardo transforms Jose's list of commodities into an image of his affective condition carrying on, embodied by the ship, and to be transformed with the ship's anticipated demolition. He "pictures gringos shaving with his tears, pulling cold cans of his bile from gleaming white refrigerators made of his hatred. A perfect immortality" (183).[70] As if giving a nod to Salgado's description of the uses of "that huge animal lying on the beach" about to be transformed through the efficient economy of recycling, Bernardo makes an important amendment to such an account by incorporating his imagined afterlife into the scrap material of the ship. He imagines his disappearance at the hands of the market; whether or not Bernardo physically survives this nonvoyage, his affective production of tears, bile, and hatred join the *Urus* as future scraps to be made immortal through their transformation into new commodities for the retail consumer economy: disposable razors, recyclable cans, more domestic vessels. Bernardo's emotional traces, alloyed with the recyclable metal of the ship, figuratively reincorporate him into the circulation of the global economy from which the crew has, through abandonment and immobility, fallen. Such an imagined future recycles the emotional traces of laborers, treated as disposable, beyond recognition for a future market. Recycling suggests a perfect economy that runs on the circulation of goods between consumers and capitalists; the labor performed for the recycling is usually absented from this economy. And while the commodity has no history or apparent network of social relations for the citizen-consumer (exemplified by Bernardo through the "gringo"), Bernardo's emotive afterlife is depicted as immortalized, smuggled into future commodities and consumer markets, through the potentially endless sequence of use, transformation, and new use that is recycling.

Recycling the material of the ship depends on an erasure of the material's history, a history incompatible with the valuing of the new commodity. Bernardo's imagined future thus illustrates the broader connection and disjuncture between labor, consumption, and ownership that make virtually every commodity a product with untraceable histories. It is the imagined and visual distance between the northern, Anglo, masculine consumer and Bernardo that the old sailor tries to subvert (though not overcome) through a mental picture; precisely because the consumer cannot see the laborer and his material and emotional fragmentation in their razor blade, their consumption does not look like the consumerist cannibalism that it is. His emotional fragmentation and its invisibility to the consumer he imagines as a "gringo" highlight his status as legal phantom, whose legal personality is disavowed except when criminalized as "undocumented." Bernardo imagines with terror his self recycled out of recognition. It is with his labor that he is also an economic phantom in the global economy. Resembling the undocumented laborers at work in agricultural fields, sweatshops, prisons, restaurants, hotels, factories, virtually anywhere, Bernardo shares something of the racialized position of Ralph Ellison's narrator in *Invisible Man*: "I am invisible, understand, simply because people refuse to see me." Bernardo's "immortality," achieved through the commodification of his affective products, suggests the eternal existence of anonymous labor rendered invisible to the public imaginary. The ship's metal, and Bernardo's tears, will be transformed beyond recognition: melted down to destroy their formal specificity, they become melded with other scrap, others' tears, as part of a process that recycles them as both the material effects of failed salvage and potentially unending resources. To remain on board the *Urus* would mean, for Bernardo, his continued enslavement, but to have the ship scrapped would mean an invisible, economical death, a disappearance-by-recycling. In either case, Bernardo's bleak meditation on the future proves prescient: he is the one crew member who will have disappeared from the *Urus* by the time the Ship Visitor finds the crew. Even before Bernardo's injury and anonymous death in a Manhattan hospital emergency waiting room, the ship venture has transformed Bernardo into a capacious figure of the disappeared.

Perhaps anticipating his entry into the world of the disappeared, Bernardo spots an elderly Argentine couple improbably strolling the otherwise deserted pier like "ghosts" and convinces them to alert an international seafarers' advocate to the crew's entrapment onboard (116). His interment in a potter's field on Hart Island, on the other side of Manhattan from Brooklyn Harbor and Ellis Island, is an uncanny return for Bernardo to a space of internment, invisibility, and death.

Bernardo thus moves from one site of exception, the ship, to another, the potter's field. If his spirit and tears stay with the iron hulk, then it is Hart Island that gets his body. Hart Island is a thin strip of land about a mile long and a quarter of a mile wide in the western part of Long Island Sound, off the coast of the Bronx. It contains the remains of more than three quarters of a million people, making it the densest cemetery in the United States. The island is administered by the New York City Department of Corrections, which ferries prisoners from Riker's Island to bury thousands more bodies at Hart Island each year. Both a public cemetery and a prison, this double heterotopia of the disappeared is also largely invisible, hidden from and closed to the general public. Prison inmates from Riker's Island, who usually serve light sentences of less than a year, bury the dead. Housing over 850,000 bodies of adults and children since its public use as a cemetery began in 1869 (plus other human parts sent from hospitals), the island is a space within which the classifications of the legal personality of the dead and the living are processed by prison authorities, who manage the living in direct relation to the dead: burial, visitation, disinterment, and records—virtually all conditions affecting the dead and the living on Hart Island.

For over 150 years, Hart Island has been serially abandoned and reused in order to manage the detainment, disappearance, and criminalization of bodies both alive and dead. Its status as public but remote city land made of it a long social experiment in the biopolitics of unwanted bodies and in the afterlife of slavery. A prisoner of war camp during the Civil War (and briefly during World War II), the island was purchased by the city in 1868 for use as a "potter's field," a biblical reference to the burial of "strangers" using Judas's thirty pieces of silver, what chief priests otherwise shunned as blood money.[71] The Bible does not mention who conducted the burials: on Hart Island, a jail housed prisoners who performed the burials for convict wages, underscoring convict labor as the afterlife of slavery, as the Thirteenth Amendment prohibited slavery and involuntary servitude except as punishment for a crime. In the nineteenth century, the island was used as an isolation ward during yellow fever epidemics, a women's "charity" hospital, and an insane asylum. Business development of the land for tourism and recreation has been perpetually considered and deferred, most notably when a black entrepreneur, Solomon Riley, got hold of land on Hart Island's southern tip in 1925 and tried to build a "Negro Coney Island" alongside the prison and burial places, a prospect denied by the city officials who revoked the man's license. Instead, the island continued to be used as a protean space of detention in the early twentieth century: a home for elderly indigent men, a women's tuberculosis hospital, a "reformatory for male misdemeanants 16–30 years old," holding cells for older male prisoners from overcrowded city jails, and "a disciplinary barracks" for the navy and camp for three German prisoners of war during World War II. After the war, the Department of Corrections regained use of the island as a prison, released it to the Department of Welfare to house male "derelicts," and again reclaimed it to accommodate the rising population of inmates in city jails, as the U.S. Army opened a Nike missile base in a portion of the island that would be abandoned by 1961, when the army barracks were converted to house family court cases and traffic offenders. In five years, the jail closed and a Phoenix House drug rehabilitation center opened before moving out of Hart Island in 1976.

From 1982 to 1991 prisoners who worked at the graveyard again were kept on the island before the jail closed a final time: inmates have since been ferried to Hart Island from nearby Rikers Island, what some call the largest penal colony in the world (and the main base of operations for the Department of Corrections), to bury the dead for about fifty cents an hour. Recently, the Rikers Island prison complex itself has become a site of disappearance not only through incarceration but also through the screening, detention, and deportation of immigrant inmates from the moment of arrest: "Every year thousands of immigrants being held on Rikers Island are transferred to federal custody and deported. Only about half of them have a criminal record, many of them are here legally, most of them have their due process rights violated and all of them are subjected to substandard conditions before being returned to their countries of origin."[72]

Throughout the island's many incarnations as city property, two constants remained: the burying of the dead and the use of prison labor to do it. The Department of Corrections apparently has discontinued the practice of reusing mass graves for some of the adult bodies in favor of a grid system. The Hart Island Project led by the community artist Melinda Hunt has cultivated greater visibility of the island, which remains unknown to most New Yorkers, including even friends and loved ones of the buried.[73]

Bernardo attains a "strange immortality" that uncannily resembles his self as the affective and material scraps of the *Urus*. His burial in potter's field is only the final act in the drama of transforming persons into the forever anonymous, detained, and disappeared: from Ellis Island's perverse proximity to the ship in New York Harbor to the island of Manhattan where Bernardo dies anonymously to Hart Island on Long Island Sound, where he is to be buried without name or kin, by laborers themselves ferried from an island prison.

Hart Island, while a seemingly minor detail in Goldman's novel, reflects the novel's broader meditation on the nexus of the disappeared, anonymous, and hidden lives of those whose legal personhood has been organized around forms of coerced labor. The attempt to erase such histories of legal personhood—and to disappear the laborers that embody those histories—is part of the particular kind of economic salvage that Mark and Elias attempt with the *Urus*, a form of nominal salvage that ultimately seeks to recycle past objects into new ones, free of their historical traces. *The Ordinary Seaman* contrasts this economic salvage with the alternative of salvage as a critical mode for reading.

Hart Island also resonates with another once-forgotten and hidden burial ground—where, during the seventeenth and eighteenth centuries, 15,000 to 20,000 enslaved and free Africans were buried deep in a six-acre swath of land in what is now Lower Manhattan, an area whose surface has been mapped, plotted, sold, and resold as real estate for hundreds of years. The history of this burying ground returns us to the temporality and problematic of salvage. A small part of what was then called the Negroes Burial Ground was unearthed in 1991 during the preliminary construction of a government skyscraper. Hundreds of human skeletal remains and burial artifacts at the site prompted the General Services Administration (GSA), which knew of the site when it purchased the land but had not anticipated significant remains would be intact, to hire a company who would undertake "rescue" or "salvage" archaeology, a process of excavation whose completion is hastened by the urgencies of capital. Salvage archaeologists aim to rescue artifacts discovered or disrupted during construction and development projects that are then put on hold, often due to legal or community pressure and at the expense of the economic projects, which in turn puts pressure on the archaeological teams to complete their work as quickly as possible. Excavation in this case is not merely an unearthing, but a disruption of the time of capital: salvage archaeology ruptures (disrupts, interrupts) the economic venture that initiates it. Salvage archaeology, then, must rescue material traces of the past from the threat of imminent future erasure even as it attempts to construct an alternative future in which the artifacts—especially the bioarchaeological material of human burials—may survive the economic imperative to build on top of them, yet ultimately without disrupting the teleology of development.

Advocates for preserving and memorializing the burial ground sought to redirect the purpose of the GSA-funded salvage archaeology toward a historiographic reincorporation of what had been estranged from and denied in historical narratives: a spiritual family genealogy of ancestors and descendants that also attested to the extraordinary productivity of African Americans in building New York City and, by extension, their crucial but underacknowledged contributions to the nation. And until the excavation of the unmarked burial grounds, the story of the African diaspora was another unrecognized, spectral layer of New York City history.

In 1664, just before the Dutch ceded Manhattan to the British, enslaved Africans [sometimes considered "half-free" by the Dutch] made up about 40 percent of the colony's local population. The British continued the slave trade [and enacted laws more rigidly regulating slavery], importing as many as 6,800 Africans between 1700 and 1774, many of whom had worked previously on Caribbean plantations. By the mid-eighteenth century, New York had become a thriving port town, and enslaved Africans loaded and unloaded cargo at the docks, wharves, slips, and warehouses along the East River. They also piloted boats ferrying produce from the farming villages of Long Island, repaired and expanded city streets, and worked in shipbuilding and construction. On the eve of the American Revolution, New York City had the largest number of enslaved Africans of any English colonial settlement except Charleston, South Carolina, and it had the highest proportion of slaves to Europeans of any northern settlement. Though seldom acknowledged, Africans were essential to the functioning, as well as the building of colonial New York.

In November 1697, New York City adopted a policy of mortuary apartheid, declaring lower Manhattan churchyards off-limits to blacks. Forced to look for a place to bury its dead, New York's African population, which then numbered about 700, chose unappropriated property outside city limits two blocks north of today's City Hall. There, from 1712 until 1790, in an area characterized by David Valentine, an early city historian, as "unattractive and desolate," Africans conducted last rites for their people. "So little seems to have been thought of the race that not even a dedication of their burial place was made by church authorities," wrote Valentine of what was known then as the Negros Burial Ground.[74]

The policy of "mortuary apartheid" not only segregated the dead but also exiled black bodies, nearly half of them infants and children but also adults who endured severe physical stress and short life expectancies—to the margins, beyond the northern city limits of Wall Street. The Negroes Burial Ground was treated by whites as a wasteland, where other "undesirables" such as prisoners of war, epidemic victims, and poor whites were also interred, particularly in a potter's field next to the burial ground. Despite grievances made by black New Yorkers, pottery makers and others repeatedly threw waste materials onto the land; later one nearby landowner erected a fence and charged black residents to bury their dead. By 1792, as the city expanded, the burial ground remained clearly marked on maps but was not recognized as sacred ground: the land was simply revalued, platted, sold, and used as building lots. To read New York through the spectral history of its racialized, alienated, and unfree laborers—whose very presence revolved around the city's development as a colonial port city—is, also, to recognize the once-central, now-marginal location of New York Harbor in the storyworld of *The Ordinary Seaman* as the ruins of a colonial slave labor and migration history spanning both sides of the Atlantic, of which New York City is but one northerly node.

The unearthing of a portion of what is now known as the African Burial Ground sparked a conflict between the GSA and New York's African American communities over the future of the excavated site—a conflict that quickly spread into a national controversy about race and nation; about the ongoing culture wars; about slavery's conventionally ignored existence in the North and the unacknowledged contributions of enslaved people to the building of New York; about the tensions between "descendant communities," salvage archaeology, and real estate development; about the scientific and spiritual reading of bones to salvage a history of people largely excluded from the historical record; and about how a country ought to care for, rescue, and retrospectively incorporate the dead into U.S. and transatlantic history. The 1991 rediscovery of the burial ground showed how colonial New York's African population built the city under both Dutch and British control and comprised 40 percent of the city's population by the eve of the American Revolution. The burial ground thus fit into a liberal recovery narrative for many African American New Yorkers even as the site seemed merely a legal and financial obligation for the GSA to salvage the physical remains as quickly as possible in order to resume pouring cement for the foundation of a new building. Despite the major archaeological significance of the burial ground as the largest colonial-era burial ground of free and enslaved Africans in North America, several grave sites were accidentally destroyed, remains hastily disinterred, and construction plans under way without the involvement of local activists, who objected to the exhumations and claimed the site as sacred ground.

How does the process of salvaging the dead inform acts of critical historiography, which trace the contours of absence in official historical narratives? What must be lost in the rescue attempt? Various African American groups offered competing responses regarding the African Burial Ground. For prominent burial ground organizers, whose work successfully led to a 1992 federal law that halted further excavation of the site and allocated funding to memorialize the burial ground, the answers lay in commemorating the dead as ancestors that share a spiritual and historical kinship with present-day African Americans, especially in New York—a move that sought to reincorporate African Americans and Afrocentric spiritual philosophies of kinship and collective genealogy into a national imaginary that values the myth of origins. The bioarchaeological method of evaluating the skeletal remains promised a kind of communion with the dead as ancestral subjects and bearers of a communal identity, history, and knowledge that science would help them to reveal (in contrast to competing archaeological methods that treated the remains as objects valued strictly for their scientific and historical value).[75]

Moreover, the state oversight committee wanted a museum that would be "a place similar to Ellis Island, something that can attest to Afro-American history."[76] Indeed, the Statue of Liberty and Ellis Island Museum are partial models for the organizers of the African Burial Ground museum and memorial who seek to honor the dead as ancestors and as a long-overdue incorporation of African American heritage in the nation's civic history. Mayor David N. Dinkins illustrated this vision at a 1993 ceremony to mark the African Burial Ground's newly granted status as National Historical Landmark.

> Millions of Americans celebrate Ellis Island as the symbol of their communal identity in this land. Others celebrate Plymouth Rock. Until a few years ago, African American New Yorkers had no site to call our own. There was no place which said, we were here, we contributed, we played a significant role in New York's history right from the beginning. . . .
>
> Now we—their descendants—have the symbol of our heritage embodied in lower Manhattan's African Burial Ground . . . Again and again I have witnessed the power this site has to move people's hearts, and to educate their minds. . . . By opening a window into a long forgotten part of New York's past, the Burial Ground has changed the past itself. All New Yorkers are enriched by the gift of history it has bestowed.[77]

The African Burial Ground (ABG) was proclaimed a National Monument, "like the Statue of Liberty," in 2006, and the 2007 memorial dedication ceremony included a ceremonial torch brought over from the Statue of Liberty for the first lighting of the ABG memorial.[78] The African Burial Ground, once the junked remains of the city's growing real estate market, is now among the highest markers of civic history. In producing the ABG's public historical narrative, the organizers who invoked Ellis Island revealed a collective desire to correct for the juridical treatment of African Americans as strangers in their own land. The appeal to a nationalist origin—a "symbol of our heritage" on the order of Ellis Island for European immigrants and Plymouth Rock for colonial Americans— suggests a desire by Dinkins and others to salvage a national history of racial oppression by emphasizing the labor productivity of the African diaspora in spite of the physical and social injury to which the burial ground's skeletal remains testify.

The strong identification of the African Burial Ground with Ellis Island and Plymouth Rock, however, suggests not only a retrospective correction but also a disavowal of the spectral histories of expulsion that animate those older monuments: the wars of aggression and acquisition against First Nations peoples at Plymouth Rock, or the federal policies of immigration control and detention at Ellis Island. These sites were structured by a human taxonomy of racial categories and modes of classification made possible by a legal culture that sanctioned the figure of the nonperson person, a form of human life rejected by the very political and social order that claims the power to name and assign it. What develops as a juridical human taxonomy becomes an instrument of the living that haunts the dead and their future descendants: the racial expulsion from New York's churchyards, for example, continued a posthumous exile designed to resemble the legal alienation and social injury of early New York's black population in life. In frequently comparing the burial ground to the mythic Ellis Island, Mayor Dinkins and other commentators suggested that the legal culture of slavery and racial oppression is firmly in the distant past, in the time of origins, with the result that visitors to the memorial site may not hear its strange echoes in the juridical sanction of contemporary forms of racialized labor and alienation that Colin Dayan and others identify in the late twentieth century and beyond. In other words, the African Burial Ground's supporters constructed a liberal recovery narrative that hides the bodies, much as Hart Island does, from being incorporated into a critical genealogy of contemporary legal personhood in the United States.

Ellis Island was the model for this liberal disavowal of the legacies of legal personhood. It is where millions of U.S. citizens trace their family genealogies to a ship embarking in the "New World." From 1890 to 1954 Ellis Island, the country's first federal "immigration station," proved enormously productive of legal classification of personhood, evaluating more than twelve million immigrants, exiles, and refugees who sought entry into the United States. Part of the island's national mythology is its reputation as an "Island of Tears" for the minority of immigrants who journeyed across the ocean only to be rejected at the gates. Suppressed from this mythology is the history of Ellis Island during periods of war and immigrant expulsion programs, when the port of entry would be transformed from an "immigration station" into a deportation center for thousands of suspected "enemy aliens, "enemy radicals," "subversives," and even "enemy merchant seamen" who were then indefinitely imprisoned at the island awaiting a final decision of release or deportation.[79] By estranging its itinerant population from national territory, Ellis Island prison thus repeated the familiar strategy of spatial marginalization as political expulsion from the nation through the power of punitive legal recognition, in which the law recognizes the personhood of the detained individual only in his or her capacity for criminal agency— a criminal agency often proved retroactively by the law's classification of the individual as somehow illegal. The experience of the anticolonial Trinidadian critic C. L. R. James as a detainee on Ellis Island in 1952 for subversive activities provides a corrective to Ellis Island as an icon of U.S. hospitality. A colonial subject who traveled primarily between his native Trinidad, Britain, and the United States, James was attuned to the unstable, uneven, and powerful classification of persons by the state. But it is his attempt to gain legal residence and citizenship in the United States that most violently subjected him to the state's classificatory powers.[80] In Goldman's novel, the crew–turned–stateless refugees detained in a legal limbo while on board the *Urus*—all within view of the Statue of Liberty—revise its enduring myth as the port for a nation of immigrants. Bernardo links their immobility to that of the statue's, predicting that "when that statue walks, chavalos, this ship will sail" (45). The crewmen's dilemma calls up a neglected national history of Ellis Island, which acted primarily as an exceptional space of detention when it served in part as an Immigration and Naturalization Service detention center where "aliens" languished under indefinite detention, held for "confidential" reasons or none at all, until Ellis Island closed in 1954 to be remade a decade later as a national monument and museum. Their situation is in contrast to the history of Ellis Island as the immigration gateway, instead evoking Ellis Island as an "island prison," as described by a dissenting Supreme Court justice in the 1952–53 case *Shaughnessy v. Mezei*.[81]

Aligning the commemoration of the African Burial Ground with the Ellis Island museum promised funds for preservation and for a permanent memorial to mark the suffering, contribution, and vitality of African Americans that have long been ignored by official historical and political narratives. In the 2003 ceremony in which the 419 African Americans whose remains were excavated a dozen years earlier were led in a procession from Howard University to their reinterment site at the new African Burial Ground Memorial, speakers repeatedly linked salvaging the bones of the dead with a renewed claim to a spiritual genealogy. Bernard L. Richardson thanked God, who has "made these bones live again." The civil rights leader Marian Bascom remarked, "I'm not too sure that those skeletal remains are not part of me, hidden and forgotten for hundreds of years and now recovered and given a sacred burial." And Dr. Maya Angelou, speaking on behalf of the ancestors, recited a poem written in their honor: "You may bury me in the bottom of Manhattan. I will rise. My people will get me. I will rise out of the huts of history's shame."[82]

Nonetheless, rescue historiography—like salvage archaeology—entails pressures to save selectively, distinguishing mere junk from the junked resources. To salvage history is to select certain historical fragments for rescue and return others to the junk heap. When an entire people's collective history has been threatened with the status of junk, the distinction between worthlessness and worthiness becomes especially divisive—all the more so when the history being salvaged is also the bones of the dead, the rescue of an ancestral imaginary. In 1993, amid growing tensions between the GSA and ABG organizers, Melinda Hunt and Margot Lovejoy designed a public artwork titled *Just Outside the City* that sought to commemorate the nearly one million buried in New York City's nine potter's fields. They planned to install the sculpture where there was once an eighteenth-century almshouse and, nearby, the city's oldest and mostly forgotten potter's field under what is now City Hall Park in Lower Manhattan, an area within the presumed historic boundaries of the ABG. A firestorm erupted between the artists and members of the African Burial Ground Steering Committee, leading to controversial roadblocks at several political levels and the ultimate revocation of the artists' official permit to install the sculpture. Hunt appealed to the historical links between the ABG and the potter's fields: not only were there a small minority of poor persons, anonymous persons, and prisoners of war who were buried somewhere among the ABG, but the "location of the African Burial Ground set a precedent for the city's potter's fields." According to Hunt, "That doesn't say anything negative about the burials or the type of burials, but that certain people were buried outside the city limits." Some ABG committee members objected to the implications that the ABG is itself a potter's field.

> Peggy King Jorde, an official in the Dinkins administration who now serves as the committee's executive director, said the objections stemmed from the parallel the artists draw between the burial ground and the potter's fields—a link that demeans the burial ground, she says, by associating the blacks buried there with those buried unceremoniously in potter's fields.
>
> "Would you call Chatham Square a potter's field?" Ms. Jorde said, referring to the city's first Jewish cemetery, remnants of which still exist in what is now Chinatown. "Symbolism is extremely important. I think we'd all agree with that."

Some of the committee's members objected because they felt that the location of the sculpture encroached on the presumed historic boundaries, violating what Ms. Jorde called "the significance and integrity" of the burial ground.

Christopher Moore, a historian on the committee who supported the proposed sculpture, said that others also saw in it unsavory connotations in the use of the writings by inmates, some of whom are black.[83]

Jorde elsewhere has claimed that the GSA had initially mistaken the burial ground for a "potter's field," a term that "divorced it from its African origin and diminished its importance."[84] As I discussed in relation to Hart Island, to call the burial ground a potter's field evokes the biblical reference to a place reserved for the burial of strangers—thereby designating those of African descent as alien, among but not belonging to society, and underscoring the unmarked burials of the racially and economically segregated. In common English usage, *potter's field* figuratively means a wasteland, a strange heterotopia of nonrecognition, where immortality does not come with a name marker but with anonymity, estrangement, and oblivion (even today, Hart Island burials are marked by numbers that correspond to names on paper records). Unlike the name "African Burial Ground," which speaks to a nationally recognized history of ancestral and historical legacy, "potter's field" leaves unmarked any principle of categorization that defines the dead or the meaning of the burial ground itself for the present. As we know from the fictional Bernardo's death, the potter's field is where bodies and things are sent to disappear, to be forgotten, not commemorated or easily visited. Most of these bodies are difficult for the living to salvage through historical narrative. As Lynne Lewis, executive director of Picture the Homeless, says regarding the organization's effort to secure permission from the Department of Corrections to conduct interfaith ceremonies for the dead on Hart Island, "Homeless people are treated like garbage their whole lives and are then thrown into pits." She adds, "It's very personal for us."[85] Yet as *The Ordinary Seaman* suggests in its depiction of Bernardo as a potential *tunshi*—a spirit that may return to haunt the shipowner Elias and lead him to waste away from fright—the potter's field is whence the forgotten, treated as refuse, return as spectral reminders to the present.

Bernardo's disappearance evokes a long history of the disappeared in New York through its exceptional sites—sites shaped by competing modes of salvaging. There is the mode of economic salvage motivated by neoliberal imperialist nostalgia suggested by Salgado's *Workers* and explicitly embraced by Goldman's shipowners, Mark and Elias. There is the liberal mode of salvage used in the African Burial Ground project. What Goldman's novel invites is a third mode of salvage: a critical mode of reading by searching for the haunting imperial and national traces, the fragments of history that animate the neoliberal present, a mode of reading that asks how these traces might bring into view the significance and operations of the debris of legal personhood across legal identities, from the corporate to the seafaring to the refugee and migrant person. It is this critical mode of salvage work that this chapter has sought to demonstrate. And it is this critical mode of salvaging that reveals what the liberal mode of the African Burial Ground opening ceremonies disavows: the persistence of the slave personality and its capacity to shape states of exceptional personhood in the present.

2 / Sugar's Legacies: Romance, Revolution, and Wageless Life in the Fiction of Edwidge Danticat and Rosario Ferré

Even within the homes of the sugar elite's descendants, where wrinkled white women recall the glorious days gone by of multiple houses, servants, and demure carriage rides to church, the cleaning women slip in their own memories, which complicate the homogenizing narrative of Ponce's grandeur and lily-white moral decency. They remind the questioner that much has been omitted from such stories. Poor women did the cooking, cleaning, and caring that sustained these expansive lifestyles. The region is dotted with families of African descent who share their employers' last names, bound to them generations ago by enslavement and in many cases by blood connections, forged in semiclandestine sex.

—EILEEN J. SUÁREZ FINDLAY, *IMPOSING DECENCY*

Imagine gathering all the sugar in the world in one location. . . . There is all this knowledge that comes with that, the learned knowledge of the men and women who have worked on this site for years and years and years, not to mention of the families of these laborers. There is a living memory of the smell and the steam—this heavy molasses odor that's still in the space.

—KARA WALKER, INTERVIEW BY KARA ROONEY

Is grace, yes. And I take it, quiet, quiet, like thiefing sugar.

—DIONNE BRAND, *IN ANOTHER PLACE, NOT HERE*

Among the crumbling industrial sites of the Brooklyn waterfront sits the vast Domino Sugar Factory refinery complex. Completely rebuilt and expanded after an 1882 fire destroyed the original Williamsburg factory, the new refinery was touted as the largest on the planet, capable of producing 1,250,000 pounds of sugar daily.[1] Between the late nineteenth and the mid-twentieth century, the American Sugar Refining Company rose to become a key player in industrializing the international sugar trade and bringing it to Brooklyn. The Domino Sugar Factory employed thousands of immigrants, pulled shiploads of raw sugar from the Caribbean into the Port of New York, and—to ensure those regular shipments—relentlessly expanded American capital interests into the "colonial and semicolonial territories of the United States, especially Cuba, the Dominican Republic, and Puerto Rico."[2] At the factory's height, it supplied a large part of the U.S. sugar market; by its sputtering twenty-first-century end in 2000, the site had closed its doors after owners defeated an especially long and bitter labor strike. The latest plans for a major redevelopment of the site into luxury residential towers, a park, and office and retail space are under way after a failed community bid to preserve the historic building. In this limbo time between working factory and luxury towers, the Domino Sugar Factory has become one stop along the sprawling U.S. road tour of architectural relics, the decaying monuments to an urban industrial past that have been so endlessly visited and photographed by urban ruin enthusiasts.[3]

It is in this refinery of accumulating colonial, industrial, and neoliberal economic debris that Kara Walker held her 2014 art installation, *At the behest of Creative Time Kara E. Walker has confected: A Subtlety, or the Marvelous Sugar Baby, an Homage to the unpaid and overworked Artisans who have refined our Sweet tastes from the cane fields to the Kitchens of the New World on the Occasion of the demolition of the Domino Sugar Refining Plant.* The installation features an enormous, approximately seventy-five-foot-long sphinx-like statue coated in white sugar: with something of the awesome powers of the Greek and Egyptian sphinxes, the face of this "New World Sphinx" is modeled on advertising images for Aunt Dinah Molasses (featuring a mammy caricature with a handkerchief tied around her head), while its bottom is raised up in air, a ten-foot vulva of white sugar crystals on full display. The sphinx-like statue contradicts its name as a subtlety through her figure's explicit presentation of breasts, butt, and vulva. "By being sexually overt," notes Walker, "she's not very subtle at all. She's discomfiting."[4] Around her are slave boy attendants, "sugar babies" approximately five feet high and sculpted out of sugar, molasses, and resin and burnt to varying degrees. These sculptures were modeled on racial kitsch statues of little smiling slave boys carrying woven baskets that Walker found for sale, made in China, via Amazon.com. The factory site and sugar's mutable states and properties led Walker to invert her signature play with color. Instead of fabricating black paper cutouts and exhibiting them on a white surface, as in her past work, here the female sphinx gleams white, its refined sugar coating the sculptural body whose rejoinder to refinement is a sly "fuck you."[5] The three-dimensional boy slaves vary from shades of a blood-like reddish-brown to burnt black to ashen gray. The unstable climatic conditions of the factory space contribute to the melting and collapse of the attendants.

In interviews leading up to the installation, Walker described how the site itself—the walls, windows, floors, ceiling—shaped her plans for the sculptures, as well as how her knowledge of the site's histories meddled, ghostlike, with her artistic response to the site.

> There are decades of molasses that cover the entire space; it's coated—it's an amazing relic or repository vessel. . . . There is a living memory of the smell and the steam—this heavy molasses odor that's still in the space[,] . . . this grassy, pungent, almost nauseating sugar smell that lives in the tissue of everyone who has worked in that plant.[6]

In contrast to the whitebox museum backdrop for Walker's black paper cutouts, the "decades of molasses" transform the factory into a space whose entire purpose was to produce whiteness, to remove the natural elements of color from sugar crystals through centrifugal force, to turn brownness into the by-product—the waste—of refinement. Walker's monument makes present the absence of human labor even as she imagines the ongoing presence of the factory within each laborer's body, as if the product of their labor were living "in the tissue of everyone who has worked in that plant." This residual history of sugar and its processing actively interfered with the installation: as her production team tried its hardest to remove the thick molasses residue from the factory floor, molasses-tinged fluid began leaking from the ceiling onto the gleaming white sphinx, running down the contours of its body and streaming it with the taint of the very color that had been so thoroughly removed in the course of refinement. In their material presence, instability, and aesthetic use by Walker, white sugar and brown molasses are and are not metaphors for economies of race, sex, and labor (slave, minimum-wage agricultural and industrial). The whiteness of the sphinx was designed to gleam against the dark walls, and the sculptures are doubly perverse "subtleties": they are ostentatious, and they are counterparts to the elaborate sugar sculptures that became fashionable in medieval Europe as edible trophies served between courses of a meal. Walker, as if rehearsing the role of medieval court confectioner, serves Brooklyn A Subtlety commissioned by Creative Time, whose editorial board includes an owner of the new development. A Subtlety becomes an interlude, an interruption, or a mediation between two courses of development—the colonial, industrial era of the Domino Sugar factory and the neoliberal gentrification of the Brooklyn waterfront. And true to the culinary metaphor, A

Subtlety is temporary, to be presented and consumed for eight weeks as public art before the site's demolition.

In its iconoclastic way, Walker's *A Subtlety* joins a broader aesthetic strategy by African American and Caribbean women artists and writers to redefine sugar's legacies through the multifarious and overlapping genres and modes of romance.[7] Taking Barbara Fuchs's point that "romance is a notoriously slippery category," this chapter draws on existing critical understandings of romance in order to think about how romance figures categories of laboring legal personhood.[8] Four meanings of romance may be brought to bear on the work of Walker and the narrative fiction by Danticat and Ferré. There is romance as love story; romance as "an operation of translation and transformation," suggested by root meanings of the term as the process of transforming "Latin texts into French";[9] romance as an "eternal and unchanging" genre, what for Northrup Frye and later Hayden White amounts to a fixed template for a story of heroic transcendence;[10] and romance as the nation-building genre that binds history to politics, the state, and ideologies of the family. The national romance combines the love story with the story of heroic transcendence as part of a strategy to construct "foundational fictions," as Doris Sommer calls them in her study of the narrative tactics that made literature so crucial to nationalist politics in the newly emerging states of nineteenth-century Latin America.

Fabricated in a defunct refinery undergoing partial demolition, Walker's sculptural monuments of—pointedly, not to—the sugar industry actively respond to the romanticization of sugar's legacies in all four meanings of romance outlined above. First, as with much of Walker's signature work, the "Marvelous Sugar Baby" is nothing if not a strategic operation of translation and transformation, in its visual translation of stereotypes and in its literal transformation of sugar, its artistic material, as well as the transformation of the factory into an exhibition space. Second, the giant white sphinx of the New World plantation complex refuses romance as love story, which binds love with sex through courtship or seduction: her face is stern and her breasts, buttocks, and vulva are on full display. Third, the installation refuses the genre of romance as defined in literature by Frye and adapted by White, in which romance refers to a mode of storytelling that ends with a triumphant resolution and an overcoming of earlier conflict. Instead of following the linear teleology of Frye's romance genre, the sticky, tarlike molasses residue of the plant visually dramatizes the condensation of temporalities (ancient, colonial slave, ex-slave, industrial, postindustrial) and geographies (Brooklyn, Cuba, Puerto Rico, the Dominican Republic, untold sugar plantations elsewhere) and racial ideologies (the tar baby; raw, sexualized brown sugar; refined white crystals) that still cling to the surfaces of the factory. Molasses becomes, in this sense, not the factory's waste product but its very surface. As literal goo and figurative register of historical accumulation, the molasses claims the space of the factory in its resistance to being scrubbed or scraped away. Fourth, the installation challenges the U.S. national romance of progress—racial, sexual, or economic. Sugar's legacies of power are embodied not only in the composite stereotypes of the sexualized white "mammy" sphinx and the kitsch-molded caramelized slave boys but also in the factory site and its impending demolition.

A Subtley operates, then, as a kind of sequel to Walker's earlier work, particularly her infamous debut piece, *Gone: An Historical Romance of a Civil War as It Occurred b'tween the Dusky Thighs of One Young Negress and Her Heart* (1994), with its black paper cutout silhouettes of stereotypical antebellum figures arranged against a white wall in violent, sexual, and "romantic" combinations. Without rehearsing the controversy around Walker and her representations of blackness here—a controversy that shows no signs of flagging, given some outraged responses to *A Subtlety*—it is worth noting that what makes her art so controversial has everything to do with romance as a narrative genre of erotic and emotional attachments no less than with romance as a way of representing African American history and people as beautiful, heroic, and unremittingly positive. Instead of subscribing to affirmative representations of blackness, observes Salamishah Tillet, Walker "takes a form like the silhouette, which in antebellum America reproduced racial taxonomies, and amplifies it further so that we can begin to see and deconstruct the exaggerated versions of the original."[11] Troubling for some viewers, Walker's art does not straightforwardly challenge or counter the "ongoing melodrama of race in post–civil rights America" but rather inscribes its viewers, with their various racial identifications, into that "melodrama" as "active and consenting participants."[12] The title *Gone* makes this artwork's challenge to romance plain: it talks back to that classic national romance, Margaret Mitchell's *Gone With the Wind* (1936), whose love story between Scarlett O'Hara and Rhett Butler unfolds amid the national romance with the antebellum South, those days *befohdawah*. As Walker says of her work, it is not "dealing with history" in a way that histories of race and racism expect, with a "hero" who comes in and solves problems. Rather, she suggests, her work is "subsumed by history, or consumed by history."[13]

Sugar's properties—sweetness, refined whiteness, presumably sexualized brownness, status as object of desire and sign of wealth and power, commodification as something everyone should be able to have—have made it a virtual master trope of the romance genre in literature and music. To everyone, perhaps, but those who work in sugar, whose bodies, sweat, and fate are bound to its cultivation and production. It is thus an especially significant object for critical responses to romance. Almost from the moment it arrived by ship from the Canary Islands to the island of Hispaniola, sugarcane bequeathed its burdensome legacies. Wherever it took root, it also for a time transformed that place in relation to global economies. The sugar industry powered the massive trade in slaves, with its attendant laws and racialized categories of legal personhood; dominated the way plantation colonies were organized; and propelled human migrations, sugar import-exports, processing, consumption, and industrialization in the hemisphere, especially in the United States and throughout Europe.[14] Since the sixteenth century, nearly every island colony in the Caribbean has at least temporarily been used as an experiment in monoculture sugar production by European and U.S. empires.[15] With the development of large-scale sugar production came major changes to categories of legal personhood and to the laws govern-ing forms of coerced labor and enslavement, which structured sugar's twin economic boom, the African slave trade. As the most basic story of Caribbean colonization would note, ship, sugar, and slavery developed as powerful nodes of a colonial network that depended on the changing recognition of human persons in relation to labor identities established by law.

Moreover, where there was sugar, there was sex; and where there was sex, there was the racial, class, and juridical politics centered on women's sexual reproduction. As discussed later in this chapter, the colonial popu-lation debates and antiprostitution laws in Puerto Rico and the constitu-tional provisions regarding the family in the Haitian Constitution reveal intense investments in biological genealogy: they are among sugar's lega-cies. In plantation colonies, the law's defining powers over personhood did the work of literally defining the inheritance of wealth or property and the inheritance of legal subjugation. Legal personhood is organized around biopolitical regimes of race, sex, and labor both openly affirmed by the patriarchal elite and clandestinely exploited by them. Legal iden-tities are not merely a direct response to economic need and political status: they gather form and substance from nation-building narratives, which in turn depend on notions of labor, race, gender, sexuality, and political belonging.[16] In the cases of Haiti, the Dominican Republic, and Puerto Rico, these nation-building narratives emerge from, and circu-late within, histories of contested and attenuated sovereignty.

This chapter explores literary responses to the collision of sugar, romance, sex, and legal personhood in Haiti and Puerto Rico.[17] Danticat's "A Wall of Fire Rising" and Ferré's *Sweet Diamond Dust* highlight how narrative tropes of rehearsal and reproduction complicate the meanings of sugar's legacies for legal personhood. Rehearsal and reproduction interrupt and respond to romantic and tragic narrative modes of emplotment in Danticat's short story and challenge the romantic conventions of Puerto Rican patriarchal literary tradition in Ferré's novella. These narrative modes are disrupted by and depend on material conditions of rehearsal and labor in "A Wall of Fire Rising" and reproduction and inheritance in *Sweet Diamond Dust*. These literary texts call into question what it means to inherit regimes of legal personhood generated in the era of sugar, slavery, and sex. They question a literary imagination shaped uncritically by the legal fictions that legitimate certain genealogies and that define family, citizen, mother, prostitute, father, and child. "Sugar's legacies" is not merely metaphorical: it refers to the material conditions of wealth, labor, sex, gender, and race as they get transferred (or altered) from one generation to the next.

The first section of the chapter shows how Danticat complicates romantic and tragic historiographies of Haiti by using the trope of dramatic rehearsal, which I read as a process of repetition that instantiates and complicates the desire to salvage liberation narratives of Haiti from their junked political legacies. I argue that rehearsal refigures sugar's long legacy in Haiti in ways that complicate generic categories and that underscore the disjuncture between anticolonial revolutionary legacies and the postcolonial, neoliberal present. Turning from a country whose large-scale sugar production and export declined precipitously with the Haitian Revolution and formal independence, I go on to consider Ferré's *Sweet Diamond Dust* and its depiction of sugar's legacy for the familial, class, and racial politics of sexual reproduction in Puerto Rico, a formerly Spanish colony seized by the United States in 1898, largely for its potential as a monoculture sugar-producing colony. The second section of the chapter analyzes Ferré's play on inheritance in her depiction of the myth of *la gran familia puertorriqueña*, so crucial to the traditional Puerto Rican letters of the elite hacendado class, as well as her challenge to that myth through the feminist mode of antiromance. As Donette Francis argues, it is through the mode of "antiromance" that "sexual citizenship" emerges as a defining feature of contemporary Caribbean feminist poetics. Extending David Evans's concept of "sexual citizenship," which stresses that "citizens have genders, sexualities, and bodies that matter in politics," Francis sees antiromance as a narrative mode that attends to different racial and gender formations and to "how the intimate domain reveals the concealed sexual qualifications of political rights for all citizens."[18] As Francis notes, "The sexual lives of Caribbean people have been matters of imperial and national state interests" and "central to colonial and postcolonial articulations of citizenship."[19] My reading of Ferré's *Sweet Diamond Dust* as antiromance extends Francis's insight not only by tracking its parody of national romance but also by focusing on how that parody is structured/shaped by the instability of the antiprostitution laws aimed specifically at the mixed-race female colonial subject.

The sparring between the Puerto Rican nationalist historical romance and a feminist antiromance gets staged by Ferré's *Sweet Diamond Dust* through the plot of a contested legal inheritance of a prominent Creole family's sugar mill and through the clash between modes of narration between characters that, for different reasons, claim the authority to tell the story of the De la Valle family as the history of Puerto Rico and a vision of its future. Ferré's play on biographical romance highlights the erotic, familial, and national investments in genealogy for a Puerto Rican nationalism in what some call the world's oldest colony. George P. Handley observes the double-edged function of genealogy as historiography in plantation societies: genealogy is "an ideological and metaphorical tool of exclusion, one that aided the plantocracy in publicly denying blacks a rightful place within the national family," but it is also "a biological tool for the writers to identify the ellipses of the planter's scheme, the moments of contact with those who have been excluded."[20] Genealogy becomes a weapon to "complete the unfinished business of decolonization throughout Plantation America."[21] It has the potential to prove Audre Lorde wrong, if only in this respect: with genealogy, the master's tools might, just might, dismantle the master's house.[22] It can certainly dismantle his household and legal legacy.

Romance, as a crucial form taken by both planter genealogies and antislavery decolonization narratives, informs my discussion of sugar's legacies. Mindful of Ann Laura Stoler's criticism of such clichéd scholarly rubrics as "colonial legacy"—where "such terms do little to account for the contemporary force of imperial remains, what people themselves count as colonial effects, and, as important, what they do about what they are left with"—the legal definition of a legacy as the money or property left to someone as stated in a will retains some explanatory power in thinking about the lasting effects of imperial formations.[23] In Danticat's and Ferré's texts, it *is* a matter of legacy: whose sons inherit their fathers' spots on the list of sugar mill workers in Danticat's short story and who legally inherits the wealth built up by an earlier colonial sugar plantation economy in the case of Ferré's novella. Legacy provides a way for thinking about the romance genre and its "foundational fictions" as they bind heterosexual unions, provide a nationalist vision for the state, and continue the transfer of wealth along reproductive lines. "Legacy," then, evokes the intergenerational transfer of wealth and the ideologies of marriage and "legitimate" and "illegitimate" offspring, as well as the sometimes unwanted continuities of material and historical conditions, that cannot be fully conveyed in the term "imperial debris." The material conditions of rehearsal, labor, and sexual reproduction cluster around the material remains of the sugar plantation as debris but also literally as legal legacies, calling attention to how debris is itself inherited in the storyworlds of both literary texts. In this way, these texts explore how the debris of legal personhood is itself a legacy, at once inherited and contested.

It is in rehearsing and responding to the genre of national romance that "A Wall of Fire Rising" and *Sweet Diamond Dust* turn to find, as with the walls of the Domino Sugar Factory, the sticky residue of the grass whose cultivation and processing did so much to shape the legal personality of the slave and its aftereffects—its centuries of molasses, its aliveness in the punishing effects on the bodies of laborers still working under terribly exploitative and dangerous conditions in mills, plantations, and refineries; in the precarious legal limbo of migrant cane cutters, seen most notoriously with Haitan *batey* in the Dominican Republic; and in the increasingly unstable positions of mill workers, as depicted by Danticat in the semi-wageless life of the character Guy outside a sugar mill.

Rehearsing National Romance in Danticat's "A Wall of Fire Rising"

At the threshold of colonial Saint-Domingue and the republic of Haiti lies the story of Bois Caïman. The many variants of the story all tell of a summer night in 1791 when enslaved and Maroon black men and women gathered in the Caïman woods to plan a revolt against the colonial slave system. The meeting involved a religious ceremony led by Boukman Dutty and an unnamed *mambo* to serve the spirits and fortify the commitment to revolt.[24] Within a few days, the sugarcane fields of Saint-Domingue's northern provinces were ablaze, the processing machinery wrecked, and the owners dead or fleeing. The uprising left the economic heart of the world's most brutally profitable colony in what C.L.R. James describes as "a flaming ruin," one that would burn for nearly thirteen years before culminating in the declaration of the free black Republic of Haiti.[25]

Competing historical narratives have proliferated around the Bois Caïman ceremony: as part of a narrative of lost possession for French contemporaries, it was denigrated as savagery and witchcraft; as part of a narrative of freedom for Haitians, it was celebrated as the origins of a revolution whose signal achievement—the establishment of a free republic—would presage future Pan-African and Pan-American liberation movements.[26] In the past few decades, the story of Bois Caïman has been recast by a minority of Evangelicals as a scene in the unfolding drama between God and Satan on a cosmic stage. For these Haitian and U.S. Evangelicals, Bois Caïman represents not a signal achievement but rather an originary catastrophe, in which Boukman calls on pagan spirits to free the enslaved in exchange for the future nation's loyalty, prompting the devil to draw up a contract for Haiti's soul.[27] And it is this demonic possession of Haiti that, for these Evangelicals, guarantees all that follows, casting the 2010 earthquake and its long-term devastation as just the latest evidence that Haiti, since its conception, has embodied a spiritual, social, and economic catastrophe without end.[28]

As Evangelicals' influence on Haitian politics increased throughout the 1990s, a minority of Haitian evangelical leaders made repeated attempts to disrupt the national commemorations of the Bois Caïman ceremony, urging their followers to help exorcise the devil from Haiti by symbolically cleansing the site and converting Boukman (posthumously, of course) to Christianity.[29] Their decision to crystallize a public crusade around the commemoration suggests the original ceremony's enormous importance to Haiti's national history, as a moment when the enslaved irrevocably took the matter of their history in their own hands.[30] To insist, as some Evangelicals do, that those were Satan's hands is to attempt to exorcise history, to expel from the national body a spiritual tradition of Vodou that also serves as a vital mode of everyday historiography.[31] The Bois Caïman ceremony ultimately resisted any easy containment promised by conventional models of commemoration, which seek to formalize a simplified relationship of the present to the past. As if to underscore this point, the Evangelicals' efforts to disrupt the commemoration were aimed not primarily at the main event itself but rather at the months-long rehearsals and preparations of the commemoration's organizers, suggesting that the contests over the performance of historical narratives is, at its core, a struggle over how to rehearse history in everyday life.[32]

If Haiti's postcolonial history involves the protracted struggle of the state and its elite against an overburdened and disavowed poor majority, then much of this struggle plays out symbolically in rehearsals of the revolution and its heroes—rehearsals that are also contests over the shape and meaning of political life. The Bois Caïman controversy demonstrates this fact no less than do presidential speeches. The cultural critic Maximilien Laroche has compared this long-standing political "ritual of identification" to an inverted Vodou practice: instead of serving the spirits, the politician makes the spirits serve him; instead of the god "mounting" (or "possessing") the believer, the politician seeks, "by means of oratory incantations," to mount the god.[33] Perhaps no president did so more fully than François Duvalier: during his notoriously brutal rule, Duvalier represented himself as possessing the spirit of Jean-Jacques Dessalines (who decimated much of the remaining white population, announced Haiti's independence to the world in 1804, and declared himself emperor) while incorporating into his public persona the Gede spirit Baron Samedi (the *lwa* of diplomats and senators, the keeper of the dead and of cemeteries, and, alongside Papa Legba, master of the border between life and death).[34] During the 2004 bicentennial of Haiti's declaration of independence, Jean-Bertrand Aristide also identified himself with Dessalines; barely two months later, on the tarmac of the Central African Republic, where he was forced into exile, Aristide restaged Toussaint Louverture's final speech to his French captors in 1802: "I declare in overthrowing me they have uprooted the trunk of the tree of peace, but it will grow back because the roots are l'Ouverturian."[35] If to invoke the spirits of Haitian revolutionaries by rehearsing their famous lines is to mount the god, then it is the public rehearsal of history that, for politicians, serves as the means for possessing the spirit of the revolution.

What these rehearsals show is that every historical narrative has a history, a story of its production, and these narratives operate not only within spectacular contests for political and cultural power but also in the everyday social life that may be hidden in the shadows of such public contests. Such a view of history prompts basic questions: How does the present place its stunning and unyielding pressure on history? How does history, as meaning both what happened and that which is said to have happened, get produced, circulated, or submerged in everyday social life? Why, moreover, do such questions gather so insistently around the *rehearsal* of historical narratives, figures, and events—around those moments, such as the Bois Caïman commemoration, when a performative repetition of history is supposed to ensure an untroubled relationship to the past, one that promises to preserve, remember, or re-create it?

In everyday use, "rehearsal" is a capacious term: it may refer to various acts of repetition, recitation, narration, enumeration, performance, practice, or preparation and to various ends, on- and offstage. One possible etymology of the verb *rehearse* highlights rehearsal as an ongoing labor of cultivation with a temporal relationship not only to the future but also to the past: to rehearse is to "harrow [rake] again."[36] The process of rehearsal may take place in the observable world or unfold in the mind, and what gets rehearsed may be something remembered from the past (a childhood memory, a list of yesterday's errands) or something imagined to be in the future (tomorrow's errands, one's own death).

Edwidge Danticat has written that, for many Haitians, "it is as though the Haitian revolution was fought less than two hundred days, rather than more than two hundred years, ago. For is there anything more timely and timeless than a public battle to control one's destiny, a communal crusade for self-determination?"[37] "A Wall of Fire Rising" asks a related question: How can the revolution feel so near, so eternal, yet so estranged from the postcolonial present? Staged near a late-twentieth-century sugar mill, the story dramatizes rehearsal as a process of salvaging among the ruins of the sugar mill and the history it signifies.[38] A foundational site of capitalism that has shaped modern trade routes, produced stunning world profits, ensured new practices of enslavement, and forged an enduring nexus of economic power and colonial ideology, the sugar mill—like the sugar refinery for which it prepares the raw sugar—palimpsestically records the traces of these histories. To follow Walker's suggestion of the Domino refinery surfaces as sticky with "decades of molasses," the sugar mill is figured as a palimpsest, but it is a palimpsest under contestation and contention over who gets to write and who tries to erase. The midway point between the cane fields and the refinery, between the smell of crushed cane and the smell of molasses, the sugar mill is caught between in other ways—between histories and how they get rehearsed and between families and how they may possess or be possessed by it.

"A Wall of Fire Rising" figures the rehearsal of historical narratives as an attempt to salvage a future from the ruins of history, an effort that also drives recent scholarship on the historiography of the Haitian Revolution by Michel-Rolph Trouillot, Sibylle Fischer, David Scott, and others. Highlighting the revolution not as a singular event but as a process of rehearsal, the short story, like Vodou, constitutes a theory of history as important as the work of national commemorations but often overlooked in the ebb and flow of everyday life. The short story dramatizes the hidden labors of rehearsing history, performed not by politicians or religious leaders but by those who cannot, in a sense, refuse their roles. Seven-year-old Little Guy has just been cast as Boukman in an upcoming school play, prompting him to rehearse his lines incessantly; meanwhile, his father's failure to gain long-term employment leads him to rehearse an escape, which he plans as a spectacular event that will vindicate his self-worth and, in death, free him from a life hidden in the shadows of the sugar mill. Rehearsal is thus figured as a process of repetition that instantiates and complicates the desire to salvage liberation narratives of Haiti from their junked political legacies. "Salvage"—as the effort to save that which nonetheless bears traces of its former ruination—informs my reading of rehearsal as a trope within the storyworld and gestures at the kind of "salvage work" I see in the narrative strategies of contemporary literature more broadly. As a literary strategy, to perform the work of salvage is, in this sense, akin to making junk art. Assembling textual fragments pulled from the wreck of the neoliberal present, Danticat and Ferré salvage histories that call into question the political and cultural terms of social life.

The Plot is Out of Joint

> *I think we live in tragic times less because of the heaps of catastrophes growing around us . . . than because of the out-of-jointness between our former languages of opposition, hope and change, and the world they were meant to criticize.*—DAVID SCOTT, INTERVIEW BY STUART HALL

> *Time here is not mere chronological continuity. It is the range of disjointed moments, practices, and symbols that thread the historical relations between events and narrative.*—MICHEL-ROLPH TROUILLOT, *SILENCING THE PAST*

The French Antillean colony of Saint-Domingue was the vaunted French jewel of the transatlantic capitalist economy, and by 1789, the year of the French Revolution, it had surpassed all others in world-record levels of sugar and coffee production through racialized slave labor. Former slaves and their free allies defeated the French, Spanish, and English imperial armies and, in the midst of internal political maneuvering and social upheaval, transformed the colonial plantation complex into a free republic.[39] More and better accounts of the revolution may be found in any number of books, articles, and essays on the subject, but like mine, all of them compel narrators to make basic choices that explain what happened no less than what its history ought to mean today, and this point serves as Scott's two-part premise: first, we have the power to choose our narrative strategies; and second, narrative modes of emplotment have explanatory power over not only the story but also what it means for imagining a future politics in the present.

"A Wall of Fire Rising" elaborates a model of historicity that takes into account not only what narrative form reveals about the production of history but also how the process of rehearsing history situates historical narratives within the lived present, which constrains the production, performance, and interpretation of such narratives. Rehearsal has two basic functions in the story: a son repeats his lines from a school play as a kind of practice performance in order to memorize them for the "real" performance, and his father mentally prepares for a future and unrepeatable act. At one level, rehearsal dramatizes people's efforts to gain some control over the telling and meaning of specific historical narratives. At another, rehearsal becomes a literary model of how narrative fiction may theorize an involvement in history as material, social process and as a narrative of that process. Rehearsal can offer us especially suggestive ways to explore the writing of history as a narrative problem (of how to connect the past, present, and future into a story) without ignoring the material conditions that shape both the narrative construction and the events that make up any historical narrative.

Reconceptualizing rehearsal as a historical labor and a social process, rather than as a simplified repetition, also undermines two narrative templates for Haitian history as either unchanging or as a series of repeating cycles. In mainstream news reports, Haiti is most often presented as a news story that escapes the fundamental features of narrative: Haiti is timelessly incomprehensible, where the present is the past is the future, a country forever giving itself over to the same abrupt and violent passions of nature—and, as Danticat observes in another context, "nature has no memory."[40]

If news stories represent Haiti as insensible to history, the academic fascination with recurring historical patterns in Haiti perversely leads to the same effect. One critic talks of Haitian history as "shaped around cycles of revenge and hatred that to this day still turn in self-destructive, self-defeating movements."[41] Another imagines a convergence of the 2004 overthrow of Aristide and the 1806 assasination of Dessalines as "a story unfolding on a single stage, a drama running circles since its beginning. From a distance of two centuries, the same scenario, ending with a similar denouement . . . in front of a comparable audience."[42] History seems to happen as an endless repetition: Aristide's forced exile restages Toussaint's kidnapping; the current divide between the Haitian elite and the majority merely continues the split between the colony's *gens de couleur* and the *nouveaux libres;* national rulers and foreigners alike repeat colonial patterns of tyranny; U.S. occupation and multinational "peacekeeping" missions restage the foreign military invasions of the revolution. Change is taken for repetition, and repetition is taken as a sign that nothing's changed.

For other scholars, the Haitian fight for independence serves as the starting point for theorizing what histories of colonialism and radical antislavery might mean for the contemporary moment, loosely organized around a paradigm of modernity. Fischer argues that the revolution's radical antislavery project proved to be paradigmatically modern even as its centrality to modernity was disavowed by its contemporaries and continues to be disavowed today. Scott contends that those of us who remain committed to liberatory politics must choose a different narrative strategy to tell the history of the Haitian Revolution since the waning of decolonization movements in the late twentieth century, a strategy that explains the signal intellectual legacy of the revolution no longer as a story of triumphant decolonization but rather as one of a paradoxical, irresolute modernity. Scott sees in historical narratives of the Haitian Revolution a shift from a romantic mode, which structures social attitudes of anticolonial longing, to a tragic mode of postcolonial irresolution, one he argues better fits our moment in the twenty-first century. While Scott deftly explores how narrative choices may help us fashion a usable past for the postcolonial present, he fails to see beyond the genres of the hero (what is tragedy if not the genre of the fallen hero?). More important, he obscures the process of rehearsal by which narratives (historical and literary) are provisionally made and remade, whatever the narrative genre.

Scott examines what he calls a double narrative strategy in C. L. R. James's classic account of the Haitian Revolution, *The Black Jacobins*, first published in 1938 and revised in 1963. The 1938 edition tells the history of the revolution in what Scott calls the exemplary anticolonial mode, that of romance, while the 1963 edition recasts the anticolonial revolution's principal hero, Toussaint Louverture, in a postcolonial tragedy. What Scott means by romance is decidedly not "a cross between our contemporary use of the word as a love story and a nineteenth-century use that distinguished the genre as more boldly allegorical than the novel," as Doris Sommer defines it in her book on the narrative overlap of the erotic with the patriotic in the "foundational fictions" of nineteenth-century Latin American novels, which I discuss in my reading of Rosario Ferré's *Sweet Diamond Dust* below.[43] Instead he borrows more strictly from Hayden White's classification of archetypal story plots, as adapted from Northrop Frye:

> [Romance is] fundamentally a drama of self-identification symbolized by the hero's transcendence of the world of experience,

his victory over it, and his final liberation from it. . . . It is a drama of the triumph of good over evil, of virtue over vice, of light over darkness, and of the ultimate transcendence of man over the world in which he was imprisoned by the Fall.[44]

"Romance," concludes Scott, "is a drama of redemption" that was clearly needed when anticolonial movements aimed strategically to cultivate a sense of unity, hope, and organized opposition to systems of oppression, but it is nonetheless a mode of emplotment that has outlived its usefulness for the present task of fashioning a future postcolonial politics.[45] We must embrace tragedy, as James did when he recast Toussaint Louverture as a tragic hero. As Scott explains:

Tragedy . . . orients us away from the assumption that the future can be guaranteed by the pasts accumulated in the present. And because action in tragedy is not guaranteed in this way by a progressive dialectical resolution, it is more willing to honor our openness to contingency, our vulnerability to luck and chance; it is more willing to recognize the frailty of will, and the dark underside of mastery, the reversibility of all achievements.[46]

Tragedy revises the feeling that history has failed us (or that we have failed history); it moves us away from a narrative of progress even as it obliges us to rethink our core assumptions about political order, justice, community, agency, and freedom.[47]

"A Wall of Fire Rising" anticipates Scott's concern with modes of emplotment in historical narrative even as it complicates the relationship between romance as anticolonial longing and tragedy as postcolonial irresolution. The story tracks three days in the life of a small family whose one-room shack lies on the outskirts of a large sugar mill. The short story metonymically references anticolonial revolutionary romance and postcolonial tragedy by casting a son and his father in the roles of revolutionary hero and contemporary tragic figure, respectively. Little Guy's role in an anticolonial romance fits the historical Boukman to a nationalist narrative of vindication. His parents are deeply moved by his rehearsals of Boukman's lines, despite the fact that the speeches sound as if they were written by a playwright "who gave to the slave revolutionary Boukman the kind of European phrasing that might have sent the real Boukman turning in his grave," despite Boukman's widely known prayer recited by heart in Haiti.[48] As Little Guy eagerly accepts his new role, his father, desperate for regular employment, has waited six months only to receive the offer of one day of work at the sugar mill. To his wife

Lili's concern, Guy talks of death and escape as if they were one and the same. Set in contrast to the son's revolutionary romance is the father's prosaic tragedy: Guy lives in a time that is "out of joint" with the earlier language of resistance available to him, a time deaf to his insistence that he could be otherwise than the part he has been consigned to play.

How well the boy performs on the day of the school performance, or whether the play is ever performed at Lycée Jean-Jacques, we never learn. Little Guy's narrative arc is interrupted when his father suddenly jumps to his death from a rainbow-colored hot air balloon floating high above the fields of the sugar mill. He flies over the sugar mill to the applause of his fellow workers below and the horror of his son and wife. It is when he is nearly over his family's heads that he leaps from the balloon to fall dramatically near the feet of Little Guy and Lili. The hot air balloon owner, young Assad (whose Levantine family owns the sugar mill), leaves the stunned crowd to recover his free-floating property, bewildered by Guy's ingenious theft and single-handed operation of the hot air balloon.[49] It is then that Little Guy fiercely recites the two speeches that he had been practicing so earnestly.

> "A wall of fire is rising and in the ashes, I see the bones of my people. Not only those people whose dark hollow faces I see daily in the fields, but all those souls who have gone ahead to haunt my dreams. At night I relive once more the last caresses from the hand of a loving father, a valiant love, a beloved friend."
>
> "*There is so much sadness in the faces of my people. I have called on their gods, now I call on our gods. I call on our young. I call on our old. I call on our mighty and the weak. I call on everyone and anyone so that we shall all let out one piercing cry that we may either live freely or we should die.*" (78–80; emphasis and quotation marks in original)

This scene of Guy's literal fall to the sugar mill fields brings the conflict between anticolonial romance and postcolonial tragedy to a head. Postcolonial tragedy thus seems to overtake and subsume the mode of the anticolonial romance evoked by Boukman's lines. If, as anticolonial romance, the school play had an institutional function to commemorate the origins of the state as emancipatory, heroic, and authentically national, the suicide transforms the context and thus the meaning of Boukman's lines into a grievous lament at the loss of one's father in the fields of the sugar mill and a prayer calling for a collective liberation that cannot be commemorated because it has not yet come. The revolutionary spirit vocalized by Little Guy now takes on the tones of tragedy. In the anticolonial romance, Boukman's cry to live freely or die is ultimately part of a narrative of overcoming made possible in retrospect: the insurrection led to a republic of free citizens, and those who died in the fight are vindicated as state martyrs by the revolution's eventual success—as was Boukman himself, who was surrounded by troops and gunned down, his body burned and his head displayed on a stake in the main square of Le Cap.[50] Spoken by Little Guy over his father's dead body, the lines can no longer properly belong to the school play's version of Boukman. Boukman's lines no longer signal the revolutionary spirit that propels the anticolonial progress narrative (from enslavement to triumphant overcoming and full political freedom) but rather eulogize its end. The father's death oddly refutes the promise of anticolonial romance by offering a still, silent response to the son's cry: a death that seems senseless, without the grand narrative of revolution to vindicate it, becomes Guy's only way to resolve the impossibility of escaping the constraints of economic and political dispossession that shape his everyday life and his imagined future.

Guy desires to wrench himself free from what Scott elsewhere calls the dead-ended postcolonial present in which Guy has been cast, for he has watched this play before, and he knows how it will end. He confides to Lili, "You know that question I asked you before . . . how a man is remembered after he's gone? I know the answer now. I know because I remember my father, who was a very poor struggling man all his life. I remember him as a man that I would never want to be" (75). Guy anticipates here his own future as a remembered past of unending tragedy, felt not as a staged drama but, perhaps more painfully, as a personal protracted failure without hope of catharsis. And it is this vision of the future that he cuts short when he jumps from the sky.

Yet Scott's embrace of tragedy as a mode of emplotment for our dismal times cannot fully account for why Guy chooses a vehicle as anachronistic or untimely as it is spectacular. Such a framework also raises a number of questions: Can the exhaustion of anticolonial romance explain how or why Guy covertly operates a hot air balloon before leaping from such heights? How might this spectacular flight complicate, rather than affirm, tragedy as the most appropriate mode of emplotment for Guy's life in the postcolonial present? If tragic times are defined by an out-of-jointness between earlier languages of resistance and the present, will the times cease to be tragic once we find the most fitting narrative frame for the present? And if Guy plans his suicide—if, as the narrative suggests, he calculates perfectly how to fly the balloon and precisely where to land—then he is not only in control of what happens, but what happens also cannot be understood solely as an effect of *hamartia* (the error that brings about the tragic hero's fall, sometimes known as a "tragic flaw").[51] Guy's suicide and Little Guy's rehearsals of Boukman that precede and follow his father's death suggest that it is not any one mode of emplotment but rather the process of rehearsing historical narratives and adapting them to present conditions that has explanatory power. Guy's suicide, then, does not simply highlight the disjuncture between anticolonial romance and postcolonial tragedy; it also embodies the tension between the double meanings of history—between the material conditions that shape the terms of his daily life and the work of cultivating a narrative under those conditions. As dramatic and seemingly inexplicable as Guy's suicide may seem, it is the result of his planning and mental rehearsal.

Rehearsal is the practice that must be concealed once the performance properly begins: as preparation for the formal performance, it is work that shouldn't be showing once the curtain rises. Exposing the labor of rehearsal is thus a little like exposing the seams that join two pieces of cloth: this exposition reveals the cloth's construction. An emphasis on the process of rehearsal thus prevents any single performance, recitation, or remembrance from attaining a purely commemorative status, as part of a ritualized and celebratory relationship to the past that official national histories encourage. For example, the short story's depiction of Little Guy's rehearsals displaces his lines from their proper institutional context of the schools, where students practice becoming good citizens in part by memorizing the nation's great achievements, onto the site of the father's death. Rehearsal, moreover, puts the performer in the unstable position of giving voice to that which is neither utterly new nor automatically learned. Even when lines are learned "by heart," rehearsal reveals the maintenance usually needed to keep those lines at the core of one's being.

How, then, does the process of rehearsal allow us to consider the subject's position in rehearsing the time and plots that have thrown their lives, like Hamlet's, so out-of-joint? Danticat's expansive figuring of rehearsal invites us to rethink how the claims of history on the present are not only made, but how they are received, practiced, worked over by its actors, by those who must live with these stories, whether in eager anticipation of a future performance or in dread that it may merely repeat an earlier one. History's most pressing claims on Guy, Little Guy, and Lili become apparent only when we consider how their relationship to the Haitian Revolution takes shape through the belabored process of rehearsing it in their lived present.

Little Guy's lines serve as a plot device to juxtapose the political ideals of the Haitian Revolution against the staggering economic burden on dispossessed rural Haitians living under the neocolonial and totalitarian state. They also draw attention to the labor required of an actor to embody, perform, and interpret a role by foregrounding the labor of rehearsing history—of reciting one's lines, of commemorating a past in a voice that does not match it. When Little Guy first recites his lines, for example, Guy and Lili feel overwhelmed, "as though for a moment they had been given the rare pleasure of hearing the voice of one of the forefathers of Haitian independence in the forced baritone of their only child" (57). But it is only "as though" and "for a moment," for his rehearsal underscores the boy's strained labor—to collapse the distance between child and forefather, neoliberal present and revolutionary past, by forcing the voice—and his listeners' labor necessary to deny the dissonance.

Little Guy's process of rehearsing within the constraints of his present is given an enormous amount of attention in the short story. Tipping his head "towards the rusting tin on the roof," he prepares his first recitation for Guy and Lili; he continues to study his lines in a corner of his family's one-room shack after school; he mutters them at supper "between swallows of cornmeal"; he reminds his parents, "I need many repetitions"; he asks to recite his lines aloud when they visit the sugar mill yard, and when Guy says no, "We have heard them," he mumbles the lines anyway and suffers punishment for it; he mutters his lines as he drifts off to sleep with his book clasped tightly to his chest; he screams in terror because he has forgotten them in his sleep; he practices with his dad before school the next day; he is given more lines by his teacher as a reward for having memorized the first speech; he recites those lines after school to practice them; he interrupts his parents' talk to tell them that he has forgotten his new lines; he is admonished by Guy for failing to live up to the responsibility of playing his part (55, 57, 59, 63). These are the kinds of work Little Guy does between the time he's assigned to play Boukman and the time he recites his lines over his father's dead body. One can trace the dramatic lines as they interrupt, are shaped by, and in turn contribute to the social contexts that delimit the conditions for the labor of rehearsal. The contexts here are familial, domestic, pedagogic, cultural, economic, gastronomic, and political, and Little Guy's rehearsals are both enabled and constrained by them.

The labor of rehearsal thus suggests that Little Guy and Guy reference anticolonial revolutionary romance and postcolonial tragedy just enough to show how ill-fitting these modes of emplotment are, how strange it is to wear a history cast in a certain mode that cannot fully explain one's messy, complicated relationship to it in the present but that shapes one's present nonetheless. Little Guy's rehearsals, in contrast to Guy's own, allow this complex relationship to come into view. Little Guy is the son who plays the father of the revolution. Guy plays the father who is the son of the dispossessed for whom the revolution had been fought—still "born in the shadow of the sugar mill" but, now, barely allowed to work there (66).

When Lili tells her son, "Remember what you are. . . . A great rebel leader. Remember, it is the Revolution," and Boukman is the hero of the play, Guy quickly establishes his skepticism of this revolutionary romance. He responds, "Do we want him to be all of that?" (54, 55). To Lili's dismay, what Guy wants is for his son to have a stable future role in the economic production in which he himself plays only an intermittent role: he wants to add Little Guy's name to the waiting list for permanent employment at the sugar mill to help secure him a job by the time "he becomes a man" (66). Lili senses the danger of casting their son in the drama of the sugar mill: putting his name on the list, she fears, "might influence his destiny" (66). Lili's pride at her son being cast as the hero of the revolution might come from this same thought: for Lili, her son's performance as Boukman promises to be a rehearsal for his future life, which she can hope takes something of the heroism, the overcoming, that classifies the play as an anticolonial romance. Guy not only recognizes Lili's interpretation of the play's significance, but resents her for it: what his son's incessant rehearsing does is confront Guy with the sense that his present is out of joint with the past, and history has eclipsed his future.

Guy's suicide brings echoes of Haiti's past to bear on the contemporary stage of the sugar mill yard. His death seems to literalize what Fischer describes as a textual symptom of disavowal: it is "an unexpected flight into fantasy where one might have expected a reckoning with reality."[52] And yet Guy's secret fantasy to float away and "*be* something new" is at once the flight from and fatal reckoning with reality. It is here that I want to consider more fully the family's story as a neocolonial and national drama performed on the real stage of the sugar mill. In "A Wall of Fire Rising," the sugar mill doubles as dramatic stage and as the now-reduced but nonetheless persistent remains on which Haiti's history has been written and written over.

A brief sketch of Haiti's postcolonial history will help make sense of the function of the sugar mill in the short story. In the Age of Revolutions, the Haitian Revolution was the only one that led to an abolishment of slavery forever (in the words of the state's constitution), making Haiti a lone free state established by former slaves in a world dominated by slaveholding nations and ideologies of white supremacy. A territory built as a plantation complex but where slavery was to be forever abolished produced internal tensions for the new state, since the export-oriented plantation economy seemed the only chance for economic survival.[53] By 1804 the Haitian state "had become the most important owner of cultivated land in the country," but its first leaders had trouble coercing, let alone convincing, the newly freed women and men to return to the very form of labor that had defined the conditions of their unfreedom.[54] During and after the revolution, the Haitian elite and its first leaders struggled to revive and maintain large agricultural estates as the country's economic base while the Haitian majority actively resisted plantation labor (even, with Boyer's Rural Code, at the point of bayonets) in favor of cultivating small plots of land. The leaders sought to reframe plantation labor as the work required for liberty rather than the slave work it had been known to be: as Toussaint Louverture noted in the forced labor decree he instituted in 1800, "liberty cannot exist without industry," and only the cooperation of the "soldier" and the "cultivator" could create a free state.[55] But at the core of Louverture's forced labor decree was a contradictory national program to yoke the category of free and full legal personhood—the fully enfranchised "citizen," to which the forced labor decree is addressed—with the economic and political imperatives that required the labor of sugar cultivators on pains of fines, arrest, imprisonment, and coercion. Louverture at once proclaims all the people citizens and collapses the meaning of citizenship into forms of labor that if not done voluntarily as a civic duty must be coerced in service to the state: like the case of *Robertson v. Baldwin*, which made an exception to free labor rights by justifying the coercion of sailors' labor as crucial to national security and that finds its echo in contemporary forms of coerced labor depicted in Goldman's *The Ordinary Seaman*, Article 1 of the forced labor decree states, "All overseers, drivers, and field Negroes are bound to observe, with exactness, submission, and obedience, their duty in the same manner as soldiers."[56] Haiti's plantation workers largely resisted this compulsion: while the first Haitian leaders fought over who would control the plantation export economy, the great majority of Haitians established subsistence agriculture and a limited export economy, an economic practice that has been, over time, severely strained by heavy tax burdens on the peasantry and neoliberal trade policies that destroyed markets both foreign and domestic, even as small-scale farming continues to characterize the majority of agricultural production in Haiti.[57]

Wide-ranging hostility to Haiti from France, the United States, and the Vatican led it to hold a "pariah status" even among newly independent states in the Americas.[58] "The inescapable truth," notes Sidney Mintz, "is that 'the world' never forgave Haiti for its revolution, because the slaves freed themselves."[59] As internal social, economic, and political contests between a factional elite and the peasantry intensified over the course of the nineteenth century, political and economic isolation by foreign powers gave way to more direct political and economic domination of Haiti by foreign powers (most notably France and the United States but also Britain and Germany).[60] By the beginning of the twentieth century, the United States secured its economic domination of the Haitian economy largely through foreign investment contracts, paving the way for future economic control and political interventions—from the harsh and transformative U.S. occupation of Haiti from 1915 to 1934 to what still goes on under the new names of peacekeeping, aid, development, and reconstruction. Ever made to feel the full brunt of national and international forces since the revolution, the rural and urban poor under François Duvalier and his son Jean-Claude were taxed so heavily that they (along with foreign loans) effectively financed the outlandish luxuries of members of the repressive state apparatus even as they struggled daily to keep from starving.[61] Meanwhile, the Duvalier regimes agreed to USAID and neoliberal trade policies that transformed Haiti into a net importer of its staples, including rice and sugar, effectively destroying Haiti's agricultural economy as the vexed promise of sweatshop labor for U.S. corporations spurred the move to the cities.

Significantly, in "A Wall of Fire Rising," the sugar mill's central importance to the family that lives on its periphery is far from a choice of narrative realism. As a system, sugar production has struggled since the revolution. It was virtually defunct by the 1980s: only a few large-scale sugar mills existed; of those few (four mills), even fewer have operated recently (as of January 2011, one mill at half capacity), and only one was organized as a large estate of cultivated land owned by the mill.[62] HASCO, the Haitian American Sugar Company, was set up during the U.S. occupation of Haiti to revive the plantation system (restoring legal foreign ownership of the land was among the first changes made by the United States to the Haitian Constitution). The United States also controlled sugar plantations in the Dominican Republic, where Haitian workers increasingly migrated to work on plantations, becoming iconic figures of twentieth-century sugarcane laborers in the Dominican Republic called *batey*, also the name of workers' shanty-towns near the plantations.

In short, the Haitian sugar mill, like the cargo ship, is a diminished remainder of history. It is an iconic palimpsest, written over by colonial world-market systems; then by the conflicted demands of the new national state; then by the occupation that revived plantations and forced labor while provoking antioccupation narratives of rural authenticity; then by agricultural decline; and now, in the short story, by a personal crisis made legible only by reading the many faded layers of history that constitute the palimpsest. Significantly, Danticat evokes the sugar mill—with its iconic images of cutting sugarcane in the fields and processing cane in the mill—only to doubly dislocate them, for Guy eventually confides to Lili that his few hours of work at the sugar mill are spent cleaning latrines. As Guy protests to Lili, "I was born in the shadow of that sugar mill . . . Probably the first thing my mother gave me to drink as a baby was some sweet water tea from the pulp of the sugarcane. If anyone deserves to work there, I should" (66). The horizon of his daily life is set by the sugar mill not because he is forced to work but because he is forced out of work by a system that reinvents the disposability of laborers (a disposability underscored by his job cleaning latrines).

For most of the short story, it is the son's new role as Boukman that repeatedly upstages his father and heightens Guy's sense of personal failing, even as Lili struggles to reconcile the two conflicting roles her son and her husband perform. Guy, for instance, has the first line in the short story. He enters his home and says to his family, "Listen to what happened today," but nobody listens because Little Guy quickly upstages his father with his own imperative: "Listen to what happened to me today!" (53). Hearing that his son is playing a hero slave revolutionary, Guy struggles to read the name "Boukman" and comments on the "hard words here." But his son has already learned an entire speech, as Lili is quick to point out to Guy before the son proudly recites it (55). It is only when Little Guy is offstage that Guy cautiously shares his feelings and secrets with Lili, namely, the certainty that, despite the role he's been given, he "can do other things" (68). And here is where Guy's own labor of rehearsal is revealed. Whereas Little Guy's rehearsal as Boukman is the work of remembering what another has written, Guy is secretly carrying on the work of rehearsal, too, for a performance of his own devising. Guy's final performance disrupts the narrative arc that he earlier anticipates of himself as like his father, someone he "would never want to be" (75). Unable to control the origins of his narrative, Guy controls its end, and by changing the end, Guy changes the way his life story can be read.

The hot air balloon becomes an object of longing and of vindication for Guy: as he insists to Lili, "I can make this thing fly" (62). This thing, which requires a crew of workers to launch, is a leisure vehicle of flight that gives the sugar mill owner's son a view directly over everyone working at the sugar mill: it represents, if not an "overseer," a kind of privileged "seeing over" the workers that they have (no doubt) observed many, many times. Guy watches the balloon even when it is deflated and fenced in the sugar mill yard, as he tells Lili repeatedly. He comes to rehearse in his mind a fantasy: to prove that he can fly it alone and land where he intends. A dream: to fly to nowhere in particular and "just *be* something new" (73; emphasis in original). A spectacle: to make his flight miraculous. But his moment of performance itself, his final death, does not offer his spectators a mode of emplotment that explains the story. It can only be understood by recognizing his secret rehearsals and his indirect cues to Lili that he has something in mind. He tells her, "Pretend that this is the time of miracles and we believed in them. I watched the owner for a long time, and I think I can fly that balloon. The first time I saw him do it, it looked like a miracle, but the more and more I saw it, the more ordinary it became" (67). The double vision of remembering a time of miracles while living in a time that no longer believes in them shows that Guy is invested in his own narrative project, to connect a past time of miracle to his future flight, but one that depends on the dramatic play of make-believe: they must "pretend." Guy wants a miraculous end, drawn from fragments of revolutionary, mythopoetic, and historical narrative, to prove himself in a time when vindication is still a sane, and needed, response. He writes himself a one-scene drama that implicitly rehearses a history of racial enslavement in a plantation system: the balloon as vehicle of modern science and leisure flight, operated by a small gas-fueled "wall of fire rising," joins the Myth of the Flying Africans (in which enslaved Africans escape their enslavement through miraculous flights, such as riding a great bird over the ocean to Africa, and jumping off cliffs to return to Africa or to reunite with ancestors, depending on the version).

Guy's rehearsals also more fully reveal "A Wall of Fire Rising" to adopt a narrative structure borrowed from its central trope—the rehearsals of history. Guy's flight of the hot air balloon over the sugar mill yard uncannily (and implicitly) rehearses an otherwise minor moment in Haiti's history. As Laurent Dubois narrates:

On April 10, 1784, a balloon rose over the thriving sugarcane fields south of Le Cap. A crowd—which included the colony's governor—watched as it rose to 1,800 feet and then descended slowly to the ground. The men responsible for this spectacle were emulating scientific pioneers across the Atlantic who, the year before, had sent the first balloon in history into the sky. As they read about this triumph in the newspapers of Saint-Domingue, many in the colony were taken with the same excitement for the new machines that was gripping France. . . . So it was that the first large balloon to fly in the Americas went up over a thriving sugar plantation. As they watched the balloon ascend, noted Moreau de St. Méry, the "black spectators" could not stop talking about "the insatiable passion" men had to "exert power over nature." They were perhaps thinking of their own condition.[63]

Odeluc, a science enthusiast, slave driver, and plantation administrator to the marquis de Gallifet (an absentee planter), helped launch the large balloon on one of Gallifet's three plantations, which were the centerpiece of the colony's prosperous sugar economy and, reputedly, a model of "happy" servitude.[64] It was at one of these plantations that on the night of August 21, 1791, soon after a secret meeting in the Caïman woods, a revolt would be launched that would retrospectively become known as the start of the Haitian Revolution.[65] Among the leaders who sparked this "wall of fire," made by sugarcane fields ablaze, was, of course, Boukman.[66] At one of Gallifet's sugar plantations, then, the scientific experiment of hot air balloon flight was funded by slave labor to "celebrate the triumph of science over nature"; at another, some years later, local slaves began the political and military experiment of organizing a large-scale insurrection to liberate themselves from enslavement, radically challenging colonial theories of science, nature, and race in the process.[67]

It is in the context of this history that Guy's flight and Little Guy's lines can be seen as converging onto the site of the plantation's surviving remnant, the contemporary sugar mill yard. In this way, Guy's miraculous operation of the balloon transforms the commemorative aims of his son's rehearsals by displacing them back onto the site of the sugar mill and so onto a site that has been shaped by colonial, anticolonial, postcolonial, national, and neoliberal economic and political formations in Haiti's history. It is the interruptive process of rehearsal that brings the play's language of the revolution (however stylized) to bear on the plot of a family's struggle to maintain a sense of dignity in the face of protracted dispossession. They are the same lines, taken from the same anticolonial revolutionary romance, but they have been wrenched from the realm of commemoration and thrown into a lamentation—of a mythical time of miracles within the shadows of the sugar mill, of a hunger fooled by sugar water tea made from scraps of cane, and of a father who achieves the spectacular flight that made life after landing an unendurable possibility.

And yet what are Lili's labors of rehearsal? No one casts her, as they do her son, in the role of revolutionary hero: such roles, anyway, are included within a largely masculinist purview of history, in which female figures are deemed heroic for their service to the men on center stage (the *mambo* assists Boukman, and even Défilée serves Dessalines).[68] Instead, the burdens of family survival push Lili to improvise daily a set of responses to the needs of the family as a whole: she keeps hunger at bay by making sweet water tea, foraging, and selling spices at the market obtained on credit; she tries to soothe the anxieties of her husband and son; and she works to cultivate in them a feeling of worth and dignity in spite of their economic and political dispossession. Her role is constrained (and made meaningful) by the struggles of her husband and son, a point underscored in a short story that appears later in the collection, in which we learn that Lili "killed herself in old age because her husband had jumped out of a flying balloon and her grown son left her to go to Miami" ("Beside the Pool and the Gardenias," 94). As Guy and Little Guy pursue two lines of flight, that of death and migration, it is Lili's position as the audience and supporter of Guy and Little Guy that pulls into view the material constraints within which all three characters must act. In the end, Guy invents his role of flying the balloon as a way to escape the constraints of a history he felt so fully, a history he felt he could neither survive nor transcend. And it is Guy's protest to the inescapable burdens of history, which includes the material conditions of the present and the stories of how the present came to be, that leads Little Guy's rehearsals of Boukman to culminate not on a school stage but on the sugar mill yard, in grief.

"A Wall of Fire Rising" explores the complex afterlives of the revolution and the dissonance between a promised legacy of liberation and its diminishment in the neoliberal present. In this context, the trope of rehearsal reveals a process of repetition that both performs and instantiates the desire to recuperate radical liberation narratives from their political legacies—to salvage, in this instance, the revolutionary effort to transform a colonial slave economy into a national one built through universal, free, and full legal personhood. What emerges over the course of the short story is the desire to salvage the promise of the Haitian Revolution by rehearsing it—in the scripted language of a school play no less than in the secret plans for an escape that, unwittingly or not, draw from at least two histories of flight: the antislavery narrative of ancestral return and the colonial technology of the hot air balloon. The trope of legacy is inscribed in the story, both in terms of the celebrated national, political inheritance of the country's founding revolutionaries and in terms of the fraught tensions that come with having a son inherit his father's semi-wageless life. The tragic action in both the short story and in scholarly recovery efforts of the Haitian Revolution thus becomes, as Édouard Glissant suggests elsewhere, "the uncovering of what had gone unnoticed": the uncovering of the rehearsals that go on in the shadows of the mill and the revealing of the labors of living with sugar's legacies.[69]

Burning Down the House: Sugar, Sex, and Law in Puerto Rico

The Haitian Revolution was more than an inspirational model of anti-slavery, anticolonial revolution throughout the Caribbean. It also led rival colonies, especially Cuba and Puerto Rico, to intensify sugar production in a bid to replace the loss of Haitian sugar on the world market. While sugar plantations existed haphazardly in Puerto Rico since the sixteenth century, it was not until the destruction of Haiti's plantation economy that Puerto Rico's Creole and emigrant elite ultimately acted on what they saw as "a golden opportunity to accelerate the economic transition from cattle ranching and subsistence agriculture to intensive production of commodities such as sugar and coffee."[70] These powerful actors in the early nineteenth century saw themselves as the natural inheritors of the sugar production promised by Saint-Domingue's demise. In a sense, the Creole and planter elite claimed a double-edged inheritance of a profitable plantation economy built on slave labor and the potential for a slave revolt that could dramatically alter the island, a potential not lost on the men who debated over whether developing Puerto Rico into a predominantly sugar economy would lead them to suffer the violence that destroyed Saint-Domingue. As the patrician Don Pedro Irisarri warned:

> The French colony, so rich and opulent, has been destroyed and ruined by the very same people who had cultivated and beautified it . . . In a moment, everything was dealt a mortal blow by the disorder of a daring and well-conceived insurrection. The mulattoes and black slaves rose en masse and, resisting all legitimate authority, executed on their masters and magistrates the most bloody and horrible massacre, and leaving no stone unturned, they have remained content in their perfect anarchy, without God, without law and without conscience. . . . It is true they will submit to force [and regulation by Spanish law] while their number does not exceed or keeps a balance with that of free men, but when that terrible moment [of numerical superiority] arrives, that is the moment when the last misfortune, the destruction of the whole Island, will ensue.[71]

Shifting the island's core economy to sugar threatened to upset the current majority Creole and free population in favor of a small but rising population of enslaved workers of African descent.[72] The fear of large-scale sugar production was located in the expectation that to produce more sugar was also to import and produce more raced workers on the hacienda—island-born as well as *bozal,* or African-born, slaves, whose enslaved personhood confirmed (for the elite) an inherent lawlessness that seemed to preclude them, unlike working-class free people of mixed racial categories, from ever being incorporated into the *patria* as citizens.[73]

The prospects of the Puerto Rican sugar economy in the early nineteenth century depended on population demographics, which registered not only a rapid population growth rate of enslaved and free black persons—including African slaves, who were smuggled to Puerto Rico and Cuba until the mid-nineteenth century, despite the legal abolition of the slave trade in 1812—but also the careful management of sexual reproduction through Spanish colonial law.[74] Haciendas had been guaranteed financially throughout the nineteenth century by legal marriages, on the one hand, which produced legitimate heirs and business alliances, and, on the other, by extramarital sex between hacienda families and their Afro–Puerto Rican workers, whether legally enslaved or in feudal-like servitude after slavery in Puerto Rico was abolished by the Spanish National Assembly in 1873. The legal management of sexual reproduction also entailed the policing of public space as a way to guard the professed purity of the legitimate family and the emergent national (if still colonial) body politic it represented: the antiprostitution campaigns that marked the shift between Spanish and U.S. colonialism thus drew on and reinforced the sexual, racial, familial, and medical discourses that made women in Puerto Rico not only important subjects of legal classification but also figures whose sexuality would either bless or doom the future of the colony.[75]

In using the trope of inheritance, Rosario Ferré's *Sweet Diamond Dust (Maldito Amor)* shows the raced, sexed Puerto Rican female body at the discursive center of Puerto Rico's economy and politics, and thus its taxonomy of legal personhood, for over five hundred years. *Sweet Diamond Dust*—populated by the De la Valle family (which has owned the Diamond Dust sugar mill and surrounding hacienda for generations), their *independentista* lawyer-friend and biographer, and a woman whose legal incorporation into the family by marriage brings the scandal of her mixed racial status and her "legendary" prostitution to the town of Gumaní—demonstrates that to trace the history of sugar's legacies is to reveal the entanglements of those class, racial, and juridical sexual politics that have come to define both the plantation economy and competing visions of Puerto Rican nationhood. These competing visions play out in *Sweet Diamond Dust* as a struggle between two narrative genres: patriarchal nationalist romance, represented by the lawyer Don Hermenegildo's romanticized biography of the De la Valle patriarch, and a feminist antiromance, represented by the "mulatta" Gloria Camprubí, which seeks to reveal the erotic, familial, and national investments in genealogy on which the patriarchal national romance depends but must also disavow. As with other postslavery novels, "genealogical inquiry" in *Sweet Diamond Dust* "attempts to follow biology rather than ideology, to follow the traces of transgression, of human errancy, of breaks or ruptures that have generated new cultures and that expose planter authority as illegitimate."[76] Ironically, Don Hermenegildo's biography seeks to affirm planter authority as legitimate even as his own history and later interviews with Ubaldino's family and their servant, Titina, reveal the genealogical threads of racial mixing in both legitimate and illegitimate family lines. Again, legacy (and sex) is not merely a metaphor here but a messy set of material and legal conditions. As with Danticat's "A Wall of Fire Rising," Ferré's *Sweet Diamond Dust* demonstrates how modes of emplotment and the forms of legal incorporation they manage are at once disrupted by and emerge out of material conditions of sexual reproduction and domestic labor.

On both island and mainland, Puerto Ricans have sought to challenge U.S. colonialism's power to delimit Puerto Rican legal personhood by cultivating versions of cultural nationalism that would be best embodied and guaranteed by three mutually exclusive political categories: independence from the United States, full and equal incorporation within the United States as the fifty-first state, or the continuation of a qualified incorporation within and exclusion from the United States through some version of commonwealth or colonial status. Legal personhood has been deeply entangled with the question of how to understand the relationship between nationhood and colonial rule for one of the oldest enduring colonies in the world. For over five hundred years, changing legal categories (and classificatory systems) made their indelible marks on Puerto Rico, which eventually gained limited forms of legal sovereignty, self-governance, and Spanish citizenship for its inhabitants before the 1898 U.S. takeover of Puerto Rico stripped native-born inhabitants of those gains won only the year before, in November 1897. The "second colony," or Puerto Rico under U.S. colonial rule, rendered non-Spanish inhabitants of Puerto Rico without any clear legal status; meanwhile, the set of U.S. Supreme Court cases known as the Insular Cases handed down a series of contradictory and ambiguous decisions regarding the legal classification of persons inhabiting the so-called unincorporated territories gained as spoils of the Spanish-American War.[77] Caught between the U.S. Supreme Court's inability to define the relationship of the United States to Puerto Rico as one of a democratic republic to the island or as one of empire, inhabitants of Puerto Rico were effectively stateless—"without a country," as one U.S. Democratic senator noted—until the 1917 Jones Act for Puerto Rico conferred on them an attenuated form of U.S. citizenship, civil rights, and a limited form of local government.[78] Only a few months later, the new legal classification enabled the state's expanded claim on those whom it recognized even under qualified citizenship, when hundreds of thousands of Puerto Rican men were to be drafted into the U.S. military's campaign in World War I.

As the legal scholar Pedro A. Malavet notes, racialized categories of legal personhood have always informed U.S. debates over the proper relationship to Puerto Rico, which has been among the nation's most economically desired territorial possessions but whose full legal incorporation was perceived by the U.S. government and courts as a threat to the very body politic of the nation. Echoing early nineteenth-century debates over whether to shift the island's economy toward sugar plantations, the U.S. congressional debates that led to the 1917 Jones Act included arguments over the nonwhite racial person as a legal person but one incapable of self-governance. As one U.S. representative in the congressional debates argued, Puerto Ricans were ineligible for statehood because their "mixed race" status—overwhelmingly either "pure African" or with "an African strain in their blood"—confirmed them as a people who could not be trusted to follow, let alone participate in establishing, the law.[79] As with the infamous 1857 *Dred Scott v. Sandford* opinion, categories of legal citizenship were delimited by an ideology of racial underdevelopment that assumed the nonwhite person ineligible for legally recognized, full political inclusion into the United States.

What Malavet and many other critical race theorists and historians of Puerto Rico tend to neglect, however, is the centrality of racialized sexual practices and norms to political and social movements in nineteenth- and twentieth-century Puerto Rico. In the epigraph that begins this chapter, Eileen J. Suárez Findlay describes the "wrinkled white women" who, in the late twentieth century, continued to reproduce sugar's gloriously white legacy as the national narrative of Puerto Rico, seemingly oblivious to the histories they share with their servants. Such whitening depends on the specific exclusion of the "semiclandestine sex" that fueled the island's economy and that supplemented the legitimate family genealogies of its cultural elite. Sugar's legacy is, again, a legacy of the classification and regulation of categories of legal personhood that centered on legitimate and illegitimate forms of labor and racial identities. Findlay notes that many episodes of political reform as well as campaigns of political repression and exclusion between 1870 and 1920 were morality and decency campaigns whose proponents targeted women according to their class and racial identification. Antiprostitution campaigns under Spanish and U.S. policy—which involved the forced registration and policing of sex workers as well as the criminalization of women whose racial and working-class status left them vulnerable to accusations of prostitution, often requiring male relatives or lovers to testify to their morality and decency—were the crucibles in which the legal personhood of "decent" citizens were forged.

> Such repressive episodes consistently centered on racially charged excoriation of unruly plebeian women, who were labeled "prostitutes." These crackdowns were selective, however. Their very harshness encouraged the political inclusion of those who did not fall within the state's repressive purview. During the late nineteenth century the harassment of alleged, darkened prostitutes went hand in hand with elites' concession of honorable, racially acceptable citizenship status to plebeian men. Several decades later, respectable bourgeois "ladies" were the new actors to enjoy inclusion in the public sphere through their participation in an antiprostitution crusade.[80]

Findlay's study demonstrates how the racial and sexual classification of women was not limited to a symbolic level, in which "women's bodies and morality served as particularly powerful tropes for the formation of discourses through which were alternatively expressed colonial dominance, emerging national or bourgeois class identities, and yearnings for the creation of effective nation-states."[81] Drawing from Stoler and Cooper's reminder that "discourse about sex was not necessarily metaphoric: sex was about sex—and also about its consequences,"[82] Findlay points out that "sexuality becomes explicitly politicized at certain historical moments" in the making of social and political orders: "the men and women who sought to regulate sexual practice . . . worried constantly about the racial, economic, cultural, and political ramifications of marriage, consensual union, prostitution, and male infidelity."[83] Racialized sexual practices and norms proved central to everyone's investment in Puerto Rico: they shaped competing visions of nationhood for Puerto

Rican men and women of all classes; Spanish colonial policies on the island; and U.S. policies, from colonization to the late twentieth-century politics of mainland migration and so-called overpopulation. It was the colonial policy on prostitution that helped give continuity to Spanish and then U.S. colonization of the island. As Laura Briggs points out, the U.S. military continued "the existing Spanish policy of protecting the families of *gente decente* (respectable people) from rowdy women, unsanitary prostitution, and the danger of contagion through quarantine in segregated neighborhoods, weekly or biweekly pelvic exams, and mandatory medical treatment."[84] Examining prostitution as a "technology of empire," Briggs focuses on how U.S. empire throughout the twentieth century has managed its colonial relationship to Puerto Ricans through the interpenetrating discourses of race, science, and sexuality.

> From the exotic, tropical prostitute (seductive but brimming with disease), to the impoverished, overlarge family (produced by ignorance and brainwashing by the Catholic Church), to overpopulation, to the notion of the "culture of poverty," Puerto Rican sexuality has been defined by its deviance. . . . [R]eproduction and sexuality have defined the difference that makes colonialism in Puerto Rico possible and necessary, what makes "them" need "our" regulation and governance.

In response to the very possibility that Puerto Ricans might be granted U.S. citizenship, "moral reformers, the military, and colonial officials had located what was wrong with the 'natives' in sexuality, as they targeted venereal disease, prostitution, and immoral sexual relations as key arenas for reform if Puerto Ricans were to become citizens."[85]

These antiprostitution campaigns reveal sexual citizenship as conceived in multiple, overlapping, eugenic regimes of legal personhood between the Spanish empire, local Puerto Rican colonial governance, and the United States. They are a political legacy even as they are explicitly concerned with the literal questions of reproduction and inheritance. They raise the question of legacy in *Sweet Diamond Dust* as a very literal one, a point made in the introduction to this chapter. The story's plot revolves around the imminent death of Doña Laura De la Valle, wife of the late patriarch and statesman, Don Ubaldino De la Valle. Doña Laura has threatened to disinherit her children in order to bequeath the family's sugar mill and attendant hacienda lands to Gloria Camprubí, her "mulatta" domestic servant and daughter-in-law, and Gloria's young son. Don Hermenegildo, a local lawyer and admiring friend of Don Ubaldino, is in the midst of writing a patriotic biography of the man when the De la Valles' servants, Titina and her brother, appeal to him to help resolve the conflict among the servants and between the family members, each of whom holds a stake in the terms of the legal will. Over the course of the narrative, the conflict over who should rightfully claim the family's legacy proves to be a conflict over who has the authority to narrate the family's history and to embody the island's future. The novella is divided into chapters, each narrated by a character that provides conflicting versions of the De la Valles' history and the present discord over the legal inheritance. Don Hermenegildo, whose biography of Ubaldino is included as select chapters of *Sweet Diamond Dust,* is the principal interlocutor for several characters' testimonies: the servant Titina, who appeals to the lawyer for help in ensuring that she and her brother receive the bungalow promised long ago by their patriarch, the late Ubaldino; Arístides, Ubaldino's sole surviving son, who provides his own version of the family's history to justify his plan to inherit the property and sell it to his brothers-in-law, who are shareholders of the U.S. Snow White Sugar Mill; and Arístides's mother, Doña Laura, who tells her story to Don Hermenegildo as he visits her deathbed. The final chapter of the novella is reserved for Gloria herself, as she sets fire to the De la Valle home while Don Hermenegildo may or may not be trapped inside.

In *Sweet Diamond Dust,* the double conflict over legal inheritance and modes of national historiography play out around the female body of Gloria—and they converge between her legs, in her reputed sexual practice, and in the child she bears. Ferré underscores the economic importance of legal as well as extralegal sexual and familial ties in *Sweet Diamond Dust* when the lawyer and biographer Don Hermenegildo writes, nostalgically and with great Hispanophilia, about the "blood ties among the most distant families" in the town of Guamaní, which generated not only heirs but also "financial and moral support, so as better to manage our sugarcane haciendas."[86] The genteel financial and familial arrangement among Creole families that Don Hermenegildo describes in his biography stands in contrast to the position of the Puerto Rican hacienda families after U.S. possession of the colony, symbolized in *Sweet Diamond Dust* in two major ways: by marriage of the De la Valle daughters to wealthy U.S. capitalists (three of them married to shareholders in the Snow White sugar mill), which represents marriage as an unequal incorporation of a feminized Puerto Rico into the masculinized U.S. family and economy—in contrast to the familial network of mutual aid among the hacienda-owning class; and by the strategies of exclusion that leave Creole family sugar mills without access to the credit that U.S.

banks so easily extend to U.S.-owned mills, enabling the latter to expand and update their machinery.

Sugar, for the Creole families, had bequeathed its doubled legacy along the lines of the legal or "legitimate" family genealogy and the "illegitimate" product of extralegal sexual relations: one line traditionally inherited property; the other, continued servitude on the haciendas. Marriage and the laws of inheritance required the cultural exclusion of extramarital "blood ties" and allowed for a labor-owner relationship shaped by the formal disavowal of those very ties.[87] As Don Hermenegildo learns from Arístides, son of the late sugarcane patriarch Don Ubaldino and one of the would-be heirs to the family's Diamond Dust mill and cane fields, many of their cane laborers were

> illegitimate sons of our father, [whom I] fired unceremoniously. They were easy to recognize because they all looked vaguely like him, except duskier in skin and sullen in countenance. . . . In this way I freed the company of a number of unnecessary expenses, as Father had always insisted on clandestinely taking care of their families, and cut the risks of a claim to our inheritance down to a minimum."(43)

The danger that the legally illegitimate family of patriarchs would make "a claim to our inheritance" is not only an imminent threat to the inheritance of Arístides and his legitimate siblings—since Gloria's marriage to the firstborn son, Nícolas, itself is considered illegitimate and a scandal—but also has happened before. In an affront to Puerto Rican society, Arístides's late grandfather Don Julio Font had nearly dispossessed his own legitimate son, Ubaldino, by giving his mistress and their illegitimate children the majority share of the Diamond Dust sugar mill and surrounding lands. Ubaldino, however, invokes the "Right of Recall," an "ancient law of the Spanish Legal Codex" unknown to the U.S. bank and sugar mill interests that nearly succeed in buying the Diamond Dust sugar mill from Don Julio's poor illegitimate family. Ubaldino thus saves Diamond Dust from its threatened loss to a series of illegitimate owners (the illegitimate family, the would-be U.S. buyers) and returns the mill to its proper place in the legitimate De la Valle family. To the great dismay of Don Hermenegildo, however, Doña Laura's death signals the dispossession and erasure of the De la Valle family and its Creole claim on Diamond Dust, regardless of who gets to inherit the hacienda and mill, since Arístides plans to claim inheritance of the mill only to sell it to his sisters and brothers-in-law—and thus to the Snow White sugar mill.[88] Arístides justifies his plan by appealing to the scandal that his mother would cause by leaving everything to Gloria and her son—a "monster," according to Arístides, because of his uncertain origins as the potential progeny of Arístides himself, his brother, Nicolás, his late father, Ubaldino, or any one of the men in the bars frequented by Gloria, whom Arístides calls a "half-demented town whore" (50).

Doña Laura leaves everything to Gloria and Gloria's son in order to challenge the national romance that the De la Valle family has been telling about itself for generations. This national romance idealizes the historical Creole elite's investment in whiteness, drawn both from Spanish colonial notions of *limpieza de sangre,* or purity of blood, and from U.S. classifications of raced colonial personhood in the early twentieth century.[89] Consider again the explicitly policed personhood of poor Afro–Puerto Rican women during the antiprostitution campaigns of the late nineteenth and early twentieth century that linked national prosperity and security to the suppression and quarantining of women perceived to be prostitutes by legal authorities. The nineteenth-century discourse on Afro–Puerto Rican female sexuality persists well into the twentieth century with Arístides's account of Gloria, his former lover, as a "half-demented town whore" (50), and Don Hermenegildo views Doña Laura's intention to leave Diamond Dust to Gloria and her son with some alarm. And for good reason, since it is in Gloria's inheritance that Doña Laura seeks the dissolution of the De la Valle family dynasty, among the last of the great Creole hacienda-owning families that form the heroes of Don Hermenegildo's national romance.

The national romance not only justifies the marginal, criminalized, and dispossessed status of Afro–Puerto Rican personhood but also requires the suppression of blackness in Creole familial genealogies. The De la Valle children's horror that a clearly mixed-race Gloria legally married their elder brother, Nicolás, is so strong that they express their contempt at his funeral (he died in a plane crash under suspicious circumstances, possibly killed by his family): "'Thank God He took him away from us, Mother. . . . This way no De la Valle will ever marry a black woman again'" (79). While the De la Valles pride themselves on their pure bloodlines as if unsullied until Gloria's arrival, Doña Laura belatedly surmises that Don Julio Font, the father of Ubaldino and the man responsible for revitalizing the De la Valles' family line and sugar mill, was not the Spanish-born patriarch that everyone pretended him to be (from the same province as the conquistadors, no less). Even as Ubaldino's elderly aunts talk endlessly about "which families of Guamaní had a strain of black blood in them, and which had managed to remain white" (70), Doña Laura discovers one family "secret" that these aunts have disavowed: with their encouragement of Don Julio Font's courtship of Doña Elvira, the aunts unwittingly guaranteed that their niece, "the refined Doña Elvira, educated in Paris amid silk cushions, had married a black man!" (74). Don Julio Font's primary position in the patriotic biography of his son Ubaldino also depends on his visual disappearance from the family's lineage. "That was the reason," surmises Doña Laura, "I could never find a single portrait, daguerreotype, or photograph of poor Don Julio Font in the house, while there were plenty of Doña Elvira, as well as of other De la Valle ancestors!" (74). And while the Creole elite would not dare publicize it, their knowledge of Don Julio Font's racial mixture was the reason Doña Laura suspected that her daughters were shunned from polite society in Guamaní, thus leading them into the arms of U.S. capitalists who did not seem to mind their incorporation into the family.

While each narrator relies on rhetorical strategies to claim the authority to relate his or her version of events as the truth, the conflict over telling the family's history is staged primarily as a conflict between two main narrative genres that, at first glance, do not seem to be by definition opposed to each other: the national biography of Don Hermenegildo and the antiromance of Gloria. What Don Hermenegildo calls "biography," Gloria derides as a "novel" and a "romance" (the two terms being interchangeable for Gloria, as they were in earlier literary historical uses). Don Hermenegildo's book—which I call a biographical romance—makes a political investment in family genealogy that is shared by nationalist biography and romance while denying the erotic politics that produce the family genealogy. Such genres, however, reveal deeply shared investments in tracing the illicit and licit genealogies of sexual reproduction, as genealogies that have the potential to shape visions of nationhood and the categories of legal persons it incorporates.

What distinguishes the conventional biography from the romance is the historical and individualist claim made by the former: as the nonfiction narrative of a life (often an important public figure), biography would seem to deny its status as romance. And yet Don Hermenegildo explicitly writes his biography as at once a history and a romance. Faced with what Don Hermenegildo calls Titina's "accusation" of family secrets and internal hostilities within the De la Valle family, the biographer sees it as his duty to disavow historical truth in favor of cultivating national aspirations and pride. He concludes, "It's better to forget these unhappy events, erasing them with the edifying accounts of his heroic exploits" (24). Noting the power of his biography to serve as a foundation for a stronger Puerto Rican nationalism, Don Hermenegildo goes on to convince himself of his narrative strategy: "Every country that aspires to become a nation needs its heroes, its eminent civic and moral leaders, and if it doesn't have them, it's our duty to invent them. Fortunately this is not the case with Ubaldino, who was truly a paragon of chivalrous virtue, and whose story I have already begun to relate in my book" (24–25). While it is difficult not to hear Ferré's parodic authorial register in the lawyer's reflections, his ostensibly earnest conviction—that the biography of a statesman ought to serve as the aspirational model of the heroic life for the rest of the nation—makes explicit Don Hermenegildo's participation in the nation-building project of romances, the foundational fictions of which Doris Sommer writes. Such romances sought to anchor legal and political independence in what Benedict Anderson has called the "imagined community" of the nation. Tasked with cultivating a national imaginary, the authors of these romances had to envision not only character types, which would serve as models of civic personhood within the new state, but also the proper forms of attachment between these characters in the effort to overcome the colonial past and make new men and women.

Scott and Sommer identify as "romance" the exemplary mode for anticolonial narratives and for newly independent nations' narratives, respectively: caught between the anticolonial and the postcolonial, Puerto Rico's ambiguous and contested status evokes both Scott's and Sommer's definition of romance. As I note in my discussion of Scott's argument that the first edition of *The Black Jacobins* follows a romantic mode of emplotment, Scott cites romance in White's terms, as a "drama of self-identification" represented by a hero who triumphs in the struggle "of good over evil" and who symbolizes man's ability to reverse narratives of decline and exile. Romance is a drama "of the ultimate transcendence of man over the world in which he was imprisoned by the Fall."[90] As if responding to this definition of romance as itself a response to the Fall of Adam and Eve and their banishment from paradise, *Sweet Diamond Dust* represents the biography of the heroic statesman, Ubaldino, as just such a drama of the *anticipated* (if not ultimately realized) transcendence of Puerto Rico over its present unfreedom as a U.S. colony—a transcendence that, moreover, is envisioned as a regaining of paradise lost, a paradise presumed to have been in full bloom during Spanish rule. Given Ferré's rejection of the paradise lost narrative of Puerto Rico, there is an added irony in defining romance as a response to the original Fall: if romance imagines a transcendence of "man" over a world shaped by Eve's original sin of the knowledge of good and evil (a sin for which she is punished by the pain of childbirth), then Ferré's challenge to romance is to insist that stories of a lost paradise fuel a delusional obsession with origins, origins that, as acts of brutality, would themselves be in need of purgation.[91] The call for unity that Scott identifies with the anticolonial romance thus presumes an untroubled vision of the paradise lost; in *Sweet Diamond Dust*, such romancing of an original paradise drives Doña Laura and Gloria to repeatedly contend that what Don Hermenegildo calls "paradise" has always been a "hell." The lawyer misses the origins to which romance seeks to return. Reading anticolonial romance abstracted from any specific literary historical context, as an allegorical narrative that plots a story of heroic overcoming and transcendence, ignores the erotic investments and sexual labor of women that are at those origins and that often are made to underwrite the triumphant endings of the anticolonial romance.

Sommer recognizes the allegorical function of romance but argues that it cannot be divorced from the erotic, familial, and conjugal logics of heterosexual romance in representing the nation. Reading romance as "a cross between our contemporary use of the word as a love story and a nineteenth-century use that distinguished the genre as more boldly allegorical than the novel," Sommer describes the "classic examples" in Latin American fiction as "stories of star-crossed lovers who represent particular regions, races, parties, economic interests, and the like. Their passion for conjugal and sexual union spills over to a sentimental readership in a move that hopes to win partisan minds along with hearts" (5). Such an account of romance resonates with Don Hermenegildo's biographical romance in some respects but contradicts its use and function in others. Romance is the literary model from which Don Hermenegildo loosely draws when he writes what he calls his biography of Don Ubaldino for a Puerto Rico in need of a cultural nationalism that will inspire a desire to be free from U.S. possession. As a public lawyer involved in cultivating a cultural nationalism, Don Hermenegildo sees it as his civic duty to write the biography, much like those authors of nationalist romances who "were preparing national projects through prose fiction and implementing foundational fictions through legislative or military campaigns," encouraged as they were "both by the need to fill in a history that would help to establish the legitimacy of the emerging nation and by the opportunity to direct that history toward a future ideal."[92]

Don Hermenegildo's book manuscript, which forms several chapters of the novella, reads as an exemplar of a distinct, would-be "foundational fiction," one that elaborates on the *gran familia* myth so well cultivated by the Puerto Rican literary tradition. Marisel C. Moreno distills the myth into three major tenets: "a unified nation built on racial democracy and harmony," the "glorification of the island's agrarian, precapitalist past under Spanish rule," and "the cult of patriarchy, embodied by a benevolent father figure" (17).[93] All three are on parodic display in Don Hermenegildo's biography of the patriarch Ubaldino and the De la Valles family. Hermenegildo's work may also be described as an example of a historical version of *la novela de la tierra*, a romance mode that participates in "a nostalgia for the paternalism of the plantation," which other narrators in the novella all seem to refuse or mock, except perhaps for the patriarch's faithful servant, Titina.[94]

Yet there are important exceptions to Sommer's account of romance that highlight the ambiguous legal status of Puerto Rico. They lend at once a certain urgency and a sense of belatedness to the struggle between Gloria and Don Hermenegildo over the historiography of family and nation. The "classic example" of "star-crossed lovers" whose unions symbolize the unity of a nation in Sommer's study are complicated in *Sweet Diamond Dust*: all four of Ubaldino's daughters marry U.S. capitalists, three of them to stakeholders in Diamond Dust's U.S. nemesis, the Snow White Sugar Mill, thus reproducing the colonial relationship between Puerto Rico and the United States. The marriage between Nicolás and Gloria may have represented the future of the Puerto Rican nation—indeed, they even produce a son, Nicolasito, whom Doña Laura sees as a symbol of a future Puerto Rico—but their love is doomed, and their son is not the confirmation of a consummated marriage but the product of Gloria's extramarital sexual practices. Nicolasito is a "genealogical nightmare, a monster."[95]

Gloria and her son function as the excluded terms that traditionally structure "legitimate" family genealogies. Doña Laura's insistence on legally incorporating Gloria into the family and on giving this widow and her son the family's inheritance is an attempt to repair the break between legal and social legitimacy, an attempt that Sommer also observes in the classic examples of nineteenth-century Latin American romance featuring "star-crossed lovers" whose unions symbolize a future national unity. But while Doña Laura's will attempts this form of legal incorporation for the De la Valle family, Don Hermenegildo's biographical romance sees the legal incorporation of a potential bastard as an abhorrence. His narrative of Ubaldino depends on the purity of the legitimate De la Valles' family genealogy and the rescue of Diamond Dust from its illegitimate by-products. Arístides's accusations (as Don Hermenegildo calls them) of his own father's bastard children, of Gloria's prostitution, of his brother Nicolás's gay desires, and of Nicolasito's uncertain paternity reveal the statesman's family to be in disarray, flouting the sexual practices that define the legitimate family. Arístides uses these accusations to bolster his claim that he is the only legitimate heir to the family's property. But even he seeks to manipulate legal legitimacy to occasion a social scandal when he plans to inherit Diamond Dust only to sell it to his brothers-in-law.

In addition, whereas Sommer argues that "without a proper genealogy to root them in the Land, the creoles had at least to establish conjugal and then paternity rights, making a *generative* rather than a *genealogical* claim," it seems that generative claims entail genealogical ones.[96] In the case of Puerto Rico—perhaps in contrast to the countries included in Sommer's study—it is the U.S. capitalists who make solely generative claims of increased economic productivity and technological modernization, as they grafted themselves onto the older branches of Guamaní society. *Diamond Dust* suggests that the generative claim of the Creole elite depends precisely on their genealogical claim back to the origins of the nation and, through state-sanctioned sexual reproduction, forward to its imagined future. In this way, Don Hermenegildo writes of the land of Guamaní as a "gift" "bequeathed" by the Taino people to "us," the landowning and professional class of the region (4). The fantasy of Creole national indigeneity relies, again, on the trope of inheritance in order to establish their authenticity and legitimacy, in contrast to the U.S. capitalists, and to suppress their own history as colonialists. The Creole elite invent a narrative of inheritance to replace the more accurate one of theft and genocide; they insert the Taino into a genealogy of the nation, figuring the indigenous people as forefathers rather than as objects of enslavement and extermination, thus portraying the elite as the rightful inheritors of the land and its natural guardians. The wealthy hacienda-owning class sees the land and its fecundity as its cultural, moral, and economic patrimony, and the language of inheritance that is meant to affirm an idealized genealogy of Puerto Rico is threatened by the secrets of the De la Valle family, a family metonymic of heroic, Creole Puerto Rico in Don Hermenegildo's biographical romance. The biography as national romance depends on these revisions and exclusions, and nobody threatens Don Hermenegildo's project more than Gloria Camprubí and the legal will she is poised to inherit.

What Scott and Sommer each leave out are the genealogical investments in romance that Ferré highlights and systematically challenges. Gloria and son are figured as truly illegitimate within the family's genealogy, and, while Doña Laura's will gives them a legal, therefore legitimate, claim to the family inheritance, it is precisely the social illegitimacy of Gloria and her son that Doña Laura affirms. Doña Laura shares Gloria's contempt for national romance, the narrative genre of choice for the Creole elite's telling of Puerto Rico's national history, a genre indelibly linked to Puerto Rico's plantation economy and the delineation of personhood and rights that the colonial plantation economy produced. She reads Gloria's sex work as a politics of the erotic, a politics that promises to embody a future Puerto Rico where there would be no longer a place for the racial, class, and gender purity figured by national romance. Unsurprisingly, then, Doña Laura sees her death as also heralding the death of the land-based plantation system of familial and sexual arrangements in favor of a thriving port economy—symbolized by what Doña Laura describes as the open hospitality and economic exchange achieved by Gloria's "cunt"—in the making of a new Puerto Rico. As she explains to Don Hermenegildo during his visit to her deathbed, she can "foresee a time when all this rivalry" between local landowners and northern investors will be "but a legend whispered by the wind, a picturesque romance of the past," while the port takes on more significance (75):

> It's our island's destiny to become the gate to South as well as to North America, so that on our doorsill both continents will one day peacefully merge into one. And it's for this reason that I'm set on leaving Diamond Dust to Gloria and Nicolasito, because they are the children of that port, their unbribably tribal offspring. From the very first day of Gloria's arrival at our house, I was very much aware of her constant visits to the waterfront canteens and bars, where she soon became a sort of legendary prostitute, offering herself to all those ruined farmers who were about to emigrate to Chicago and New York, as well as to the new entrepreneurs who came from the north, and thus Nicolasito can be said to be the child of all. In her body, or if you prefer in her cunt, both races, both languages, English and Spanish, grew into one soul, into one wordweed of love. She's a priestess of our harbor; pythia of our island's future. (75–76)

By figuring the future of the island as the "gate" and "doorsill" of the Americas—a threshold that not only joins the Americas but also functions as an indiscriminate and potentially generative site of sexual, cultural, and linguistic union—Doña Laura seeks to challenge *independentistas* like Don Hermenegildo, who figure Puerto Rico through the dynamics of rape, as a chaste woman unfairly possessed by the brutish United States, and who fit the past into the genre of national romance. Whereas Don Julio Font invents a heroic genealogy for himself to pass as Spanish, Gloria's mulatta status also explicitly threatens to delegitimize the national romance by (re)incorporating racial mixture into the Creole elite's family genealogy, to Doña Laura's satisfaction (11).

Ultimately, however, Doña Laura's fantasy of indiscriminate incorporation merely inverts Don Hermenegildo's biographical romance: rather than undo the genealogical logic and the disavowed sexual politics at the core of the lawyer's nationalist vision, Doña Laura reinforces it through the sexual and economic gifting of Gloria's body—and the land she stands to inherit—to migrant farm laborers. Gloria ultimately rejects her mother-in-law's insistence that Gloria be legally incorporated into the family—and then sexually and economically incorporated into the making of a new Puerto Rico—by refusing the legal inheritance and Doña Laura's instruction to "sell our land progressively, piece by piece, to aid those who have already begun to emigrate to the mainland by the thousands, fleeing from the hell of the sugar plantation, to lend the honest effort of their arms and legs to other harvests more generously repaid" who may return with money to buy back a piece of their "lost paradise" (76). Whereas Doña Laura seems to be opposed to the De la Valles' romance promulgated by Don Hermenegildo, she ultimately represents another version of it, with an alternate conception of Puerto Rico as a paradise lost, to be regained.

In the end, Gloria fulfills neither Doña Laura's fantasy for redistributing the land nor Don Hermenegildo's wish that Diamond Dust remain in the De la Valle family. Instead, Gloria tears up the will and instructs Titina, who first alerted Don Hermenegildo to the conflict over the will, to help set fire to the house and the surrounding cane fields—with Don Hermenegildo still inside the house. Gloria explains to the "faithful" De la Valle servant (81):

> If Don Hermenegildo came to the house, if he agreed to leave his elegant, leather-upholstered solicitor's office where he's locked himself up for years writing a sentimental romance about Don Ubaldino, he certainly didn't intend to help us, or to hand us Diamond Dust on a silver platter, but rather to let Arístides and his sisters know about Doña Laura's secret will. Although in a way I'm not sorry he came, and I'm glad you invited him to do so, because now Don Hermenegildo will never be able to finish his novel. He's probably still sitting next to the dead woman, staring into the dark and inventing new lies, new ways of twisting around the story he heard from the lips of the protagonists of this tasteless melodrama. And if he should get away, if he should somehow manage to escape from the river of blue benzine that we poured a minute ago over the

mounds of dry cane stalks[,] . . . we'll still have the satisfaction of knowing that nobody will believe his tale about the man he maintained was a leader and a statesman, and who had been corrupt for so long. Facts have a strange way of facing down fiction, Titina, and if Don Hermenegildo's aborted novel was to have been a series of stories that contradicted one another like a row of falling dominoes, our story, the one we've taken the authority to write, will eradicate them all, because it will be the only one in which word and deed will finally be loyal to each other, in which a true correspondence between them will finally be established. (82)

Gloria does not merely reject or challenge Don Hermenegildo's "sentimental romance" or "novel." She wants it destroyed, "aborted," as a lie. For Gloria, the biography would have been, in any case, a failed attempt at romance: instead of possessing the structural coherence and unity that romance requires to fulfill its social function as a foundational fiction for the nation, Don Hermenegildo's book would have collapsed upon itself, structured as "a series of stories that contradicted one another" (82). Admonishing Titina for weeping, Gloria adds, "You must understand that everything he wrote about us was a lie, and that the only thing that will remain of his novel will be the allegiance between fire and words" (85). Gloria claims her act of burning down Diamond Dust is an act of writing its "true" story—a kind of perfect unity of the two meanings of the term "history," in which that which is said to have happened and that which happened share a "true correspondence" and ultimately eradicates the conflicting versions of the De la Valles' legacy that Don Hermenegildo includes both in his biography and in his interviews with Titina, Arístides, and Doña Laura. The gaps and contradictions between the stories Don Hermenegildo hears during his investigation, while they disrupt the unity of his narrative of romance, do not effectively undermine or counter the narratives of the nation that Gloria seeks to destroy. Gloria embraces the capacity of antiromance to reveal the "sexual citizenship" so crucial, as Francis argues, to the political formations of personhood in the Caribbean.

Don Hermenegildo's biographical romance relies on the network of cultural narratives that crisscross and reinforce each other. With torch in hand, Gloria enjoins Titina to sing with her "that old song" (85), the *danza* "Maldito Amor" ("Damned Love"), by Morel Campos. Campos, a nineteenth-century mixed-race Puerto Rican composer whose work hangs heavy with the perfumed aura of the Creole nationalist romance, of a Puerto Rico imagined as a paradise before the Fall, and with a harmony of European and African-inspired musical rhythms, composed in the decades leading up to the Spanish-American War, died just two years before the 1898 U.S. takeover. His music, then, represents the time before U.S. colonization. Ferré's reference to "Maldito Amor" (the title of the novella in its original Spanish) is part of the novella's status as a "parody of this paradise," noting in her preface to *Sweet Diamond Dust* that the *danza* "exemplifies better than any work I know the seigniorial paradise of the sugarcane planters, without ever mentioning that the greater part of the islanders lived in Hell" (Ferré viii). The erotic themes of romance in "Maldito Amor" frame the novella, whose opening chapters are also the opening chapters to Don Hermenegildo's biography of Ubaldino. The first chapter sets the stage of Guamaní as a (Spanish colonial) paradise, and the second establishes Ubaldino's origins in the courtship between Doña Elvira and Don Julio Font, when the newly love-struck Doña Elvira would spend all her time "daydreaming of Don Julio's amber-colored eyes and returning to reality only when she sat down at the piano to sing her favorite *danzas*," especially "Maldito Amor," which she would sing "at least ten times a day" (9). Far from a return to reality, the *danza* structures the courtship through a popular genre of national romance, without regard to the irony of the song's title or its quoted lyrics ("Your love is now a songless bird/ Your love, my dear, is lost in my heart / I don't know why your passion wilts me / And why it never flamed!").[97] After marriage, Doña Elvira finds that her husband is violent and cruel, and his stubborn cheapness indirectly causes her death soon after childbirth.

"Maldito Amor" takes on new meanings through Gloria's command to Titina to stop crying and instead sing the *danza* that Gloria and Nicolás sang "as we made love long long ago in these same cellars which you and I are lighting up now" (82), as if the lovers had understood that not only their love but also the mythical paradise of Puerto Rico were "damned." Imploring Titina again to sing the song with her as they set fire to the cellar, Gloria revises the lyrics to the *danza*, reclaiming the language of love by wresting it from the forms of national romance that for so long nourished the families of sugar planters and watered their fantasy of an original Puerto Rican paradise. She sings the final words of the novella:

Your love is a bird which has found its voice
Your love has finally nested in my heart;
Now I know why it burns
When I remember you.

Gloria's lyrics suggest that only with the destruction of Diamond Dust and the De la Valles' romance with genealogy will the bird, songless in Campos's version, find its voice. For Gloria, to accept the legal inheritance is to accept the national romance narratives of the type that Don Hermenegildo has been so earnestly writing. She seeks not merely to disrupt such narratives, but to destroy them outright: death by fire in *Sweet Diamond Dust*, death by drowning in Ferré's later novel, *House on the Lagoon*. *Sweet Diamond Dust* reveals that biography and romance participate in the myth of *la gran familia* and thus are invested in the familial and sexual logics of genealogy even as they deny the ideological consequences of this investment in its modeling of personhood and nationhood.

Where will she and her son be, after all, once the house, fields, and mill of *Sweet Diamond Dust* are destroyed in the fire she sets? Amid a blazing house and cane fields, *Sweet Diamond Dust* culminates with Gloria affirming her romantic love for Nicolás, in contrast to the repeated dismissals of the very possibility of love between a mulatta prostitute and a gay dandy, as Aristídes hatefully describes them both. Gloria reveals marriage alliances as the racist and sexist business arrangements that build legacies among the elite even as she claims a love match between Nicolás and herself that refuses to carry on the tradition of inherited wealth and racial purity. And yet this love marriage proves impossible, a relation to be destroyed, leaving Gloria with no refuge.

PART TWO

SALVAGE AESTHETICS

3 / Fugitive Personhood: Reimagining Sanctuary in Gayl Jones's *Song for Anninho* and *Mosquito*

Memory in our works is not a calendar memory; our experience of time does not keep company with the rhythms of month and year alone; it is aggravated by the void, the final sentence of the Plantation; our generations are caught up within an extended family in which our root stocks have diffused and everyone had two names, an official one and an essential one—the nickname given by his community. And when in the end it all began to shift, or rather collapse, when the unstoppable evolution had emptied the enclosure of people to reassemble them in the margins of cities, what remained, what still remains, is the dark side of this impossible memory, which has a louder voice and one that carries farther than any chronicle or census.

—ÉDOUARD GLISSANT, *POETICS OF RELATION*

I'm only telling y'all as much as I am telling y'all because this is supposed to be kept in the archives of the Daughters. The archives keeper is supposed to be trustworthy, but being a hidden agenda conspiracy specialist I have still employed everything that I've learned. My first love is the love of language, though, and whilst I defends the rights and privileges of the new Underground Railroad and maintains as much of they secrets that they ain't revealed they ownselves, I wants to maintain they privacy, conquer my own ignorance, and to tell y'all a story about South Texas.

—GAYL JONES, *MOSQUITO*

Emphasizing the power of sovereign law to adjudicate and recognize certain forms of human life as excluded from the body politic, death-bound theories of personhood provide influential paradigms for explaining why and how citizenship and international human rights law fail to ensure the dignity and rights of all human lives. These theories take seemingly exceptional categories of the legal person—slave, prisoner, fugitive, stateless refugee, de facto stateless person, undocumented alien, all of which bar persons from full participation in political life—to represent the normal institutional operations of law. Death-bound paradigms reveal that the ideal abstract citizen figure that stands as the normative legal person in traditional liberal politi-cal thought is a deceit; instead, they identify the figure on the horizon of political thought as some version of *homo sacer*, as the exemplary figure of biopolitics, and some version of "bare life" as its paradigmatic condition. Sovereign violence reveals itself to produce and to be con-stituted by the threshold of indistinction, a boundary or entryway of the modern political order, a zone between inside and outside, life and death, human and beast, homicide and sacrifice, law and fact, nature and right, exception and rule, licit and illicit, and so on.[1]

The figure of the living dead has come to embody the legacy of the political relation between the person and the state—whether it is the leg-acy of legal slavery in the Americas that inheres even now in the category of the natural human person or the exclusion (what Agamben calls the originary "ban") of he who once had been included in political life. As discussed in the introductory chapter, death-bound paradigms strategi-cally conflate the threshold of legal personhood with that of biological life, as in Hannah Arendt's image of the stateless as figures who, in the "abstract nakedness of being human," are bereft of social and political life; Orlando Patterson's study of how legal slavery effected a form of "social death" for slaves despite their limited status as legal persons; Saidiya Hartman's argument that the "states of injury" inflicted by law's restricted recognition of the enslaved body merely reinscribe the condi-tion of social death; Colin Dayan's tracing of a continuity in civil death between a rhetoric of law that invents "legal slaves" and one that renders the contemporary felon "dead in law"; Sharon Patricia Holland's work on cultural representations of death and black subjectivity; Achille Mbem-be's theory of necropolitics; Russ Castronovo's reading of "necro citizen-ship" as the core political discourse of the nineteenth-century U.S. public sphere; Abdul JanMohamed's reading of "the death-bound subject," born into a lifelong imminent threat of death, as it shapes the body of work by Richard Wright but also African American literature from its inception.[2] Of concern are the aftereffects of this imminent threat of violence and death initially authorized by law, which held black lives captive to the violence that the category of legal black slave enabled—for, as Hartman reminds us, "*the recognition of the slave as person depended upon the calculation of interest and injury.*"[3] While this list evokes the pervasive-ness of figurations of bare life, it does not mean to flatten the distinctions between the forms of life they conceptualize. Nor does it suggest that these theories are merely repetitions of the figure of "bare life" or "social death" so much as that they draw on, if sometimes also actively depart from, that figure. What these and other theories of contemporary forms of life do is pull, insistently if also variously, from the core trope of death to delimit the conditions and limits of political life.[4]

What recourse is there for refugees seeking to escape the imminent threat of biological death? Within the death-bound paradigms of personhood, there can be no outside to legal violence: sanctuary becomes a product of the state of exception, an affirmation of bare life rather than its alternative. Waligora-Davis contends that for the refugee, described as bare life or "merely flesh," "sanctuaries are spaces of internment in the fullest sense: they are spaces realizing social—and sometimes literal—death."[5] Adapting transhistorical theories of bare life to a culturally specific analysis of U.S. law's "historic alienation of black bodies," she argues that African American citizenship has been defined not by its approximation of full citizenship but rather by its overlap with the legal identities of the refugee and the stateless person.[6] The black body "is the body around which civil protections and human rights are delineated, but for whom they remain unconferred," and it is in response to this "anomalous relation to the law" that African American writing and politics have called for sanctuary as a safe space from the violence of the law and an alternative juridicial-political order.[7] In this way, Waligora-Davis provocatively reconceptualizes sanctuary in light of the political theory of bare life and civic death: sanctuary not only references an idealized state, but also a "space of the legally anomalous [within which] African Americans have historically been locked."[8] This second quality of sanctuary reveals it as a zone of indistinction for the black body—a limit-space, threshold, ghetto, detention camp, site of internment, place of arrest and of indefinite incarceration, but an "unlocalizable space" nonetheless.

> Simply put, sanctuary is an anomic legal state predicated on the rupture of blackness from legal personality that is achieved by denying the humanity of the black body. In this sense, sanctuary, as an "anomalous zone" or a "state of exception," guarantees black rightlessness. Sanctuaries are spaces that mirror the violence that constitute them.[9]

Sanctuary, as the exceptional granting of protection to refugees or fugitives under certain conditions and within certain spaces, presents itself as a utopian respite from a legal order that historically has denied human and civil rights to black bodies but is, ultimately, a dystopian space, complicit with the very legal order that defines sanctuary as its exception. Sanctuary affirms the authority of the law through its very status as an exceptional, extralegal space, "calling into question the presumed safety culturally associated with these sites."[10] Ostensibly a space of refuge from violence, sanctuary itself reflects the violence from which the fugitive seeks protection.

This reading of sanctuary, while convincing, prompts questions about how to think about the radical potential of antislavery movements that rejected an appeal to law for sanctuary and insisted on making unauthorized, fugitive forms of sanctuary. What of the efforts of enslaved, formerly enslaved, and free blacks to make—for themselves, and as much as possible on their terms—their own refuge from legal subjugation? What of those African Americans who rode or assisted the Underground Railroad, and what of the former slaves, the escaped fugitive slaves whose *marronage* led to the establishment of societies that made their own claims to sovereignty, and in the process radically redefined the meaning and purpose of sovereign power in the Americas? In thinking about enslaved persons who sought refuge in an unauthorized, fugitive, and thus seemingly precarious form of freedom, one might consider this sanctuary as a practice rather than a space—a practice that challenged the existing legal order by performing a new if fugitive mode of sanctuary.[11]

This chapter contends that Gayl Jones's book-length narrative poem, *Song for Anninho*, and her late novel *Mosquito* perform narrational acts of creative *marronage* as a way to challenge death-bound theories of personhood by envisioning an alternative "poetics of relation," Glissant's term for the aesthetic and political formation of identities and narratives through relation and errancy rather than isolation and linearity. *Marronage* is the term in French slave colonies for the act of fugitive slaves in Martinique, Jamaica, Haiti, Brazil, and elsewhere who escaped into forested hills or mountainous regions. This "historical *marronage*," writes Glissant, "intensified over time to exert a creative *marronage*, whose numerous forms of expression began to form the basis for a continuity" of Caribbean literatures, with all their strategic detours and errancy—their "processes of intensification, breathlessness, digression, and immersion of individual psychology within the drama of a common destiny."[12] This creative *marronage* is also marked by "geographical connectedness," memory through oral forms and Vodou ritual, and "all the canny detours, diversions, and ruses required" to keep this practice of cultural flight and world-making from losing its subversive power.[13]

In *Song for Anninho* and *Mosquito*, this poetics of relation is quite distinctive among the wide-ranging, heterogeneous literary imagination of Jones's oeuvre. Jones experiments in these texts with a distinctive narrative poetics, one that gives voice to the fugitive refugee in search of sanctuary: what emerges through this creative *marronage* is a revision of the meanings, forms, and functions of sanctuary as a practice. Her poetics of narration, what Jones elsewhere calls "liberating voices," refigure the politics of fugitive personhood in *Song for Anninho* (1981) and *Mosquito* (1999)—two texts that, along with her pivotal novel *The Healing* (1998), depart from her better-known novels, *Corregidora* (1975) and *Eva's Man* (1976), which grappled with the injurious legacies of legal racial slavery through the sexual as well as psychological assaults on black men and women.

This chapter begins by reading *Song for Anninho* as a meditation on the failure of sanctuary as a place, prompting the speaker of the poem to locate sanctuary not in any one place but rather in the practice of her spiritual and bodily healing. *Song for Anninho* is explicitly concerned with the aftermath of a catastrophe in which the seventeenth-century Maroon community of Palmares is destroyed by a colonial military expedition charged with eradicating the sanctuary, leaving the speaker, Almeyda, to narrate her escape as a fugitive and her process of healing from the wounds of catastrophe. In both *Song for Anninho* and *Mosquito*, the principal narrators explore fugitivity in relation to sanctuary and to alternative models of the storytelling archive as they evade, exceed, refuse, and otherwise seek to undermine the power of the law to delimit human personhood. The latter part of the chapter examines *Mosquito* as it extends and revises the philosophy of sanctuary begun by *Song for Anninho*. *Mosquito* uses the trope of the talking book to critique the history of legal sanctuary, as part of the eponymous narrator's reenvisioning sanctuary as a spiritual, political, and aesthetic practice for fugitive personhood. The narrator redefines sanctuary across legal, national, and racial identities: in the storyworld of the novel, the historical Underground Railroad becomes revitalized for a new sanctuary movement to help any and all seekers of refuge crossing into the Southwest from the U.S.-Mexico border (Central Americans and, in Jones's novel, Zapatistas from Chiapas, Mexico). Jones invokes but also refigures the historical Sanctuary movement of the 1980s—"one of the most important acts of civil disobedience of the late twentieth century"—in which thousands of U.S. citizens actively assisted Central American refuge seekers who eluded Border Patrol agents and crossed the U.S.-Mexico border, with great peril to their lives and with horrific stories of war, bombings, kidnappings, rapes, murders, mutilation, and threats of death.[14] Early on, historical Sanctuary movement organizers invoked the Underground Railroad and the moral good in offering "safe spaces," or sanctuaries, for fugitives when state law conflicted with divine laws of compassion, hospitality, and justice. Like the Underground Railroad, the historical

Sanctuary movement is thus the embodiment of the liberal response to sanctuary. Jones's work, as the chapter examines, responds to both death-bound and liberal conceptions of fugitive personhood and sanctuary.

In redefining sanctuary, *Mosquito* also redefines archival memory. In contrast to the archival turn in studies of slavery that reflect on and perform narrative failure, as discussed in the introduction, *Mosquito* is all narrational maximalism—a nonstop narrating that accumulates into a storytelling archive that radically undermines models of the archive as haunted or as a repository of law, order, and death. *Mosquito* also challenges models of personhood that tend to affirm as absolute the sovereign power to define the scope, quality, and vitality of personhood: in challenging the reduction of personhood to its juridical meaning, the character Mosquito recuperates a variety of aesthetic, spiritual, and non-nationalist models of extralegal personhood that historically have enabled forms of everyday resistance to legal exclusion. Expanding the extralegal dimensions of personhood as a way to contest its legal dimension is thus formative to Jones's broader project of decolonizing the novel and the concept of the person. This decolonization is an ongoing process that cannot rely on legal or political correctives, such as an expansion of legal recognition or civil rights: instead, it depends on deconstructing the concept of sanctuary so that it is no longer a space of temporary protection from legal punishment structured by the law and mirroring its violence. Rather than serve as an extralegal space for the fugitive who must flee or evade the law, sanctuary in Jones's novel becomes an open archive of stories, composed of potentially infinitely expanding authorial personae, that is paradoxically contained within the self. Jones, then, transforms the concept of sanctuary into an aesthetic, decolonial practice of "minding the word."[15]

Rather than reaffirm the form of bare life, embodied in a kind of nonperson or living dead, as the paradigmatic human condition in our modern political order, Jones appeals to the aesthetic and political dimensions of extralegal personhood as a means of contesting the juridical logics of legal personhood. In particular, Jones conceives of the extralegal persona as a fugitive and a refugee that seeks sanctuary from the law and in doing so challenges the cultural logics underpinning taxonomies of legal personhood. The fugitive flees from the law that marks her as criminal; the refugee, from the legal order that fails to keep her safe. The history of the legal personhood of African Americans is one of a collapsed distinction between the fugitive and the stateless refugee in relation to the U.S. legal order—a collapse most strikingly demonstrated by the 1850 Fugitive Slave Act, which turned black bodies into fugitive bodies, as their legal status came to occupy a zone of indistinction subsequently distinguished by the law, which almost always recognized the black body as a slave body. Solomon Northup's narrative (and now a major motion picture) *Twelve Years a Slave: Narrative of Solomon Northup, a Citizen of New-York, Kidnapped in Washington City in 1841, and Rescued in 1853*, testifies to this racial vulnerability, as one example of a freeborn black "citizen" who was kidnapped, whose legal status was reclassified by corrupt police authorities and courts, and sold "back" into slavery as part of the political economy of racialized legal personhood—as easily as if he always already was a fugitive slave.[16]

Jones seeks to reconceptualize the human person's relation to the law by salvaging histories of fugitive legal personhood in the Americas, in which individuals excluded from the political order survived in ways that challenge the overdetermined condition of bare life. Counter to "bare life," which Agamben identifies as the "protagonist" of *Homo Sacer*, Jones's protagonists—which are paradoxically excluded from and yet captured within the political order in ways that might, to Agamben, resemble the condition of bare life—simply talk too much to evoke the condition of bare life.[17] Mosquito, in particular, claims countless political, cultural, and social opinions in her effort to recapture the scope and meanings of personhood from the state. Such extralegal or fugitive persons challenge death-bound theories of personhood no less than the juridical logics that structure modern politics, suggesting that creative and spiritual aesthetic modes of salvaging among the debris of legal personhood provide an alternative to the critical obsession with death-bound personhood.

Fugitive Healing

Song for Anninho performs a double act of creative *marronage*: it takes historical *marronage* as its subject matter but begins in the aftermath of its failure—the destruction of one of the largest Maroon communities in the history of the Americas and the largest fugitive refuge from legal chattel slavery in seventeenth-century Brazil. Its Maroon leaders envisioned this refuge not only as a sanctuary but also as an independent, sovereign state whose existence and political structure would pose an explicit challenge to the logics of enslaved personhood in colonial Brazil. The poem opens with the destruction of the Quilombo or Republic of Palmares, the largest and best-secured society of fugitive settlements in colonial Brazil, after enduring nearly one hundred years of Dutch- and Portuguese-sponsored assaults. Zumbi, leader of the now-defunct political order of Palmares, is stripped of his role as sovereign and reduced to a fugitive captured by colonial law: sharing the fate of Babo in *Benito Cereno*, Zumbi's severed head is publicly displayed after his capture, not only "to kill the legend of his immortality,"[18] but also to evince in the flesh his reduction from black fugitive leader to the figure of the "sacred" in the archaic Roman legal sense, in which "human life is included in the juridical order [*ordinamento*] solely in the form of its exclusion (that is, of its capacity to be killed)."[19]

What follows is the song of Almeyda, a *palmarista* who has survived the catastrophic destruction of the Palmares refuge, the loss of her lover/ husband, and the mutilation of flesh. As with Zumbi's severed head, her mutilation is made to speak through what Hortense Spillers calls "a hieroglyphics of the flesh" that mark the captive body as a stolen body, the product of "externalized torture" that turns gendered stolen bodies into a common "territory of cultural and political maneuver."[20] In a variant of Spiller's formulation, Almeyda's breasts, having been cut off and thrown into the river by a Portuguese soldier, represent the theft of flesh intended to symbolically reinscribe Almeyda into slavery even as her body is caught between captivity and liberation, in a state of fugitivity. Like the scarring of her lacerated chest, Almeyda's song testifies at once to her wounding and her healing, as the singing of her lost refuge itself becomes a refuge, one no longer bounded by the constraints of her time and place.

As the subject of Almeyda's song, Palmares has been displaced from a geographically situated reality into a spiritual icon of past resistance, affirmation of the enduring African presence in the Americas, and future liberation. A brief discussion of its geographic time and place, as well as its changing place in historical narratives, will situate the multiple meanings of time and place in the poem—of the life span of Palmares, of its historical excavation, and of the futurity it has come to signify. Overwhelmingly, during its existence and since its destruction, in histories and literary depictions Palmares has been iconic of the "resistance to New World slavery and its legacy," although there are no surviving written documents from Palmares itself in the historical record.[21] What is less often emphasized, however, is that Palmares was neither spatially bounded nor insular, being often damaged and rebuilt in different locations in the Serra da Barriga. It was a refuge but also a distinct social system—not only an escape from "a slave-holding society entirely out of step with forms of bondage familiar to Africa" but also an alternative to colonialist modes of governance and models of personhood.[22] In other words, Palmares challenged the colonial, political, and economic system.

It did not, however, isolate itself from that system; it was, instead, intimately connected with surrounding communities in trading and social life. After 1640 Palmares grew to become a formidable republic of tens of thousands of free people, strategically positioned in forested mountain terrain in the interior of the coastal states of Pernambuco and Alagôas but able to make repeated contact with surrounding trading partners and plantation slaves. As it grew, Palmares society developed a complex, predominantly Africanist practice of governance. It also served as a refuge for various outcasts: slaves, freeborn blacks, Indians, mixed-race persons, religious minorities, and poor whites would seek out Palmares as a hideout, or *mocambo*. While some slaves escaped to Palmares and were recognized as free by the welcoming *palmaristas*, others were "stolen" from slaveholders in raids and taken to Palmares—and they would not be considered free until they, in turn, stole another. In other words, one could not become liberated by having another person grant one's freedom. Instead, Palmares developed a certain economy of exchange premised on the notion of freedom as an active, self-authorizing process that also extends itself in a potentially unlimited way: a "stolen" slave became free only by stealing another and thus beginning the process for that other to become free by stealing another, and so on.[23]

After a particularly brutal campaign against Palmares in 1678, the military leader Ganga-Zumba offered the Portuguese a peace treaty that would reverse the self-authorizing process of becoming free in favor of the colonial model of determining slave or free status based on criteria of birth: he offered to return all *palmaristas* not born in the *quilombo* (mostly women) in exchange for allowing Palmares a claim to limited self-sovereignty.[24] A Palmares military leader named Zumbi (also known as "Zambi") led a revolt against Ganga-Zumba in order to prevent such negotiations and refused to surrender to the Portuguese. Palmares was destroyed soon after a Portuguese advance led some two hundred *palmaristas* to fling themselves over a cliff, in a move that evokes the myth of the flying Africans, anticipating Guy's suicide in Danticat's "A Wall of Fire Rising," discussed in the previous chapter.[25] "In its time and place," the historian R. K. Kent concludes, "Palmares had only two choices. It could continue to hold its ground as an independent state or suffer complete extinction."[26]

The dominant concern of the historiography on Palmares, up until the early 1990s, has been to answer two related questions: how important was Palmares, and how was it distinctly African even in the "New World"? Historians such as Kent have tried to answer both questions by arguing that Palmares was not merely a network of fugitive settlements but in fact a state or republic with mostly Central African systems of governance, law, economy, and society. Pan-African intellectuals since the 1960s, such as Abdias do Nascimento, have used the methods of official commemoration and preservation to keep alive the memory of Zumbi, and the promise of a future Pan-African society. Nascimento organized efforts such as erecting a bust of Zumbi and (in 1980) declaring the anniversary of Zumbi's death, November 20, National Black Consciousness Day. Pan-Africanist movements seek to keep Palmares alive in memory as the remembered promise of an as yet unfulfilled future, "an icon to be pursued, a society which we must dream of and fight for."[27]

While Jones draws from primary colonial documents and recent Pan-Africanist historiography to depict Palmares, she does so in order to amplify its historical, mythical, and lyrical registers as sanctuary rather than its political resemblance to a sovereign state or republic. Thus, while King is right to describe the poem as a tribute to Palmares and a complement to "the contemporary cultural movement and excavation project that Abdias do Nascimento helped to organize on behalf of Brazilians of African descent worldwide," I suggest that Jones also points out what is missed by celebrations of Palmares that claim its significance on the basis of its establishment of sanctuary in the form of a sovereign state.[28] With *Song for Anninho*, Jones turns away from models of personhood focused solely on its politico-juridical function, thus giving humanity its meaning solely in terms of a system of legal personhood formed by the state, which may affirm, deny, attenuate, retract, or otherwise burden it. The poem instead focuses on the difficult process of affirming a creative, spiritual personhood in the absence of Palmares's political sovereign authority and as a challenge to Brazilian colonial sovereignty. It is notable, then, that Jones prefaces the poem with a written address to the Portuguese sovereign in the voice of its agent: the epigraph is a military petition dated 1695 from Domingos Jorge Velho to "His Majesty," the Portuguese crown, whose money funded the campaign at the request of local colonial governors. Velho, an infamous *bandeirante* ("follower of the banner"), led the army that would eventually destroy Palmares after years of Portuguese failures and many, many dead.[29] In the petition, Velho confirms that Palmares has been destroyed even as he warns that the war is not yet over: there are "survivors . . . in the great depths of these forests" whom he must "hunt" down. "If not," he warns His Majesty, "another stronghold will suddenly appear either here in Barriga or in any other equally suitable place."[30]

The poem quickly turns away from this official register and toward the voice of Almeyda, one such survivor hidden in the Barriga mountains, who has been mutilated by a Portuguese soldier and has been separated from her lover and husband, Anninho, after the chaos of the military invasion.[31] Zibatra, a healing woman who can "hear beyond ears," prompts Almeyda to "find" Anninho. Almeyda must now perform a quest to heal from the wounds of catastrophe. The quest demands from Almeyda a poetic effort to transform "time" into a spiritual fluidity and "place" into a location of not only lost but also future possibilities. When considered in relation to how she constructs the image of sanctuary, Jones's formal experimentation produces startling results: "I've always been interested in getting the greatest flexibility in the rendering of time/place/space in fiction . . . trying to maintain a kind of 'coherence' at the same time there is a looseness and flexibility of dramatic structure—the coherence and flexibility of jazz improvisation."[32] The song, in its dream-like shifting between past, present, future, remembered voices, visions, dreams, and desires, becomes Almeyda's spiritual process of searching for Anninho—and thus, for a relation of love, a spiritual stronghold of a sort Velho had not imagined.

Germane to Almeyda's healing quest is the recurring question of how best to bear the burden of personhood "in this time and place." Jones sets up a relationship between the act of freeing oneself from the burden of enslavement and the act of giving birth, of delivering oneself of a burden, or "that which is borne in the womb."[33] In one sense, the womb is a met-onym for Palmares, located as it is in the Barriga mountain range. *Barriga* means "belly" generally in Brazilian Portuguese and Spanish, and "*estar de barriga*" colloquially refers to being pregnant. Palmares is fig-ured by both its survivors and Velho as a fertile site that may conceive of a new refuge: Velho notes that survivors may create another "stronghold" somewhere else in the belly of this forest or another, and before they are separated, Almeyda and Anninho repeatedly speak of their hopes for rebirth, for "a New Palmares." This hope is transformed into song: with the help of the healing woman, Zibatra, whom, as Madhu Dubey notes, is a "surrogate mother" who fills the matrilineal gap and enables Almeyda to heal through spiritual transcendence and wholeness, Almeyda begins the process of refuging, of seeking refuge not in a place of shelter but in the very process of seeking refuge, of fleeing from the law.[34]

Almeyda's grandmother and the healing, or conjure, woman, form a matrilineal line that Almeyda must actively construct; in contrast, Almeyda repeatedly recalls a woman who refuses to bear the burden of children, the self-mutilated woman whom Almeyda knew when she was enslaved on a sugar plantation with her grandmother and mother. It is through this figure that Jones stages an argument between Almeyda's grandmother, Almeyda, and the unnamed woman over how best to imagine liberation and futurity when the black female body was subjected to the burden of reproducing the slave system, whether as slaves whose personhood was delimited by the law or as fugitives whose freedom was extralegal. Both women insist on a certain kind of unity of person, but they belong to two different times: Almeyda, having known Palmares, wants to open herself to bearing the burden of carrying Anninho's child as a way to become spiritually whole, by extending herself for a future possibility, while the unnamed woman, held captive, seeks to guarantee her wholeness by closing off her body from the potential of bearing the burden of another's flesh.[35] In Almeyda's song, at once a eulogy of remembrance, a prayer for future healing, and a call for the return or a renewal of what has been lost, a motif emerges of birth and rebirth. The poem links healing with rebirth and Almeyda's love for Anninho with her desire to bear him a child—a desire now impossible to realize after the war has taken her lover and the flesh of her breasts.[36] It is in this context of healing from loss, and of the violent mutilation of her flesh by an agent of the sovereign power, that Almeyda repeatedly returns to the story, told by her grandmother, of this unnamed woman on the sugar plantation, long before Almeyda was taken to Palmares.

> "There was a woman, Anninho, who mutilated herself,
> so she wouldn't have to have any man at all.
> She had done it, because she didn't want
> any man at all, not the black ones or the white ones.
> There was something that she did to herself so that
> no man would go near her."

Almeyda struggles to affirm the self-mutilated woman's gendered personhood, which has been delinked from sexual and reproductive instrumentality. The woman provides a stark contrast to depictions of Gloria's sexualized citizenship in Rosario Ferré's *Sweet Diamond Dust,* in which Doña Laura equates Gloria's "cunt" with Puerto Rico's open port and the fruit of cultural bilingualism that both, in Doña Laura's vision, produce. In *Song for Anninho,* Almeyda recounts a conversation with her lover Anninho, in which she raises the subject of the self-mutilated woman.

> "I think as soon as she discovered how they would use her,
> she did that horror to herself."
> "Did away with her womanhood."
> "She was still a woman."
> "You know what I mean."

"Yes. But there was nothing about her that was not a woman,
except the thing she had done to herself. She wore leather
bracelets and necklaces of trumpet shells. Men found no way
in." (54–55)

In a very physical way, the unnamed woman contradicts the logic that
to be without sexual love and childbirth constitutes a loss: caught within
the slave system, reproduction would transform her into a "breeder"
rather than a "mother," to borrow Angela Davis's distinction.[37] Whereas
enslaved women in both Brazil and North America sometimes resorted
to contraception, abortion, and infanticide in order to "obstruct reproduction of the slave system," the self-mutilated woman also closes the
metaphorical wound of the vagina as a way to protect herself from
another kind of loss, that of her formal unity.[38] The woman paradoxically
mutilates herself in order to stay *formally unified*, impenetrable, impreg-
nable. "They [the other women] think I have mutilated myself, but," she
tells Almeyda, "I have kept myself whole" (73). The spatial unity of form
here forecloses the biological time of futurity through bearing a child.
The woman explains to Almeyda that female personhood has value only
in the economy of sexual reproduction, for its promise of reproductive
labor, whether with white or black men: "This is a time, young one, when
a woman / is worth nothing if her body can't / produce for them, or bear
the burden / of their flesh. Not ours. But theirs" (70). The enjambed lines
emphasize female personhood as a value conditional to what her body
can do, can produce, can bear, as able acts and as sexual imperatives:
a woman "is worth nothing if her body can't." The unnamed woman's
personhood is circumscribed totally by a model of bare life produced by
the plantation system, which in multiple ways forces enslaved persons to
bear the burden of "their flesh."

The women deliberate over the burdens that weigh specifically on
the status of enslaved female personhood: is the womb a sanctuary—
or a prison—for cultivating future generations? Is the body a sanctuary
for the self *only* if it is protectively bounded, and thus not violated by
sex—and what sex might lead to? A woman's womb is metonymic of the
Maroon community; both are sanctuaries weighted by "the burden of
time" and "the burden of their [men's] flesh." Early in her song, Almeyda
announces to an absent Anninho, "I will plant my womb in the earth, /
and it will grow, / and this feeling we have made between us / will grow
as deep" (16). Almeyda's human flesh becomes the flesh of the earth, and
the image of Almeyda planting her womb in the earth suggests generation no less than burial. The unnamed woman's story unfolds as a series

of remembered conversations: Almeyda remembers telling her story to Anninho, she remembers her grandmother arguing with the woman over "what she has done," and, in the final section of the poem, when times and places converge onto a single plane of memory, Almeyda envisions her lover Anninho speaking intimately with the self-mutilated woman, healing her with his touch, his eyes, his understanding of her. It is then that Almeyda envisions the woman confiding to Anninho that if she "had seen Palmares in her future, / she would never have done that thing" (102). The disagreement between the self-mutilating woman and the grandmother, a *macumbeiro* who insists that they must all "bear the burden / of our time," arises from thinking through the best ways to liberate oneself from the historical burdens of retractable personhood (68).

Palmares, as a state, and the self-mutilated woman both represent a closed form of sanctuary, an exceptional space of protection that nonetheless mirrors the violence of racial slavery and sexual violence that shape its boundaries. Almeyda seeks to transform sanctuary, however, from a bounded place into an open, relational practice: the poem ends with Almeyda's address to her lover, "Now I make roads for you, Anninho. I make roads" (119). For Almeyda and a faction within Palmares, self-authorizing freedom has to be realized in connection with another, whether through the historical process of successive freedom (freeing oneself by freeing another) or through giving birth to another. The process of healing from the destruction of Palmares involves moving beyond protective, bounded spaces to multiple "roads" whose endpoints must remain undefined even as they figuratively reconnect Almeyda with her lost lover. Sanctuary remains a condition for healing from the retraction of one's personhood, but the form of sanctuary has been transformed from enclosure to an open path that must not only be remembered, but also sung.

Mosquito's Sanctuary Movements

The storyworld of *Mosquito* takes this process of "making roads" literally, and in directions that critics have often found dizzying: the novel is presented as an exuberant, digressive, often slyly humorous narrative told to us by Sojourner Jane Nadine "Mosquito" Johnson, an African American truck driver whose routes take her into the Southwest borderlands, where she participates in a "not-mainstream" movement to provide sanctuary to unauthorized refugees from the Mexican border, in violation of U.S. immigration and asylum policy. Critical of how the historical sanctuary movement of the 1980s used transnational affiliations to reaffirm existing liberal modes of governance and the state authority they underwrite, Jones depicts a shadow sanctuary movement—a "not-mainstream" sanctuary movement that obliquely counters the politico-juridical system of legal personhood by evading its mechanisms of both the exclusion and the incorporation of the human person.

Favorable and unfavorable readers alike have neglected the significance of sanctuary to the novel's aesthetic and political project.[39] Few have considered how the novel reconceptualizes sanctuary through the rhetorical tactics that structure it; instead, sanctuary is noted as merely a plot detail, an occasion or excuse for the complex series of digressions that structure the narrative. Indeed, tens, sometimes hundreds, of pages of narration come between one sentence that advances the political sanctuary movement plot and the next, and Mosquito's narration frequently gives way to other characters' voices or their writings at some length, including letters between friends, journal entries, songs, even text by Jones's mother, Lucille Jones.[40]

An independent trucker by occupation and personal philosophy, Mosquito collects the texts and stories that constitute the novel.[41] Mosquito's narration is heteroglossic, digressive, accumulative, associative, and relentless in its inclusion of a vast array of knowledge and discourse from television, newspapers, rap videos, fast-food signs, and junk mail: anything and everything, it seems, becomes incorporated into Mosquito's narration. The novel is structured by such digressions, along with embedded texts typographically set apart from the principal narration, and a generally nonlinear, incorporative play on the encyclopedic drive to take "everything" as its focus (even as it refuses a key function of the encyclopedic novel to delimit the scope of knowledge). The result is a book that critics, with the important exception of Deborah McDowell, have faulted for its length, its seeming formlessness, its "stilted" political content and wildly heterogeneous discursive content. Henry Louis Gates Jr., for instance, describes the novel as "a late-night riff by the Signifying Monkey, drunk with words and out of control, regurgitating half-digested ideas taken from USA Today, digressing on every possible subject." Mosquito's inconsistencies, excesses, and "hidden talents," are taken by Gates to indicate Jones's failure to construct a figure of the human personality. Gates leads a chorus of reviewers who fault Mosquito for its thematic and formal experimentations with orality. Conducted mostly in an ostensibly black Kentucky vernacular, Mosquito's narration has been described as difficult to "read"—difficult to read the words on the page and hard to figure out in terms of Jones's textual deconstruction of oral narrative tactics. Gates, whose theory of black vernacular and oral narrative forms has been seminal to African American literary critics, faults Jones for trying to write her own "dissertation about orality."[42] *Mosquito* clearly does not give its readers the "illusion of speech," as Gates would have preferred. He expresses irritation at Jones's aesthetic theories of improvisational and polyphonic narration, which are expressed frequently by characters, as when Mosquito wonders if "it be possible to tell a true jazz story, where the peoples that listens can just enter the story and start telling it and adding things wherever they wants. The story would provide the jazz foundation, the subject, but they be improvising around that subject or them subjects and be composing they own jazz story."[43]

The novel's narrational structure gives voice to Mosquito as the figure of a nonrealist human personality and, as I suggest, a model of personhood that challenges the logics of legal personhood. Yet critics have tended to assume that Mosquito is merely a portal into Jones's inner self. Published after the death of her mother, Lucille, and only months after Jones's husband committed suicide during an altercation with police, the novel serves as evidence for Gates that Jones is in need of literal sanctuary, in the form of a psychiatric asylum.[44] Gates's review is the most prominent, but several others read the novel through Jones's family tragedy: reviewers strained to "discern" in the novel, as Gates writes, "clues to Jones's feelings about the recent tragic events of her personal life," while apparently unfazed by the fact that Jones would have completed the novel before the tragic events of 1998.[45] Moreover, critics such as Gates and the reviewer Greg Tate bristle at Jones's desire to create what she describes, in her essay on the decolonized novel, as a "multicultural, multilinguistic, multi-vernacular novel and at the same time . . . a self-defined African American novel, that is *la verdadera historia,* an African novel born in the New World."[46] Tate reproaches Jones for her lengthy engagement with Latina/o culture by way of the Sanctuary movement plot and Delgadina, Mosquito's girlfriend, described in another review as a "paper cutout of a Chicana who exists only to voice stilted political views." Bypassing the novel's treatment of sanctuary altogether to reproach Jones for her interest in Chicana, Mexican, and Central American cultural politics in the Southwest, Tate accuses Jones of unleashing her inner "Racial Authority . . . [which speaks] on behalf of our Latin American brothers and sisters too and [does] it at a length" he finds "self-indulgent" and "incredibly demanding of even her most sympathetic readers' time, tolerance, and intelligence."[47]

Whereas the novel's initial reception faulted its heterogeneity and multicultural experimentation at the level of character and narrative structure, recent critical essays focus primarily on the cultural intersection of U.S. African American and Latin American cultures and characters, to the exclusion of the novel's formal experimentation. Such critics rightly identify *Mosquito* as a continuation of Jones's interest in hemispheric America and its histories of racism, slavery, colonialism, liberation struggles, and cultural syncretism, but they also tend to gloss over Jones's depiction of sanctuary in the novel, including her reference to the historical mainstream Sanctuary movement (with a capital *S*) in her fictional plot of a "not-mainstream" sanctuary movement (with a lowercase *s*). Essays on the U.S. African American and Latin American connections in the novel at times describe its sanctuary movement plot vaguely or incorrectly, without considering reference to the historical movement, thus failing to consider how and why Jones constructs the image of a broader and inclusive sanctuary movement in contrast to the historical one.[48] Sanctuary, for Jones's readers, is everywhere and nowhere, self-evident (as plot) or evidence (as symptom) that an authorial self has taken refuge from the world. Critical accounts of the novel that reduce the sanctuary movement to the plot, only to consign the plot to the margins of critical attention, make it easy to miss the relationship between the sanctuary movement and Jones's aesthetic project in the novel. Such readings miss the significance of sanctuary and archive in Jones's engagement with knowledge, coloniality, power, and aesthetics as part of her attempt to write a novel that attempts to perform its own decolonization.

Mosquito eventually reveals to readers her motive for saying so much aloud: her "hidden talent" is a perfect auditory (rather than photographic) memory, which proves crucial to her involvement in both the not-mainstream sanctuary movement and the Daughters of Nzingha, a tongue-in-cheek spiritual organization that collects an archive of a potentially infinite number of stories from the African diaspora and friends around the world. Mosquito is the archive keeper for the Daughters of Nzingha due to her perfect auditory memory, which obliges her to act as a "minder of the word," as she incorporates her personal stories into the special archive. Analysis of Mosquito's depiction of the sanctuary movement and the Daughters of Nzingha archive reveals the formal coherence of the novel and its ambitious project to rethink sanctuary and archive as embodied and decolonial aesthetic practices of narration. In the novel, archive keeping mirrors sanctuary work; each relies on reading and narration to challenge the legal and political management of personhood by the state. I want to suggest that *Mosquito* reconceptualizes sanctuary and the archive by centering on the figure of the fugitive person as a demonstration of Jones's broader aesthetic project—what she describes in a 1994 essay as a "Third World aesthetics" waging a "war for independence" from colonialist and state logics of personhood and authority. If "Mosquito refuses to shut up," as McDowell notes, in contrast to Jones's earlier female characters, perhaps it is because the process of decolonization must be narrated and yet incomplete, always oriented toward unrealized possibilities.

Rooted in Hebraic definitions of community, and then later in medieval Christian definitions of the church as a sacred place, "sanctuary" refers broadly to any place, understood by law or established custom, to provide immunity from the law to fugitives who enter that place. In adapting Hebraic traditions of communitarian sanctuary, the Christian church emphasized the hierarchy of the clergy—instead of the community—as the source of authority. In early and medieval Europe, the contest between the state and the church over which was the superior authority—and which could define and classify the sort of person one was—played out in this practice of sanctuary. The anthropologist Hilary Cunningham notes that in "the early days of ecclesiastical sanctuary, the church mainly assisted runaway and abused slaves" who fled disciplinary punishment from masters. The cleric acted to intercede between fugitives and civil justice—between slaves and masters, "sinners" and state authorities—by evaluating the fugitive's plea for sanctuary and deciding on the appropriate level and form of pardon or punishment, and at whose hand (God, the slave master, or the state).[49] By the eighth and ninth centuries in Europe, church sanctuary, as a sacred place and as an institution that intercedes between individual and state, began to erode. Civil authorities produced categories of fugitives and delimited which categories could seek sanctuary, under what conditions, and to what ends. Church sanctuary—and so, ecclesiastical authority—became increasingly limited, bureaucratized, and subsumed within the civil realm until it was finally abolished in England in 1624.

The practice of sanctuary (like that of archive keeping) is governed by a principle of authorized entry and authorized guardianship. Likening the space of sanctuary to the narthex, the entrance part of the church traditionally used as a place of penitence where those excluded from full membership in the church could still hear the service, Waligora-Davis argues that both are "spaces that remain beyond reach—part of a distant future. As both legal and political interstices, they delimit the boundaries of the law."[50] The history of sanctuary law suggests that sanctuary reinscribes the fugitivity of the refuge seeker and affirms the authority of the state—and the church, a core sanctuary site—to determine what categories of personhood deserve what sort of protection and under what terms. Although largely considered a holy space and thus alternative space to civil law, sanctuary highlights how civil authority and the ideology of citizenship draw on the same notions of paternalistic and pastoral care that have defined the authority of the Christian church. In 1967 the Arlington Street Unitarian Church in Boston reclaimed the earlier history of church sanctuary as a sacred space and alternative to state authority when it became the first church to publicly declare sanctuary for nearly three hundred Vietnam draft resisters.[51] In this case, U.S. citizens became fugitives seeking immunity from their government on the grounds that their government was engaging in an immoral and unjust war. It was similarly in the name of a higher moral law that a number of white, middle-class U.S. citizens of multiple Christian denominations challenged the policies of the Reagan administration when they began to declare church sanctuary within the United States for Central Americans seeking refuge from the devastating wars of the 1980s, in which the Reagan administration itself was deeply involved. The movement, led according to sometimes-conflicting visions by its Tucson and Chicago branches, was publicized by sanctuary workers and journalists as a national struggle over America's conscience and ultimately its soul. The most publicized actors were white U.S. citizens. The journalist Ann Crittenden affirms the vision of an America whose (tacitly white) citizens fight for the freedom of others and maintain the essential national tradition of hospitality when their government falters.

> Ordinary citizens, coming face-to-face with the refugees, stepped into the government's shoes and welcomed the sojourners in their midst. In this they represented their country at its best. As the *Arizona Daily Star*, a Tucson daily newspaper that was sympathetic to the underground railroad, commented, "America at its greatest has always been America as a refuge from persecution, as a protector of the helpless, and a voice for justice. America has won wars and flexed its military power, but it's the enlightened attitude toward basic human freedom that gives us our special status in the world."[52]

Crittenden reflects, "In the end the sanctuary story is about a battle between Americans, between two radically different visions of the kind of country we are [one based on law or one based on morality] and our place in the world."[53] The *Arizona Daily Star* invokes the need of the "persecuted" for refuge, protection, and a voice but finds this need fulfilled by "America." In a familiar move, the *Star* justifies U.S. military aggression by appealing to U.S. exceptionalism, represented by the special, self-proclaimed status of the state that defends human rights. The metaphor of citizens stepping into "the shoes" of the state suggests that the citizen and the state are interchangeable partners in maintaining good moral governance. Major national conflicts over slavery and civil rights are often fitted into the ideology of liberal exceptionalism: the big shoes of national tradition are always filled, sometimes by citizens and sometimes by the state. The shoes march to the beat of freedom regardless of whose feet fill them. What must go unspoken in the article is that the flexing of U.S. power in Central America, however covertly, was inextricable from the plight of the refugees; that the U.S. sanctuary movement represented an idealized "American" space of human rights–based hospitality, a sanctuary that not only offers protection but also mirrors the violence that constitutes it and, moreover, engenders the violence that necessitates the very call for sanctuary.

The well-publicized work of the movement thus sought to provide refuge for Central Americans fleeing war as well as to affirm the moral terms of the nation. As Cunningham notes in her important study of the U.S. Sanctuary movement, "like their right-wing counterparts," sanctuary church committees "tended to view state as a moral entity that produced policies with moral implications."[54] Crittenden's account of sanctuary workers as interchangeable with state authority is telling: in this contest over who has the authority to categorize individuals into deserving political refugees or undeserving economic migrants, the Sanctuary movement workers came to act as informal gatekeepers that relied on a set of categories strikingly similar to those of the state, if not the Border Patrol.

Sanctuary workers, in testing the boundaries of citizenship and seeking to enlarge it with the authority to welcome non-nationals into the nation, were literally put on trial by the state. And it was when the INS sought to prosecute movement workers for human smuggling—when their status as free citizens was threatened by the state's charge of committing an economic crime of smuggling "economic migrants" rather than a moral act of providing sanctuary to "political refugees"—that the ideological contradictions within the Sanctuary movement became irrepressible, and the rhetoric of hospitality to strangers, of the global family, and so on, gave way to an increasingly bureaucratized system that stressed the legality of their work from the perspective of international and even national law. The workers continued to hold meetings to review underground refugee applications but adopted United Nations High Commission on Refugees (UNHCR) criteria and made a list of additional stipulations to use for determining the refugee status of applicants, many of whom were denied assistance by movement workers. Derrida reminds us that hospitality requires a host who claims the authority to welcome the stranger, or guest, into the home or the country and who, at some level, controls the terms of hospitality and thus the condition of the guest.[55] If the ideal of hospitality—as an unconditional welcoming of the stranger as guest, an open invitation to cross the threshold, free from the host's control of the situation and judgment as to who is deserving or undeserving of hospitality—is impossible to realize in the world, then the kind of hospitality that is possible all too readily reproduces its opposite condition. The Sanctuary movement workers claimed the authority to establish categories of refugee personhood and then to manage individuals into those categories. In the effort to challenge the state, then, the Sanctuary movement came to impersonate it.

Historical sanctuary work publicly and actively contested U.S. state power, regularly dealt with and provoked the INS, and sought to challenge the conservative Christian alliance with President Reagan and the state in favor of the vision of a *"global* church" whose values and actions "surpassed the boundaries of nationalism."[56] If historical sanctuary workers and journalists took an opportunity to make transnational identification and organization but used that opportunity to reaffirm national identification and U.S. exceptionalism, Jones imagines a way to reenvision what has been a nationalist story of statelessness in the Americas as an antinationalist story of decolonization, of helping counter or evade the everyday oppressions structured by modes of governmentality, which in this case refers to a logic of governance that makes use of the state and its system for delimiting and producing legal persons as citizen or alien.[57] *Mosquito* highlights the effective exclusion of unauthorized persons from the category of the human by depicting the noncitizen seekers of refuge as hunted prey. Mosquito's involvement with the sanctuary movement begins when she finds a stranger—a pregnant woman named Maria "Barriga" Rodriguez—hiding in her truck. Playing on the multiple meanings of the words *"coyote"* and *"shape-shifter,"* Mosquito describes a pregnant woman "darting her head around" and "scurry[ing] back into the back of the truck." Mosquito hears "this commotion in the back of my truck. Sounded like a coyote or something, or maybe one of them prairie foxes. I think they call them prairie foxes, don't ya?" Mosquito plays on the term *coyote* as wild animal, as mythic spirit, animal self-protection, both animals and humans that play at camouflaging or changing color for protection or survival, and also for love, as when Mosquito thinks about how animals change colors at Marineland during their mating ritual (*Mosquito* 21). Mosquito peers into her truck with the flashlight and a stun gun and spots a pair of sandaled women's feet, reminding her of the shape-shifting "nayatls" her Chicana friend Delgadina told her about, "humans that can really change theyselves into coyotes and coyotes that can change theyselves into humans too" (23). Evoking the animal coyote, Maria is also apparently her own *coyote*, or human smuggler.

Jones complicates the figuration of unauthorized refugee characters by the law as at once "unnatural," alien and threatening to the body politic, and all *too* natural, abjected by the border system that, as Mary Pat Brady argues, serves as "a proving ground not simply for citizenship but for humanness as well."[58] Maria "Barriga" Rodríguez, from Chiapas, Mexico, gets figured as a woman whose border crossing transforms her from human subject to nonhuman prey even as she insists on her human fugitivity by repeating to Mosquito the only word she knows in English: "sanctuary." Moreover, her nickname, "Barriga," links her to the story of Palmares within the Barriga mountains, when the border collapse (rather than a crossing) between sanctuary and slave law leaves Almeyda and other survivors to a condition of human fugitivity equivalent to hunted prey.

By depicting unauthorized border crossers as nonhuman animals, Jones affirms the function of the border as abjection machine only to complicate the border's power over the human: as Mosquito ventures, flashlight still in hand, on first encountering Maria in the truck, "Don't look like no coyote feet, I says out loud, signifying, you know . . . I know you ain't no prairie fox. And you shore ain't no chameleon" (24). Maria importantly also evokes the trickster figure, able to move between human and nonhuman forms to evade the punitive violence of the law, thus affirming the creative dimensions of extralegal personhood. Maria seems reduced to a figure of social and civil death, the nonhuman animal, even as her figurative reduction to the nonhuman becomes a way to incorporate her within literary traditions of the trickster figure, as one who, without political power or recognition, nonetheless manages to slip through and manipulate the logics of power.

Whereas Mosquito narrates the effect of Maria's border crossing as if it transforms Maria's behavior and appearance into that of hunted, nonhuman prey, she later tells the story of Maria's cousin's detention in a "Middle America" jail to show how the cousin's imprisonment underscores the collapsed distinction between the legal identities of the refugee and the fugitive. With the citizens of "Middle America" unable to determine her proper classification after asking for her papers, and after hearing an accent they struggled to identify, Maria's cousin falls into an ambiguous zone of criminality for which the local residents have no proper place of containment.

> The reason Maria's cousin got throwed in jail was because they didn't have no detention camps in Middle America. . . . Plus, they didn't know what kinda illegal she was. They thought she mighta been Cuban, and the State Department policy then was that Cubans was supposed to be processed into America, and they had to send for somebody from one of them states that was usedta dealing with illegal aliens, and to even import an immigration lawyer, 'cause there weren't any in Middle America that knew anything about the immigration laws. . . . Well, she was an illegal alien, so they couldn't just let her go free. Somebody suggested that they put her in the women's wing of the state asylum. That didn't seem the thing to do 'cause she seemed pretty sane. They might be crazy peoples in the state asylum but they was all documented citizens. They did have a Texan who thought he belonged to the Republic of Texas and was a free and sovereign citizen, but even he were a documented citizen and a United States American even if he thought hisself a Texan. . . . But it was illegal to be an undocumented citizen, so one of the documented citizens, one of the true Americans, suggested that she be put in jail till somebody could adjudicate what to do with her. So they put her in jail and forgot about her. (345–46)

Challenging the language of alienation and criminality, Mosquito calls the cousin an "undocumented citizen" (346). But, as even the Texan experiences, it is the document—and not the human form or political will—that is the necessary condition for one's classification in the taxonomy of legal personhood. The prison, the insane asylum, and the detention camp all become synonymous sites for suspending the human who contests his or her relation to a given legal identity, in a state of indefinite detention: but it is ultimately the cousin's status as "illegal" that has her put in jail rather than in the asylum. Even as the state reserves the power to produce legal national identities and define modes of governmentality, it is left to the documented citizens of "Middle America" to recognize the "illegal" in the name of the law, with their attendant fear, loathing, and plain confusion about whom the law recognizes as "illegal." Moreover, the locals figure the cousin's detention as a protective sanctuary against the truly punitive site of detention, Mexico itself: as Mosquito tells it, the local officer and his cohort claim "how rather than being jailed against her will she willingly went to jail[,] . . . rather than return to her poor old can't drink the water you better bring bottled Mexico with all them wild Mexican bandits, drug smugglers, and corrupt police and government officials. Control the border! . . . The Rio Grande is shallow only four feet deep there's too many Mexicans crossing over they must think it's the Jordan!" (353). Here, Jones clearly evokes the violence of sanctuary in the detention of the "undocumented human" while linking it to the history of the enslaved humans who crossed the Ohio River, into a fugitive form of freedom.

While Maria's cousin was jailed for being some kind of "illegal," it is her detention itself that may be illegal but ultimately not punishable, underscoring the association of citizenship with legality when confronted with the presumed criminality of the alien or refugee. Maria's cousin is rescued by an "expert immigration guerrilla-lawyer" who inexplicably appears "to prove that Maria's cousin's arrest was illegal. That even though she was an alien and stranger in a strange land among strange people dressed in strange clothes she still had certain inalienable human rights. She couldn't just be kept in jail and forgotten about 'cause the citizenry didn't have a clue" (347). While the lawyer, Linda Chong, uses the language of human rights to scare the locals into releasing Maria's cousin, the locals have the authority of the state behind them: to Mosquito's outrage ("I thought Middle America would be put on trial for their inhumanity and crimes against the humanity of Maria's cousin"), the lawyer cannot actually prove any crime had been committed against the cousin (347). As an immigration guerrilla lawyer, Linda Chong is at once an interpreter of the law and an exile from it. While she "tried every legality to get copies of the documents to prove that they had illegally kept Maria's cousin," it "seemed that the documents on the arrest of this undocumented human had disappeared" (347). The lawyer cannot access the closed archives of indefinite detention and immigration *practice*, even as she has mastered the archive of immigration law.

Maria's initial plea for sanctuary eventually leads Mosquito to Father Ray, an eventual love interest who persuades Mosquito to participate in the not-mainstream sanctuary movement—what, for her, becomes a chance to respond to the abjection machine of the state border, which reads her own U.S.-born body as alien and thus always potentially criminal. She sees sanctuary work as a way to be "thumbing my nose at them . . . border patrol sons of bitches" who are always "harassing me and shit" (239, 238). Mosquito frequently turns the distinction between citizen and foreigner into an unsolvable national question of who is a U.S. citizen and who a "sojourner."[59] Mosquito complains repeatedly of the chain of misrecognitions of people of color, as a result of the image of U.S. citizens as "white." The Border Patrol agents sometimes think Mosquito is Mexican and sometimes a smuggler, and later, when Ray introduces her to not-mainstream sanctuary workers, one of them mistakes her for a refugee. The misrecognition goes all around: Mosquito, too, mistakes an Asian American citizen for a foreigner. In refusing to delimit the terms, conditions, and identities of the deserving refugee, the not-mainstream sanctuary movement is delinked from any one historical or political context, suggesting that seeking refuge is figuratively to participate in the process of decolonization: "[We] help all sorts of people. The Mexicans, for sure. But also Haitians, political refugees of all sorts. Conscientious objectors even. Not just the Third World. Well, I guess anyone who needs to be a refugee sorta becomes part of the Third World, you know" (225). Ray's "group," as Mosquito calls it, helps anyone seeking to free himself or herself from oppressive ideologies and practices. The not-mainstream movement also helps redefine the U.S. Southwest as part of the hemispheric history of decolonization in and beyond the Americas, as Carrie Tirado Bramen and Ifeoma Nwankwo note.[60] Ray is a conductor within a fictionalized composite of multiple historical networks more inclusive, radical, and transnational in their purpose to provide sanctuary to conscientious objectors, Salvadoran refugees, and disenfranchised people in need of legal advice or psychological healing of the wound caused by their status as undocumented, as much as the "guerrilla personality" types looking for a movement (426).[61]

Mosquito, initially wary of Father Ray's sanctuary movement, assumes it is like the mainstream movement of television documentaries, a movement of white religious people helping Mexicans (thus playing on the dynamics of misrecognition, as the historical Sanctuary movement gave sanctuary to Central Americans crossing the U.S.-Mexico border) (63). Father Ray is her first big surprise—"'cause I'm expecting a white priest and this a African-American priest. Leastwise on television when they tells you about the Sanctuary movement, they's always some white priest" (74). Mosquito alludes to the dominant historical narratives of the Sanctuary movement, which drew parallels to the Underground Railroad for the purpose of heroizing the participants but minimized the role of people of color within both movements. In contrast to the historical Sanctuary movement, Jones's novel depicts a "not-mainstream" sanctuary movement as an underground, radicalized network largely of people of color for whom sanctuary work involves the transport, legal assistance, and harboring of refugees as part of an enigmatic and non-centralized, indefinable, loosely collective quest for full decolonization of people in the Americas. The not-mainstream movement rejects the authority to establish or assign legal identities to those fugitives who call for sanctuary; in fact, the not-mainstream movement rejects the values and principles of authority even when it uses them as masquerades. The movement is profoundly disorganized, without hierarchy or refugee application reviews. It depends on much being undeclared: its members use false names even when they know each other (outside the movement) by their real names, and its mission is not centralized or authorized by representatives. The "not-mainstream" sanctuary thrives on its invisibility to both state power and "mainstream" discourse, as it is composed of politically marginalized people of color who have learned to use the effects of their enduring exclusion from the nation, a condition portrayed by Jones when Mosquito and other people of color are more likely to be confused with the refugees themselves and ignored altogether by the national press, to form a "guerrilla personality." The "guerrilla personality" wages its "little wars" against the legal personality through tactics of indirection, secrecy, and mobility—tactics of the less powerful who use nonrecognition by the state to their advantage.[62]

Ray's veiled remark to Mosquito, that "there are certain ways that we're known to each other," evokes the underground or coded language of the antebellum Underground Railroad. The not-mainstream movement, which (like the mainstream movement) claims this legacy, leads Mosquito to withhold information that she should not share to "y'all," her readers: "y'all gots to remember that I can't tell y'all everything for security purposes" (551). Mosquito must keep some things secret from even her longtime best friend, nicknamed Monkey Bread, and even in a "coded letter" addressed to her. Responding to Monkey Bread's request that she describe her truck, Mosquito writes, "They is security reasons that I can't describe my truck. I can't tell you the reason for even the reasons for they being security reason is a security reason" (561). Mosquito freely parodies the discourse of national and corporate security, which leads to a receding line of unspoken reasons in the name of "security," a euphemistic codeword for secrecy, bolstered by "reason," which falsely legitimates the need for secrecy. The parodic register at once highlights the different politics of announced secrecy, its necessity and its teasing effect. The not-mainstream movement is only declared to one's own self, which is part of an open and undisclosed collectivity, its workers linked to each other through undeclared affinities. Sanctuary, like the textuality of historically marginalized cultural traditions, must be open-ended, both centric and eccentric. Whereas Agamben collapses the threshold into a zone of indistinction, Jones imagines a tension between the inside and the outside that gives the threshold its structural integrity and also marks it as a site of play between the two sides of the metaphorical doorframe.

Ray does draw on the names and publications of the mainstream movement, as when he tells Mosquito, "We're sort of like a modern Underground Railroad. In fact, there's a book I'll let you read called *Sanctuary as Metaphor: The New Underground Railroad*. I'm not the mainstream Sanctuary movement, though" (225). Ray's book reference plays on the title of *Sanctuary: The New Underground Railroad*, published in 1986 by two prominent, radical, Chicago-based sanctuary workers in the midst of the movement, Renny Golden and Michael McConnell.[63] Ray reveals his complete identification with the not-mainstream movement by insisting that he is "not" the mainstream one. Ironically, Jones takes several lines directly from the mainstream book and gives them to Father Ray, and it becomes impossible to determine precisely how the not-mainstream movement operates differently or independently of the mainstream one, since it uses their tools, publications, and rhetoric. As with the archive that Mosquito keeps for the Daughters of Nzingha spiritual organization—an archive that comprises Jones's novel—Ray includes such texts without the authoritative categorizing procedures that organize them. He also reclaims the legacy of the Underground Railroad, which mainstream Sanctuary movement activists such as Golden and McConnell historically appropriated as their common heritage. The first half of the book's title, *Sanctuary as Metaphor,* gently mocks the historical Sanctuary movement's rhetoric while describing Mosquito's own narrative riffs, which make extended use of the metaphorical reserves of "sanctuary" through her various digressions and speculations. *Sanctuary as Metaphor: The New Underground Railroad* comments on the analogical reasoning according to which sanctuary workers were to refugees what conductors were to slaves—a promise of freedom based on the alliance of citizen and noncitizen to force the United States to live up to its true ideals of human equality and freedom. The title also makes plain the uses of metaphor, reminding us that the Underground Railroad itself is a code name for the flexible network of temporary hiding places for runaway slaves fleeing the South—the railroad having been run by metaphorical language and coded talk as much as anything else.

Jones claims the "new Underground Railroad" for the not-mainstream movement and, in the process, implicitly critiques its prevailing historical narrative. Like the historical Sanctuary movement, the real Underground Railroad was retrospectively celebrated and adopted as part of the national story of courage and morality: as the historian Charles L.

Blockson notes of the antebellum movement, "the most assiduous organizers of networks to freedom were black freemen. . . . They organized
their own network quietly and well," in contrast to the "throng of lectur-
ers" who claimed the public sphere as the center of the struggle.[64] Insofar
as the law operates within the public sphere, secrecy is a survival tactic of
both the fugitive slave and the provider of refuge, who in the act of providing refuge also becomes fugitive. In contrast to the historical sanctuary workers who publicly claimed their rights as citizens and Christians
to provide sanctuary, Mosquito notes, "my mama didn't raise the sorta
fool that would tell y'all the whole story, 'cause that would be like if I was
a fugitive during the time of the old Underground Railroad I got myself
free, then I comes telling everybody all the secrets. I got to defend the
rights and freedoms of them that ain't got they freedom yet" (601). Mosquito tells us part of the story and part of the reason for not declaring the
rest. Her declaration contrasts with the historical Presbyterian minister
John Fife, who ignited the Sanctuary movement by "declaring sanctuary
for undocumented refugees" as a way to "get the story out to the American people."[65] Ray further distinguishes the not-mainstream movement
and explains the reason for stories and people to remain undeclared:
"The mainstream Sanctuary thinks that the more they're known the
safer they are. That's why most sanctuaries declare themselves. We're
more like what they'd call the Nicodemuses of the movement," by which
Ray means that they don't declare themselves but do find ways of becoming known to each other (307).[66]

The not-mainstream movement relies on secrecy rather than visibility,
fugitivity rather than legality, and digression rather than directedness.
The digressive, riffing narrative style of the novel structures Mosquito's
own reading of the politics and aesthetics of sanctuary. Mosquito opens
the novel by telling a story the way anyone might begin: "I was on one
of them little border roads in South Texas" when—except that Mosquito
doesn't say when; instead, she digresses on the geographic, financial, and
colonialist landmarks of the Southwest, "a landscape full of power." Her
apparently random break in the narration to read "me some of my mail"
is merely a shift in registers, as her mail reviews Southwest borderlands
politics and the politics of citizenship, statelessness, sanctuary, and freedom. As a rarity in the trucking world, an African American woman
trucker receives unlikely junk mail: there are the Texans who declare
their independence from "imperial Mexico" and the "corporate United
States" and try to set up their fictional Texas as a refuge from history.
There is the union flyer she accepts that says "una union fuerte incluye a
todos," even though the man who hands out flyers "knows that I'm not

recruitable." And there are the institutional sanctuaries—Marineland, where Mosquito focuses on the glass that protects and holds back the marine life ("Got to be a mighty powerful glass to hold back the ocean like that"), and the "new Nature Sanctuary" Mosquito and Delgadina visit, a sanctuary for desert plants sponsored by a wealthy "gringo" couple appropriately named Powers and visited by tourists who come to visit a staged version of authenticity (Mosquito and Delgadina overhear a Dick-and-Jane-type couple chatting, "everything they have here is natural, Dickey, no artificial lakes like that other sanctuary," and comparing the food and souvenirs at the "Mexican village," the "Zulu village," and so on (46–47).[67] Such natural and cultural sanctuaries of staged authenticity, in short, leave Mosquito skeptical. These are ideologies for preserving living and aesthetic forms as things, sanctuaries in the sense of confinement or embalming. Mosquito's long list of sanctuaries exhausts the definitions of "sanctuary" as some thing or some place in order to suggest that "sanctuary" is not a place you can visit.

To counter the border system and the legal system that would produce abject "aliens," Mosquito's work for Ray's sanctuary movement involves her use of doubletalk, "coded" and "real" (Mosquito's distinction). Coded epistolary writings in particular come to make Mosquito's "love of language"—along with the love of her truck—central to her involvement in the sanctuary movement. It also joins her sanctuary work to her obligations to the Daughters of Nzingha archives. Mosquito is mindful of her obligations to the movement as to what to narrate, to put into the Daughters' archives, and what to "tell" her readers she is withholding. An expert in signifying, including digressing, her use of code becomes extensive as her involvement with the sanctuary movement grows. She learns to be a "hidden agenda conspiracy specialist" (552–56, 600), and as part of her training she practices writing and reading "coded letters," which are also "real" letters in ordinary, meaningful English. These codes use "almost any book as a official code manual . . . They say that it is okay for me to tell y'all this, unless they is countries that starts banning every book and newspapers . . . but we can even make official books and newspapers subversive" (560). Mosquito, like Ray, appropriates mainstream discourse, suggesting that encoding and decoding refers more to a way of reading or listening, deconstructing, and telling unintended stories through "official books and newspapers" than to an invented system of symbols and correspondences used to communicate secret messages.

In Mosquito's secret code reading of "official" documents in her sanctuary work, Jones's novel establishes a relationship to the public sphere that challenges the traditional social function of the novel as a narrative genre that represents the public sphere and, in doing so, ratifies and regulates the relationship of the individual to the state in the cultivation of citizenship—and thus, an idealized participation in rational debate and consensus in the making of law and political order—as the height of human personality development. As Slaughter notes, the liberal public sphere "is not just a space that processes, regulates, and circulates stories and their generic narrative forms; it mediates between the realms of political governance and private life, fixing the terms of separation and interaction between the state's administrative institutions and the social world of the people."[68] Slaughter goes on to complicate human rights and democratic theories of the liberal public sphere as charged with the responsibility of "vigilating the state and its observance of human rights" by observing that the public sphere, while idealized as the space of human rights enjoyment and protection, is also "a primary site of human rights violation," a place of "discrimination, disadvantage, and vulnerability."[69]

Historically, Sanctuary movement workers participated in the public sphere as an act that was a "hallmark of citizenship—the highest form of the human personality's self-expression in traditional human rights discourse—that is exercised through storytelling and story-listening."[70] In testing the capacities of storytelling in the liberal public sphere to shape U.S. democratic and human rights norms, a proportion of the historical Sanctuary movement workers did not merely tell their own stories of civil disobedience; they asked Central American unauthorized refugees, and hence fugitive, to participate in the U.S. public sphere by telling their stories of political repression as a way to produce public awareness of the refugees as victims of human rights violations and, thus, refugees deserving of legal asylum. Yet legal status legitimating one's political membership in a society is a crucial condition of participation in the public sphere—and it was the refugees' classification as illegal aliens, rather than as legal refugees, that was in question.[71] This paradox was underscored by the need for refugees to literally hide their faces, usually with bandannas, when they told their stories in public. Their legal identities were as noncitizen fugitives, in contrast to the U.S. citizens of the movement, who could fully claim their place in the public sphere even as they publicly rejected U.S. immigration and asylum laws.

Jones's novel highlights the public sphere as a space of vulnerability and alienation for those not categorized as ideal citizens before the law. Mosquito's narration highlights this skepticism of the idealized space of the public sphere, which, she and Ray note, is claimed by the mainstream Sanctuary movement as a space for rational debate between citizens over the proper relationship between the state, the citizen, and the refugee. The not-mainstream movement's relation to the public sphere has been shaped by the historical violence of the law in its alienation of human persons, from slave to citizen, from the constitution of the nation. Far from presuming an idealized, ahistorical space of rationality and communicative speech acts among citizens, the not-mainstream workers of the novel work through indirection, code, secrecy, and the repurposing of official documents.

Mosquito's strategically digressive (as in digressing from the mainstream) narration is itself a gathering together of all the stories, including her own, that comprise an archive of stories for the semisecret Daughters of Nzingha, the spiritual and textual "cult," as Mosquito sometimes calls it, that consistently deflates or reverses every officious or mystical aspect they cultivate. The Daughters' organizational structure, its newsletters edited by Monkey Bread, and Monkey Bread's aesthetic theories (as published in the newsletters)—as well as the archive itself, which includes everything Mosquito narrates in the novel and beyond—all challenge the representation of the public sphere in both political theory and literary form. The public sphere and the novel, in its traditional social function, ratify each other: together, they plot and naturalize a certain story of the development of the human personality as one whose potential is realized in the idealized rights-and-duties-bearing citizen, who is fully incorporated into the public sphere, as part of "the people" that constitute the liberal state. Those excluded from the "community of speech" are not only exiled from the polity but also effectively refused recognition as persons. They are outcasts, conventionally written out of those novels that plot a story of an individual's social incorporation into the public sphere and thus the state.[72] Rather than focus on this exclusion from the conventional story of an individual's incorporation into the public sphere, Jones turns the convention of incorporation on its head: the novel plots a story of the public sphere's incorporation into the individual, one who simultaneously refuses her full incorporation into the state. Here, Jones brilliantly takes a detour around the sharp divide between debates over whether critics ought to theorize the form of the archive or whether they ought to recuperate the actual stories and voices of the enslaved. *Mosquito* reconceptualizes the archive as a decolonial project that recovers not the history of slavery but rather the highly self-reflexive narratives of the African diaspora. Mosquito's auditory memory is crucial to this form of the archive. Her auditory memory works through Mosquito's body and memory, which incorporates but does not alter other voices and languages, and there is no single ideological position put forth by all the stories in the narrative. Mosquito's inclusive drive is thus a variation on the dialogic, which Mikhail Bakhtin suggests is an aspect of the public sphere and which Mae Gwendolyn Henderson defines as the "ability to speak in the multiple languages of public discourse."[73]

The not-mainstream sanctuary movement and the Daughters of Nzingha are engaged in a small war with the logics of legal personhood, which sanction the public sphere and underwrite the novel's conventional representation of liberal democratic norms. *Mosquito's* dialogic narrative structure—interspersed as it is with other characters' letters, stories, and voices, not to mention newsletters and junk mail, which are sometimes presented typographically to interrupt Mosquito's narration, as if included in a literal archive of papers—constructs a heterogeneous image of public life vastly different from Habermas's idealized space of rational debate and consensus making. The public, as represented in the novel's version of the archive, reveals itself to be formed by histories of legal personhood, including the history of church sanctuary, that have been underwritten by a legacy of oppressive logics; moreover, the public sphere of the novel seems unaware of those it has effectively excluded, even as those same figures of exclusion actively but covertly shadow the public sphere in the spirit of what Mosquito cryptically calls "the revolution." The Daughters of Nzingha archive also works against the meanings of sanctuary as a bounded place and as an exceptional space that mirrors the violence of the law from which it seemingly provides refuge. It is Mosquito's work as keeper of the archives, or minder of the word, that makes the novel itself a kind of textual sanctuary that is also living, mobile, and necessarily incomplete, thus linking the not-mainstream sanctuary movement with the work of keeping archives as intimately related practices of a decolonial aesthetics. Rather than ratify the public sphere and the logics of incorporation that Slaughter finds in the traditional social function of the novel no less than of international human rights discourse, Jones's novel constructs the images of sanctuary and archive that challenge the traditionally institutional, discursive functions of both.

Rooted in fourteenth-century European Christian definitions of the church as a sacred place, "sanctuary" may refer broadly to any place, understood by law or established custom, to provide immunity from the law to fugitives who enter it. In the late nineteenth century, its usage was extended to refer to any area of land that protects and encourages the growth of wild animals or plants. The conventional meaning of sanctuary is that space which protects life as an exception to established rules or practice (whether, for example, a church provides sanctuary for a fugitive or an endangered species is protected from an otherwise hostile ecosystem). It is the archive that traditionally houses, represents, and protects those established rules or practices. Sanctuary, in this sense, becomes the exception to the laws of the traditional archive, even as both sanctuary and archive represent spaces of protection for that which is included.

Jones's concept of the archive may be usefully contrasted to that of Foucault and of Derrida. Foucault conceives of the archive in its discursive, institutional function; using the language of law and governance, the archive represents the "law of what can be said, the system that governs the appearance of statements as unique events."[74] Derrida stresses the archive as a juridical and ontological concept, tracing the etymology of *archive*, which derives from the Greek *arkheion*, "initially a house, domicile, an address, the residence of the superior magistrates, the *archons*, those who commanded."[75] The *archons*, as "citizens who thus held and signified political power," also held the authority "to make or to represent the law."

> The archons are first of all the documents' guardians. They do not only ensure the physical security of what is deposited and of the substrate. They are also accorded the hermeneutic right and competence. They have the power to interpret the archives. Entrusted to such archons, these documents in effect state the law: they recall the law and call on or impose the law.[76]

Such a concept of the archive also suggests that the *archons* possess the authority to "recall" the law by acting beyond its bounds but with its sanction nonetheless—as do the officers who jail Maria's cousin illegally but who also, as agents of the law with the power to make official documents disappear, are effectively empowered to delimit legality and illegality and to erase their own illegality from the archive. As archive keepers working on a very different principle from that of Middle America, Mosquito and the Daughters of Nzingha refuse the right to make, call on, or impose the law (they are not the *archons*, and their archive does not house the official documents of the law). Moreover, they construct an archive that deflates the conventional institutional, discursive, and juridical principles of the archive by caring for its junked stories, the subjects and stories excluded from official archives, even as the Daughters of Nzingha archive indiscriminately incorporates and appropriates the official documents that construct a certain image of the liberal public sphere. The Daughters of Nzingha archive is a kind of fugitive counterpart to the archive as law, and its archive keepers act as an extralegal counterpart to "those who command." What Derrida, in his encounter with the Freudian archive, names "archive fever"—"the desire and the disorder of the archive," the obsessive return to, and forgetting of, origins, the scene of writing, the inscription or trace left where memory breaks down—is noticeably absent in the novel.[77] Mosquito simply remembers without forgetting, and her archive keeping is capacious, indiscriminate, and yet insistent on the decolonizing function of providing refuge for stories in the hopes of keeping them and their authors "whole."

Consisting of the Daughters of Nzingha archive, *Mosquito* represents Jones's vision of the "decolonized novel." Her 1994 essay, "From *The Quest for Wholeness*: Re-Imagining the African-American Novel: An Essay on Third World Aesthetics," tells the story of how the novel became decolonized from the novel's point of view. Making literal the claim by Henry James that "[a] novel is a living thing, all one and continuous," the novel asserts itself as a figure for thinking human personhood: "I am not your idea of the 'well-made Jamesian novel.' I am the very idea of being human in a complex world, or complex universe" (510). The "decolonized novel" searches for multiple relations of language and culture and resists enclosing itself or those multiple relations within a singularizing national tradition, identity, or a state authority. The novel is not a sanctuary and does not seek out ostensibly protective enclosures of status or homogeneous community. It does not search for preservation, to maintain itself in an unchanged condition, so much as it seeks survival in forming connections with other elements without asserting control over them. A tricky form of wholeness for literary art to aspire to, a relational rather than a bounded wholeness (as was the self-mutilated woman from *Song for Anninho*), something between compositional boundaries and the spirit of potentially infinite associations with "everything." Jones envisions the decolonized novel as an "Afrocentric, Afro-eccentric" novel (510). This joke defines the Afrocentric novel as centered on the African diaspora even as it is, in an Afrocentric way, decentered, always aware of and engaged with what appears marginal or peripheral from any one perspective. The decolonized Afrocentric novel is eccentric, as it whimsically shifts away from its center, as well as ex-centric, as it moves beyond identifications based on a perceived center. The decolonized novel frustrates the distinction between inclusion and exclusion, and between figure and background, baldly declaring, "I take for my focus everything" (96). Jones's essay performs this inclusion of imaginative cultural forms through the unlikely pairing of the language of "third world" decolonization struggles with a sort of double-talk or playful deconstruction of her own claims. Take the title of the essay, for example: she embeds the claim for wholeness within a fragment. The essay reads as a complete piece and is not excerpted from a published work but is named a fragment in search of wholeness. That quest is invoked in the title of the larger work, but it appears contained, within the fragment. Jones claims eccentricity and centrality: for every claim or principle she asserts, she jokingly leaves an escape hatch.[78]

The story of how Mosquito gained her perfect auditory memory illustrates the decolonial aesthetic practice that organizes both sanctuary and archive in the novel. Mosquito—a.k.a. Nadine Sojourner—explains that, as a preschooler singing "Down by the Riverside" in church, she became the object of a verbal contest between her mother and Mizz Cajun, a root or conjure woman, over whether Mosquito would study war or the word/Word. As Mosquito says, "*I don't know if she say word with a small w or a large W*" (568; emphasis in original). Disrupting the murmured approval of the congregation over the song's key lines, "I'm gonna *lay down my sword and shield /Down by the riverside / Study war no more*," Mizz Cajun points her finger at Nadine and "reads" her as prophetic text.

> Now my mama she don't want Mizz Cajun to read me, and although she knows the power of Mizz Cajun from all the narratives in which Mizz Cajun is the force and power . . . she gets up to shield me from Mizz Cajun . . . but Mizz Cajun gives me my reading anyways. She says to me, Sojourner, I'm going to tell you who you was back in Africa . . . [when] you started singing that song, then I remembered who you is. You is the one of us warrior womens that usedta do battle back there in Africa when they was trying to bring us over here for slavery. I knowed you before the Middle Passage and I know you now . . . That's who you is. You is the warrior class. You don't take no shit. You is the warrior class. You don't take no shit. (566)

The root woman's strength derives from her practice of African spiritual and healing techniques; the "root" refers to multiple meanings relevant to Mosquito's story. The poet and critic Harryette Mullen notes that the root in ritual practice might "indicate the strength that comes of being rooted in a coherent culture and kinship structure," but the magic of the root might also lie in "the power of language to aid in visualization as a healing technique, or as a psychological tool for self-affirmation" (633). Mullen considers the root doctor's art as an art of "survival for slaves" who rely "upon their own visionary powers of imagination to 'make a way out of no way' and thus conjure a better future for their descendants" (633). Here, Mizz Cajun "reads" Mosquito by rooting her in a warrior culture and by implicitly identifying her kinship to Nzingha, the most well documented and legendary African queen of the eighteenth-century, romanticized by Angolan and African American nationalists in the 1960s and 1970s as a legendary "proto-nationalist" heroine who valiantly fought Portuguese colonization and slave trade.[79] Mizz Cajun asserts that Sojourner (Nadine) was "*a warrior women to keep us from slavery,*" from both white slavers and the Africans who were "*enslaving us ownselves.*" Mizz Cajun did not know "*they*" had even "*captured you . . . But they is going to come a day . . . when you is going to have to pick up your sword and shield and study war again*" (566; emphasis in original).

Mizz Cajun claims Nadine as a warrior. But Nadine's birth mother claims her for studying the word/Word. Verbal sparring ensues: When Nadine's (real) mama says that "*Words is mightier than the sword,*" Mizz Cajun responds, "*Only when you controls the medium and the message.*" But then Nadine's mama one-ups her, "*When you takes the s off the beginning of sword and puts it at the end you's got words*" (567). A hush falls on the congregation as they wait to hear Mizz Cajun's response. Mizz Cajun, laughing, then declares her judgment on Mosquito: "*If she is going to have to mind de word she is going to have to remember all of dem dat she hears*" (568; emphasis in original). Mizz Cajun then turns and turns, like a whirling dervish (or a trope), as she transforms herself "into all the different colored peoples" of the world. By turning, she performs revolutions, returning to herself even as she fleetingly embodies all the colors of personhood within her person. The conjure woman's name, "Cajun," also alludes to Arcadia, figured as an idyllic place and refuge. In becoming all colors of human, Mizz Cajun gives flesh to the political liberation movements that she calls into being through her words. As she spins, Mizz Cajun chants the lines, "*Peaceable she'll be / Until the words come forth / Enough is Enough / Then she'll do her warrior stuff*" (568). It was then that, as Mosquito tells us, "all over the world the colored peoples started new freedom movements." Mizz Cajun, in conjuring Mosquito as "a minder of the word," simultaneously inaugurates the mid-twentieth-century wave of decolonization and civil rights movements: Mosquito's gift for remembering all the words she hears and the world's decolonization are twins birthed by the same cultural mothers. Mosquito's gift becomes the origin story for the novel, itself part of a potentially infinite archive that includes anything Mosquito hears. Mosquito thus reconceptualizes the archive from its legal and colonialist principles of collection to a newly begun, living body of stories collected by the processual art of listening as part of her prosaic (in both senses of the word) life. Rejecting sanctuary as a closed, anomalous space of protection from a fundamentally unjust legal system, the two mothers also link the call for sanctuary to hemispheric and transnational movements for decolonization. "The plea for Canaan has marked African American letters since its earliest inscriptions, shaping the character of African American intellectual thought and underwriting critiques of U.S. democracy, governance practices, legal culture, and imperialism," notes Waligora-Davis; moreover, "This cry for sanctuary bound U.S. race relations to larger international projects."[80] Mosquito's story of her hidden talent at once participates in and parodies the African American ex-slave narrative tradition of secular literacy as a tool for political empowerment and the African American tradition of "visionary literacy," in which literacy was acquired by "supernatural means" and served as the sign of a miraculous gift to a spiritual visionary. Stories of visionary literacy had the effect of figuring the Bible as the sacred text and God as directly bestowing a person with the power to read its signs.[81]

The novel shifts between the mid-twentieth-century decolonization movements to the decolonial project of the Zapatistas in the neoliberal era. Mizz Cajun's chant, "enough is enough," anticipates the rallying cry of the Zapatistas and their early use of electronic media to introduce themselves to the world and participate in the spirit of radical liberation movements around the world. "Enough is enough" alludes to "Ya Basta!" The Zapatistas "went public" with their struggle in Chiapas, Mexico, upon the signing of the North American Free Trade Agreement in 1994. The Zapatista Army of National Liberation, or Ejército Zapatista de Liberación Nacional (EZLN), has operated on militant, political, economic, and cultural fronts to challenge the Mexican state's neoliberal and anti-indigenous politics. The play on sword and word also echoes the Zapatista slogan, "Our word is our weapon," from the movement's principal authorial persona, Subcomandante Marcos.[82] Mizz Cajun's invocation highlights the movement's interrelated aspects of textual creativity and political resistance to regimes of racialized personhood and economic exploitation, in which the very act of indigenous people marching to the capital to claim the right of legal personhood—to have a public voice—was a spectacular political act. Moreover, the Zapatista movement has become distinctive in its radical human rights vision of decolonization, which involves delinking sovereign states from the absolute power to recognize or deny legal personhood, calling for states to recognize the full personhood not only of indigenous peoples but also of all humans, regardless of nationality and citizenship status; encouraging peoples to form transnational networks and relationships that do not depend on national allegiances; and showing that anticolonial struggles need not demand a new nationalism. Mizz Cajun's invocation also seems to anticipate Maria's encounter with Mosquito: from Chiapas, making dolls, and repeatedly crossing the U.S.-Mexico border, Maria is obliquely coded as a Zapatista who seeks sanctuary from Mosquito. Mosquito's encounter with Maria thus leads to Mosquito's literary and quotidian double roles in the purposefully disorderly "not-mainstream sanctuary movement": she decodes messages in creative ways, and she uses her truck to secretly transport refugees outside the systems of either the mainstream church Sanctuary movement or the state asylum proce- dure. In the novel the mainstream movement is there to divert attention from what its shadow is really doing, a shadow that nobody, including the mainstream movement, can really see—a shadow whose outlines are indistinct even to Mosquito because the "not-mainstream" movement is at some level ethically anarchic, not really an organized "movement" so much as an improvisational and digressive play of narrative movements. It is, as I mention above, a movement for those with a "guerrilla person- ality," those who use the law's failure to recognize their personhood to their advantage as they wage a "little war" against the prevailing logics of legal personhood.

Mizz Cajun's line that Mosquito will do "her warrior stuff" once "the words come forth" is hokey but also serious, in that it links her future work in the "not-mainstream sanctuary movement" with her "perfect auditory memory." From the day Mizz Cajun "read" her, Mosquito started "remembering every word and Monkey Bread started writing as her way of minding the word" (569–70). She remembers everything that she hears, all the stories her girlfriends tell her, all the stories she reads aloud, all the snippets of discourse she hears while channel surfing on TV: all of it goes into the Daughters of Nzingha archives, which is dedi- cated to including the potentially infinite stories of all survivors of what gets called the African Diaspora Holocaust but also anything else that comes to the ears of Mosquito and to the other, potentially innumerable authorial personae that act as caretakers for the archive. The archive, then, is a prosaic sanctuary that is as unfinalizable as the personae that make it up.

Mosquito's self-described "love of language" recovers the root mean- ings of the term *person* without abandoning its juridical-political mean- ing. Mosquito is a fugitive persona that performs the processual act of seeing what the law and its agents cannot see—or must not see, must deny—and that is the shadows cast by categories of legal personhood, the fungible border between those categories, and the indistinct con- tours of borderlands that throw into question the form, the shape, the definitiveness and definition of the concept of legal personhood upon which the citizen and the modern political order depend. Far from being a bounded self, Mosquito's "guerrilla personality" is relational, but deliberately vaguely so, without an original or central persona from which the others spin outward. Instead, the authorial personae are mutually constitutive of each other. Mosquito and Monkey Bread, for instance, have a complementary responsibility toward minding the word that could not exist without the other: the two girlfriends act as literary alter egos, as oral and written minders of the word in symbiotic relation to each other. Monkey Bread says in a printed interview with the Daughters in the newsletter, "Nadine is sorta like my own personal archives." The matter of alter egos gets more complicated if we move from the level of plot and character to the form (or rather, format) of the book and its note of authorship. The epigraph labels the book as part of the archives and constructs a genealogy between Jones's mother and grandmother that Jones identifies as her own in the "Author's Note" at the end of the book. It seems that Jones, Monkey Bread, and Mosquito are each "daughters" of spiritual mothers who charged them with keeping a protective archive that is also aware of a sense of possibility.

Mosquito further identifies herself with Nzingha, suggesting that she in some sense "is" her own "spiritual mother." Spending the night in the sanctuary of Nzingha's house, or temple, Mosquito has a dream encounter with Nzingha that is at once reverent and hilarious. Asleep in the Africa room, Mosquito sees an African-looking woman who says proudly, in the "accents of Africa America, of Caribbea, of Africa itself": "I salute you, Mosquito. I am Nzingha, warrior queen. Do not think of me as your leader. There are no leaders here. We are here to serve each other" (417). Mosquito, entertained but skeptical of such a stereotypical character, repeatedly asks Nzingha: "who are you?" Nzingha responds, "I am who you imagine me to be . . . Perhaps I'm your own exemplary self" (417). Nzingha believes everyone has "many selves," and one "was an exemplary self" among the other selves. Later, Mosquito thinks, "if it is her [Nzingha], it is in the form of my own thoughts talking to me. Nzingha? I ask. I am here, she says. We know who we are, don't we, Sojourner?" Mosquito transforms the story of a dream encounter within herself to become the story of her many selves.

Mosquito ends her dream story with the warning, "I should not tell you this. For some among you will think I'm a nut"(417). As Mosquito suggests, the Daughters deflate or reverse every officious or mystical aspect they cultivate. Self-parody may be their defining feature and their version of a decolonized aesthetics. The Not for Members Only membership card, for instance, is only valid if unsigned, and cards are valid even if you choose not to carry them—"that is, you do not have to be a card-carrying member . . . to be a Daughter of Nzingha" (413, 439). The newsletter is a hilarious, irreverent parody of societies, foundations, nongovernmental organizations, and social clubs. The humor and teasing between Monkey Bread and Mosquito, through personal letters and the Daughters newsletter, help constitute the imaginary ideal principles of the archive and of storytelling for the survivors of the African diaspora holocaust all over the world. The newsletter's officiousness is part of the joke and part of its serious philosophy, too, as are the multiple tricks about the Daughters and the authorship of the newsletter. Here the Daughters and the sanctuary movement share features that parody institutional spiritual and political organizations. At the same time, they extend the potential of spiritual and political organization to become a freed and freeing, imaginary ideal of a decolonial sense of collectivity that is also open and uncoerced. As Mosquito's involvement with the Daughters and Ray's sanctuary movement suggest, *Mosquito* is both a parody of preachification and a spiritual quest to decolonize the self and the story, not through bounded protection, but through an open relation to the world.[83]

Mosquito reads as representing the universe and the world of Jones. The real or implied author notes in the epigraph as well as in the "Author's Note" at the end of the book a complicated self-referential genealogy that mixes Jones's mother and grandmother with the characters and texts they have written. These latter texts come to figure as part of a matrilineal genealogy in the Daughters' archives, as stories that mostly have not been published by Jones's mother or grandmother, and they serve as part of the mysterious "Electra project" in the novel (see, e.g., 440–46), further suggesting complex bloodlines displaced onto literary lines that go on "keeping" the word. The Daughters newsletter make references to Jones's earlier texts but also to Jones's mother's texts, and her mother's mother's texts. Though *Mosquito* does not center on family or genealogy, the mother-daughter relationship is here invoked and transformed in multiple ways, especially through Jones's incorporation of her late mother's work into her own. Jones creates a whole literary network through letters, which figure mother-daughter friendships and woman-woman friendships. While it's true that Mosquito says little to nothing about her family, kinship is present in the metafictional aspect of the novel. After reading the newsletter, Mosquito comments, "To tell the truth, I think it's a confabulatory newsletter and that it's really a story written by Monkey Bread but in the form of a newsletter, and that she added that seemingly real letter to herself [accompanying the newsletter] to make it seem like it were a more realistic story when it is probably more surrealism than reality" (447). Both *Mosquito* and Jones are trickster storytellers, and it seems very likely that Mosquito "is" or makes the Daughters, and maybe Mosquito, Gayl Jones, and Monkey Bread are all alter egos of one another. Mosquito's evidence for her charge includes names in the newsletter that belong to characters she has played in plays; the reader may recognize names from Jones's earlier fiction, such as Joan Scribner Savage (*The Healing*) and news from Palmares (*Song for Anninho*). McDowell, who notes that Mosquito adds "Nzingha" to her signed name at the end of the narrative, asks "Who writes here—Gayl Jones? Her late mother Lucille Jones? Kate Hickman [character created by Lucille Jones]? Electra? Delgadina? Monkey Bread? They all come together to tell a polyphonic story, but it's impossible to tell them all apart."[84] Jones complicates the relationship between author, narrator, character, and reader through a potential series of characters who may be alter egos of the real and implied author and one another. The Daughters become an imagined transnational collectivity defined by self-parody and Afrocentric (and Afro-eccentric) friendships. Its decolonizing potential becomes apparent through a relationship between narrator and the world, in which the archives keeper is a narrator whose memory potentially stores the idea of all the stories in the world and at the same time submits to the ignorance of being merely one character in a universe full of stories that have their own unknowable sense of possibilities.[85] A narrator obsessed with metafictional concerns, she sometimes imagines her authorship of future novels; however, she frequently refers to herself as an archives keeper. If her narration comprises the Daughters' archives, the "archive" makes an open offer to keep and tell stories rather than to operate as a mechanism of law, an ordered repository, or a delimiter of discourse. The Daughters is multiple, made of authorial parts that may be fragmentary but not fragmented, for the multiple authorial alter egos of Mosquito, Monkey Bread, Gayl Jones, Lucille Jones, and so on, exist in relation to each other, part of a paradoxically open and unfinished wholeness in which each author shares in the making of the narrative.

A "history of violence compelled the longing for a safe space—a sanctuary—within the African American imaginary," notes Waligora-Davis, "yet sanctuary has so often proved tragically untenable—even dystopian."[86] Ultimately, Jones's work responds to the long history of the violence that has shaped the sanctuary no less than the archive, a violence inflicted by the law and its representatives on the meanings of human personhood. *Mosquito* transforms sanctuary from a paradoxical space of safety for, and violence against, the fugitive body, into an aesthetic, decolonial practice of keeping an archive of all the stories offered by all the survivors of what Jones names the "African Diaspora Holocaust" and their friends.[87] It is in keeping this archive—one that appropriates the institutional functions of the archive in order to challenge the authority of the law—that Jones demonstrates her vision of sanctuary as a textual, archival practice of openness that also refigures the African American body from the object of legal violence to a living, narrating, and polyphonic network of personae. Jones thus redefines the institutional, juridical, and discursive functions of both sanctuary and archive. The body and memory of the eponymous narrator of *Mosquito* becomes an open archive involved in sanctuary work, holding the stories of other personae whose voices are ignored by the law and whose bodies are rendered fugitive. *Song for Anninho* and *Mosquito* both advance a hemispheric vision of the histories of legal personhood that, following W. E. B. Du Bois's concept of a "semicolonial world," locates the black body at the interstices of democracy and empire, of citizenship and statelessness within and beyond the United States.[88] It is in this broader context that Jones outlines her project to elaborate an aesthetic practice capable of decolonizing the mind, to borrow a phrase from Ngugi wa Thiong'o. Sanctuary thus is transformed into a decolonial practice, as part of a broader project to "decolonize" both the novel and its author from political and cultural legacies of colonialism, as Jones outlines in her essay on Third World aesthetics. Such a project works to reveal the assumptions that structure the semicolonial legal personality and tries to heal the wounds created by the juridical logics of legal personhood by elaborating an extralegal, aesthetic model of personhood.

4 / Masking Fanon

*So maybe with Fanon a chance to start fresh. Start at the beginning—
paint Fanon on my face, wear the mask of him. Pretend he's real because I
am. Pretend I'm real because he is. Or was once. Behind a mask he might
become real again.*

—JOHN EDGAR WIDEMAN, *FANON*

John Edgar Wideman's 2008 novel, *Fanon*, finds its genesis, according to
Wideman's self-named writer-narrator John, in a remembered image of
Frantz Fanon's face under erasure.

> I encountered your stenciled, spray-painted image, an image like
> my project, almost effaced, so I didn't recognize you until two days
> after you popped up in the middle of nowhere, a field where cows
> grazed near the beach.[1]

A fugitive image, Fanon's face surprises John as all the more present for
being barely there. Fanon's image is spray-painted on the "concrete mini-
bunker" of an energy company supplying electricity to the tourist section of Martinique, a former colony and now an overseas department of
France (4). It was from this island that the young Fanon secretly fled, early
in 1943, eager to escape the pro-Vichy government of Admiral Georges
Robert and fight against fascism, only to be repatriated a few weeks later
to newly pro-Gaullist Martinique. Fanon fled the island again in 1944,
this time successfully enlisting in a colonial unit of the Free French
army that trained in Morocco and Algeria before landing in southern
France—an experience that would leave him embittered by the hypocrisy of French humanism and would eventually lead to his radically anticolonial, antiracist humanist thought and work. The image of Fanon's
face in Martinique, then, suggests his figurative return to the island as an
icon of radical decolonization. Yet spray-painted by an unknown graffiti
artist within a hidden locus of power of the neocolonial tourist economy,

Fanon's image, like his legacy, is at once faced and effaced. The image has as its apparent audience only grazing cows and the occasional wandering tourist, albeit one who has been chasing Fanon's spirit for decades.

John's belated recognition of Fanon amplifies his own distance from the revolutionary spirit that had inspired him since his youth in the 1960s: far from the position of the radical anticolonial visionary, John finds himself in tropical Martinique as a melancholy African American in the uneasy position of the privileged U.S. tourist, accompanied by his white French lover, Chantal, for a travel writing assignment for *National Geographic*.[2] In Wideman's first version of this encounter, told in *The Island: Martinique* (2003), his writer-narrator persona Paul repeatedly fails to recognize "this somehow familiar face staring back at us."[3] Paul betrays a complicated desire to recognize and disavow, to look to and look away from the face of Fanon: "Could the face be there and not there. One of the island's fabled ghosts playing us. If we stopped looking, if we blinked, would it go away" (122).

Like Paul, Wideman's writer-narrator John in *Fanon* has been burdened by a Fanon project that has been stalled for decades, a project that "continued to simmer, however, never forgotten, never achieved, often lamented," and that inspired in John "a deep dread that someday my nation and I must endure a shattering reckoning" (*Fanon* 4). If Fanon's face is the sign of the ghost that haunts John as unfinished business—as "that which appears to be not there is often a seething presence, acting on and often meddling with taken-for-granted realities"—then it is only years later in writing *Fanon* the novel that John is ready to face Fanon, in the double sense of reckoning with the man and giving him a face.[4] Addressing Fanon, John wonders, "if your words and deeds alleviate one iota the present catastrophe of hate, murder, theft, and greed, where else should I start looking besides the mirror. Where should I search if not in faces of people I love. Will I find an answer in your eyes, behind me in the mirror, gazing into the face I see seeing yours" (5). The problem of connecting with Fanon is cast repeatedly in the novel as the problem of whether and how to conjure his presence and incorporate it in John's lived present, forty years after Fanon's death, when the continuation of imperial wars, racial violence, and the disappointment in postcolonial regimes have led to a sense of melancholy in evaluating the legacies of anticolonial, antiracist revolutionary narratives. At the crux of *Fanon*, then, is the dissonance between the legacy of Fanon's vision of a liberatory future and Wideman's neoliberal, neoimperial present.[5] And, I contend, it is the imagined face of the human person as a cultural and juridical construct that serves as the site for registering this dissonance.

The person is a figure shaped by conditions of literal life and figurative death, biological existence and social recognition, legal status and cultural representation. A figure whose plasticity, artificiality, and instability is often obscured by its apparent naturalness as a synonym for any human being, the legal person—as a subject of certain rights and duties recognized before the law—is the originary legal fiction and the foundation of modern politics. As noted in the introduction to this book, the root meaning of *persona*, a mask worn by actors on stage and through which their voices can be heard, highlights the person as a paradoxical figure of concealment and disclosure, in which the mask stands in for the human as one whose voice may be heard before the law.[6] Moreover, as Randall Williams argues, the figure of the person in human rights discourse is shaped by narratives of normative human personality development that assume and require imperialism, undermining radical decolonial politics and evading the fundamental problem of rights-bearing personhood as a category delimited by the state. The person is, then, a mask for the human composed of the material traces of our colonial, imperial, and racial legacies.[7]

This chapter reads Wideman's *Fanon* as a novel that challenges the narrative structures and social logics that undergird the legal personality in civic and international human rights law.[8] It contends that in linking the complex legacies of anticolonial struggles to the neoliberal present— a time when states are attenuating or eviscerating the legal rights of human personhood even as international human rights discourse claims to broaden those rights—Fanon refashions personhood as a highly constructed, artificial mask that enables the wearer to evade or exceed the law's defining powers. John and his persona, who is named Thomas, are the principal narrators of the novel. They fail to provide the story of Fanon's life using exemplary genres of individual development (such as the bildungsroman, biography, and biopic). As the narrators self-reflexively turn to prosopopoeia to try to get on with the story, they disrupt the originary act on which political rights depend: the act of giving the abstract figure of the person a human face and voice and attributing to the person (as a rights-bearing subject) a normative process of development and civic incorporation. Prosopopoeia—to make a face, or a mask, through which one may give voice to the dead—specifically depends on this gap between the human and the person that liberal human rights discourse seeks to close by merely disavowing. As John seeks to "paint Fanon on [his] face, wear the mask of him," Fanon emerges as a complex figure of prosopopoeia in the novel, a mask voicing a radical decolonial future even as the historical Fanon relied on models of psychological human personality development that may be reinscribed by the legitimating mechanisms of colonial violence.

Fanon is thus an invocation of the dead and a meditation on the labors of salvaging the revolutionary personality, of repurposing the political legacy of Fanon to challenge the developmentalist logics of the human personality. The result is a novel whose masking of Fanon complicates the distinction between mask and skin, cover and flesh, by elaborating what I call the masks of legal personhood. The masks of legal personhood stand in contrast to the historical Fanon's trope of the (white) mask as a psychological disavowal of one's own (black) skin. Rather than take the form of a duality, the masks of personhood take the form of collage, which disrupts the teleological narratives of personal development that have given shape to the image of the normative human personality at the heart of both literature and the law. I show how Wideman uses narrative collage, adapted from the civil rights–era visual collages of Romare Bearden, in order to construct the image of the person as a mask composed of fragments in new relations with each other, re-placed and repurposed through the aesthetic effects of collage. Wideman's use of Bearden-inspired narrative collage is well known to his readers. Here I am interested specifically in how Wideman's narrative collage constructs persons as masks, an effect produced by Bearden's own use of collage while a member of the Spiral Group. I examine the effects of John's strategic failure to sustain narratives of development in favor of constructing narrative collages for his Fanon project. The failure to develop serves as a narrative tactic for structuring the novel and a call to reexamine the shape of the person in a world defined by an ongoing discursive violence done to those caught within the legal framework of personhood, with its promise of human rights.

Developing Persons

It is a daunting task to search for Frantz Fanon, not least because so many competing versions of him may be found in the writings and politics of others. During his lifetime, Fanon was known to relatively small circles of professional colleagues, political contacts, friends, and family. Born in Martinique in 1925 and eventually a veteran of the Free French army working as a psychiatrist—in Lyon, France, and then in Blida-Joinville, Algeria, before resigning in order to commit himself to the Algerian War for Independence—Fanon also published papers in psychiatry and wrote three books, none of which were widely reviewed at the time of initial publication. After his death from leukemia in a Bethesda,

Maryland, clinic, Fanon's body was transferred for burial to the outskirts of the land that would in a few months become an independent Algeria. Also within months of his death, he would be transfigured into an apostle of violence by the French press even as his role in the revolution as a delegate, pamphlet writer, and liaison for the National Liberation Front (FLN) was unknown or unimportant to most Algerians.

It was with the first translation of *Les Damnés de la terre* into English by Grove Press in 1965 that Fanon's *The Wretched of the Earth* became a bestseller and the name *Fanon* a dislocated flashpoint for U.S. racial politics. Advertised as "The handbook for a Negro Revolution that is changing the shape of the white world," "a fiery manifesto," and "a revolutionary bible for dozens of emerging African and Asian nations," *The Wretched of the Earth* was read—by mainstream reviewers no less than by Hannah Arendt—as a threatening contagion for racial and class violence whose arguments "are spreading amongst the young Negroes in American slums and on American lecture platforms."[9] The word *Fanon* became a battle cry and badge of honor for an urban politics of radical liberation: Eldridge Cleaver famously claimed that "every brother on a roof top" could quote Fanon, and Stokely Carmichael invoked Fanon as among his "patron saints" of black nationalism. The intellectual historian David Macey tartly notes, however, that "most of Fanon's American readers appeared not to have noticed" that *The Wretched of the Earth* is, at least in part, "a book about Algeria and not America" and that Fanon "was simply not a black nationalist." John Edgar Wideman suggests how the name "Fanon" circulated in the 1960s and 1970s as a floating signifier for black radical politics when he notes that his brother never read one of Fanon's books but "stole it, carried it around with [Fanon's] name sticking up in [his] back pocket" (Wideman, *Fanon* 63). Fanon has proven to be an enduring, mutable, and extraordinarily malleable object of prosopopoeia—what Henry Louis Gates concludes is "a Rorschach blot with legs"— through which a variety of political, cultural, and aesthetic arguments are voiced, from Third Worldist to U.S. radical black politics to postcolonial theory since the 1980s.[10] In the documentary film *Frantz Fanon: Black Skin, White Mask*, director Isaac Julien embraces rather than deplores the semiosis of *Fanon*: as Julien writes in an essay commentary on the film, he seeks to extend the project of making Fanon "a more open sign," inviting the audience "to project their own Fanon into the film" by staging the visual representation of him as a "ventriloquist" performance by the actor Colin Salmon amid a montage of texts, including scenes from *The Battle of Algiers*.[11] Fanon is, in short, an elusive and spectral figure, simultaneously invoked and under erasure, subjected to an endless process of academic, cultural, and political prosopopoeia.

Wheeling through genres of personal development—especially biography, memoir, bildungsroman, biopic screenplay, and nonfiction essay—John stages the artistic labor of his "Fanon project" as an extended case of writer's block. He writes in a letter to Fanon, "I'm reluctant to say whether my evolving project is fiction or nonfiction, novel or memoir, science fiction or romance, hello or goodbye. A little tweaking and maybe it would fit in one category or the other" (Wideman, *Fanon* 136). "Dazed" by "the implacable either/or categories" that he has been trying to "write [his] way out of" throughout his career, John finds genre systems as intractable as the racial ones the historical Fanon had sought a "way out of" through his writing (94). What these categories of genre and race presume is a model of development that reaffirms the system of categorization as merely descriptive of reality rather than productive of it: wary of committing his project to any one categorical line of development, John suggests that his narrative has the potential to develop in alternative ways that, with "a little tweaking," could morph across categories and thus undermine the very system of categorizing texts and persons (136).

The category of the legal human person itself encapsulates a narrative of development, that of an individual who is educated and incorporated into civil society as a full, productive citizen. *Fanon* the novel obliquely echoes recent critiques of developmentalist discourse as it produces the logics of governance and capitalism that delimit norms of human personality development. In particular, it invokes the ways in which developmentalist discourse has been projected onto the legal personality of racialized minorities as an ongoing legacy of the apparently defunct legal regimes of racial slavery and empire. These norms structure modes of informal class apartheid within contemporary society and give shape to the normative human subject of rights, as Wideman makes clear in his literary representations of urban renewal and social development projects. John's meditations on the effects of neoliberal state and private interests on the racialized urban poor are incorporated into the narration of his struggle with the Fanon project. In a conversation about the Fanon project when John visits his incarcerated brother, Robert, for example, Robert interjects to explain how the state has outsourced the prison's food service to a private company. In turn, this company hired nutrition experts "to figure how much a grown man needs to eat to stay alive. . . . Ain't nobody I know starved to death yet, but they keeping us lean, bro, mighty lean" (Wideman, *Fanon* 61). Robert's account prompts John to shift from carefully managed hunger to its obverse, the overabundance of cheap junk foods in poor neighborhoods. Imagining a dialogue with his mother over the biopolitics in neighborhoods like Homewood, John comments, "*There's a war going on, a war being waged against people like us all over the world and this prison visiting room one of the battlefields and Esther Morris* [a widow who died alone with her hand in a bag of pork rinds] *one of its millions of casualties*" (62; emphasis in original). Esther and Robert become figures of a biopolitical regime that—while fat or lean, respectively—does not find its visual image in an aesthetics of bare life. U.S. urban development policy hides the long shadow of racialized personhood cast by the nominally race-free figures of the abstract citizen and the normative person of human rights law, producing instead a discourse on the black "underclass," the "culture of poverty," inherent criminality, and the failure of "individual responsibility" to explain their exclusion from civic incorporation.[12]

Fanon the novel turns to collage instead of development narratives as an alternative form of incorporation, seeking not only to construct the mask of Fanon but also to paste imagined fragments of Fanon's life into John's own, refusing conventions of unity and chronology in order to produce new relations between Fanon and John's lived present or between an anticolonial revolutionary legacy and the diffuse, often untraceable violence of the neoliberal present. Fanon is everywhere and nowhere on the streets of John's Pittsburgh: in his visits to prison; during a pitch to Jean-Luc Godard while the pair take a tour through Homewood; while narrating extended scenes from his never-to-be-completed screenplay of John's mother witnessing the murder of a teenager (recalling Omar, Robert's son) by gang violence, juxtaposed to Fanon's case summary in *Wretched of the Earth* about two Algerian boys who kill their European friend; and while narrating a panning shot of Homewood's darkening streets while words from Fanon's *The Wretched of the Earth* scroll in split-screen below. *Fanon* the novel uses collage to put the complicated national legacy of U.S. urban and racial development in relation to the broader legacies of radical liberation movements of the 1960s, encapsulated in the prosopon of "Fanon." In the postscript to *Fanon*, for instance, Wideman addresses a letter to his mother in Pittsburgh about riots in the suburbs of Paris: "Immigrants burning up in government hotels. Algerian kids and kids from Mali, Senegal, Ivory Coast, Martinique burning cars. Economic woes. People trouble—Muslims vs. Jews, Jews vs. Christians, Christians vs. Muslims, blacks vs. whites, immigrants vs. natives" (226–27). The structural violence of racialized incarceration and food biopolitics that organize everyday life in places like Pittsburgh—with people getting choked "past the point of seeing themselves anything much like a human person, more like an article of clothing rolled, twisted, squeezed as dry as hands could squeeze, then fed through the rolling-pin wringers of the washtub" (102)—evince a world whose "Manichean violence," with its legacy of differential personhood, flattens the human and its legal personality beyond recognition (6).[13]

John extends his depiction of hidden racial colonial legacies animating the neoliberal, postindustrial present when he juxtaposes Pittsburgh to the French city of Lyon. Lyon is the city in which Fanon trained in psychiatry—an "untidy city of fractious workers," with its soldiers fighting colonial wars in Dien Bien Phu and Algeria, and with its ghettoized "quarter housing Arab immigrants in kennels and hives" (Wideman, *Fanon* 196). During his time there as a young veteran of the Free French army, Fanon received an unexpected kind of colonial education, which inspired him to write an essay on the dis-alienation of the black man for his graduate thesis: the essay was rejected but was published as *Black Skin, White Masks* in 1952. John reveals the city's narrative of material development as indebted to French colonialism and its legacy of postcolonial immigration but concealed in the gleaming high-tech twenty-first-century cityscape.

> Unpeeling Lyon an endless tumbling through history. Like unpeeling your skin. Down which path should your biographer pursue you to catch a glimpse of your true face. The same question dogging you, Fanon, as you pursued your many faces, through many cities, many pairs of eyes. Will I get lucky and unearth a definitive portrait of you. A view of you freeze-framed on the screen, like I chanced upon Emmett Till's battered face once upon a time, a closeup, millions upon millions of fugitive dots momentarily aligned just so to represent a conundrum recognizable as a human face and also undoubtedly your particular face, your likeness, a still photo fixed so I can study it, you know, like an image from the Lumiére archives, an original print stuttering, impaled on the end of a quivering spear of light, a ghost face, dead leaf, its stare crossing mine, staring back as I stare, staring till the ancient stock overheats, begins to smoke and curl. (197)

Lyon becomes a possible way to "unearth a definitive portrait" of Fanon, but what flashes at John in his imaginative act of searching for Fanon's story in the city's own—an act as corporeal, intimate, and painful as flaying one's skin—is not Fanon's "true face" but instead a "conundrum," a puzzle or a problem, resembling a human face at once Fanon's and not Fanon's. The search for Fanon's face is spliced with a remembered image of Emmett Till's mutilated, water-logged corpse following his 1955 murder, his face barely recognizable as such and captured in the form of a "still photo" of "millions of fugitive dots momentarily aligned." These dots are "fugitive" in multiple senses of the term, at once outside the law and seeking refuge from its violent capacity to define categories of racialized personhood that produce those who may be killed but not legally recognized as murdered and those who may kill but not be legally recognized as criminal. They produce an image of the face as hidden and mutable, dots to be scrambled or reorganized into other faces and other legacies.

The "fugitive dots momentarily aligned" also represent the failure to connect them, just as the murder trial so notoriously failed to recognize the body and the murder of Till: instead, the grainy image of Till's battered face represents an open wound that cannot be closed by court-determined justice. Till's legal personhood was illegible when defense attorneys argued in 1955 that there was no murder because there was no body, despite Mamie Till's identification of her son's remains. As Myisha Priest puts it, "The illegibility of Till's body made him illegible as a legal subject."[14] And it remains illegible in the 2004 reopening of the case, when the broadest legal conception of harm "cannot be addressed in the context of new criminal prosecutions," leaving a "lack of closure in the case [that] cannot be ameliorated through criminal proceedings."[15] Till's legal illegibility is in stark contrast to its haunting force for John and for Wideman, Till's agemate. In his 2005 essay, "Looking at Emmett Till," Wideman writes of the shock of recognition produced by seeing the image of Till's face in *Jet* magazine: the face that "has haunted me since I was fourteen, and [in which I] saw myself reflected in the dead—horribly transformed."[16] Even when John imagines looking at Till's face with the critical distance of an academic spectator, as one who would "study" it as if it were unearthed from the cinematic archive, it continues to haunt him, and the film stock, heated by an otherwise endless staring contest, "begins to smoke and curl."

Christopher Metress has noted Till's function in African American literature as either a figure of the sacrificial lamb or as "a figure of disturbance and disruption."[17] It is the latter figuration of Till that Wideman pursues. He concludes his essay on Till by claiming, "We have yet to look upon Emmett Till's face. No apocalyptic encounter, no ritual unveiling, no epiphany has freed us. The nightmare is not cured."[18] The novel incorporates these dots, which momentarily align to form the horrific transformation of Till, into the "peeling" of Lyon's history. This incorporation highlights, collage-like, the relation between two contemporaneous but otherwise distinct contexts: the racial colonial violence Fanon would witness and the contemporaneous extralegal but sanctioned racial violence in the Jim Crow U.S. South. And it brings them both to bear on Wideman's present of racist, xenophobic unrest and war.[19]

The spectral images of Fanon and Till become metonyms for anticolonial revolution and the U.S. civil rights movement, respectively, even as they signal in Fanon their overlapping legacies in the "war on terror." This latter sanctions what Patricia J. Williams calls "privatized violence" not only by contractors but also by soldiers and governmental agencies on the ground, most emblematically in the form of the tortured body, while deploying a racializing discourse on the need to help Afghan and Iraqi populations in their political and cultural development.[20] Williams suggests as much in her commentary on the 2004 U.S. Justice Department decision to reopen the Till murder case in an election year and in the wake of the Abu Ghraib torture and abuse scandal.[21] The pictures of Abu Ghraib recalled scenes from Gillo Pontecorvo's *The Battle of Algiers*, the film screened by the Pentagon at the start of the Iraq invasion in a stated effort to learn lessons from the French army's mistakes in counterinsurgency warfare (not, apparently, in relation to the French army's extensive use of torture). Moreover, the Military Commissions Act (2006) deprives noncitizens under indefinite detention and possible torture of the rights of habeas corpus (literally, "that you have the body [in court]"), thereby reinforcing legal personhood as the vanishing point of international human rights law and state taxonomies of the person.

Under indefinite detention and without their bodies or voices allowable in court, human detainees are effectively excluded from the normative right of the person to have its voice heard in court but are nonetheless captured as exceptional persons within the law. It is the recognition that these humans are persons—but an exceptional category of persons—that makes them subject to legal state violence. This point often gets lost in the conflation of the legal personality with the human as a subject, as when Judith Butler observes of Guantánamo detainees (and others in U.S.-organized secret detention centers),

> These prisoners are not considered "prisoners" and receive no protection from international law. . . . [A]s a result, the humans who are imprisoned in Guantánamo [detention camp] do not count as human; they are not subjects protected by international law. They are not subjects in any legal or normative sense.[22]

Fanon's "ghost face" haunts the current spate of neoliberal imperialist wars; it also marks postcolonial melancholy, as becomes evident when Fanon's hopeful call that the newly decolonized countries "turn over a new leaf" becomes for John a desiccated figure of a former life, a "dead leaf."[23] Ultimately, the true faces of Fanon and Till elude John: the close-up remains all surface and light, a pointillated mask exchanging John's stare.

Wideman's *Fanon*, I argue, suggests that the relationship between developmentalist logics and the legal human personality is structured by the masks of personhood. Because what I call the masks of legal personhood complicates the metaphor of the mask evoked by Fanon's title *Black Skin, White Masks*, it is worth pausing to consider the historical Fanon's use of the figures of face and mask to advance his theories of human personality development. For Fanon, this mask hides a real face; unmasking the black colonial subject becomes the unintended culmination of his personality: "We have seen in fact that the Antillean who goes to France pictures this journey as the final stage of his personality. Quite literally I can say without any risk of error that the Antillean who goes to France in order to convince himself that he is white will find his real face there."[24] Embittered by his own cold reception in France after having fought in the Free French army, Fanon takes pains in his early writing to show normative civic incorporation as an impossible fiction for the black man who is caught within a racialized taxonomy of personhood, even as states and human rights law cling to the fantasy of an abstract personhood freed of race. That this abstract personhood disavows the very white skin encapsulating it, thus giving the person its form and its mask, becomes clear once the black colonial subject discovers his "real face" in the eyes of white French citizens: the black man is left to feel his real face as a "crushing objecthood" (Fanon, *Black Skin, White Masks* 109) that nullifies any claim to the formal equivalence promised by abstract legal personhood and the human rights personality. Efforts to erase the "burden" of blackness are part of this "historico-racial drama" of civic incorporation. "For several years," writes Fanon, "certain laboratories have been trying to produce a serum for 'denegrification'; with all the earnestness in the world" (111). For Fanon, the fact of legal personhood is itself the product of the "white man" having "woven me out of a thousand details, anecdotes, stories" (111). The story of the "denegrification" serum reveals the racial entanglements of persona, mask, and cultural narratives of development. What the lab scientists of Fanon's anecdote share with liberal democratic actors and human rights activists is an inability to recognize how the normative, abstract legal personality depends on the selective labor of denying this entanglement while weaving racialized subjects out of history. Fanon himself was invested in a shared logic of developmentalism even as he challenged its racialist and colonialist manifestations. At a time when Third Worldist political actors and movements appropriated the language of human rights for national independence struggles, aiming to expand the narrow Eurocentric boundaries of the human personality of the UDHR, Fanon diagnosed in his psychiatric patients the alienating effects of colonialism and racism on consciousness, the body, and social life. Joining his psychiatric with his revolutionary work for the National Liberation Front, Fanon also envisioned personhood in its truly postcolonial condition, in the form of a kind of "new man" that required for his existence a new social order.[25] Fanon was invested as a psychologist in a model of human personality development freed from the terror of colonialism and its deforming effects on the colonizer and the colonized, the torturer and the tortured, the white and the black. Nonetheless, his thought on human personality development overlaps with liberal human rights discourse, such as the language in Article 22 of the UDHR, which declares the right of everyone to the "social and cultural rights indispensable for his dignity and the free development of his personality." Psychology, psychoanalysis, and liberal notions of human subjectivity are premised on the claim that mechanisms for psychological development are universal. Borrowing this universalist humanist template for psychological development to elaborate a political argument about human personhood, Fanon specifically identifies the mirror stage as a key moment in the narrative of personal development that gets disturbed by racial colonialism. For a colonial or racial subject to pass the mirror stage successfully, he must recognize the real black face beneath the white mask: this successful development entails a political transformation that, in turn, makes possible Fanon's "new man" and a new society freed from colonial racial violence as well as the pitfalls of nationalism.

The psychological model structuring Fanon's theory of decolonization also contends that the full potential of the human person can only develop freely in a decolonized world that refuses existing European models of political, economic, and cultural development: "We today can do everything, so long as we do not imitate Europe, so long as we are not obsessed by the desire to catch up with Europe. . . . When I search for Man in the technique and the style of Europe, I see only a succession of negations of man, and an avalanche of murders" (Fanon, *Wretched of the Earth* 312). As Fanon, already ill with leukemia, concludes in *Wretched of the Earth*: "For Europe, for ourselves and for humanity, comrades, we must turn over a new leaf, we must work out new concepts, and try to set afoot a new man" (316). Fanon's "new man" depends on narratives of development that overlap with liberal human rights discourse, presenting a tension between radical decolonization and an internationalism that depends on and furthers new imperialisms.[26] Fanon's model of human subjectivity is put in the service of finding an alternative political result to a universal mechanism of development: in this way, psychological development is key for Fanon to reconceptualize the person as a figure before the law and defined by it and thus produced by the political order. As Diana Fuss observes in her critique of Fanon's problematic sexual politics, among his most important contributions to political thought is "the notion that the psychical operates precisely as a political formation," thus insisting on the "historical and social conditions of identification" so that "what Fanon gives us, in the end, is a politics that does not oppose the psychical but fundamentally presupposes it."[27]

Core contradictions within Fanon's political thought, especially having to do with gender and sexuality, arise when Fanon seems to forget the relation of the psychical to the political in personality development. Fuss charges that

> Fanon's own politics takes the multifarious form of an extended investigation of the psychopathology of colonialism that not only describes imperial practices but also, where sexual differences are concerned, problematically enacts them. When addressing the politics of sexual identifications, Fanon fails to register fully the significance of the founding premise of his own theory of colonial relations, which holds that the political is located within the psychical as a powerful shaping force.[28]

The limitations of Fanon's models of personal development similarly become the implicit locus of Françoise Vergès's critique of Fanon's masculinism and his vision of a revolutionary new man. Vergès analyzes the trope of the mirror in *Black Skin, White Masks* to show how Fanon's use of the mirror stage depends on the desire for a total truth that could be revealed under the mask, and on a normative development of the individual's conception of the self that fails for the black man in a society where legal (and thus politically recognized) personhood is delimited by whiteness. For the black man whose mirror hallucination of the other should reflect a white face but instead reflects a black face, the mirror reflects back onto him an experience of racial alienation and depersonalization. If, as Fanon accepts, hallucination occurs when the unity of the white self is threatened, the black Antillean man's hallucination suggests that the unity of the self—the sense of a wholeness to be protected from the racial other for whom the self is "suffused with attraction, repulsion, denial, and anxiety"—is an impossible fiction as long as he remains a racialized colonial subject.[29] Beyond the ideology of personal development through racial colonial education, the misrecognition of the mask for one's "real face" is perhaps a foundational fiction and, in *Black Skin, White Masks*, a necessary condition for the conflation of the human with the legal person. Vergès argues that "Fanon aspired to a universal—the universally human—and difference could only be invidious."[30] In seeking to "destroy the white mask on black consciousness," the "political project born out of this approach was to achieve not singularities but a totality. Behind the mask, the revealed truth."[31]

Wideman draws from but significantly revises Fanon's use of the Lacanian mirror stage. Riffing on the mirror as an object into which both John and his persona Thomas repeatedly gaze, Wideman writes:

> Masks do not disguise truth. Masks are true. The pure, absolute, reassuring truth of black or white. Pure illusion. Pure white or pure black. Masks truer than the gray shadow staring back from a mirror, your unconvincing reflection that does not disguise the lazing emptiness behind it you pretend not to see. (*Fanon* 219)

Wideman's use of collage to construct the masks of human personhood enables him to formulate an alternative to the normative narrative of personal development and civic incorporation: legal persons are revealed to be highly constructed masks, formed by collage, that resemble and then substitute for the human face. In contrast to the historical Fanon's theories of racialized flesh and the white mask that covers it, *Fanon* the novel suggests that a mask is all there is before the law: as the root meaning of *persona* suggests, a mask does not stand in for the human; a mask is the person before the law, and it is forged by legal identification at least as much as by one's effort at creative self-making. The mask for Wideman is neither a true face nor the face of the ideal individual subject of development fully incorporated into civic society (the hero of an ideal bildungsroman): it is instead a collage of disparate materials in everyday life whose coherence lies in paradox; in the distortions of scale, proportion, and perspective; and in the new relations that arise when each fragment is made to connect with all the others. Rather than naturalize, normalize, or decry the paradoxes of personhood in civil and international human rights law, Wideman takes paradox as the mode of his artistic labor by placing contradictory elements alongside each other, highlighting their tension as productive of a relational mode of authorship among personae.

Assemblages: Faces and Masks

Prosopopoeia is the paradoxical labor of masking the author's voice so that he may speak. Disguising himself with the authorial persona Thomas, John projects the Fanon book as a series of borrowed voices disguising the author's own, with the borrowed voices made to speak through the images of borrowed faces, as it were. But the mask in Fanon denaturalizes the figure of the human face by lingering on its construction through the processes of fragmentation and incorporation. As an imagined patient's plea to Dr. Fanon—*"Heal the divisions within me my enemies exploit to keep me in a place I despise. Myself cut up, separated into bloody pieces, doctor. Like you. Fractured, dispersed, in death as in life"*—suggests, the fractured psyche of the colonial subject may be healed (*Fanon* 47; emphasis in original). The wholeness that emerges will resemble a reconstitution of the body in the form of collage: the person in Fanon is constructed as a mask of fragments, dispersed and brought together again, the divisions healed but outlined by their former cuts.

Collage becomes a form for the literary construction of the masks of legal personhood, explicitly highlighting what the construction of the person in civil and human rights law disavows: the relation among otherwise disparate elements that produces contradiction, paradox, and dialogue in any composition. Bearden's civil rights–era visual photomontage and collage aesthetics serves as Wideman's aesthetic model for his own narratorial collage techniques, as Wideman himself has made clear in several of his writings, including *Fanon*. In an interview, Wideman explains that "Romare Bearden is more or less an aesthetic hero. His main mode or form was collage. And certainly collage is a very suggestive art form, because it means you take bits and pieces from every damn thing and start throwing them together, and if you do it in the right way, maybe something new is created."[32] In the novel, John reflects on the ethical effects of Bearden's collages and his mother's collage-like stories, which "flatten and fatten perspective. She crams everything, everyone, everywhere into the present, into words that flow, intimate and immediate as the images of a Bearden painting. . . . Bearden's collages and my mother's narratives [are] truly democratic—each detail counts equally, every part matters as much as any grand design" (Wideman, *Fanon* 21–22).[33] While it is a famously Modernist (and, in terms of ordinary art-making such as collage scrapbooking, then also a Victorian–era) artistic practice that marks the art of Bearden and the stories of Wideman's mother, the formal operations of collage cannot be isolated here from their challenge to conventional visual representation and narration of the legal and social conceptions of African American personhood.

Bearden's reinvention of the collage form emerges from a direct concern with the effects of racialized personhood in the United States, when Bearden proposed a collaborative collage work during a meeting of the Spiral Group, whose artists gathered to discuss the relation of art to racial injustice. "We hoped," recollects one member, "with our art to justify life."[34] Here I want to pay special attention to Bearden's influence on one specific effect that his and Wideman's collages produce, and that is the masks of personhood. A rare letter from Bearden to a dismissive art critic highlights the potential for the cultural form of collage to refigure the human legal personality. In response to the critic's description of Bearden's collage as simply "peopled by black faces cut out of magazines," Bearden carefully explains how his collages transform the face, that quintessential metonym of the human person whose voice deserves to be heard before the law, into a mask: the faces are built "from parts of African masks, animal eyes, marbles, mossy vegetation."[35] Bearden suggests something of the collage form's potential to respond to the distortions of black civic personhood when he argues that, along with the fracturing of visual details that are then integrated into a different space and form, "such devices . . . as distortion of scale and proportion, and abstract coloration, are the very means through which I try to achieve a more personal expression."[36] At the same time he insists, "It is not my aim to paint about the Negro in America in terms of propaganda. It is precisely my awareness of the distortions required of the polemicist that has caused me to paint the life of my people as I know it."[37] This explanation at once naturalizes the personal as the emotional and social conditions of everyday life (highlighting the artifice of Bearden's work while paradoxically claiming its realism) and suggests that it is precisely the distortions of the African American figure within the political realm—whether through the denial of, or the insistence on, the African American's full legal personhood and membership in the national body politic—that have delimited the person. Moreover, it suggests that the visual distortion of scale and proportion might be salvaged from racist polemics and repurposed to figure genealogies of personhood and the personal.

It is only by narrating Fanon's death (narrated as an impossible cinematic collage directed by Godard) that John seems to fully embrace the possibilities of narrative collage to mask Fanon, to transform Fanon into the proper subject of prosopopoeia. In other words, the scene of his death becomes the necessary condition for his reanimation as mask. It is only in the final chapters that John and Thomas attempt to give voice to the mask of Fanon. Until then, he is depicted as the elusive subject of their speculation, with only other writings by or about Fanon from which to work. As these sections shift in and out of Fanon's imagined (mostly inner) voice, Fanon emerges as a persona who exists only through the prosopopoeic relationship he has to others. Fanon—filled with the urgency of a writer determined to envision a new man emerging from colonial violence while knowing he may not have long to live—dictates his last book to his wife, Josie. Her typing "nail[s his flying thoughts] to a noisy machine"; the staccato violence of her act seems to qualify his authorship by changing his relationship to his own voice, prompting him to wonder whether it is even really his voice he hears when he says his book out loud (Wideman, *Fanon* 187). Fanon becomes, paradoxically, the subject of his own act of prosopopoeia. His dictation to Josie, who types under the sign of "Fanon," transforms him into the very persona to which he gives voice. His already mediated relationship to his own voice, echoed by his wife's dictation, prompts Fanon to consider the ethics of representing his patients in the case studies that make up the final section of *The Wretched of the Earth*, titled "Colonial War and Mental Disorders." He initially reminds himself—and Josie—to "be certain the text distinguishes the patient's voice from mine" but soon begins to question that possibility, not only for the text, but also for the very notion of authorship.

> I don't want to fall into the trap of treating my patients as the beke [*sic*] treat me. Never letting me speak for myself. Or turning my words into evidence against me. The proper representation of these cases is immensely complicated. Perhaps hopelessly compromised by any form of writing. I suppose in some sense I'm always speaking for my patients. Though, in fairness to myself, I often feel the patients speak for me. Not only do I quote them at considerable length. I also find myself splicing into my accounts their exact words or words not exactly theirs not mine either, words I try to imagine the patient might employ in a particular situation. An odd, secondhand, alienated structure's being formed as we proceed in these book sessions. A process that controls me as much as I control it. A sort of bricolage of free-floating fragments whose authorship is unsettlingly ambiguous. (191)

For the character Fanon, the relations of psychiatrist to patient and of author to dictated text threaten to be defined wholly by a mode of one-way representation, a "speaking for" that reminds Fanon of the colonial relations of the black Martinican to the white Creole, or béké. The term *béké* may derive from an Ibo word meaning both "white" and "foreigner," and békés supported the Vichy government of Admiral Georges Robert when the seventeen-year-old Fanon made his failed escape to Dominica.[38] Speaking for the other in this sense eviscerates the other's personhood, enabling "some groups of people [to] rule other groups of people by transforming those others into phantoms" (Wideman, *Fanon* 167). John's Fanon addresses his fear of reproducing the colonial relation in his own work by recognizing that all such relations are not only mutually transformative but also permeable: while there is a distinction between the physical bodies of the psychiatrist and the patient, or Frantz and Josie, what we call the "voice" of these persons proves to be a composite of migrating words. The "splicing" of words into the represented speech of Fanon and that of his patients (and even the sound of Josie's typing) evokes the kind of unaffixed, ever-changing work of collage. It constitutes a "bricolage of free-floating fragments" made of whatever is to hand (his patient's speech, Josie's hands, the typewriter), fragmented into words and joined together to produce new relations. What emerges is not some idealized union but a third thing built from these fragments that cannot be traced to their original sources, an "alienated structure" that fundamentally changes notions of authorship and voice: Josie, Frantz, and Frantz's patients contribute to and incorporate each other's words in a process not simply mutually transforming, but alienated from its sources. Fanon, like all of those invoked in the process of dictating the case studies, is revealed to be an author whose persona is itself a collaborative composition made from ordinary materials. While I suggest the possibility that such collage making can defamiliarize the human personality in ways that enable a more open political imagination, the process of opening oneself to the violence of splicing also does violence to the body and psyche, especially when those voices cannot escape colonial experience and racial fantasy.

John depicts the authorial persona of a Fanon struggling with the ethics of prosopopoeia before he presents the image of Fanon as a public persona, serving as a delegate to the 1960 Conference on Positive Action.[39] Scanning his audience as he prepares to speak on the importance of the Algerian war for independence, Fanon gives voice to the connection between epistemologies of personhood and sovereignty, or between systems that claim the power to name and classify the human figure and the geographic body in the name of cartographic truth. He visualizes the representational strategies of early Western maps of the world, drawn to reflect the psychic life of European colonialism.

A cartoon map, really, outmoded then and now, Beware, drag-
ons be here, a map with distortions of scale, flat-out lies and con-
scious misrepresentations, embedded superstitions and ignorance,
a map of dreams, a prettied-up picture of Europe's unspeak-
able nightmares and aspirations. . . . [A] fairy-tale map abiding
till today . . . drawn by a few dreaming hands . . . who retain the
power in their hands, their heads to draw the old map again and
again and squeeze a whole world onto a parchment grid, making
it, then and now, everybody's map, white brown black red yellow
green, establishing scale and relationship among peoples, . . . the
map missing the sea of faces Fanon looks out upon, and no matter
how deep and dense this sea appears to him, that immensity does
not exist, cannot be located, a blank site, a terre inconnue, emptied of meaning once and forever by the mapmakers because they
chose to render no shape for it, appended no names but theirs, left
it as an invisible island floating, drowning, a hole, a fearful void in
a greater sea that surrounds it, washes over it, conceals it from sight
and time. Unless the map, as Fanon understands it, the map that
erases him by erasing itself by erasing him, can be flipped over to
its unwritten side and then perhaps you could begin a fresh drawing of the world. (Wideman, *Fanon* 221–22)

The legacy of colonial cartography comes to resemble the counterpart
to the ethics of Bearden's collage art: distorting scale and proportion of
land and its inhabitants, these maps constructed different masks for different others and called it "skin." These acts of prosopopoeia have worked
to hide the constructedness of personhood even as they reveal, in this
sequence, their own distortions, anxieties, desires. In "establishing scale
and relationship among peoples," Fanon considers how the map failed
to recognize as normative juridical persons the faces of those who, like
the faces in the audience, recognize their own personhood even as it is
"missing" from the map, included only as unreadable and unknowable,
the subject of erasure. The map cannot be thrown away. The persona of
Fanon here imagines, instead, the blank space of the map's "unwritten
side" as holding the decolonial potential to figuratively redraw the world.
The hope of starting "fresh" depends on using the existing map to trace a
new image; and yet, if Wideman's novel is any suggestion, the promise in
that new image is not to offer a more realistic survey of the globe and its
inhabitants but to explore the depth and density, the tensions and continuities, the distortions of scale and perspective, that function to convey
the complexity of a new conceptualization of personhood. It is to tell

stories like John's mother, whose philosophy of storytelling in everyday life shapes his ethical imagination; or to make space like his artist friend Charley, who insisted on painting each new canvas blue-black before "scrubbing, rubbing, scraping, licking, erasing, flogging, and washing" the dark skin back to light, until "the tortured canvas"—now a darkly painted skin under erasure—"would collapse in tatters and droop from its frame" (Wideman, *Fanon* 20); or it is to write on John's childhood magic slate, in which lifting the plastic sheet promised to erase whatever had been written even as its traces were left as impressions on the board underneath, never really erased but operating as a multilayered palimpsest.

To figure personhood as a mask made by collage requires the violence of fracturing and joining, and of adopting an "alienated structure" for one's persona. Unlike Fanon's own writings, *Fanon* is not as invested in a normative model of development that presumes a fully humanized (masculine) personhood, one that would be ultimately free of masks altogether. In the novel, the mask can imprison or liberate: what matters above all is the condition of its making and its subsequent relation to the wearer and to the voice. Wideman's narrative collage offers a rethinking of the trope of the mask in Fanon's writing by suggesting that it is not enough for black skin to cast off the white mask and the colonial racial epistemology it signifies in order to access a truth, an authentic existence. *Fanon* takes Fanon's ridicule of the "denegrification" serum to its limits by suggesting that the skin is itself always a kind of mask, and that one's persona is, as its etymology suggests, the mask that amplifies the voice and makes a face to be recognized by the law and society. There may be the possibility of a new kind of persona for the individual who undertakes the difficult creative labor of constructing a collaged mask for himself or herself, but this persona is made from the materials of his or her complex social reality. It is therefore incorporated in ways that challenge the Manichaean colonial relation or any single epistemological, ideological, or legal-political order. Collage thus provides an alternative way to construct personhood: rather than rely on the fiction of absolute equality promised but never delivered by abstract personhood, the collaged mask of personhood becomes a multifaceted reflection of a social reality that recognizes the link and the likeness between all masks. John gives voice to this sentiment through the persona of Fanon, who approaches the podium and thinks, *"My brother, my likeness.* He often recites those words of Baudelaire to remind himself that what he despises most in another is also always his own face mirrored in their features, his actions doubled by theirs" (Wideman, *Fanon* 219; emphasis in original).

The masks of personhood, constructed as collages of historical fragments, are the products of a kind of salvaging work that challenges both
liberal narratives of development and current critical theories of personhood, which see it as always and already death-bound or as caught
within various thresholds of indeterminacy, as discussed in the introduction to this book. Critical of existing paradigms of liberal rights at
the national and international scales, the novel suggests that the problem
of legal recognition is not simply that some are recognized as persons
and others are not: dispossession, exclusion, and occlusion inhere in the
very category of the legal person. The abstract person's formal equality before the law emerges from an ideal model of human development
that disavows the history of racial taxonomies and of the persistently
uneven categories of national belonging produced by the law—often
cobbled together from older laws whose spectral presence can be seen in
the revisions and expansions of legal personhood. The broad histories of
legal slavery, incarceration, and colonialism have shown that legal personhood works not only to protect or enlarge individual rights but also
to subject individuals to punitive conditions of enslavement, imprisonment, or civil death.

The novel therefore brings into view the sovereign violence—rather
than benign liberal development—that constitutes the person. But it also
suggests that fixing our eyes unwaveringly on the threshold of "bare life"
may eclipse the prosaic ways in which persons excluded from political
life but captured within the law (Fanon's colonial subject or Wideman's
incarcerated brother) might maneuver, evade, exceed, or challenge the
law's recognition of them as exceptional persons, legally undeserving
of rights.[40] Calling into question the taxonomic logic and textual representation of the liberal model of legal personhood without resorting
to death-bound theories of personhood, Fanon turns to mid-twentieth-
century anticolonial revolutionary thought in the hope of salvaging a
conception of the human person that would help (as Wideman says of
Fanon's thought) find "a way out of this goddamn mess" of structural,
racist, taxonomic violence against human life (Wideman, *Fanon* 94). The
novel invites us to consider how we might form an ethical politics and
poetics of personhood under the present conditions of coerced labor and
neoliberal privatization, refuge and asylum, criminalization and detainment, and other institutional practices that make us visible as particular
kinds of persons before the law.

Moreover, the formal reliance of collage on juxtaposition might help
to highlight what Joseph Slaughter, following Wendy Brown, imagines
as a more productive future-oriented human rights project that would

"recognize paradox's figurative role in human rights instead of treating it as a shameful limitation of human rights discourse and practice."[41] Fanon's formal experiment in collage lies in thinking anew the figure of the person in both the law and the letter at the start of the twenty-first century. For John, it becomes all the more urgent to salvage the ruins of personhood in the effort to piece together a mask that might free the human from the political legacies that have shaped the normative personality in sovereign law and human rights discourse. Collage works across the historical periods of mid-twentieth-century decolonization and late-twentieth- and twenty-first-century neoliberal globalization to reveal relations between their times and their fractured incorporation into the contemporary political imaginings of personhood and human rights. Ultimately, Fanon is a novel of endless address, of prayers and pleas to connect with absent others before trying to "wear the mask" of them (Wideman, Fanon 86). Focalized through Fanon and detailing his thoughts as he approaches the podium, the novel ends with an apostrophe, an imperative, a plea, a desire for the imaginative act of prosopopoeia without the voicing that would satisfy the desire: the final word of the novel, addressed by John to Fanon or by Fanon to the mask of himself, is "Speak" (222).

Epilogue: The Ends of Legal Personhood

*Which direction does language point—past or future. Are words and
stones equally unquiet, restless, swirling, bloodstained and dangerous
even when they seem to be asleep. . . . A vast field of stones scattered in the
desert, meaningless fragments and fragments of fragments, indecipherable
signs of disorder, waiting for someone to imagine what they once were,
what they might become. Stones disappearing as fast as dreams if you step
closer and try to touch, count, weight and measure.*

—JOHN EDGAR WIDEMAN, *FANON*

*Who gets banned and expelled so that we can live in reasonable
consensus? Let us name them now. Criminals. Security Threats. Terrorists.
Enemy Aliens. Illegal Immigrants. Migrant Contaminants. Unlawful
Enemy Alien Combatants. Ghost Detainees. These are new orders of life;
they hover outside the bounds of the civil, beyond the simple dichotomies
of reason and unreason, legal and illegal. The receptacles for these outcasts
are in the wilderness, the desert, or islands cut off from sociocultural
networks of daily life.*

—COLIN DAYAN, *THE LAW IS A WHITE DOG*

*Where am I to be classified? Or, if you prefer, tucked away? "A Martinican,
a native of 'our' old colonies." Where shall I hide?*

—FRANTZ FANON, *BLACK SKIN, WHITE MASKS*

To make the dead "act, speak, answer as is our wont": beyond the rhetorical power it grants the writer—a power Wideman performatively
struggles to claim throughout *Fanon*—prosopopoeia may also evoke
the desire not to speak for but to recover the voices lost to the archives
of Atlantic slavery, to have through literature a form that, like cinema,
"animates the dead, revives dead images of things, the images people and
all other things discard" (194). It evokes the related promise to jumpstart
the narrative failure Saidiya Hartman laments in her inability to find a
mode for telling the story of enslaved girls killed at sea, the promise to get
the heart of narrative beating again in spite of the ongoing political and

economic assaults on human life made possible by law's defining powers over categories of the person. Put as a question, the problem of narrative failure raised in the introduction also has been what each chapter of this book seeks to address in its readings of the contemporary literatures of the Americas: What narrative modes, and which literary forms, might best give shape to stories in which human forms of life fall into systems of legal personhood composed of seemingly defunct taxonomies of difference and apparently discarded fragments of earlier law and political ideologies?

There is a narrative sequence in *Fanon* that forms something of an echo, one that may perhaps also be heard as a response, to Hartman's "Venus in Two Acts." It is only in the final section of the novel, itself structured as a series of abandoned beginnings, that John the narrator shifts tactics and tells the story of the historical Fanon's own false start—his first attempt to leave *béké*-dominated Martinique and fight alongside the Free French in early 1943. "A false start," John narrates, "the first time Fanon risks the sea" (151). In what one might imagine to be an ironic form of *marronage*, the seventeen-year-old Fanon, despising the pro-Vichy government in Martinique but believing deeply in the high ideals of France, tries to escape the island to join the Free French army on the other side of the Atlantic. Fanon secretly gains passage to Dominica in the hopes of being sent from there to the front to help liberate the metropole.[1] To pay his way, he steals bolts of cloth his father had bought and intended to have fashioned, as Wideman imagines it, into a suit for the father to wear at his son Felix's wedding.[2]

> Thread by thread, [the father] paid for that wedding suit never cut from cloth the son stole[,] . . . unraveled by the son's thieving fingers, picked apart thread by thread, respun into gold, the gold traded for a ticket, the ticket a passage to a different life a different fate for Frantz who must wear it forever as he wears the father's skin no matter how far from the island of Martinique the stolen ticket transports him. (147)

Fanon's conviction that he is French, a defender of liberty, fraternity, and equality, motivates him to spin, like the young girl in the West Indian version of Rumpelstiltskin, cloth into gold.[3] His unraveling of the cloth's threads, respinning them into the gold that would promise him "passage to a different life," suggests a series of transformations whose alchemy fails.

Drawing from the details of David Macey's biography (a form that, as Macey acknowledges in an interview, borrows its structure of development from the bildungsroman), Wideman invokes a crucial convention of the coming-of-age hero, in which the hero takes his destiny in his own hands by moving from a peripheral hometown to the metropole. But in this case the "stolen ticket" does not take Fanon very far. After a few weeks of languishing in nearby Dominica in the hope that he'll be taken to fight, Fanon is sent back to Martinique and made to return to school.[4] Rather than develop a narrative of progressive incorporation of the self into a civic national order, even an anticolonial aspirational national order, by making that move from the periphery to the metropole, the novel underscores false starts and paradoxically recursive trajectories in the development of an ideal human rights personality. Fanon's effort to shed his genealogical inheritance—his father's skin, his kin cut from the same cloth—in favor of a national one—the purported race-blindness and abstract legal personhood of French national belonging—eventually returns Fanon to the experience of his black skin, with its legally authorized and psychological binds (an experience condensed into the famous line from *Black Skin, White Masks* reporting the response of the French child who sees the newly arrived Fanon and says in fear, "Look, a Negro!").[5] The skin his father hoped to cover with a suit that, unlike his skin, he could take on and off—the skin Fanon had hoped to transcend in his civic union with the nationalism of a free France—becomes "Skin father like son had no choice about, except to slip inside and wear" (146). The experience of racial classification is translated into a costume, a textile of skin that the coming-of-age hero—whose successful self-development of an international human rights personality ostensibly realizes an enfranchised personhood fully and equally integrated into civic society—does not wear, and a skin that Fanon cannot shed. Fanon's "Great Escape" is not recounted using the character development and teleology that conventional biography provides. Instead, Wideman narrates a scene in which a young Frantz's future is being read by the local market woman who silently cuts the father's order of a bolt of cloth, "a tale like Braille she reads in the nap of the fabric, the man's fate, the fate of Frantz, his son, bound and twisted in the threads of this good cloth, cloth the father thinks is one thing, a thing purchased and owned, when in fact it's another, a story the market woman sees and the man can't" (148). Wideman's play on a life as lines of thread—"bound together as threads in a fabric," worried, subject to "wear and tear," "the whole pattern known" before it's begun, measured and cut by the Fates—displaces the fiction of free and full, self-sponsored development affirmed by the conventional coming-of-age story and desired by the young Fanon (146). Like the threads of a life, the textile of skin can never be woven, as a bildungsroman hero must believe, by the one whose life it is, highlighting the tension between the hero's full and free self-development and his normative civic incorporation into the nation.[6] *Fanon* thus provides a response to Slaughter's study of the mutually enabling fictions of the bildungsroman and international human rights law: rather than work to present a normative human personality as the proper subject of human rights, *Fanon* historicizes and disrupts normative models of the legal human personality and its development.[7] Slaughter's contention that the bildungsroman gives narrative shape to the legal personality within international human rights discourse means that narrating Fanon's life story means binding him to, or tearing him from, the fabric of legal recognition.[8]

In Wideman's novel, the local market woman's vision of Fanon's future becomes the counterpart to the narrator's effort to both read and weave Fanon's life into a narrative of development—a text that is expected to render the life into a story, with a sense of purpose and direction, plot and coherence.

> Yes, all threads connect. Yes. No way you can follow how or why. No. You can't choose, even if you could guess where this particular thread or that one might lead. The same step leads everywhere, nowhere. To France. Back home to his island. Glory. Shame. Hitler's fatherland. The motherland. War. Peace. The bottom of the sea. . . . Are there semblances of plot, of direction, purpose, and necessity, in Fanon's story. Someone or something in charge—weird sisters, a deity, Progress, History—wouldn't that be preferable to no one, nothing in charge, only random permutations and combinations of desire and fear, slaughter and love, the relentless cannibalizing of ourselves, our offspring. Why not you in charge, Doctor Fanon. A physician who first cures himself, then cures us, the world, of its ills. Why not you. Seize the bit in your teeth, horse and rider, and ride. (151)

John the narrator not only undercuts his own fantasy of Fanon as heroic maker of his own destiny whose powers of self-direction, self-healing, self-movement go global; he also highlights the artifice required to order a life retrospectively when there is "no one, nothing in charge," directing Fanon's life as it unfolds. Threads, woven together without a discernible beginning or end, form a cloth that perhaps would unravel if the tension produced by their different directions did not hold them together. Wideman tugs on these narrative threads, pulling them into other scripts of romance as heroic transcendence: Fanon imagined as the hero scientist, the gifted psychologist, the doctor with the cures for everything wrong with the world; Fanon imagined not only as the gutsy hero outlaw straight out of a spaghetti Western but also as one so attuned to the horse that, as with Yeats's dancer inseparable from the dance, one cannot tell the rider from the ride.[9]

Against such imagined ends for Fanon are John's bleak sense that neither fiction nor biography can transform a reality that offers no order, progress, or transcendence: "all threads connect," but only in "random permutations and combinations of desire and fear, slaughter and love, the relentless cannibalizing of ourselves, our offspring" (151). Wideman's protracted narrative struggle to make Fanon speak underscores the ethical dilemma in making the absent present only to serve as instrumental figures, as masks for authorial will.[10] The bottom of the sea for all those drowned in the course of the Atlantic slave trade is the same "bottom of the sea" Fanon risks when he sails on the unsteady vessel used to smuggle him to Dominica, the same bottom of the sea Danticat figures as an echo of the middle passage when an unseaworthy vessel carrying Haitian refugees sinks before reaching Miami in "Children of the Sea," and the same fate risked by the Haitian refugees confronted in Brathwaite's "Salvages" by the Coast Guard cutter *Salvages*, which is not at all "trying to save, or salvage, the refugees."[11] Literature as the art of saving, rescuing, or even partially salvaging is never an easy position taken by the writers whose texts I have explored in this book. They are not out on rescue missions so much as they are keyed into the problems and the perils of a system that decides what forms of human life, and what narrative forms, are authorized to be rescued. For the literary texts explored here, narrative form and narrative failure are crucial modes of responding to the archives of legal racial slavery and the categories of legal personhood they have helped construct in the Americas. The readings of contemporary literature in this book have aimed to show how contemporary literature uses narrative forms and aesthetic modes to tell the story of the legal person in a critical way. Wideman's novel questions the complicated ends of salvage in the performance and ultimate refusal of narrative failure in its invocation of the assemblage of masks through which the dead or lost speak: the mediation of narrative and of the mask is always insistently present, never allowing readers to fall into the romance with history that a realist reconstruction of Fanon's life story promises; but never, too, falling simply into the despair that one cannot listen to what the mask has to say and learn something about the spirit.

This book has sought to examine literary responses to the ruinous effects of neoliberal globalization on human life, evoked in the critical discourse on wasted lives, wageless life, disposable people, imperial debris, precarious life, negative personhood, bare life, necropolitics, necro-economics, and so on. These tropes underscore the precarity of the human person and seek to displace the rights-bearing abstract individual legal citizen—or its counterpart, the ideal consumer—from the center of political thought. At the same time, this book suggests that such waste- and death-bound theories of personhood threaten to eclipse the taxonomic logics and contingencies that have shaped the histories and literary imaginings of legal personhood—and, in doing so, eclipse from view the various legal fragments that constitute its masks. The trope of the mask as an assemblage of legal and extralegal fragments is one exemplary figure of the aesthetics of salvage for the literary texts examined in *Salvage Work*. Disrupting generic narrative conventions of the immigrant novel, the bildungsroman, or the postcolonial novel, these literary texts highlight the conventionality of personhood as a legal fiction organized not only by liberal and neoliberal logics but also by its capacity for malleability and metamorphosis, translation, and adaptation across categories, legal and economic systems, and sovereign power.

Where personhood emerges as a generative problem for narrative forms and modes of narration in contemporary literature, it raises challenging questions about the ethics, poetics, and politics of a legal fiction that has had coercive and violent effects on human life throughout the world. Such literature does not provide solutions or calls to action so much as take very seriously the need to delineate the historical and geographic lines of violence, the zones of ethical quandary, and the forms of beauty and value that have shaped the problems of legal personhood. It is work whose importance and potential is felt all the more by its absence in the contemporary political imagination more broadly concerning exceptional categories of legal personhood.

When then U.S. Secretary of State Condoleezza Rice defended the CIA practice of extraordinary rendition, in which unknown numbers of people suspected of terrorist involvement were secretly captured, transported, and detained in undisclosed locations, she argued it was not only lawful but also absolutely necessary to liberal democracy. Invoking the "statelessness" of terrorists and state sovereignty's first and foremost duty to protect its citizens, she explained that these individuals "come from many countries and are often captured far from their original homes. Among them are those who are effectively stateless, owing allegiance only to the extremist cause of transnational terrorism. Many are extremely dangerous. And some have information that may save lives, perhaps even thousands of lives." "The captured terrorists of the 21st

Century," she noted, "do not fit easily into traditional systems of criminal or military justice, which were designed for different needs. We have to adapt. Other governments are now also facing this challenge." Rice's use of the phrase "effectively stateless" was an important linchpin of her argument that rendition "saves lives," citizens' lives to be specific, without violating the rights of other citizens. Even before they are kidnapped and secretly detained, the people who undergo rendition have been tactically relegated to the legal limbo of statelessness, of being a national of no political state on earth. For those kidnapped and detained by the United States or its partners, challenging detention would be to reduce him or her to shadowboxing, as even those detainees allowed hearings are not allowed to hear the full charges or review the evidence against them. From the early modern use of "sovereignlessness" to identify those who may be captured into slavery to the invocation of statelessness to identify those who may be captured in the war on terror, Rice draws on a long history of figuring the stateless person as criminal even as the Bush and then Obama administrations invent new categories of captivity. Naming these categories seals the value of lives and makes of the figure of legal inclusion par excellence, the citizen, a "precarious privilege" that recognizes the stateless and the citizen alike as persons who may be assassinated by drones or indefinitely detained and tortured.[11] The effectively stateless terrorist—effectively denationalized by a performative speech act—is not merely vulnerable to being disposable or wasted but *must* be so, must be disposed of and eliminated.

As is by now well acknowledged by critics of juridical personhood and human rights law, exceptional categories of personhood reveal the unjustness that drives the core operations of unexceptional personhood. If one cannot accept Rice's justification for extraordinary rendition—a justification tweaked, revised, and reused for the current acts by the United States of drone killings as part of what some now call not a war on terror but, more ambiguously and more honestly, the "terror war"—then it must also become impossible to embrace legal personhood as the aim and end goal of movements for political change. Two movements that would seem to have nothing else in common in their politics or their methods share just this belief in the power of law to protect any subject that attains the status of legal personhood: the movement to grant nonhuman animals legal personhood and the movement to expand legal personhood to human fetuses—or even more dramatically, to fertilized human eggs, or the moment of conception.

As the Nonhuman Rights Project, whose objective is to persuade a U.S. higher court to grant legal personhood to a nonhuman animal, puts it,

"The passage from thing to person constitutes a legal transubstantiation. On the outside a legal person appears unchanged from the time she was a legal thing. But she has been transformed and brought to legal life."[13] A 2012 campaign to amend the Mississippi state constitution to define legal human personhood as beginning at the moment of "conception" or its functional equivalent makes a similar case: by voting on Mississippi Amendment Initiative 26, Mississippi can "be the first in the nation to protect every human being from the very beginning of life, whether that life begins by natural or artificial means. By recognizing the personhood of our tiniest brothers and sisters, we will ensure that the preborn receive equal protection under the law regardless of their size, location, developmental stage or method of reproduction."[14] The liberal promise that to be granted legal personhood is to be "brought to legal life," to be moved from the position of an inanimate thing to that of a living rights-bearing subject, has driven two otherwise disparate political movements—one for fetal personhood and the other for nonhuman animal personhood—to a common strategy of expanding legal personhood in unprecedented ways, beyond its current limit to "natural" born persons, or humans, and "artificial" persons, or corporations and other entities. The debate over fetal personhood in particular raises questions about how the conceptual limits of the person arises out of the intimate relations between categories of legal personhood that my book explores in the context of labor identities, national histories, and literary narrative.

Since 2007, Personhood USA, a right-wing grassroots movement based in Colorado, has been working to pass ballot measures in every U.S. state in order to amend state constitutions to include the definition of a person as any fertilized human egg, cloned human genetic material, or "the functional equivalent thereof."[15] A pregnant woman and the zygote/embryo/fetus would then be recognized as two separate and equal persons before the law. Personhood USA calls on supporters to "Stand with us as we declare before the whole world that every person is uniquely created in God's image and deserving of the full protection of the law!"[16] The complexity of the pregnant woman's body, which sustains itself and a developing organism, gives way to a radical extension of the meaning of personhood: it is not only a matter of life and death but also a matter of the Christian spirit and the sovereign law bound to protect it—even as it is unbound by corporeality, at once transformed into an irreplicable representation of an image and a microscopic cluster of cells preceding the recognizably human form.

While Personhood USA's state ballot initiatives have not yet succeeded, prosecutors and legislators in dozens of states have been quietly but effectively affirming the personhood of the fetus over and against the personhood of the pregnant woman in common law court decisions across the country since the Supreme Court ruling in *Roe v. Wade* in 1973.[17] During the 1980s, a rash of cases tested the limits of fetal personhood against that of the mother.[18] Perhaps most notorious was the case of Angela Carder, a previous cancer survivor who was newly diagnosed with lung cancer while pregnant. Carder chose aggressive treatment for her cancer that posed risks to the fetus, which by this point had virtually no chance of being viable. When hospital administrators learned of these developments, they held a hearing with separate counsel representing Carder, her fetus, and the hospital, and determined that an effort to save the fetus was justified even if it caused the death of the mother. Against her wishes and those of her husband, parents, and doctors, Carder was forced by court order to undergo a cesarean-section delivery of her twenty-six-week fetus, although it was known that the surgery would likely end her life and give the fetus little chance for survival. Carder, who cried on learning of her baby's death, lapsed into a coma and died two days later. In recent decades, fetal personhood legislation has only intensified, leading to cases including that of Marlise Muñoz in 2014. Muñoz was fourteen weeks pregnant when she collapsed and was rushed to a hospital in Fort Worth, Texas. Hospital officials refused to disconnect her from life support, even after they acknowledged the woman was medically and legally dead and her fetus was not viable. Hospital officials pointed to Texas state law regarding the "protection" of the unborn child and fought the Muñoz family in court until a district judge finally ruled that the hospital misinterpreted Texas law by keeping a dead woman on life support.[19]

Categories of personhood carry with them not only specific histories (in this case, *Roe v. Wade* and the biopolitics of legislated motherhood) but also the potential for transforming the meanings of legal personhood in new ways. While the discursive framework of such legal cases tends to emphasize the woman's bodily integrity and right to privacy, it is the conceptual problem of the "person" as a necessary yet ambiguous legal fiction, as well as the image of the human personality as presented to and by the law, that lie at the core of fetal and maternal personhood debates. The mother gains a legal personality that makes her at once absolutely responsible for, and always potentially criminal toward, the fetus—and the fetus gains a legal personality as, in the words of one assistant district attorney, "the most innocent of victims."[20] Fetal personhood discourse makes the deceptively simple claim that the offspring of two humans is human, whether birthed or not, independently viable or not, and thus deserving of personhood. In revising the taxonomy of legal personhood to introduce and then delimit the fetal person, the law would paradoxically transform the figure of the maternal person into an always potential criminal guarantor of the life that develops from her eggs. As the 1988 Illinois Supreme Court decision in *Stallman v. Youngquist* concluded, interpretations of fetal personhood could make "mother and child . . . legal adversaries from the moment of conception until birth."[21] Moreover, the mother would be created as a new class of persons, one whose personhood is not only automatically subordinated to that of the fetus from the elusive moment of conception but also has a "legal duty to guarantee the mental and physical health of another," a duty of one person to another "never before . . . recognized in law."[22] In this case, the expansion of personhood to the fetus depends on its alienation from the personhood of the mother: commenting on another court case, the *Stallman v. Youngquist* opinion worries that such expansion "would have the law treat a pregnant woman as a stranger to her developing fetus."[23]

Although legal decisions like the court order affecting Carder were eventually overturned or vacated in the 1990s, a number of fetal personhood cases in more recent years have been brought against pregnant women in a resurgence of fetal personhood claims that depend on a toxic mixture of institutional biopolitics, the legacy of the drug wars as played out largely on the bodies of low-income women and women of color, and the reinterpretation of current state laws originally passed to protect children from abuse and injury or to acknowledge the special harm done to pregnant women by third-party assailants.[24] For example, since the 1997 South Carolina State Supreme Court decision *Whitner v. South Carolina* held that pregnant women who allegedly "risk harm" to their fetuses may be prosecuted under state child endangerment laws, women have served jail time for stillbirths whose causes may be medically unproven but assumed to be related to illegal drug addiction.[25] In 2006, a sixteen-year-old girl in Mississippi whose stillborn baby tested positive for cocaine was charged with "depraved heart murder," or killing with "a callous disregard for human life," and faces a life sentence without the possibility of parole until the age of sixty-five. The state of Alabama—what one reporter calls "the national capital for prosecuting women on behalf of their newborn children"—has aggressively prosecuted and sentenced pregnant women for violating a "chemical endangerment" law, even if their babies are born healthy, by interpreting the term "environment" to also mean the "womb," and "child" to also mean "fetus."[26] A woman in Indiana was charged with fetal homicide for the premature birth and loss of her daughter following her attempted suicide. And a woman in

Iowa was arrested on suspicion that she deliberately fell down a flight of stairs in order to end her pregnancy.[27]

Efforts in state and federal legislation, no less than common law court decisions, have been strengthening fetal personhood claims. One Georgia state representative, for instance, introduced a 2011 fetal personhood bill that redefines the "product of human conception" as "prenatal human person," the "induced termination of pregnancy" with "prenatal murder," and every miscarriage into a potential crime required to be reported and investigated.[28] Drafted in the same year, a congressional bill, the Life at Conception Act, echoes the Personhood USA amendment initiatives at the federal level: it affirms that "the terms 'human person' and 'human being' include each and every member of the species homo sapiens at all stages of life, including the moment of fertilization, cloning, or other moment at which an individual member of the human species comes into being."[29] In this new approach to fighting *Roe v. Wade*, biological human life at the cellular level becomes the sole requirement, measure, and purpose of legal personhood. The person becomes, simply, all that is absolutely and irreducibly human from the moment of biological "conception" or legally fictive "conceptualization." The language of personhood proves itself mutable, transforming not only legal and biological relationships between bodies but also the very meaning and shape of those bodies and the categories of personhood that represent them before the law. Personhood, moreover, proves itself doubly mutable—both changeable and vulnerable to being rendered silent or unheard—as legal cases and jurisprudence establish the terms under which one may be heard as a person before the law. And this mutability itself suggests that, as conceptions of personhood shift into new forms, there is a history of hidden continuities, instability, and paradox that shapes the current taxonomy of persons before the law.

Explicitly invoked and claimed as part of the genealogy of fetal personhood and nonhuman animal rights advocacy, slavery and abolition, as well as, to a lesser extent, incarceration, have been central to subsequent debates over the meanings and bounds of personhood, property, and labor (in its free wage and its reproductive forms). The history of racialized legal personhood in the United States has been appropriated by personhood advocates, who adapt this history to fit an array of political projects to reform, revise, remake, or redefine the meanings of personhood in the law. Fetal personhood groups, for instance, claim to have inherited the political legacy of the abolitionist movement: likening the aborted zygote to the antebellum slave, Bryan Longworth of Personhood Florida asks, "Where do you go to buy a good slave today? . . . You can't get one. Why? Because people now see slavery as abhorrent, and one day people will see abortion as equally abhorrent, if not more abhorrent."[30] Lynn Paltrow, founder and executive director of National Advocates for Pregnant Women, argues that rather than benignly expand the rights of personhood to all forms of human life, "fetal separatism, in the guise of adding one group to the Constitutional population, will do something unprecedented in US history: subtracting another."[31] She emphasizes, "Women are being stripped of their constitutional personhood and subjected to truly cruel laws. . . . It's turning pregnant women into a different class of person and removing them of their rights."[32] Fetal personhood initiatives have little to say about potential effects on the legal personhood of the pregnant woman, which opponents such as Paltrow compare to the dystopia of Margaret Atwood's *Handmaid's Tale*, in which women become refigured as depersonalized vessels of reproduction. The legal construction of the uterus may be understood in the related context of what Alan Hyde calls "the legal vagina," a "hiding place, full of secrets the eye cannot behold from outside, where drugs or other mysterious narratives lurk," and which, in its discursive construction, "turns out to be [among] the least private, most specularized body" constructed by law.[33] It is as if the intimate biological relationship of the in utero fetus and the pregnant mother, when defined in the language of legal personhood, makes a slave of one or the other.

Slavery has also become a defining analogy for animal rights activists who challenge the status of nonhuman animals as property in law. These advocates seek to expand the limits of the person to nonhuman animals, which, as a category of beings, cannot speak for themselves and have historically been treated as objects, things, and property in law.[34] If supporters of fetal personhood challenge the temporal axis of human development when identifying the boundary of legal personhood, animal rights activists challenge the taxonomic border between the human and other animal species in their bid for a liberal expansion of personhood rights.[35] As the general counsel to PETA argues, "Slavery is slavery, and it does not depend on the species of the slave any more than it depends on gender, race, or religion."[36] The legacy of slavery and abolition is invoked here in order to make the moral claim for expanding personhood where the humanity of the legal person, as a moral agent, is presumed in law even when the "person" is not identified in law, as in the Thirteenth Amendment, which prohibits slavery and involuntary servitude except as punishment for a crime but makes no mention of "persons" or "humans." It is on this basis that PETA has filed a lawsuit against Sea World alleging that the aquatic entertainment park violated the Thirteenth Amendment by literally enslaving orca whales that were kidnapped and forced to live and work in the park, technically bypassing the legal question of whether orca whales are constitutional persons while effectively proving them to be so.[37]

But the history of legal slavery also haunts the discourse in ways that fetal or nonhuman animal advocates may not invoke or even recognize. Although the Nonhuman Rights Project imagines that the legal "transubstantiation" from thing to person would guarantee the rights of the nonhuman animal, the legal status of the slave as a person once again suggests that dispossession and exclusion inheres in the very category of legal personhood. It is a strange irony that the haunting aftereffects of legal racial slavery continue to be felt so painfully in contemporary black life and across racial, labor, and national categories of personhood, even as the legal abolition of racial slavery becomes a pervasive metaphor for the moral victory and the master precedent for extending the boundaries of legal personhood.

It is in response to these fundamental contradictions of legal personhood—to the wreckage and debris of legal personhood in the history of the Americas—that contemporary literature speaks. Significantly, Wideman's *Fanon* does not feature a single moment of uncomplicated recuperation. It does not find the real "Fanon." What it does do is perform the labor of salvaging the cities and persons who have forgone the promise of salvation but who refuse the dismissal as ruined. This salvage work invokes the creative powers of assembling discarded fragments, of tracing the marks of ruination, and of thinking anew the politics and poetics of personhood that holds our lives and shapes their courses in times both ordinary and not. Salvage work is what prompts John the narrator to think—on watching Jean-Luc Godard's film *Our Music* and amid John's efforts to give words to Fanon's legacy during the invasions and occupations of Afghanistan and Iraq and during spikes in racial and class violence in the zones of empire—about the meaning of archaeological efforts to read the meanings of Sumerian stones. He wonders, "Are words and stones equally unquiet, restless, swirling, bloodstained and dangerous even when they seem to be asleep . . . A vast field of stones scattered in the desert, meaningless fragments and fragments of fragments, indecipherable signs of disorder, waiting for someone to imagine what they once were, what they might become" (104–5). It is a creative practice both attentive to and fraught with the burden of recognition and transformation, as Sibylle Fischer suggests in a dedication to Destimare Pierre Isnel (aka Louko). Fischer quotes Louko, a sculptor in Port-au-Prince's Grand Rue neighborhood who died in the January 12, 2010, earthquake in Haiti, as saying, "There are no limits here, there are so many things here. No limits to what I can do. Anything you find—just give it to me. Everything they throw in the garbage, I use it. This is the thing you see: old stuff. And then the transformation of objects into new things."[38] It is a response to catastrophe that makes use of the rubble to build an aesthetic and political imagination made of, but also beyond, that catastrophe that began with the flickering of persons and money, biological life and civic death. Legal personhood reveals itself to be an ethical failure and definitional impossibility that nonetheless constitutes the contours and limits of every person before the law. It is left to the literary and artistic imagination to perform the work of salvaging personhood, responding to current debates over the legal status of workers, refugees, prisoners, and corporations by exploring how the terms of legal personhood have formalized the uneven shuttling between agency and abjection, economic life and civic death, authority and criminality that continues to animate the Americas.

Notes

Introduction: Contemporary Literature and the Legal Person

1. For Joseph Slaughter's distinction between the legal person and the common meaning of personhood and personality that is synonymous with the self and psychological behavior, see his *Human Rights, Inc.,* 17–18. I discuss the distinction between legal personhood and psychological personality in my reading of Fanon in chapter 4. See also Noonan.

2. Colin Dayan reads John Locke's inquiries into personhood in *An Essay Concerning Human Understanding* (1689) as a potential challenge to the philosophy and science that sought to prove human inequality and racial inferiority, suggesting that his inquiries into the person as a "thinking thing" had the potential to destabilize or call into question the boundaries between thing, animal, and human self. Locke's argument "that differences between animal and human consciousness are only differences of degree," Dayan argues, "skewered prejudicial judgments about the mental and physical history of the types of mankind, especially popular in theories of human inequality and pro-slavery ethnographies that saw blacks as akin to brute creation" (*The Law Is a White Dog,* 123). She argues that Locke's thought experiments about what constitutes personhood were then misused by Edward Long and others in the development of civil and penal law in North America and the Caribbean (116–27). Dayan's reading of Locke's potential provides a counterpart to contemporary readings of Locke's philosophies of personhood as excluding the African slave. Sibylle Fischer's reading of Locke through his discussions of slavery in his *Two Treatises of Government* (1690) and in his *Fundamental Constitutions for the Government of Carolina* (1669) is helpful here. Fischer notes that in Locke's *Second Treatise,* political slavery—in which a prisoner taken in a just war may be used as a slave—is justified as "a continuation of the state of war" (Fischer, "Fantasies of Bare Life" 6), while the racial slavery protected in *Fundamental Constitutions*—in which he states, "Every freeman of Carolina shall have absolute power and authority over his negro slaves, of what opinion or religion soever"—becomes an exception to political slavery (Locke, Art. 110, quoted in Fischer,

"Fantasies of Bare Life" 7). As Fischer notes, "What we see in Locke is a cleavage opening up between two kinds of slavery, one defined in relation to the sovereign, and one defined in terms of interpersonal domination. The first relation opens toward the space of the political, where slavery will be banned. The second one opens toward the space of property relations, where slavery will be admitted. . . . Ultimately, this cleavage, which separates politics from race and makes race a nonpolitical issue, became crucial for the foundation of modern politics in the Atlantic World" (7).

3. Dayan, *White Dog*, xvii. Dayan draws in part from an account of the masks of law as magical in Noonan, 20.

4. Dayan, *White Dog* 41.

5. Best, "Neither Lost nor Found" 157.

6. Ibid., 156. See my brief discussion of the archive in chapter 3. Here, Best goes on to quote Michel-Rolph Trouillot, who importantly points out that there are never merely absences or presences in the archive "but mentions or silences of various kinds and degrees" (Trouillot, *Silencing the Past* 48, quoted in Best 156). For his study of silences and the production of historical narratives, which informs chapter 2 of this book, see Trouillot, *Silencing the Past*. For a mode of reading the presence of absence and the significations of blackness in U.S. literature and culture that also informs my use of salvage as a mode of reading, see Morrison, *Playing in the Dark*.

7. Hartman, "Venus in Two Acts." Hartman's essay reflects on the "ubiquitous presence of Venus in the archive of Atlantic slavery," inasmuch as "Venus" becomes the name for any and all the enslaved women and girls subject to sexual violation in the context of the legal and racial degradation of slavery. The historical slave girl that forms the subject of Hartman's essay is thus one instantiation, one guise among many that "Venus" has been made to assume. See also Hartman's memoir, *Lose Your Mother*.

8. Hartman, "Venus" 10–12. The defense rested on the claim that the girls had "the pox" (10–11).

9. Ibid., 4.

10. Ibid., 13.

11. Ibid., 4. The word *person* additionally refers to the commonsense meaning of the physical human body (as in references to "one's person") and to human genitalia (specifically, the penis in nineteenth-century vagrancy laws and laws on indecent exposure). For his readings of the legal discursive construction of bodies and body parts, especially as they relate to rights and property, see Hyde, especially chapter 9, "The Legal Vagina," and chapter 10, "The Legal Penis," 165–86. See also "person, n," *Oxford English Dictionary*.

12. Hartman, "Venus" 4. As Hartman notes, "Two girls died on board the *Recovery*. The captain, John Kimber, was indicted for having 'feloniously, wickedly and with malice aforethought, beaten and tortured a female slave, so as to cause her death: and he was again indicted for having caused the death of another female slave'" (7). Hartman here quotes from *The Trial of Captain John Kimber for the Murder of Two Female Negro Slaves, on Board the Recovery, African Slave Ship* (1792), 2.

13. Hartman, "Venus" 8.

14. See Glissant and see Brathwaite, *Contradictory Omens* 64. I take the phrase "haunted Atlantic" from Fehskens 409. See also Deloughrey's comparative study of Pacific and Atlantic island literatures and cultural theories, which includes extended readings of Brathwaite's poetry and essays as well as its resonance with a broader

understanding of Caribbean Atlantic and Pacific Island archipelagos as "a submarine rhizome" (*Routes and Roots* 25).

15. Walvin 157–58. Walvin quotes from the testimony of Colonel James Kelsall. According to the former first mate, an African who spoke some English told the first mate that the captives were begging to endure starvation and thirst on board rather than be flung into the waters to drown or be devoured by sharks: they were denied, perhaps because such "natural" deaths could not be classified as recoverable losses under maritime insurance (157–58). The *Zong* finally arrived in Jamaica, where the 208 African survivors were sold. There is some question as to whether it was the captain, or whether it was the idea of Robert Stubbs (See Walvin chap. 8).

16. According to Ian Baucom, 440 captive Africans and the slave ship were insured as property for a total of 15,700 pounds (Baucom 11). For his book-length exploration of the *Zong* case, from which he elaborates a theory of accumulation, see Baucom.

17. The retrial was granted, but no evidence exists as to whether it was ever held or whether the underwriter ever paid the Gregson group its insurance money.

18. Alerted to the killings by Olaudah Equiano, the British abolitionist Granville Sharp worked to publicize the horror of the *Zong*: he insisted on recording the courtroom proceedings as evidence with the unsuccessful aim of prosecuting the captain and involved parties for murder.

19. All quotations are from *Sharp Transcript*, 30–32, quoted in Walvin 145–47.

20. Philip 211. Justice Buller, in favor of a retrial, counters this claim by, curiously enough, dismissing the relevance of murder to the judgment of this case: "the argument drawn from the law respecting indictments for murder does not apply. There the substance of the indictment is proved, though the instrument with which the crime was effected be different from that laid" (211).

21. Conventional historical narratives of Britain's abolition of the slave trade in 1807 do not seem troubled by the absence of voices from the African victims of the *Zong* catastrophe: rather, their absence serves a triumphal story in which the *Zong* case and the cultural representations it inspired led a once-ignorant but essentially moral British public to a growing awareness of the horrors of the transatlantic slave trade and ultimately its abolition. Even aside from the erasure of Africans in the archive, the abolition of the transatlantic trade in humans did not end the trans-Atlantic trade or the mass killings of captive Africans so much as shift the economy outside the law, into illegality. Captives continued to be abused and killed at sea when ships needed to lighten their weight or eliminate the evidence of their illicit trade. Ships once registered and flagged in the financial capital of the slave trade, Liverpool, began to fly under other flags, anticipating the modern system of flags of convenience that I discuss in chapter 1. This conventional narrative of slave trade abolition is troubled by the very icons it celebrates. Consider J. M. W. Turner's masterpiece, *The Slave Ship*, also known as *Slavers Throwing Overboard the Dead and Dying—Typhoon Coming On* (1840), depicting a slave ship amid tumultuous waters, with the small figures of enslaved Africans only gradually discernible as they are being thrown into the sea. Often assumed to be a painting of the *Zong* that helped to stir public sympathies against the slave trade (and the subject of writers' reflections, from John Ruskin to Paul Gilroy), Walvin convincingly argues that Turner's painting depicts this period after the abolition of the slave trade—and not the *Zong*, as is often believed (Walvin 1–12).

22. Mbembe 40.

23. Glissant 6. Glissant conceptualizes the experience of Africans who endured the "deportation to the Americas" as a delving into the abyss (5). Before encountering the abyss of the ocean where slaves were thrown overboard, an ocean "whose time is marked by these balls and chains gone green," the Africans were thrown into the potentially world-making abyss of the slave ship or "open boat" (5): "What is terrifying partakes of the abyss, three times linked to the unknown. First, the time you fell into the belly of the boat . . . the belly of this boat dissolves you, precipitates you into a nonworld from which you cry out. This boat is a womb, a womb abyss. . . . This boat is your womb, a matrix, and yet it expels you. This boat: pregnant with as many dead as living under sentence of death" (6). For an insightful reading of Glissant's meditation on the abyss as a generative making of a "new world"—as an "experience of the world as entirety" and as "inspir[ing] a kind of thinking-knowledge that extends itself almost physically across the world," see Radović 475–76.

24. In his 1882 lecture, "What Is a Nation?," Ernst Renan suggests that the need for forgetting—even for "historical error"—is, paradoxically, necessary to invent the shared legacy of national memories he argued was necessary for his vision of nationalism as a spiritual principle. Historical knowledge threatens national unity because, for Renan, "historical enquiry brings to light deeds of violence which took place at the origin of all political formations, even of those whose consequences have been altogether beneficial. Unity is always effected by means of brutality" (11).

25. Best, "Neither Lost nor Found" 156.

26. Ibid., 159. Best reads Foucault's method of historical ontology that has shaped critical attention to the form of the archive. Foucault treats "kinds of persons" as objects generated by and circulating within discursive systems that cannot exist outside those systems: for those objects, "the archive exists as their sole condition of possibility" (159). For Best, who draws from this thought but also presses against it, Foucault's thinking on the archive establishes the "payoff for scholars of the slave past" in this way: "since the remnants of slavery always exist inside the regimes of power that produced them as such, they are never purely there as objects. They are never simply approachable. Rarefied, obscured, simultaneously emergent and lost: these are the fictions of the archive that have provided a structure to the broad historiography of slavery and that shape slavery in the visual imagination" (159).

27. Moten 742.

28. On studies of representations of slavery in contemporary US and Caribbean literature and culture, see, for example, Spillers, *Black, White, and in Color;* Rushdy, *Neo-Slave Narratives;* Dubey, *Signs and Cities;* Holland; Keizer; Tillet; Russ; and Handley.

29. Stoler, *Imperial Debris* 2; emphasis in original. Stoler notes the limitations of such ready-made and pervasive terms such as "colonial legacy" as opposed to "imperial debris": a "legacy" makes no distinction between what holds and what lies dormant, between residue and recomposition, between what is a holdover and what is reinvested, between a weak and a tenacious trace. Such rubrics instill overconfidence in the knowledge that colonial histories matter—far more than they animate an analytic vocabulary for deciphering *how* they do so. Such terms do little to account for the contemporary force of imperial remains, what people themselves count as colonial effects, and, as important, what they do about what they are left with" (12). I follow Stoler's use of "imperial debris" but also point out the usefulness of thinking about "colonial legacy" as a way of understanding the law's temporal effects on personhood, especially when

what is at stake is literally a legal inheritance of property and the politics of gender, sex, and reproduction that shape the claims to, and exclusions from, such legal inheritance, a point detailed in my reading of Ferré's *Sweet Diamond Dust* in chapter 2.

30. Stoler, *Imperial Debris* 2.

31. Caleb Smith 17.

32. Here I borrow Rob Nixon's phrase for environmental crises not recognized as such because they happen in unspectacular ways, slowly over time, and on the bodies and geographies of the global poor and people of color. See Nixon.

33. As I discuss in chapter 3, Gates rejects Jones's novel *Mosquito* as an exemplary mode of the "talking book" or the signifying monkey. On the trope of the talking book, see Gates, *Signifying Monkey* 127–69.

34. Stoler, *Imperial Debris* 19.

35. See my discussion of DeLombard and Waligora-Davis in chapter 1.

36. The failure to develop, what I explore in chapter 4 as a narrative tactic that structures Wideman's novel *Fanon*, has become part of the material history for other kinds of cultural and economic salvage work in postindustrial cities such as Detroit: that of international photographers who in recent years have documented the city as itself a colossal contemporary ruin; that of the Detroit artist Tyree Guyton, whose Heidelberg Project has transformed his residential property into a living exhibition of junk art and a community-building effort, against city ordinances for over twenty-five years; and that of Detroiters who, as the rapper Danny Brown describes in his track "Scrap or Die," strip valuable materials from abandoned buildings, salvaging the material remains of the city in order to survive. For readings of Detroit as ruins, see McGraw and Leary. For books of ruin photography, see Austin and Doerr, the more widely discussed book by Marchand and Meffre, and Levine and Moore.

37. Kara Walker, *A Subtlety*, 2014.

38. Walker's *A Subtlety* is discussed further in chapter 2, along with narrative fiction that rehearses and contests the romantic narrative mode that have shaped sugar's legacies.

39. Sharpe xii. In this way, a salvage aesthetic is informed by Morrison's account of her historical novels as "a kind of literary archeology," excavating what has been hidden or even absent from the historical record (Sharpe, xi). See Morrison, "Site of Memory." See Sharpe for her readings of literary and historical representations of Afro-Caribbean women, especially Jamaica's windward Maroon leader, Nanny, who is the subject of Michelle Cliff's fiction, and Mary Prince, the fugitive slave and narrator "of the only known English-language testimony by a West Indian slave woman" (xii).

40. Walcott, "The Antilles."

41. Shockley 808. For a more detailed reading of the poetics of *Zong!*, see Shockley.

42. Philip 196–99.

43. I am reminded of the etymology of the word *existence* by Campbell and Sitze, who note the distinction between existence and life in their reading of Foucault's "anatomo-politics" and the notion that politics no longer qualifies existence but "now appears to have become *autonomous* from existence," thus making "man" an "animal whose *loving* is in some sense separable from its *existing*" (Campbell and Sitze 15).

44. Hartman, "Venus" 13.

45. See Wagner on blackness as "an adjunct to racial slavery," 1. See also the concept of racial melancholia in relation to civic alienation, as discussed in Tillet 3–14; Eng and Han; and Cheng.

46. *detritus*, OED n. 1 and n. 2.

47. Best and Hartman 4. See Best and Hartman on the limits of seeking legal redress within liberal paradigms of justice.

48. Césaire 61. Also quoted in Cliff, *No Telephone to Heaven*, 13.

49. See Cliff, *No Telephone to Heaven*; and Chamoiseau. See Melas for a reading of modes of comparison and Caribbean writers' relation to histories, including Walcott, Césaire, Glissant, and Chamoiseau.

50. Wideman, *Sent for You Yesterday* 168.

51. Finding in the Atlantic Ocean a convergence between the neoliberal, neocolonial global market and the international slave trade, Jamaica Kincaid uses an apparent non sequitur to imagine tourists' fecal waste and African bones fed into an ocean that resembles an archive only in that it is an indiscriminate receptacle of waste. The "contents of your lavatory," she tells the tourist to Antigua, "might, just might, graze gently against your ankle as you wade carefree in the water. . . . But the Caribbean Sea is very big and the Atlantic Ocean is even bigger; it would amaze even you to know the number of black slaves this ocean has swallowed up" (14).

52. Bales, *Disposable People*; Bauman 6, 5. Bales begins his preface to the revised edition of his book with the African Burial Ground in Lower Manhattan, a site I discuss in chapter 1 in my reading of exceptional spaces in *The Ordinary Seaman*. The African Burial Ground not only reveals evidence from the bones of those buried there but also, for Bales, illustrates how "slavery," while illegal, "still exists in New York and around the world. Today it is often hard to see, but it is there. And like the slaves of the African Burial Ground in New York, the slaves all around us today have waited a long time for us and our governments to come awake to their existence" (Bales viii).

53. As the second half of the introduction suggests, the rhetoric of waste relies on the limit cases of civil death and bare life with limited attention to the ways in which the dead or the past may actively haunt the present as a meddling force, to borrow from Avery Gordon's description of haunting in the social imagination. Such rhetoric obscures from view the genealogies of legal personhood that emphasize the unfinished legacies and burdens of colonialism and legal slavery (rather than the premise of the citizen as the normative figure of the political) as they shape contemporary legal identities. On haunting, see Gordon, *Ghostly Matters*.

54. Noonan quotes Chief Justice Marshall's claim that "the vessel acts and speaks" and notes the ship's gendered personification as feminine in law (3).

55. See Franco.

56. Ibid., 193.

57. Torres Rivas, quoted in Franco 192.

58. Walcott continues, "The sigh of History rises over ruins, not over landscapes, and in the Antilles there are few ruins to sigh over, apart from the ruins of sugar estates and abandoned forts." Walcott, "The Antilles."

59. Brathwaite, "Caribbean Man in Space and Time," quoted in Russ 4.

60. See Glissant 5–10, 63–76.

61. Cliff, "Caliban's Daughter" 40.

62. Ibid., 45.

63. Wacquant 113, quoted in Bauman 81.

64. Berger 4–5, quoted in Nixon 18.

65. Nixon 10.

66. Deloughrey, "Heavy Waters" 708. Critics note that the 1981 interdiction agreement between Ronald Reagan and Jean-Claude Duvalier is in violation of international law and U.S. policies on asylum seekers. For an insightful study of the figure of the refugee and the ethics of hospitality, especially with respect to the treatment of Haitian refugees in their encounters with the U.S. Coast Guard, see also Shemak.

67. Deloughrey, "Heavy Waters" 708. For a study of the politics of refugee policies for Central Americans, see also María Cristina García. On how law constructs borders and categories of legal identity, see Dudziak and Volpp.

68. Deloughrey, "Heavy Waters" 710.

69. Deloughrey examines the Atlantic Ocean's "submarine history and its material decay" (Glissant, *Poetics* 6, quoted in Deloughrey, "Heavy Waters" 703) in the context of oceanic space that, increasingly since World War II, has been marked by enlarged state boundaries, militarization, the legal dumping of radioactive materials and heavy metals, and military weapons testing. Building on a long tradition of Caribbean writers who render oceanic modernity "in terms of pollution as well as the wasted lives of slaves and refugees," Deloughrey draws from but promises to complicate the rhetoric of wasted lives by reading waste as a "constitutive process and product of the violence of Atlantic modernity" (710).

70. Fischer, "Fantasies of Bare Life" 12.

71. The impulse to salvage resonates, for example, with the philosophy of history that Zamora reads as energizing twentieth-century U.S. and Latin American fiction—a philosophy of history marked by an "anxiety of origins" and the impulse to construct a usable past from America's many histories (6). As discussed in chapter 2, this impulse to salvage also responds to Scott's view in *Conscripts of Modernity* that "we live in tragic times" after "the end of anticolonialism's promise," a time when postcolonial thought can no longer imagine the present as "a mere transitory moment . . . from a wounded past to a future of salvation" (210).

72. On "sovereignlessness," see Bennett 18–19. On "wageless life," see Denning.

73. Denning argues against Bauman's formulation of humans as waste and as inevitable by-products of globalization. "Bauman's apocalyptic denunciation of our culture of waste is powerful, but it misses the mark," writes Denning, first, "in its overly glib linking of material waste and human waste," thus repeating "one of the oldest tropes regarding the wageless—that they are akin to garbage, rubbish. . . . And indeed there is a connection: for those without wages have long worked as scavengers" (96). Second, Denning contends, discussions of wasted life, precarious life, and bare life are really about how "globalization produces redundancy," which inquiry "would be better understood not through the deceptively concrete image of wasted lives, but through Marx's two dialectically related concepts: the relative surplus population and the virtual pauper" (96). And yet Denning's point ultimately may be too subtly different, for he concludes with yet another offering for more names to give the figure of "bare life" (97). The "virtual pauper," Marx's term for the free wage laborer and what Denning describes as Marx's account of bare life, is "the spectre of wageless life [that] still weighs upon us" (97). See Marx, *Grundrisse* 604.

74. For Noonan, "property," applied to humans, "is a perfect mask," and other masks include such legal categories as "sovereign" and "court," "plaintiff" and "defendant" (20).

75. U.S. Constitution, Art. 1, Sec. 2. Thanks to Michael LeMahieu for his discussion of this point.

76. Slaughter 18.

77. See Noonan on the history of the Latin *persona* as "the disguise adopted by the actor" that "came to mean an intelligent, self-subsisting being." In this way, Noonan fears that "in the law, masks concealing persons" are "being replaced by them, the acceptance of masks being the greater sin" (27). By "fabrication," I evoke its meanings as both a construction and a lie, following Morrison's discussion of the "fabrication of racism" (*Playing in the Dark*, 11) and Haney López's extension of Morrison's term in his study of the "legal fabrication of race" (94).

78. Noonan 26.

79. See Noonan 19–25. His reminder, "No person itself, the law lives in persons," aims to make human beings the properly acknowledged center of law (Noonan 4, also quoted in Dayan 25 n. 37).

80. Noonan 25, 19.

81. Ibid., 19–20.

82. Ibid., 26. In this way, he disagrees with the early-twentieth-century legal theorist Hans Kelsen's contention, "The concept of physical (natural) person means nothing but the personification of a complex of legal norms" as a kind of pure constructivism, what Noonan describes as an "imaginary universe corresponding to nothing in existence" (Kelsen 95, quoted in Noonan 27).

83. For her incisive study of the blood logics of legal native Hawaiian status and its consequences for politics of sovereignty, indigeneity, and ancestry, see Kauanui.

84. Here it may be helpful to remember Foucault's contention that "racism" functions as a biopower of the modern State "to fragment" the species by creating "the break between what must live and what must die," and to see in one's life the need to kill the inferior other, establishes the "indispensable precondition that allows someone to be killed" (Foucault, "Society Must Be Defended" 74–75).

85. On the limits of historic arguments for inclusion and equal rights rhetoric, see Robyn Wiegman, *American Anatomies*.

86. Tillet 3.

87. Cheng 10, quoted in Tillet 8.

88. Tillet 4, 10.

89. Cameron ix.

90. In pointing to how purportedly race-neutral laws and jurisprudence support the architecture of social injustice rather than dismantle it, critical race theory and American studies scholarship provide important critiques of liberal legalism by recognizing the limits of redress and bringing into view the process by which legal identities are experienced by those subjected and multiply constituted by the law. What post–civil rights narratives of triumph disavow is thus revealed to be that with which court cases for legal redress or reparations cannot reckon: even before slavery was abolished, "it was too late to imagine the repair of its injury" (Best and Hartman 1). The "signature of violence" cannot be unwritten; the injury created by the category of the legal slave as blackness could not be undone (Wagner 77). It is an injury that appears in new contexts, is changed by them, and yet recalls the threat of the slave mask and the iron ankle cuff, as Cliff's *No Telephone to Heaven* evokes in the body a black veteran from Alabama traumatized by his time in Vietnam. Despite the passage of years, a flesh wound on his ankle whose original cause he could not remember remains open: "The wound was livid and refused to heal" (145). If the language of injury informs our thinking of legal personhood and the subjects it figuratively covers with the sign, the

mask or the vestments, of the law, it is not to suggest the promise of healing and whole-ness that is sometimes part of liberal paradigms of redress and democratic inclusion. The fracturing of black personhood into three-fifths, for example, cannot be made whole by arriving at a whole number.

The rhetoric of injury has been redefined and deployed in important ways in criti-cal race theories. Yet, as Carl Gutierrez-Jones contends, their critiques of the liberal imagination, by being "too reticent to pursue the interpenetration of legal issues and larger cultural questions," leads the critical race studies project to "duplicate uncriti-cally the legal institution's fantasy of autonomy" (95). Like a flesh wound, the injury that inheres within the category of the legal black slave personality brings not only pain but also the peril of economic devaluation, and of being assigned a legal sta-tus equivalent to waste—but, crucially, injury is not equivalent to becoming waste. The metaphor of injury in the law evokes an instability in valuation and thus in the rights, duties, and conditions in which the voice of the person may be heard by the law. Wounded bodies live with injury, and injury alters the body over time, even if invisibly. Gutierrez-Jones proposes that, instead of "reinvoking the legacy of slavery as a paradigmatic injury," readers of race and culture should work on "complicating the rhetorical uses of injury," which "marks an act against . . . the law, rights, and accepted privilege" but also produces a rhetorical ambiguity between injury as an intentional wounding and injury as caused by an act without a particular agent (76–77).

91. Fanon, *Black Skin, White Masks* 9.

92. Then-presidential hopeful Mitt Romney was quoted as saying, "Corporations are people, my friend." See Rucker.

93. Morrison, *Beloved* 82–84.

94. On the slave and on blackness as being in a "negative relation" to law, see Dayan, *White Dog* xii.

95. As with the conventional narratives of how the *Zong* led to the abolition of the British slave trade in 1807, the conventional political account of U.S. abolition and Jim Crow reinforces assumptions that underwrite political liberalism. The violence of the slave system and of Jim Crow laws get figured as aberrations from the benign democratic norm: according to this kind of accounting, once the collective moral conscience of citizens is awakened, and the people are thus reminded of the moral founding principles of the nation, the aberration is rightly destroyed.

96. A salvage aesthetics may resemble Foucault's discussion of historical geneal-ogy—not as a genealogical search for origins or a legitimating narrative of the biologi-cally reproductive family but rather as a gathering-together of histories, in the form of narrative fiction, that calls into question the political terms of social life. See Foucault, "Nietzsche, Genealogy, History."

97. Wald reads the language of U.S. legal cases and legislation as constructing inco-herent, unstable, and indistinct categories of personhood for women, tribal nations, immigrants, descendants of Africans, and those living in Puerto Rico and other "unin-corporated territories" of an imperial nation. See Wald's *Constituting Americans* for her discussion of the contradictions in law and personhood that nineteenth- and early twentieth-century U.S. literary writers, politicians, and judges attempted to negotiate.

98. Wald 8.

99. For a collection of essays on Puerto Rico's legal status, see Burnett and Marshall.

100. Mbembe points to the variations of this subject that depend on the need for violence to come into being: "The subject of Marxian modernity is, fundamentally, a

subject who is intent on proving his or her sovereignty through the staging of a fight to the death. Just as with Hegel, the narrative of mastery and emancipation here is clearly linked to a narrative of truth and death. Terror and killing become the means of realizing the already known telos of history" (20).

101. Agamben, "Beyond Human Rights" 16, 21.

102. Ibid., 21.

103. Ibid., 26.

104. Waligora-Davis, *Sanctuary* 5.

105. Ibid., xvi.

106. Ngai 4; emphasis in original.

107. Perry 63–84.

108. See Fischer, "Fantasies of Bare Life," for her helpful gloss on *nuda vita* as a translation of Walter Benjamin's term *das blosse Leben* in his early essay "Toward a Critique of Violence." She writes, "Like 'bare' in English, *bloss* in German can mean 'mere,' but it is etymologically related to terms like *Bloesse* and *entbloessen*, hence to the idea of an exposure or vulnerability due to a (limited) nakedness. But *bloss is not* synonymous with 'naked.' By contrast, *nudo* in Italian can mean both 'mere' and 'naked,' thus shifting the weight toward the dramatic, fully exposed nakedness." Binetti and Casarino translate *nuda vita* as "naked life" rather than "bare life" in Agamben, *Means without End*. See also Norris.

109. Arendt 300. Arendt here reads Burke and exposes the paradoxes of human rights as conceptualized by the French revolutionary Declaration of the Rights of Man, with its secular sacredness of the human, and the subsequent work of international human rights.

110. Arendt 300. The legal term "natural persons" to denote any human being implicitly relies on the notion of human rights—that merely being human is enough to be a recognized as a person. Following Joseph Slaughter and other critics of human rights discourse, I understand the person to be a legal fiction distinct from, but linked to, the human being.

111. Agamben, *Homo Sacer*.

112. Ibid., 64.

113. Ibid., 174.

114. Bare life also occupies the "threshold of indistinction" between itself and the political life of the citizen; it is a form of life included in the political order only through its exclusion. As Agamben notes, "Precisely because they [the *Versuchspersonen*, humans subjected to Nazi scientific experimentation in concentration camps] were lacking almost all the rights and expectations that we customarily attribute to human existence, and yet were still biologically alive, they came to be situated in a limit zone between life and death, inside and outside, in which they were no longer anything but bare life" (159). The indistinctness of borders is a result of the sovereign power to continually redraw or blur them. In the state of exception, law becomes fact and fact becomes law, resulting in yet another "threshold of indistinction," that of juridical rule.

115. Agamben, *Homo Sacer* 174.

116. Ibid., 159, 174.

117. Agamben's later work involves an effort to think of forms of life and collectivity freed from law—see, for example, *The Coming Community* and *The Highest Poverty*, in which monastic life becomes the exemplary form of life to lie outside the law and its mechanisms of violence.

118. Norris 41.

119. Agamben, *Homo Sacer* 181.

120. Ibid., 12. *Homo Sacer* was published to call this political order into question, at a time when the official end of the Cold War, the dissolution of the USSR, and the breakup of the former Yugoslavia spurred a renewed sense of urgency, of crisis, in which the very fabric of the global political order seemed to unravel, threatening to leave its critics with nothing to grasp. See also Jacques Derrida's *Specters of Marx,* which takes the same perceived crisis as its starting point.

121. Agamben, *Homo Sacer* 8, 181.

122. Mbembe 21.

123. Ibid., 40; emphasis in original.

124. Montag 213.

125. See Dayan, *White Dog* 42–43. See also Patterson's opinion piece arguing that black young men suffer from a "cool-pose culture." Patterson, "A Poverty of the Mind."

126. Dayan, *White Dog* 268.

127. Vincent Brown 1234. Where Best questions treatment of the archive as absence, Brown challenges the invocation of "social death" as a substitute for examining the actual "experience of life in slavery" (1236), including forms of sociality and "the political activity of the weak" (1235). Like Best, who question the treatment of the archive of Atlantic slavery as absence, Brown calls for renewed attention to the historical knowledge that *is* available on the lives of the enslaved but that has been subsumed by paradigms of absence, silence, and social death. But recuperating the slave's humanity or actually lived experience, while an important call for rethinking the possibilities of historical knowledge and historiography, misses exactly what makes the legal slave such an important figure for thinking about legal personhood in the present, with its continued instability, contradictions, and continuing animation by laws presumed to have been obsolete long ago.

128. Ibid., 1235.

129. Dayan, *White Dog* 43. These questions are not limited to the contemporary period, as Dayan's own work situates the slave in a long history of multiple legal systems from medieval European notions of blood taint and the *deodand* to French and English colonial slave codes in the Caribbean to contemporary U.S. laws on the personhood of ghosts and objects and the civil death of those marked as prisoners or enemy combatants. The sheer heterogeneity of forces that converge, or collapse, upon the category of the slave at any particular space and time should not be forgotten. Against the origin myth of the transatlantic slave trade, for instance, which says that European colonial interests relied on Roman law and perceived African savagery to easily convert savage into slave, the historian Herman Bennett argues that early modern canon law delineated juridical differences among Africans as either "sovereign," and thus precluded from "unprovoked aggression," or "sovereignless," and thus legitimately vulnerable to enslavement as recognized by both Europeans and Africans (Bennett 18–19). What soon emerges from the fifteenth-century Portuguese slave raids in "Guinea" and competing laws and discourses is a "taxonomy," delineated from the body of a black woman captured in one early raid, "that distinguished Moors from blackamoors, infidels from pagans, Africans from blacks, sovereign from herrschaftlos (sovereignless) subjects, and free persons from slaves" (Bennett 22–23).

130. Here I borrow from H. Bruce Franklin, who writes that the Thirteenth Amendment "actually wrote slavery *into* the Constitution of the United States, but only for

those people legally defined as criminals" (4). Blackmon reads the Thirteenth Amendment's clause allowing involuntary servitude for those "duly convicted" as a way to resubjugate African Americans, an explicit goal of many leading white Southerners after Reconstruction. See Blackmon 53. For critiques of convict labor and the use of prison as a form of racial control, also see Lichtenstein; Alexander; and Davis, *Are Prisons Obsolete?*

131. Caleb Smith 6.

132. Wagner 78. Dayan similarly asks, "What does it mean to exist in a negative relation to law?" (*White Dog* xii).

133. Woody Ruffin was a convict (of apparently unknown racial category, suggesting to me his whiteness) at a work site—he was owned at the time by a private railroad company—and participated in an attempted escape that led to the death of one guard. Convicted but pleading not guilty, Ruffin was sentenced to death. The 1871 case concerned whether the jurisdiction in which the murder trial was held violated Ruffin's rights (Dayan, *White Dog* 60). The case would be used as precedent later for the courts' deference to prison authorities in matters involving prisoner rights and punishments.

134. *Ruffin v. The Commonwealth* (1871). The court opinion further distinguishes between "freemen" and the civilly dead: "The bill of rights is a declaration of general principles to govern a society of freemen, and not of convicted felons and men civilly dead. Such men have some rights it is true, such as the law in its benignity accords to them, but not the rights of freemen. They are the slaves of the State undergoing punishment for heinous crimes committed against the laws of the land. While in this state of penal servitude, they must be subject to the regulations of the institution of which they are inmates, and the laws of the State to whom their service is due in expiation of their crimes."

135. See Carter 1325.

136. Hartman, "Seduction and the Ruses of Power" 552; emphasis in original.

137. Dayan, *White Dog* 43–44; emphasis in original.

138. Ibid., xii. The zombie in Haitian thought is many things—among them, "a momentary and reversible transformation of life" that is a symbol of "a spiritual as well as physical alienation; of the dispossession of self through the reduction of the self to a mere source of labour" (Laroche, "The Myth of the Zombi" 56). The zombie, as a particular trope for the slave and the colonized subject, is importantly a *laboring* vessel, a shell whose selfhood has been hollowed out until there is nothing but the covering, a mask resembling the once human. I suggest that this depersonalization strangely comes to resemble the figure of the legal person. For Dayan, the zombie is the product of a "transgression": zombification may be the "punishment for ambition, greed, disrespect, or slander" (*White Dog* 22). Their social function as, in Dayan's words, "highly contextualized spectacles of alienation" is "to inspire horror in the minds of the community" (*White Dog* 22). In Haitian spiritual life and cultural production, the zombie also—crucially—is not inevitably permanently alienated and living death. Tasting a grain of salt, the zombie can recross the threshold of the living, independently of the controlling power and explicitly to challenge it. If the zombie is the "remnant of loss and dispossession" and in the social context "represents the self undone," then, according to Dayan, "we can use the image" of zombification "in order to understand how things legally emptied of personhood can be repossessed or turned into vessels" for social beings that are "intelligent, aware" (*White Dog* 21–22). These vessels, shaped by the theft of the spirit by the law, may nonetheless be repossessed

with forms of life that in their very being challenges the law. Laroche, "The Myth of the Zombi" 59. On the theme of zombification in Haitian literature, see Lucas, "The Aesthetics of Degradation." For a more anthropological study of the zombie figure, see Ackermann and Gauthier, "The Ways and Nature of the Zombi." For a wide-ranging study of zombies in transatlantic cultures and its relation to a politics of living death, see Lauro.

139. UNHCR, "The World's Stateless People." "Proving statelessness," one UNHCR expert observes, "is like establishing a negative. As the UN report notes, the individual must demonstrate something that is *not* there." UNHCR, "The World's Stateless People"; emphasis in original. Article 1 of the 1954 United Nations Convention relating to the Status of Stateless Persons defines a stateless person as "a person who is not considered as a national by any State under the operation of its law." The UNHCR has tried to establish a legal identity for stateless people, but only a few countries have ratified the convention, underscoring the dilemma of the UNHCR, which is committed to reducing cases of statelessness but only by respecting the terms of state sovereignty as set by individual states.

140. These spaces, including the prison but also work sites and other places where prisoners are managed, are akin to the "anomalous zones" that Waligora-Davis examines in her work on sanctuary. She draws the concept of anomalous zones from Neuman.

141. Dayan, *White Dog* xii.

142. While Fischer in *Modernity Disavowed* reads the constitutions for their anticipatory rhetoric, as manifestoes outlining a possible future, Gulick nonetheless helpfully reminds us that the constitution as a legal document "does have something important to say to us about law" (Gulick 812).

143. 1801 Constitution, Art. 3, Title II, "Of the Inhabitants."

144. 1801 Constitution, Art. 14, 17–18, Title VI.

145. See my discussion of the Haitian Revolution and Trouillot's reading of the revolution as inconceivable within Western epistemologies in chapter 2.

146. 1805 Constitution, Arts. 1–4, quoted in Fischer, *Modernity Disavowed* 275.

147. 1801 Constitution, Art. 4. In the 1805 Constitution: "blackness" was linked to loyalty to the state (including through the multiracial sexual reproduction of white women with black men and the political alliance of white men during the revolution, all of whom now fall under "the generic denomination of blacks," 1805 Constitution, Art. 14, quoted in Fischer, *Modernity Disavowed* 276.

148. 1805 Constitution, Arts. 21–22, quoted in Fischer, *Modernity Disavowed* Appendix A, 281.

149. Peck 15.

150. Harvey, *Neoliberalism* 68.

151. Ibid., 64–65.

152. *Spectator.*

153. Ibid.

154. "The past is never dead. It's not even past." Faulkner 17.

155. Waligora-Davis, *Sanctuary* 12.

156. Jones, *Mosquito* 225.

157. For studies of legal slavery and its racial legacies in the United States and/or the Caribbean, see Fischer, *Modernity Disavowed*; Dayan, *Haiti, History, and the Gods* and *White Dog*; Best, *The Fugitive's Properties*; Waligora-Davis, *Sanctuary*; Wagner;

Gordon; Hartman, *Scenes of Subjection;* and Wong. For examples of studies that read American literatures and cultures in relation to race and ethnicity, labor, migration, and national belonging, see Lowe, *Immigrant Acts;* Camacho; Dubey, *Signs and Cities;* and Schlund-Vials.

158. These genealogies, organized around the trope of salvaging the ruins of the economic present, are the subjects of chapters 1 and 2. And, as I contend in chapters 3 and 4, even when sovereign power has wrought upon the person (or the meanings of personhood) such catastrophes as legal enslavement, social death, death-in-life, civil death, bare life, and various states of injury, there may be room for more vital forms of personhood to emerge in response.

159. Shemak provides a clear critique of the rhetoric that distinguishes an economic alien from political refugee status; she proposes the category of "economic refugee" (12) to better describe the imbrication of politics and economics that compel refuge seekers. See also her reading of the crew in *The Ordinary Seaman* in the legal category "refugee seamen" (179).

160. These texts neither participate in the commonplace of "giving a human face" to them (in which the face enables the presumably indifferent reader or viewer, secure in her own humanity, to discover the same core humanity of those otherwise "faceless" human beings) nor enact a Levinasian theory of the Other (in which a face shows itself as the failed effort to represent the human, a face that might be any part of the body evoking human suffering) on which Levinas structures his theological ethics. See Butler's critique of Levinas in *Precarious Life.* I draw from her reading of Levinas in her essay "Precarious Life."

161. Wideman, *Fanon* 219.

1 / The Free, the Slave, and the Disappeared: States and Sites of Exceptional Personhood in Francisco Goldman's *The Ordinary Seaman*

1. Salgado 12.

2. Ibid., 7.

3. The vessel itself is depicted in the photos as scaled to the globe of an earlier capitalist era. On global scale as "a construct of the circulation of capital" established during the imperial market expansion of the nineteenth century, see Neil Smith, "Contours of a Spatialized Politics" 76. See also Marston 219–42. For her theorizing of the "scale and scope of narcospatiality," see Brady, *Extinct Lands, Temporal Geographies* 172–201.

4. Stallabrass 148.

5. Clifford 73. In Goldman's novel, one of the secret shipowners, Elias, simultaneously celebrates, consumes, and appropriates Amerindian cultural experiences and cosmologies. He poses as a spiritual student of the Amazon while harnessing its names and cultural practices in order to enhance his economic progress and establish his personal superiority over his teachers. Elias frequently exhibits what Renato Rosaldo has called "imperialist nostalgia," a "compelling, contradictory, and pernicious" affective ideology that "uses a pose of 'innocent yearning' both to capture people's imaginations and to conceal its complicity with often brutal domination": Elias "valorize[s] innovation and then yearn[s] for more stable worlds" (Rosaldo 108). See Ana Patricia Rodríguez for a reading of Elias in the context of U.S. robber baron capitalists.

6. Salgado 7.

7. Stallabrass 133. Some globalization theorists would contrast the manual labor of the ship breakers against the so-called immaterial labor of the cultural producer-photographer. Here, immaterial labor refers to "the labor that produces the informational and cultural content of the commodity." See Lazzarato, "Immaterial Labor" 133–47.

8. The technology magazine *Wired* has contributed to the rhetoric of celebration and newness on globalization that became familiar in privileged business and new venture capitalist discourse by the early 1990s—a rhetoric Salgado largely accepts even as he displays nostalgia for that which the rhetoric refers to as the past. "When we talk about the new economy," say *Wired* editors, "we're talking about a world in which people work with their brains instead of their hands. A world in which communications technology creates global competition . . . A world at least as different from what came before it as the industrial age was from its agricultural predecessor. A world so different its emergence can only be described as a revolution." Browning and Reiss, *Encyclopedia of the New Economy*. For an account of global capitalism since the 1970s, see the geographer David Harvey, *Postmodernity* 201–308 and *Neoliberalism*. See the feminist geographer Doreen Massey's critique of Harvey's disavowal of the colonial and gendered conditions of fragmentation, alienation, and displacement that predate what Harvey identifies as contemporary conditions of postmodernity.

9. As Sekula observes, the symbolic death of cargo shipping by disappearance symptomatically disavows the labor and materials that continue to power globalization: 'The arrogant conceit of the cyber-economy, for that matter of the very idea of the *postindustrial era*, is that we disavow our dim but nagging awareness" that most large energy sources originate as "solids, liquids, and gases that are extracted from the earth and transported in bulk." Sekula 32–33. The antislavery advocate Kevin Bales highlights the incidence of contemporary slave labor used internationally to supply basic materials for building computer hardware and other essential components of the cyber-economy. See Bales, *Disposable People*.

10. Cooper is one of many scholars who criticize the recent scholarly attention to globalization and the global, advocating instead that scholars examine specific networks and the specificity, contingency, history, and limits of interconnectedness and other large-scale, long-term processes. Cooper argues that scholars who use "globalization" as an analytic category confuse a discursive category with actually existing conditions in the world, conditions which are neither quite "global" nor in the process of becoming global (a process signaled as occurring in the present, as distinguished from the past, by the suffix -*ization*). Cooper complains that globalization (like its predecessor term, *modernization*) "defines itself by naming a future as an apparent projection of a present, which is sharply distinguished from the past" (97). He points out that any globalization theory, whether celebratory or condemnatory, suffers from "totalizing pretensions" and "presentist periodization" (94). Cooper, *Colonialism in Question*.

11. Goldman, *The Ordinary Seaman* 97, 105, 38, 20. Subsequent references are cited in the text.

12. Revolutions in Nicaragua, El Salvador, and Guatemala became international crises by the 1980s, but they erupted after long-standing struggles over land, resources, and power. In Nicaragua in 1979, the leftist Sandinista National Liberation Front (FSLN) eventually overthrew the right-wing dictatorship of Anastacio Somoza Debayle, whose dictatorship was substantially financed, trained, and supported by the U.S. government and its military. Honduras served as a staging ground for the

U.S.-supported secret paramilitary war against the Sandinistas, thereby turning it into an extension of the battlefield. In El Salvador and Guatemala, where right-wing, anticommunist dictatorships held power and pursued internal leftist guerrilla movements, U.S. support took the form of huge aid packages, military training, and the backing of security forces and death squads responsible for a devastating system of massacres, kidnappings, and torturing in Guatemala, particularly of its indigenous population. For an account of the Central American wars with respect to their effects on migration and refugee and asylum policies, see García.

13. See J. L. Austin.

14. Gruesz 76.

15. Brady 80.

16. Shemak 179. See especially 177–212.

17. Dayan, "Legal Slaves and Civil Bodies" 23.

18. Section 688 of the 1920 Jones Act.

19. Legal Information Institute details the guidelines of maritime salvage as "the reward given to persons who voluntarily assist a ship or recover its cargo from impending or actual peril or loss. To make a valid claim of salvage, a claimant must prove: the event involved a ship and its cargo, or things committed to and lost at sea or other public, navigable waterways; the ship or its cargo have been found or rescued; the service performed by claimant must have been of benefit to the property involved in the rescue." See "Law of Salvage."

20. DeLombard 37.

21. See also Waligora-Davis, "Phantom Limbs."

22. See chapter 3 for a longer discussion of Waligora-Davis's reading of sanctuary as site of violence, which I argue gets reconceptualized by Jones.

23. Waligora-Davis, *Sanctuary* 54.

24. Ibid., 55. As Waligora-Davis argues, "Melville mines this central problem that has shaped the relationship between blacks and U.S. legal culture (i.e., law and jurisprudence). He reveals how legal recognition serves the state as an instrument buttressing rights and conferring citizenship. Melville's attention to the racial politics and political effects of legal recognition adumbrates the critique written by Supreme Court Justice John Marshall Harlan in his 1883 dissent to the Civil Rights Cases in which Harlan opined that challenges to black civil liberties have arisen from a failure to recognize blacks' 'legal right' to citizenship, to see 'them as a component part of the people for whose welfare and happiness government is ordained'" (45).

25. Ibid., 50.

26. Sailors' Union of the Pacific.

27. In 1895 a writ of habeas corpus was issued upon the petition of four seamen who, taking advantage of the Maguire Act passed earlier that year allowing sailors "the right to quit a ship while in domestic ports," quit the vessel *Arago* before its voyage to Chile. The court decision conflicted with the Maguire Act (Sailors' Union of the Pacific).

28. For a lively study of seafarers' social practices and material conditions, see Rediker, *Between the Devil and the Deep Blue Sea*.

29. On the enduring racialization of the seaman since the eighteenth century that was important to the *Robertson* case, see Rediker and Linebaugh. No longer racialized by way of the visible marks of seafaring experience on their flesh or tongues, seafarers undergo racialized conscriptions by other names, as flags of convenience ships

hire the cheapest laborers from the racialized global South vulnerable to situations of forced and unpaid labor, violence, and other forms of subjection through the production of statelessness for the workers. Under the burden of vague and contested definitions of what constitutes a "seaman" or seafarer, what is the relation of the "seaman" to the law? How has "seaman" as a legal identity shared in the histories of effectively stateless figures, such as the convicted criminal, the slave, and the ward, as subjects who may be confined legally and forced to labor, and who are excluded formally from the nation yet bound to it?

30. See also Steinfeld.

31. Sailors' Union of the Pacific continued with mixed success to lobby Congress for seamen's rights after the *Robertson* case.

32. See Sailors' Union of the Pacific.

33. Colin Dayan traces the unstable duality between "the civil body—the artificial person who possesses self and property" and "the legal slave—the artificial person who exists as both person and property" through the legal fiction of the incarcerated body's civil death. See Dayan, "Legal Slaves and Civil Bodies" 3–39.

34. Bush 1413, referencing Steinfeld 251 n. 36.

35. Bush 1413.

36. Ibid.

37. See Shemak for a detailed reading of Esteban and the crewmembers as "economic refugees."

38. Dayan, "Legal Slaves and Civil Bodies" 23.

39. See Abu-Lughod's study *Before European Hegemony*.

40. Linebaugh and Rediker 150.

41. Foucault, "Different Spaces" 185.

42. Ibid., 185.

43. Gilroy 17.

44. Originally referring to any augmentation of a band of armed men, the word *crew* came to mean a supervised squad of workmen bent to a particular purpose (*crew*, *OED*).

45. The narration makes no remark on the strange name of the *Urus*, which points to multiple invocations of excluded and excluding figurations of law and belonging, but its meanings seem to determine the ship that receives it. The name functions implicitly in the narration at multiple associative levels. The word may present an ominous address to the reader of the crew's universal condition ("you are us") or the primal foundation of contemporary U.S. dominance (an Ur of the United States), or even an extinct wild ox (Gruesz 67). "Urus" perhaps most importantly invokes hemispheric history by referencing the Uros, or Urus, people who largely continue to live on man-made floating islands since their precolonial displacement from land. Elias, as secret owner of the ship and enthusiast of South American indigenous spirituality, also presumably has named his cargo ship for the indigenous Uros people and their "islas flotandas," or floating islands. The Uros live on Lake Titicaca, divided by Bolivian and Peruvian sovereignty. I suggest that the name also references this real namesake, intimating thematic connections and commenting on the naming as an imperious renaming, an appropriation of the name but an incomplete recycling of it, as the name is taken but not transformed beyond recognition for its new use. A "floating island" on which the novel's crewmen are marooned, the ship is an inhospitable home that demands the constant maintenance of its crew, particularly of Bernardo,

Esteban, Jose Mateo, and the others who help in their survival on board. The Urus name also indirectly calls up contemporary indigenous relationships to the nation-state and the global economy, which is often akin to a colonial relationship that takes indigenous peoples' displacement and threatened social and economic order as stages within the national narrative of progress and development.

46. See Linebaugh and Rediker 150.

47. DeSombre 73–76.

48. See DeSombre 72–73.

49. Shemak 186.

50. Quoted in Carlisle 181; cited in Shemak 186.

51. "Report on colonizing the free people of color of the United States, of the House of Representatives," n.p.

52. Ibid., 103.

53. Shemak 187.

54. DeSombre 4.

55. Elias's power to name is just as indebted to what the Argentinian philosopher Enrique Dussel claims to be the originary instance of modern Western subjectiv-ity—the Spanish-Portuguese "I" of *ego conquiro*, "I conquer," instantiated practically through the Spanish and Portuguese imperial invasion of the "New World" since 1492. For Dussel, *ego conquiro* "imposed its will (the first modern "will-to-power") on the indigenous populations of the Americas" (471). See Dussel, "Europe, Modernity, and Eurocentrism." For a sustained engagement with Dussel's philosophy, see Mignolo.

56. Elias's appropriation of the Uros and Achuar Amerindian tribal names for his global capital venture signals his indebtedness to what Ana Patricia Rodríguez identifies as "the legacy of filibustering and mercenary adventurism that has driven many white male entrepreneurs to intervene in Central American politics and his-tory . . . [including] William Walker, filibuster; Samuel Zamurray, banana corporate venturer; Cornelius Vanderbilt, train baron; Oliver North, arms racketeer." Rodríguez 403.

57. Since the early 1800s, ships have had a nationality as legal "residents" of states. As the U.S. attorney general declared in 1854, "The Law of Nations and common sense require that every ship shall have a nationality." Cited in DeSombre 69. It was not until the Geneva Convention on the High Seas (1958) that this link was codified into a requirement that ships must have a national identity, which may be granted by states. DeSombre 70.

58. DeSombre 71.

59. The Seamen's Act of 1915 introduced a number of protections for seafarers, including an end to the imprisonment of sailors for desertion or an early breaking of their work contract. The Jones Act of 1920 is known as the Merchant Marine Act of 1920, and among its statutes introduced the legal responsibility of shipowners to seamen injured in the course of their duties. In Goldman's novel, the Ship Visitor notes that the only legal recourse Bernardo or the entire crew would have had would be through the Jones Act, which required the owners to attempt to treat and also to compensate Bernardo for his injuries. This act is the one law that haunts Elias. It is also a moot point, as Elias withheld his own full name from the crew as well as any of the paperwork that would have recognized Bernardo or the crew as "seamen" before the law.

60. Shemak 186.

61. Gruesz 79–80.

62. Sekula 32–33.

63. Ibid., 31.

64. Ibid., 29.

65. Ibid., 29–30, emphasis in original.

66. Ibid., 30.

67. See Gruesz 74, on the future anterior tense in relation to Donald Pease's reading of the future anterior temporality of C. L. R. James's *Mariners, Renegades, and Castaways*.

68. In a significant move to both gesture beyond and control the boundaries of the narrative world he has created, Goldman refers to extratextual sources but does not include them, such as the *Daily News* article, the real-life Bernardo's twelve-page account of the crew's trials, whose title translates as "The Last Days of an old Sea Wolf" ("Los ultimos dias de un viejo lobo de mar"), and some of the differences between historical accounts and his fictional narrative. Also referenced is Paul Chapman's informative and sensitive book-length study, *Trouble on Board: The Plight of International Seafarers*, which details the case of the abandoned crew that serves as Goldman's model. Goldman acknowledges Chapman, who works at the Seafarers' Institute, as a model on which he based John the Ship Visitor.

69. Such operations are most evident in the foundational history of private property in the United States, in which settlers conquered space and then drew up deeds and land titles where there were none before, and thereby became legal owners of property (the law itself drawn up to legitimate theft and act as a partner to violence).

70. Salgado writes of a similar process for the ship in Bangladesh: "Everything from that huge animal lying on the beach has a use. Iron and steel will be melted down and given new roles as utensils. The entire ship will be turned into what it once carried: machines, knives and forks, hoes, shovels, screws, things, bits, pieces" (7).

71. The passage from Matthew is as follows: "And he cast down the pieces of silver in the temple, and departed, and went and hanged himself. And the chief priests took the silver pieces, and said, It is not lawful for to put them into the treasury, because it is the price of blood. And they took counsel, and bought with them the potter's field, to bury strangers in. Wherefore that field was called, The field of blood, unto this day. Then was fulfilled that which was spoken by Jeremy the prophet, saying, And they took the thirty pieces of silver, the price of him that was valued, whom they of the children of Israel did value; And gave them for the potter's field, as the Lord appointed me." Matthew 27:5–10 (1769 King James Version).

72. Stringer and Friedman, "Unfair to Immigrants, Costly for Taxpayers."

73. Among those not adequately informed are the thousands of mothers who signed papers authorizing their stillborn children to receive a free city burial. See Melinda Hunt, *The Hart Island Project*. See also an interview with Hunt by the Banff Centre; and Hunt, "Potter's Field."

74. Harrington.

75. For discussion of the debates between the white archaeological firm and the black archaeologists at Howard University, see Sarah R. Katz, "Redesigning Civic Memory."

76. Harrington.

77. In Kaufman 1; cited in Hansen and McGowan 114.

78. Lopez; see African Burial Ground.

79. For more on the history of Ellis Island, see James, *Mariners, Renegades, and Castaways*; Behdad, *Forgetful Nation*; Ngai. See also "Ellis Island, National Monument."

80. The FBI classified James as a security risk since his arrival from Britain to the United States in 1938 with plans to lecture on the "Negro Question" (and meet Trotsky in Mexico City to discuss black revolution). Accounts differ as to the extent of James's time as an unauthorized alien. His status as a noncitizen made him especially vulnerable to the new immigration and deportation policies of the Cold War state enshrined in the McCarran-Walter Act of 1952, an ambitious federal act that sought to consolidate federal immigration laws, reform the racist national origins quota system of 1924, and put in place a policy of political discrimination against anyone perceived to be "radical," "subversive," or simply "Communist." James was taken to Ellis Island by Immigration and Naturalization Services authorities, where he awaited his appeal "on the claim that this change of venue had denied him due process" in his quest to prove his fitness for citizenship (Pease xiii). The McCarran-Walter Act would be used to reclassify James from an alien with minor "passport violations" or legal would-be naturalized citizen (there are conflicting accounts of his status prior to his arrest) to a "subversive" Communist who advocated revolution against the federal government: his citizenship application was denied, and he was forced to leave the United States. It was during his six-month detention at Ellis Island that C. L. R. James wrote *Mariners, Renegades, and Castaways,* his analysis of Melville's maritime fiction against the subtext of the Cold War state and the illegality of the McCarran-Walter Act.

81. Ellis Island was important to the 1924 restrictive immigration act and the new documentation procedures of aliens. INS and court decisions helped to define Ellis Island as an exceptional space of indefinite detention, thus producing subjects who could neither be "naturalized" as U.S. citizens nor freed from a punitive relation to the United States. Cold War persecution of "Communists" and other "subversive" actors involved indefinite detention on the island. For more on the indefinite detention of James and Mr. Mezei, see James, "A Natural but Necessary Conclusion," in *Mariners, Renegades, and Castaways* 125–26. See also *Shaughnessy v. Mezei* (1953). Included in the INS's official list of "subversive activities" for which James was deported to Trinidad was the study of Melville written during his detention.

82. "An African American Homecoming."

83. Steven Lee Myers.

84. Harrington. Hunt values the term "potter's field" precisely for its inclusivity, envisioning the potter's field as at once the site of abandoned social historical fragments and "a great pot of history with people all smooshed up. But today no one wants to be smooshed together; every group wants to be distinct" (Hunt, quoted in Dubin 5).

85. Tarleton.

2 / Sugar's Legacies: Romance, Revolution, and Wageless Life in the Fiction of Edwidge Danticat and Rosario Ferré

1. Schneider 25. This was the first and largest of the many sugar refineries in a rapidly industrializing Brooklyn, boosted by the Civil War and powered by the brisk shipping trade through the Port of New York.

2. The refinery was first built in 1856 and then again after an 1882 fire. The Havemeyer family's involvement in establishing the Sugar Refineries Company—the notorious Sugar Trust—was challenged by antitrust laws even as the owners found legal

ways to successfully evade antitrust regulation. Schneider suggests that the Sherman Anti-Trust Act of 1890 led to the Havemeyers family "controlling an astonishing 98% of the sugar business in America and presiding over a total monopoly on an essential commodity" (26). In cooperation with U.S. officials overseeing U.S. interests in Cuba after the Spanish-American War, they "carved out the world's largest sugar plantation" (26). On the Havermeyer family dealings, see also Ayala, *American Sugar Kingdom* 37–47.

3. In response to the interviewer's question about her work "being used as part of the gentrification process," because the real estate developer of the site is also a sponsor of the exhibit, Walker imagines her work as, in a sense, haunting the new development or making it sacred in a new way: "I don't see how that could succeed. I have this fantasy that once the installation comes down, the sphinx's presence will somehow remain. That people will remember something legendary happened here, and that the legend contained histories of sugar and of slavery, and representations of femaleness and sweetness. Sugar is so much a part of our world. It's this kind of goddess who we give ourselves over to." Interview by Paul Laster, "The Whole Reason for Refining Sugar."

4. Walker, interview by Paul Laster, "The Whole Reason for Refining Sugar."

5. This "fuck you" is also signaled in the sphinx's hand gesture of a *figa*. Walker explains, "In Portugal or Brazil, you will find these wooden, carved hand symbols with the thumb through the four fingers. Depending on where you come from, in Portugal it's a good luck charm or for fertility, and in other places, it means 'fuck you.' It is also a crude name for a woman's genitalia, which is also very present on the back. It's keeping with my work that is sometimes reduced but has quadruple meanings. The hand gesture means good luck and fuck you." Walker, interview by Antwaun Sargent, "Kara Walker Decodes Her New World Sphinx."

6. Walker, interview by Kara Rooney, "A Sonorous Subtlety." Walker responds in ways that echo Avery Gordon's notion of haunting, in which the ghost is a force that meddles with the present: Walker says, "It messes with them. It messes with the space, or rather, it messes with the histories, which I always do too." On the history of sugar "subtleties" and their move from the Middle East to European monarchy, court, church, and, with the rise of the sugar industry, their use as bourgeois entertainments, see Mintz, *Sweetness and Power* 88–94.

7. In this way, U.S. and Caribbean feminist art and writing are in contrast to major studies of the plantation school, which look to the economic and political but exclude the significations of gender, sexuality, and romance that make sugar such a potent cultural trope. See Russ (175 n. 1) for her gloss on the plantation school, or the "plantation system studies" largely of social scientists and economists.

8. Fuchs 1. Thanks to Emily S. Davis for bringing Fuchs's work to my attention.

9. Fuchs 50, 37.

10. E. S. Davis, 5.

11. Tillet 89.

12. Ibid.

13. Art21 Exclusive, "A Subtley, or the Marvelous Sugar Baby."

14. Sugarcane's global importance has been documented in well-known histories, chief among them Sidney Mintz's classic study *Sweetness and Power*.

15. As César J. Ayala states in *American Sugar Kingdom*, "In one way or another, all of the islands of the Spanish, British, and French Caribbean experienced plantation booms at some point in their histories since the initial European conquest of the

archipelago. The place of the islands in the history of the world economy since the time of the conquest lies in its plantation-based sugar production" (2).

16. Referring to the use of law to produce divisions, Handley notes, "The innumerable legal codes regarding racial identity and social rights," while they "were intended to segregate and thereby mitigate cultural development," often inadvertently served to "create cultural syncretism" (16).

17. Emily S. Davis, in *Rethinking the Romance Genre,* notes the instability of the romance genre as one that makes it especially suited to "representing fluid political, sexual, and racial identities and coalitions in an era of flexible global capitalism" (2), leading to her argument that the "global romance" provides a crucial form for a "transnational feminist politics" even as it is consistently misread or dismissed by critics who immediately discount the romance genre as an escapist alternative to politics. This chapter has a different aim: it examines feminist responses to uses of the romance genre in political historiography and anticolonial literature that reinforce patriarchal ideologies (particularly with the Haitian Revolution and the Puerto Rican literary tradition).

18. Francis 4.

19. Ibid., 2.

20. Handley 15.

21. Ibid., 16.

22. Audre Lorde, "The Master's Tools Will Never Dismantle the Master's House" (1984).

23. Stoler, *Imperial Debris* 12.

24. Some identify the *mambo,* or Vodou priestess, as Mambo Marinette; others identify her as Cecile Fatiman. It is Boukman, however, and not the priestess who has been incorporated in a largely masculine pantheon of hero revolutionaries.

25. James, *The Black Jacobins* 88.

26. By 1804 literate Haitians were producing their own narratives of the revolution to defend the revolution against French defamation and establish a story of national origins that would bolster legitimacy of the new state while conceptualizing "a new Black American Republicanism" in the process (Lewis, cited in Renda 46). Subsequent generations of Haitian historians also continued to produce narratives of the revolution whose versions were rehearsed until they were learned by heart. The Caco armed resistance to the U.S. occupation, as well as Haitian intellectuals, frequently invoked the revolutionary spirit to make sense of the present-day occupation (Renda 53).

Vodou enters the written historical record through the only known account of the Bois Caïman ceremony written by a contemporary, Antoine Dalmas, an exiled French colonist who sought to prove the revolution illegitimate and persuade France to retake the colony (Dubois 100; Dayan, *Haiti, History, and the Gods* 29). Following Dalmas, two important nineteenth-century Haitian historians, Beaubrun Ardouin and Thomas Madiou, incorporated the Bois Caïman ceremony into their national histories.

27. Elizabeth McAlister provides an insightful account of how "neo-evangelicals" came to rewrite the Bois Caïman story (and circulate it, from the United States to Haiti and back again) as part of a transnational neo-evangelical Spiritual Mapping movement—one that could transform the "blood pact with Satan" narrative into an "anticolonialist narrative in which *Satan is the colonial power who must be overthrown,*" thus locating Haiti at the center of a global battle for freedom (48; emphasis in

original). Thanks to McAlister for sharing her unpublished work with me. For evangelical versions of the pact-with-the-devil claim, which abound in an echo chamber of evangelical reports, blogs, and religious conservative online commentary before Pat Robertson's inflammatory recitation, see Bryan Fischer; Compass Direct Staff; John Mark Ministries; and Barrett. For news reports on the most recent growth of evangelical Protestant influence in Haiti, see Caistor; Tarr; and Caroit.

28. Evangelical pastors seek to advance a rival approach to this quotidian historiography when they denigrate Vodou as holding the Haitian majority "back" from cultural and material progress. Danticat sums up this attitude well in one short story in *Krik? Krak!*, in which a middle-class Haitian couple comments on their house servant as one of "those stupid people who think that they have a spell to make themselves invisible and hurt other people. Why can't none of them get a spell to make themselves rich? It's that voodoo nonsense that's holding us Haitians back" (95). The Dominican pool cleaner joins in the vilification of Marie, the servant, when he accuses her of killing a baby and keeping it with her "for evil" (99). The general disavowal of Vodou does not contradict the rise in power or influence of individual *houngan* and *mambos*, or the long-standing manipulation of Vodou by Haitian presidents, most notoriously François Duvalier.

29. Historians have speculated that Boukman was a practicing Muslim (hence the name "book man," referring to the Qu'ran) who adopted Creole Vodou practices in his political organizing. At its core, Vodou serves as a vital means of making sense of everyday life, largely by making sense of history through everyday labors of religious practice. As "a series of philosophical postulates about reality," Vodou theorizes history by giving shape to the ways in which ancestral spirits join with the present in everyday life (Mintz preface to Métraux 13, cited in Dayan, *Haiti, History, and the Gods* xvii). See also Johnson on Vodou structured as a "government of God," in that it involves a military and governmental system of organization developed over time since the colonial period.

30. McAlister notes the effort by evangelicals to appropriate nationalist mythmaking in Haiti after the 2010 earthquake: "Nationalist mythmakers ritualize remembering when children line up to sing and chant for flag days, memorial days, and independence days, and when Pastor Yvette and others led their congregations in prayer and song to clear their tent camps of *lwa* (spirits), to reclaim Haiti in the name of Jesus after the earthquake, they ritualized evangelical nationalist mythmaking" (12).

31. Dayan provides a gloss on the meaning of the word *Vodou*: the Fon tribe of southern Dahomey use the word to mean "spirit," "god," or "image," and in Haiti, Vodou refers to the powerful being "upon whom depends all of the events that come to pass on earth" (*Haiti, History, and the Gods* 288 n.7).

32. The political stakes of historiography become clear if one considers that such efforts were part of the pastors' rivalry with the government of Jean-Bertrand Aristide, a rivalry bankrolled and lent organizational support by right-wing U.S. think tanks and state policy objectives.

Pastor Joel Jeune conducted a "holy invasion" of Bois Caïman and reportedly told this story in evangelical circles: "It was a significant spiritual battle to reach the tree under which the pig was sacrificed in the original ceremony. We formed a Jericho march, circling the magic tree seven times. On the seventh time around, God gave many people a vision of the Devil fleeing from the area. The Christians were overjoyed. We cancelled the satanic contract and broke the curse, before celebrating communion and dedicating the area as a place of prayer. We also declared 14 August to be a national prayer day, on which people should pray that Haiti will return to God" (Barrett). See also *Deutsche Presse-Agentur*. In the months leading up to the bicentennial commemorations of national independence, Haitian pastors involved in the Bois Caïman controversy (including Jeune) reported fears that Aristide was planning "to renew a 200-year-old national 'pact with the devil' on January 1, 2004" (*Christianity Today*). Aristide was overthrown barely two months after the opposition organized violent disruptions of the bicentennial.

The "pact with the devil" narrative (notably recounted by the U.S. evangelist Pat Robertson during his television show's charity drive for Haitian victims of the 2010 earthquake) is thus only the most recent version of anti-Vodou campaigns carried out in the name of reforming the poor Haitian majority and marching the country toward progress, often with the effect of furthering their dispossession while policing their social well-being and cultural and historical creativity. For example, see *Haiti, State against Nation* for a mention of the antisuperstition campaigns of 1941–42 by the Catholic Church and Haitian state authorities under President Lescot, which led to the physical destruction of shrines but also amounted to a major land grab from the peasantry. On the link between the antisuperstition campaigns, national folklore performance, and the growth of Protestantism, see Ramsey (n. 50). The Catholic Church finally became more accommodating to the incorporation of Vodou practices in the 1980s, when evangelical Protestants, bolstered by Reaganite bankrolls, targeted Vodou even more directly.

33. Laroche, "The Founding Myths of the Haitian Nation" 14.

34. See Johnson for a study of Vodou in relation to François Duvalier's rule.

35. Farmer, "Who Removed Aristide?" Farmer recounts Toussaint's famous declaration to his captors before he embarked on the ship that would carry him and his family to France, where he later died in a dungeon: "In overthrowing me, you have cut down in San Domingo only the trunk of the tree of black liberty. It will spring up again by the roots for they are numerous and deep." On Aristide's invocation of Dessalines, see Sourieau.

While critics of Aristide describe his later years in power as increasingly resembling the very repressive police state that he once stood against, his early career as a charismatic Catholic priest committed to the poor and to the civilian democratic process had marked him early on as an enemy by the business elite, the repressive political and military apparatus, and the United States under Reagan. Organizers of the Bois Caïman commemoration identified the evangelical crusade as a "plot which IRI is planning with Macoute forces, through Joel Jeune under the cover of the Protestant church, . . . to organize all the reactionary forces in the country" (*Haiti Progres*). The U.S. International Republican Institute (and its arm, the "Group of 184") would be implicated heavily in the February 2004 ousting of President Jean-Bertrand Aristide. See also Farmer, "Who Removed Aristide?"

36. See *OED* entries "rehearse v." and "herse n."

37. Danticat, *Create Dangerously* 104.

38. For two sweeping studies of the role of sugar in the global economy and the relationship between colonial slavery and the rise of capitalism, see Mintz, *Sweetness and Power*; and Eric Williams, *Capitalism and Slavery*. See also Dubois; and Trouillot, *Haiti, State against Nation*. Vincent Ogé's rebellion for the rights of

gens de couleur in 1789, rather than the slave revolt of 1791, is sometimes credited as the start of the revolution.

39. For a fascinating study on how Haiti's drafts of its constitution defined citizenship and state sovereignty, see Fischer, *Modernity Disavowed*. See also my brief discussion in the introduction to this book.

40. Danticat, *Farming of Bones* 309.

41. Munro 42.

42. Sourieau 27.

43. Sommer 5.

44. White, *Metahistory* 8–9, quoted in Scott, *Conscripts of Modernity* 47.

45. Scott, *Conscripts of Modernity* 47.

46. Scott, Interview by Stuart Hall.

47. Scott, *Conscripts of Modernity* 206.

48. Danticat, *Krik? Krak!* 56. Hereafter cited by page number in the text. Boukman was known as both a "book man" and a man of imposing stature. Sold from Jamaica to Saint-Domingue, Boukman served as a slave driver and then coachman before becoming a leader of the 1791 uprising. On Boukman's role in the Bois Caïman ceremony and revolts of 1791, see Dubois 91–114. In Haiti, Boukman's prayer is widely known and recited in Kreyol. The following is one translation: "The god of the white man calls him to commit crimes; our god asks only good works of us. But this god who is so good orders revenge! He will direct our hands; he will aid us. Throw away the image of the god of the whites who thirsts for our tears and listen to the voice of liberty that speaks in the hearts of all of us" (Dubois 100). See also Fick; Geggus.

49. The Levantine Haitian owners in "A Wall of Fire Rising" are part of the history of neocolonial Haiti: between 1890 and 1905, Levantine immigrants quickly became important traders and importers through access to U.S. contacts, sources of credit, and passports (while in return boosting U.S. imports and political influence as permanent U.S. residents in Haiti). Levantine Haitians were among the white and light-skinned immigrants to Haiti who (despite a series of expulsion laws culminating in 1905) quickly became part of the prominent *mulâtre* merchant families (*Haiti, State against Nation* 234 n. 6).

50. Dubois 124.

51. Scott's understanding of tragedy draws from his account of James's use of tragedy, as culled from Aristotle, Hegel, and Elizabethan models. On the importance of plot for Aristotle and on *hamartia*, see Scott, *Conscripts of Modernity* 153–54.

52. Fischer, *Modernity Disavowed* ix.

53. Trouillot notes that colonial Saint-Domingue foreshadowed limits that "still constrain the Haitian state: external limits—territorial and demographic; [and] internal limits—the balance between subsistence and commodity production and the dominance of coffee as a crop" (*Haiti, State against Nation* 36).

54. Trouillot, *Haiti, State against Nation* 45.

55. Ibid.; see also Renda 48.

56. Louverture.

57. The first Haitian leaders agreed on two basic but contradictory principles: first, "slavery as an institution was to be forever abolished from Haiti and from anywhere else the Haitian state could reach," and second, the state had a "need to maintain large-scale export-oriented plantations and a labor system that would produce results similar to those of the slave regime" (Trouillot, *Haiti, State against Nation* 49). Peasant

modes of organized work was a tradition of slaves in the French colonial period, and repeated attempts by Haitian leaders to get Haitians to return to the plantations— even at bayonet point—were never successful (60). Such peasant agriculture has been in overall decline almost from independence, with the exception of a few historical spikes, as a result of the combined actions of repressive Haitian governments and U.S. and international monetary and trade policies, which have targeted Haiti's sugar, pig, rice, and other domestic and export products (49, 212–16).

58. Renda 50.

59. Mintz, "Whitewashing Haiti's History."

60. Renda 51.

61. In *Haiti, State against Nation,* Trouillot argues that François Duvalier transformed the Haitian state, hitherto run by authoritarian governments, into a totalitarian state apparatus that systematically set itself up against the nation.

62. The mill is not named in the short story; but as I suggest, it most likely references the Haitian American Sugar Company mill. Apparently the only mill in Haiti that owned a surrounding sugar plantation, it was an enterprise of the U.S. occupation of Haiti, in which a coalition of Marines and businessmen from 1914 to 1934 sought to secure Haiti as a neocolony. HASCO was part of an effort to revive the foreign control of large agricultural estates in the country, an effort that involved changing the Haitian constitution prohibiting foreign ownership of the land and attempting to break up the Haitian peasant-style work organization through the corvée, a program of forced labor on the plantations and in other land development projects, notably the railroad but also clearing land for large estates (such as the Dauphin plantation, what Suzy Castor calls a classic colonial enclave). In recent years, Haiti has been a net importer of sugar, due to a combination of the nineteenth-century decline of the plantation system and twentieth-century U.S. sugar policies that artificially raise the price of U.S. domestic sugar and establish import quotas for sugar-producing countries. In 1987 one sugar mill—belonging to Darbonne Sugar, an Italian enterprise—was opened only to be closed down, reopened by Castro-sponsored Cuban engineers, and sputtering even in 2010. It proved more profitable to import sugar from the Dominican Republic and then export it to the United States under the sugar quota system (Cloutier). For more on the occupation, see Castor; and Trouillot, *Haiti, State against Nation.* For a related study on the culture of U.S. imperialism during the occupation of Haiti, see Renda.

63. Dubois 91.

64. Ibid., 92. Dubois notes that, at least in elite discourse, by the second half of the eighteenth century "the Gallifet plantations were so famous . . . that to describe something sweet, people in Saint-Domingue said 'as sweet as Gallifet sugar.' And to describe utmost happiness, they said 'as happy as a Gallifet negro'" (92).

65. Ibid., 94.

66. Ibid., 99.

67. Ibid., 92.

68. Defilé, or Dédée Brazile, was called a madwoman, and she followed Dessalines's army and served them until Dessalines's assassination and dismemberment, when, according to various versions of the story, she turned sane and somber, picking up his pieces, helping lay them to rest, and condemning her people for their reckless destruction of the flesh and blood of the nation (Dayan, *Haiti, History, and the Gods* 41). Further into Danticat's collection of short stories, there is a brief reference to Lili's life

after her husband's suicide that connects the national with the familial—not through the Boukman romance, not through the sugar mill tragedy, but through the figure of Défilé: before the main character, Marie, is arrested and accused of shedding her skin at night and sucking the life from infants (of being a *lougawou* or *soucouyan*), the spirit of her mother and ancestors visit her, from her grandmother Défilé to "her godmother Lili who killed herself in old age because her husband had jumped out of a flying balloon and her grown son left her to go to Miami" ("Beside the Pool and the Gardenias" 94). On the position of women in Haitian historical narratives more generally, Dayan comments that their stories "are something of an interlude in the business of *making history*" (47; emphasis in original). For feminist revisions of the traditionally masculinist historiography of the Haitian Revolution, see Dayan; and Braziel.

69. Glissant 52.

70. González Mendoza 58.

71. Don Pedro Irisarri, "Informe dado por el alcalde don Pedro Yrisarri al Ayuntamiento de la Capital. 1809," in *Ramón Power y Giralt Diputado puertorriqueño a las Cortes Generales y Extraordinarias de España 1810–1812 (Compilación de documentos),* ed. Aida Caro de Delgado (San Juan, 1969), 45–69; quoted in González Mendoza 61–62.

72. Already by 1800, decades before the peak of the illegal (but thriving) importation of African slaves to Puerto Rico, the slave population's annual growth was greater than that of the general population. "Puerto Rico's population had an impressive rate of growth of 3.6 percent per year, while the slave population's annual growth had been even more pronounced at 4.3 percent" (González Mendoza 60). Unlike in primarily plantation export colonies, such as Haiti, the enslaved black population was still relatively small: in 1812, for example, there were 183,014 people in the free population and 17,536 people in slave population, which was concentrated in the fertile coastal areas of the island (60).

73. González Mendoza 59.

74. See Scarano 78. The owners were compensated with 35 million pesetas per slave, and slaves were required to continue working for three more years. See Library of Congress.

75. For detailed studies of the antiprostitution campaigns in Puerto Rico under the local government when Puerto Rico was a Spanish and then a U.S. colony, see Findlay; and Brigg.

76. Handley 17.

77. Malavet 38. For an extended analysis of the Insular Cases, see Kaplan, *The Anarchy of Empire*; and Burnett and Marshall.

78. Malavet 33–38.

79. Ibid., 24.

80. Findlay 10.

81. Ibid., 8.

82. Stoler and Cooper 614, cited in Findlay 8.

83. Findlay 9, 8.

84. Briggs 32.

85. Ibid., 4, 8.

86. Ferré, *Sweet Diamond Dust* 6. Subsequent references are cited in the text.

87. There are important exceptions in the history of Puerto Rico's Spanish legal codes regarding slavery, wills, and the purchasing of freedom in, for example, the

Royal Decree of Graces (1789 and again in 1815) as well as in El Código Negro, or Black Code (1789).

88. Moreno explains the political valence of major Puerto Rican writers who sought to cultivate a national Puerto Rican identity against U.S. colonialism: "In searching for that common denominator that embodied anti-U.S. resistance, members of the *generación del treinta* turned their gaze backward to the island's Spanish past, which they posited as the true essence of Puerto Rican culture"; and "thus, Hispanophilia became a privileged site in the consolidation of the canon. In this process, several totalizing metaphors, such as the family and the house, became instrumental in evoking the perception of unity that literary traditions often strive to achieve. The patriarchal myth of *la gran familia* reemerged as a foundational narrative that continues to inform Puerto Rican letters even to this day" (16–17).

89. For a study of the disparity of whiteness claims on census forms over time, in part due to the dynamics between the general population, Puerto Rican census takers and supervisors, and U.S. Census Bureau authorities, see Loveman.

90. White, *Metahistory* 8–9, quoted in Scott, *Conscripts of Modernity* 47.

91. Here I borrow Ernst Renan's formulation that nations are founded on acts of originary brutality: "Unity is always effected by means of brutality" (11).

92. Sommer, *Foundational Fictions* 7.

93. See Moreno for an extended study of the myth of *la gran familia* in Puerto Rican literature, as well as a detailed reading of Ferré's systematic dismantling of the myth of *la gran familia puertorriqueña* in *Maldito Amor/Sweet Diamond Dust*.

94. Handley 164.

95. Handley 169. Handley draws from Aristídes's reference to "the monster Gloria was carrying" (Ferré 49). See Handley for a reading of Laura's will as the vision of a Pan-American future that was popular in the 1920s and 1930s throughout the hemisphere (169).

96. Sommer, *Foundational Fictions* 15; emphasis in original.

97. For an extended reading of the function of the *danza* in *Maldito Amor*, see Ortega 89–90.

3 / Fugitive Personhood: Reimagining Sanctuary in Gayl Jones's *Song for Anninho* and *Mosquito*

1. Agamben, *Homo Sacer*. See, e.g., 19, 37, 64, 83, 107, 109, and 170.

2. Arendt, *The Origins of Totalitarianism* 295; Patterson, *Slavery and Social Death*; Hartman, *Scenes of Subjection*; Dayan, "Legal Slaves and Civil Bodies"; Holland, *Raising the Dead*; Mbembe, "Necropolitics"; Castronovo, *Necro Citizenship*; JanMohamed, *The Death-Bound-Subject*.

3. Hartman, "Seduction and the Ruses of Power" 552; emphasis in original.

4. Informed by Afro-pessimism (a term coined by Frank B. Wilderson III), Jared Sexton has noted the nuances that emerge from a tension in critical black studies between "Afro-pessimism," with its focus on blackness as negation and form of social death, and "black optimism," with its affirmation of the cultural formations of blackness. Fred Moten seeks to revise the premises of Afro-pessimism, while Achille Mbembe revises, or departs from, the figure of bare life by introducing the concept of "raw life" in the postcolony as "a place and time of half-death—or, if one prefers, half life . . . a place where life and death are so entangled that it is no longer possible to distinguish them, or to say what is on the side of the shadow or its obverse." (Mbembe

197, cited in Sexton). Sexton reads Mbembe's "raw life" as a departure from Agamben's bare life.

5. Waligora-Davis, *Sanctuary* 56.

6. Ibid., 5.

7. Ibid., 17, 5.

8. Ibid., 54.

9. Ibid., 54–55.

10. Ibid., 12.

11. For a detailed study of the effects of the Fugitive Slave Act and the freedom suits filed in law on behalf of enslaved persons who traveled to free jurisdictions, see Edlie Wong, *Neither Fugitive nor Free*.

12. Glissant 71.

13. Ibid., xxii–xxiii.

14. García 98.

15. *Mosquito* 569–70. Subsequent references are cited in the text. In Jones's essay "Quest," a discourse of control, imposition, and dominance loosely identifies the colonialist of a "colonized" novel. She writes simply, "What is a colonialist? A colonialist controls" (511).

16. The vulnerability of black men, women, and children to fall into slavery translated into the vulnerability of falling into the convict lease system in the post-Reconstruction U.S. South.

17. Agamben, *Homo Sacer* 8.

18. Kent 187.

19. Agamben, *Homo Sacer* 8.

20. Hortense Spillers, "Mama's Baby, Papa's Maybe" 67.

21. See Lovalerie King 764 n. 1. For a reading of Palmares in Jones's work, see Rushdy, "Relate Sexual to Historical." See also Kent; writing in 1965, Kent says, "No written document originating in Palmares has come to light. It probably does not exist" (170). See also the film *Quilombo*.

22. Kent 166.

23. Kent writes, "According to Pitta, the only slaves in Palmares were those captured in razzias. But they had the option of going out on raids to secure freedom by returning with a substitute. This is confirmed by Nieuhof, who wrote that the main 'business' of palmaristas 'is to rob the Portugueses of their slaves, who remain in slavery among them, until they have redeemed themselves by stealing another; but such slaves as run over to them, are as free as the rest'" (169).

24. The governor and council could not have allowed Palmares's sovereign existence—it "would have meant to reverse a 150-year-old policy of exclusive Portuguese claim to Brazil"—and it also could not have coordinated the return of some 15,000 to 20,000 *palmaristas* (173). Instead, the Portuguese sent a draft treaty "extending peace, the requested liberties, and the release of palmarista women who seem to have constituted by far the largest group of captives" to Ganga-Zumba, who was "confirmed as supreme ruler over his people" (Kent 172).

25. For a reading of *Song for Anninho* that explores the *palmaristas'* jump in the context of the legend of the Flying Africans, see King.

26. Kent 173.

27. De Carvalho 7.

28. King 755.

29. In February 1694, Palmares was finally defeated: "Some 200 palmaristas fell or hurled themselves—the point has been long debated—'from a rock so high that they were broken to pieces'. Hand-to-hand combat took another 200 palmarista lives and over 500 'of both sexes and all ages' were captured and sold outside Pernambuco. Zambi, taken alive and wounded, was decapitated on 20 November 1695. The head was exhibited in public 'to kill the legend of his immortality'" (Kent 174).

30. Jones, *Song for Anninho,* epigraph; ellipses in original. Hereafter cited in the text.

31. Jones's play with language includes appropriating names from the historical archive in order to cast them with new meanings, without erasing the historical traces of those names. King details the significance of the names "Almeyda" and "Anninho": Jones "bestows upon Almeyda the name of both the Pernambucan governor who took office at the pivotal historical moment of 1674, D. Pedro de Almeida, and the infantry colonel in the 1694 destroying force, Matias Cardoso de Almeida. This device, or strategy, functions for Jones in several ways. It endows her protagonist with official status, changes the meaning (or historical significance) of the name, and repositions a woman victimized by slavery from a marginalized space to a centralized one. She utilizes a similar approach in naming Almeyda's husband, Anninho. Anninho is pronounced the same as the singular form of anninjos, which translates literally as 'little angels.' Anninjos, in the context of Brazilian slavery, refers to thumbscrews used to punish or torture enslaved persons. Jones modifies the form of the word to signify in a lover's language what Anninho means to Almeyda. As her little angel, he is associated with the divine in the tender loving care that characterizes his earthly relationship with her. In the present and future moments of the poem, she is in contact with Anninho only in the spiritual sense" (761).

32. "An Interview with Gayl Jones," by Charles Rowell (44).

33. *OED* burden, "burthen, n."

34. Madhu Dubey, "Gayl Jones and the Matrilineal Metaphor of Tradition," 262.

35. Jones, *Song for Anninho,* 54. Subsequent references are cited in the text.

36. For a recent discussion of black female personhood, breast milk, and the slave economy, see Yaeger, "Circum-Atlantic Superabundance."

37. Angela Davis, from *Women, Race, and Class,* quoted in Dubey, "Gayl Jones and the Matrilineal Metaphor of Tradition" 246.

38. Dubey, "Gayl Jones and the Matrilineal Metaphor of Tradition" 246 n. 1.

39. The collection of essays *After the Pain* attempts to redress this absence of criticism on *Mosquito* and Jones's other understudied works, *The Healing* and *Song for Anninho.*

40. Bramen reads Gates's hostility to *Mosquito* through his "political investment in realism" (129). I would qualify Bramen's explanation by noting the particular trouble that gender stirs. See Bramen 127–34.

41. See Gates, *Signifying Monkey* 127–69.

42. Gates, "Sanctuary."

43. Jones, *Mosquito* 93. Subsequent references are cited in the text.

44. See McDowell, "The Whole Story." Dubey points out that Jones (along with Morrison) "consistently employ[s] nonrealist modes of characterization that are unreadable within the terms of images-of-black-women criticism." Dubey, *Black Women Novelists* 5. Few reviewers take the time that McDowell does to contemplate Jones's experiments with language and storytelling. Of Jones's personal life, McDowell

writes, "Critics who have habitually pondered the connection between Jones' fiction and her life couldn't resist the speculation that, with *The Healing*, Jones had broken the spell, had 'healed' herself . . . and headed toward a more affirmative vision" (9–10).

45. Gates, "Sanctuary." Gates ends his review of the book with the wish for a matrilineal model of authorship: "Would that an editor like [Toni] Morrison had helped Jones locate where she wanted her narrator to be, and to bridle in this sprawling, formless, maddening tale." Gates describes Morrison as "the midwife" of young women writers during her time as senior editor at Random House, among them, Gayl Jones, Toni Cade Bambara, and Angela Davis.

46. Jones, "Quest" 509. Subsequent references are cited in the text.

47. Tate's review, titled "Going Underground" or "Gayl Jones's Literary Sanctuary," longs for the by now more familiar type of women's writing from the younger "Gayl," "a reclusive and enigmatic sister from Kentucky who wrote books that explored scar tissue from the inside." He ends his review with a call to "all those who believe in keeping the faith . . . to say a little prayer for Gayl." Jones appears to have completed most of *Mosquito* by late 1996, and worked on the novel as she was writing *The Healing*. For a more detailed and largely sensitive news article on Jones's personal and publication history in the 1990s (despite its location in the Mental Health section of the *New York Times*), see Lanso. On the Chicana as "stereotype," see the reviewers Cole and Schillaci.

48. On the hemispheric vision of Jones, see also her novel *Corregidora*; her unpublished novel manuscript on Palmares (Gotlieb archives); *Liberating Voices*; and "Quest." For a detailed study of the inter-American commonalities and engagements in these texts, see Coser. For a reading of Jones's hemispheric vision in *Mosquito*, see Nwankwo. On *Mosquito* as an Afrocentric novel, see Clabough. See also Terry; Chandra; Mills. For a reading of characterization and *latinidad* in the novel, see Bramen.

49. Cunningham 73–74.

50. Waligora-Davis, *Sanctuary* 12. For Waligora-Davis, the narthex, like the sanctuary, is a space that precedes sanctuary proper, signifying "the legal and social dislocation of the refugee or the stateless whose rights remain perpetually deferred" (56).

51. Cunningham 84.

52. Crittenden xvii.

53. Ibid., xviii.

54. Cunningham 206.

55. Derrida, *Of Hospitality* 151–55.

56. Cunningham 206.

57. See Foucault for his coinage and theorization of "governmentality." *The Foucault Effect*.

58. Brady 53.

59. Father Ray, early on, recognizes that Mosquito has the "potential of being Sojourner," has "proven [her] ingenuity . . . [and is] trustworthy" (237, 238). Ray means here that Mosquito has the potential of living up to her given name, but Mosquito already is Sojourner, at least in name. Moreover, she is a common-noun sojourner, a traveler without permanent membership or home with any one group.

These conversations between Mosquito and Ray contain an erotic subtext, and Mosquito's responses to Ray also prolong her flirtation with him while she resists his efforts to recruit her for the movement. Mosquito repeatedly describes Ray's "hieroglyphic eyes," as when she recounts her come-on line to Ray at the restaurant: "Father

Raymond. Is it Raymond or Raimundo? I asks, leaning towards him. Like I told you, he got them hieroglyphic eyes" (213). Mosquito also evokes the black nationalist and internationalist claim on Egyptian civilization. With those Egyptian "hieroglyphic eyes," Ray is Afrocentric, yet not defined by national or racial categories. The Raimundo's eyes, then, suggest a worldliness and a consciouness about race that attracts Mosquito to Ray, despite her skepticism about his politics. Ray's name, homologous to the Egyptian deity Ra, further evokes a mythic undercurrent that signals wholeness, healing, and protection. A single "hieroglyphic eye" refers to the eye of Ra, a powerful deity associated with the sun. In ancient Egyptian myth, Ra's right eye is the sun; his left eye was destroyed by another deity but was restored as the moon. As an amulet, the *wedjat* eye symbolizes "the process of 'making whole' and healing," and the word *wedjat* literally means "sound" or "the sound one." Mosquito, then, reads the idea of a complex universe and a healing world in Ray's eyes.

60. The narrator's nickname "Mosquito" itself belongs to Spanish and English, as "a diminutive of the Spanish *mosco* which means fly and from the Latin *musca*," and "there're people in Honduras and Nicaragua called Mosquitos and mosquito's a language too" (*Mosquito* 242). The international Mosquito Coast is populated by the indigenous Miskito people, among others, whose culture and Miskito language reflect a long history of incorporating outsiders, through both cultural encounter and violence. For more on Miskito society in relation to Sandinista Revolution, see Dennis. On Miskito's friendly relations with English buccaneers and history of slaving, see Helms.

61. In an early interview, Jones explains her interest in personality: "I like the focus to be personality and what Sterling Brown in *The Negro Caravan* calls 'the revelation of personality.' This doesn't mean that the work has to ignore the social-historical landscape that may affect personality and circumstances; it just doesn't have to take up the whole space so that, as Alice Walker said finely in an interview in John O'Brien's *Interviews with Black Writers*, it makes invisible the people's own 'dreams, imaginings, rituals and legends' or relegates them to the background as seemingly 'insignificant'" ("An Interview with Gayl Jones" by Rowell 41–42).

62. The phrase "guerrilla personality" as used elsewhere is also an oblique reference to Toni Cade Bambara's *Gorilla, My Love*.

63. Golden and McConnell. Golden and McConnell are part of the Chicago Religious Task Force on Central America, at times in conflict with the well-publicized Tucson movement.

64. Blockson 4. The Underground Railroad assisted slaves fleeing the South, both before and after the Fugitive Slave Act of 1850. Blockson wrote on the railroad for *National Geographic* before publishing his book in 1987. He draws his material largely from a history of the Underground Railroad written by the black historian William Still, who published a volume of his interviews with fugitive slaves in 1872 but whose work was overshadowed by Wilburg H. Siebert's *The Underground Railroad: From Slavery to Freedom* (1898).

65. As Crittenden describes it, "The rancher [Corbett] had always been an advocate of openness; secrecy, he believed was first cousin to the lie. He wanted to build a grassroots faith community that would empower people to act in accordance with their consciences, and in his view, secrecy would smother the opportunity to develop such a consensus" (62).

66. Mosquito, at this point not an insider, retorts, "Say what? What's a Nicodemus?" To which Ray repeats, "The ones who believe the more secret we are the safer we are" (307). Nicodemus pops up in Mosquito's subsequent narration as a kind of secret code, as when Mosquito wonders whether characters like Delgadina, Maria, and Monkey Bread are "Nicodemuses"—though of course she "ain't so ignorant" to let any one of them "know that I know that she a Nicodemus, or at least I think I know that she a Nicodemus" (500). Nicodemus refers primarily to a biblical figure marked by indeterminacy and ambiguity in his relationship to Jesus. Jones imagines in *Mosquito* an open assemblage of Nicodemuses in a shadow sanctuary movement—one that uses its marginal status and its partial invisibility to its advantage—and this comes to describe all sorts of survival and rebellious tactics of marginalized people in "real" life who know ways to reveal or to communicate with each other. Mosquito's belief in "Nicodemus" as a codeword leads her to test whether her friends recognize the word—but the response is usually, "Nick who?" (494). For Mosquito, codes are not secrets one has to "keep"; they can be spoken aloud because they confuse outsiders while they identify insiders as a kind of code-switching. Other historical references to Nicodemus may be relevant. The oldest continuously occupied black town west of the Mississippi River is named Nicodemus in honor of the first freed slave in the United States whose slave name was said to be Nicodemus. Freed blacks founded the town Nicodemus following Reconstruction, and Nicodemus was poised for economic success when the (literal) railroad skipped over the town, causing its economic ruin. This Kansas town of Nicodemus is now a national historical monument. In a humorous move, the section of the novel describing the problem of Maria's jailed cousin in "Middle America" is titled "This Ain't Nicodemus," which sounds like a play on Dorothy's famous phrase, "We're not in Kansas anymore" (345). The biblical Nicodemus is represented with dark brown skin by the major African American painter Henry Ossawa Tanner in *Nicodemus Visiting Jesus*, and his conversation with Jesus has been recounted by Martin Luther King Jr. in his 1967 speech, "Where Do We Go from Here?," on the interrelatedness of America's oppressive domestic and foreign practices. King addresses the United States when he says, "Your whole structure must be changed."

67. The museum is an institution created by colonialist modes of order and knowledge production. At an African art exhibition in a Toronto museum, an African man waxes eloquently about African aesthetics as he lectures to Mosquito on the museum's powers of preservation and on the originality and singularity of Africa. Even when "you African Americans talk about jazz," he says to Mosquito, the African masks on display show that jazz is derivative, that it is already present in the masks (333). This "dissident and disillusioned African in exile" warns Mosquito, whom he names "Beautiful," to resist colonization. "Don't let anyone invade your essential self, your transcendental self. Them or us. We're both of us, Beautiful, exiles in the New World." Mosquito deflates such appropriation and bristles at his rhetoric. He speaks for her and at the same time addresses her as a representative of all Africans and as an exile. Obsessed with a singular origin, he finds all the elements of black culture in an ancient African mask, thus denying the dynamic cultural creativity of African Americans. "I am not sure which them he means or which us. I be thinking he a strange man . . . Exiles in the New World." What Mosquito notices about the museum is the mancala, or African game board, she starts to pick up before noticing the display warning, "do not touch" (334). The African exile resembles the authoritarian novelist

Jones refers to in "Quest" in his attempt to co-opt Mosquito in the effort of decolonization, in contrast to Ray, whose engagement with Mosquito was based on conversation
and sexual attraction.

68. Slaughter 148.

69. Ibid.

70. Ibid., 144.

71. Justice Anthony M. Kennedy's Supreme Court opinion upholding the core of
the 2010 Arizona immigration law—what its critics have called the "show me your
papers" provision, which "requires state law enforcement officials to determine the
immigration status of anyone they stop or arrest if there is reason to suspect that the
individual might be an illegal immigrant"—suggests the space of the public sphere as
a privileged site where, it is imagined, law is formed to represent a public will. Ruling against minor provisions of the law, Kennedy writes: "The national government
has significant power to regulate immigration. . . . With power comes responsibility,
and the sound exercise of national power over immigration depends on the nation's
meeting its responsibility to base its laws on a political will informed by searching,
thoughtful, rational civic discourse." Liptak and Cushman, "Supreme Court Rejects
Part of Arizona Immigration Law."

72. Slaughter 158–59.

73. See Henderson, "Speaking in Tongues."

74. Foucault, *The Archaeology of Knowledge* 126, 129.

75. Derrida, *Archive Fever* 9.

76. Ibid., 9–10.

77. Ibid., 52.

78. Ray laughingly figures out that Mosquito is a "jokester" (241) after she says,
"I'm ignorant about everything except," but then goes on to qualify at length, ending with her critique of James Weldon Johnson: "I agrees on some things with the
ex-colored man, but I still considers myself colorful. I ain't shitting you, Ray, excuse
my French . . . I remember reading that preachifying, though, and thinking why they
keep all that preachifying in that book, because it seem like to me it would have been
a better book without all that preachifying" (241). Jones's own novel, of course, is full
of preachifying, even if it is done with tongue in cheek.

79. Scholars since the 1970s have presented a more complex and deromanticized
history of Queen Nzingha (aka Njinga, Nzinga). John K. Thornton writes, "Pre-colo-
nial Africa's most famous, and certainly her best documented queen. She is also surely
the most romanticized. . . . By the 1960s and 1970s she had become firmly entrenched
in Angolan nationalist and much of liberal Africanist historiography as a proto-
nationalist heroine" (25). For a challenge to celebratory accounts of Nzinga, see Joseph
C. Miller, "Nzinga of Matamba in a New Perspective."

80. Waligora-Davis, *Sanctuary* 11–12.

81. Mullen, "African Signs and Spirit Writing" 623–43. Mullen critiques Gates's theory
of the "speakerly text." She notes the tradition of visionary and sacred literacy in African
American art and discusses the overlooked role of African sign-writing systems in notions
of black orality. Mullen worries that an emphasis on the "speakerly" text "will inevitably
exclude certain African-American texts that draw more on the culture of books, writing,
and print than they do on the culture of orality," and the general reception of *Mosquito*
affirms this claim for me (624). See also Mullen's discussion of Nat Turner's account of his
ease with words as a sign of his prophetic, revolutionary leadership.

82. Subcomandante Marcos, *Our Word Is Our Weapon: Selected Writings*. Subcomandante Marcos, the persona of the Mexican academic Rafael Guillen Vicente, who is of European descent, became the (masked) face and voice of the Zapatista radical indigenous movement. In 2014, twenty years since NAFTA and the Zapatistas' official launch, they have gained some limited autonomy but continue to have a fraught and sometimes violent relation to the Mexican state, which they say still harasses them. See Duncan Tucker, "Are Mexico's Zapatista Rebels Still Relevant? Twenty Years after the Uprising, Activists Say Zapatistas Have Influenced Radical Movements Around the World," *Al Jazeera,* January 1, 2014. See also BBC, "Mexico's Zapatista Rebel Leader Subcomandante Marcos Steps Down," May 25, 2014.

83. In addition to an archive, the Daughters offer the not-mainstream sanctuary movement something it needs to become a truly decolonizing movement: playfulness and humor. Mosquito's playfulness contrasts with Ray, who often misses it or gets thrown off by it and rarely joins her. Mosquito "reads" Ray as someone who, as a person of color in white mainstream society, "rejected they humor and playfulness so's not to be confused with the stereotype" (571). One of Mosquito's warrior tactics is to "face my audience and play with them, I says, even if they does think I'm a stereotype" (572), despite the angry readers in that audience. Here and elsewhere, Mosquito's archive keeping is part of a prophetic and visionary process of transforming ideas about the sanctuary and the archive that is also insistently playful.

84. McDowell, "The Whole Story."

85. The Daughters may be a sign of a multiplied notion of authorship that Jones articulates in response to Roland Barthes's 1968 announcement of the "death of the author," when he asserted, with Julia Kristeva, the radical intertextuality of all texts, an intertextuality that replaced intersubjectivity and that liberated the reader as it spelled out the death (i.e., the social irrelevance) of the role of "author" in making texts meaningful. Where there was an author, there is now the scriptor. What would the narrator and archivist Mosquito be in this case—author or scriptor? Alongside the "death of the author" comes Foucault's response to Barthes, "What Is an Author?," in which Foucault traces the creation of the modern author through his relationship to the text as well as to societal power relations. For a helpful discussion of these theories of authorship, see Pease, "Author."

86. Waligora-Davis, *Sanctuary* 12.

87. The language of control and the labor of freeing oneself from another's control preoccupies Jones's writing. Often this struggle is cast in terms of heterosexual relationships structured by slave, colonial, and gender relations. In "Quest" a discourse of control, imposition, and dominance identifies the colonialist of a "colonized" novel. She writes simply, "What is a colonialist? A colonialist controls" (511).

88. Du Bois, *W. E. B. Du Bois on Asia* 158–59.

4 / Masking Fanon

1. John Edgar Wideman, *Fanon* 4. Subsequent references are cited in the text.

2. See Coleman for a reading of *The Island* in relation to Wideman's earlier auto/biographies. For a reading of racial melancholy as a narrative strategy in *The Island*, see Bergevin. For a more critical evaluation of Wideman's position as tourist and the limitations of his travel narrative, see Chancy.

3. Wideman, *The Island* 121. Subsequent references are cited in the text.

4. Gordon 8.

5. Interestingly, in *The Island*, Wideman's persona, Paul, recounts the memory of encountering Fanon's face as having "intruded" on him in the midst of drafting his Fanon book, immediately followed by "a churning black cloud of smoke, skyscrapers on fire," what Paul interprets as one response—in the form of the terrorist attacks of September 11, 2011—to Fanon's call "that the Third World's *project* must be to resolve problems to which Europe has found no solutions" (Fanon, *Island* 124; emphasis in original).

6. See, for instance, Slaughter's reading of the wording of the 1948 Universal Declaration for Human Rights, in which "the term 'person' became a kind of mask for the human, a rhetorical feint for not naming the human itself as a question" (18).

7. As W. E. B. Du Bois noted, the new international human rights discourse "combine[d] the interest in colonial peoples with the interest in imperial objects and is too strongly weighted on the side of imperialism," a tipped scale that operates through the unequal force of political states to administer, enforce, and otherwise make of international human rights an instrument of sovereign power (Lewis 53; quoted in R. Williams xiv). Randall Williams and others have argued that the postwar human rights regime has served to secure U.S. global hegemony while defusing radical decolonization movements around the world and within the United States. For a study that points to the Southern white strategy of keeping racial oppression to the language of civil, rather than international, human rights, see Anderson. For a more critical study of the legal personality of African Americans and imperial logics throughout the twentieth century, see Waligora-Davis, *Sanctuary*.

8. Slaughter provides a gloss on the term "personality": "a technical term that means the quality of being equal before the law—to put it tautologically, the quality of being a person." While Slaughter is right to distinguish this meaning from "the thick, multi-faceted differential category of individual identity and self-expression contemplated in psychology and popular culture" (17), it is the relay between the legal and the psychological that becomes particularly important to the anticolonial thought of Frantz Fanon specifically. See also Cameron for readings of personality and its negation. For an introduction to legal personhood, see *Harvard Law Review* (2001).

9. Quoted in Macey 23–24.

10. Gates, "Critical Fanonism" 458. Gates has noted that postcolonial theorists such as Edward Said insist on situating the colonial subject in a historically specific context only to restyle Fanon himself as "global theorist *in vacuo*" (459). Fanon becomes a mask that morphs into whatever the critic wants to see, as when Homi Bhabha famously claimed *Black Skin, White Masks* for postcolonial theory by "turning Fanon into *le Lacan noir*" (462). A decade later, Macey finds that few have answered Gates's call to historicize Fanon in his specific lived context: "The Third Worldist Fanon was an apocalyptic creature; the post-colonial Fanon worries about identity politics, and often about his own sexual identity, but he is no longer angry" (28). The problem for Macey as an intellectual historian and biographer is that nearly all scholarly and artistic representations "construct a Fanon who exists outside time and space and in a purely textual dimension" (27), so that the "specifically French and Martinican dimension of Fanon's [Algerian] colonial experience," apparent in careful readings of his texts, is repeatedly effaced (29). Françoise Vergès is a notable exception for Macey, who otherwise deplores the dehistoricization of Fanon by Said and Bhabha, among others (27).

11. The documentary film *Frantz Fanon: Black Skin, White Mask*, directed by Isaac Julien, experiments with representing Fanon explicitly through prosopopoeia in what

resembles a cinematic collage: interspersing talking-head documentary interviews and historical photographs with scenes from *The Battle of Algiers*, the documentary features the actor Colin Salmon as the mask, the highly artificial presentation of the image of Fanon. Presenting a nonrealist image of Fanon, Julien explains, has "the effect of both drawing him back into the past—of the documentary image of Fanon—as well signaling his availability for the future. . . . [H]e is both representing Fanon and is not Fanon. Colin Salmon literally speaks Fanon's text, bringing it alive so to speak but in a ventriloquist manner—he speaks and is spoken. Restaging in this way avoids creating character or interiority as in the conventional fiction film." In Julien's effort to open the image of Fanon from its historical functions in the U.S. context "as a black icon to produce and prop up African-American philosophy," he must highlight the use of Fanon as a mask by presenting the image of Fanon as ever and only a mask, at once the image of a face and not a face (Julien and Nash, "Fanon as Film" 15–16).

12. Neoliberalism since the 1970s has represented a shift from the previous decade of increased federal funding, government-sponsored studies, and development programs that ostensibly sought to address problems facing urban African Americans. While structural racism and uneven patterns of urban development were frequently acknowledged in such studies, the origins of such problems were often naturalized as inherent to a black legal, cultural, and familial personality in desperate need of proper civic development. The notorious Moynihan Report (1965) exemplifies this pattern in its conclusion that, despite the formal equality of personhood gained by the civil rights movement, the black mother thwarts black men's ability to be recognized and treated as adults and full persons in social and political life. The emphasis on the pathology of the black personality persists in public discourse and underpins a range of neoliberal policies. Such policies seek to correct perceived racial pathologies by increasing punitive forms of control sanctioned by the state and managed by private industry, a dynamic pointedly at work in the still publicly run prison of Pittsburgh's Western Penitentiary, where John's brother Robert is incarcerated. The penitentiary envisions its social mission as one of corrective developmentalism—re-forming the criminal personality into a normative civic one—as begun in the world's "first penitentiary, Philadelphia's Quaker-inspired Walnut Street Jail." See Dubey for her reading of urban politics in Wideman's *Philadelphia Fire*. See also Denise Rodriguez for a study of Wideman's Homewood Trilogy as a "re-inscription" and extension of the tradition of the "black urban novel." For an insightful and lively critique of "black underclass" discourse, see Kelley.

For a critique of developmentalist logic in both leftist revolutionary and counter-revolutionary movements, see Saldaña-Portillo; Escobar; and Kapoor.

13. Wideman's figurative language here echoes Claude Lanzmann's account of Fanon on the day of his death, when, referring to the hospital staff he distrusted, he told his wife Josie, "They put me through the washing machine last night." Macey 485.

14. Priest 3.

15. Russell 2131.

16. Wideman, "Looking at Emmett Till" 46.

17. Metress 89.

18. Wideman, "Looking at Emmett Till" 46.

19. The published image of Till's face, along with his murderers' acquittal on all charges, evinced the violence of differential legal personhood in Jim Crow Mississippi and the illegibility of such violence in U.S.-led international human rights law, despite

the European press's widely expressed outrage at the racist hypocrisy of the United States. It became a haunting icon from the civil rights movement to the present (Russell 2121). The Emmett Till Unsolved Civil Rights Crime Act of 2007 (HR 923) was passed in early 2008 to enable the Justice Department to investigate and prosecute civil rights–era crimes; many of those cases remain unsolved. See Barry et al.

20. P. Williams.

21. Patricia Williams writes, "Let us consider the state of our own maximum security prisons when we hear our President promise to build the Iraqi people a brand-new, American-style facility on top of Abu Ghraib—'Camp Redemption' some in the Administration propose to rename it. . . . Let us think about the proposed sovereignty giving Iraqis responsibility for every last bit of the chaos, but no veto power over US military action within their borders." For a genealogy of the prisoner as a figure of civil death, see Dayan, "Legal Slaves and Civil Bodies" and *The Law Is a White Dog*.

22. *Precarious Life*, xv.

23. The historical Fanon evoked the liberatory potential in turning over a new leaf (*Wretched of the Earth* 316); in *Fanon* the novel, John the narrator riffs on the imagery of cinema as "dead leaf" (Wideman 197).

24. Fanon, *Black Skin, White Masks* 153 n. 16. Subsequent references are cited in the text.

25. Fanon, *Wretched of the Earth* 314; see 33–35 on decolonization. Subsequent references are cited in the text.

26. R. Williams 1–23, 94–110. Williams productively reads human rights discourse as in full contradiction to Fanon's theory of radical anticolonial violence. What I want to point out here, however, is the shared conceptions of the human person and its political development in both liberal human rights discourse and Fanon's theory of radical decolonization.

27. Fuss 39.

28. Ibid.

29. Vergès 580.

30. Ibid., 589.

31. Ibid. Vergès argues that Fanon's appeal to a true consciousness waiting to be unmasked enables his supposed disavowal of Antillean history in what she identifies as Fanon's "family romance" (589–90). Fanon "re-created his family, reinvented his filiation, and situated his symbolic ancestry in Algeria. The Creole filiation, a site of anxiety and ambivalence, was displaced, and a revolutionary filiation took its place; the heroic fighters of the national struggle became his fathers and brothers" (579–80). Fanon's "family romance" leads to a politics of gender and racial difference that Vergès describes as a theory of masculinity that assumes "only one conception of masculinity, one that requires female submission" and one that can recover "through stages of progressive development" from an emasculation caused by the wounds of colonization: "It was in Algeria that Fanon found the virile male that would belie the colonial construction of emasculated masculinity," one who could "attack the castrating master, the French man, and to castrate him in return." Vergès concludes that Fanon's family romance of invented filiation and the recovery of a wounded masculinity is "a story among men with women's bodies as hostages in the racial war" (593).

32. Lydon 2008.

33. For mention of Bearden in Wideman's work, see, e.g., Coleman and TuSmith.

34. Schwartzman 209.

35. Ibid., 212–16.

36. Ibid.

37. Ibid. 204.

38. Macey 43.

39. Ibid., 432.

40. See Agamben, *Homo Sacer*; see Mbembe, "Necropolitics," on death-bound personhood and forms of modern sovereignty in the context of the colony and slave law. For a genealogy of civil death in medieval European, colonial slave, and contemporary prison law, see Dayan "Legal Slaves and Civil Bodies" and *The Law Is a White Dog.*

41. Slaughter 13.

Epilogue: The Ends of Legal Personhood

1. Martinique was not a colony but an Overseas Department of France.

2. The conventional starting point for the story of Fanon's political and intellectual development may be in 1944, when he leaves Martinique to fight alongside the Free French, only to have his allegiance to French ideals betrayed by a growing awareness of French colonialist racism. Wideman pointedly does not include this crucial moment in his novel: instead, he turns to a seemingly minor detail recounted in David Macey's biography of Fanon—not the "proper" start of Fanon the revolutionary but the "false start" of a seventeen-year-old boy from Martinique who steals from his father to serve his mother France.

3. In Fanon's case, he spins cloth into gold not with the help of an imp but with the power of self-development affirmed by the conventional bildungsroman.

4. It is in 1944 that he leaves again to fight alongside the Free French after Admiral Robert's downfall in Martinique (see Macey).

5. Fanon's experience fighting with the Free French, and his observations of French colonial soldiers in life and in media advertising (the image of the grinning black soldier on the *banania* posters), also worked to undermine his belief in French color-blindness and civic equality. A letter to his parents while in the military reveals his bitterness about those ideals for which he was risking his life (see Macey). Also see "The Fact of Blackness" in *Black Skin, White Masks.*

6. Slaughter points out that the ideal bildungsroman invents a narrative device of a "wholly benevolent overseer who [secretly] manages the protagonist's development behind the scenes" until which time the young hero "is judged to have completed its social apprenticeship and to have thereby become capable of self-narration and self-determination, at which point the story and the narrator's work end" (213–14).

7. Extending Barbara Harlow's contention that the UDHR "can be read as recharting the trajectory and peripeties of the classic bildungsroman," Slaughter demonstrates how both human rights discourse and the bildungsroman share, produce, and project a normative ideal of the development of the human personality (quoted in Slaughter 30 n. 78)

8. As Slaughter and others have observed, the notion of the human personality contains and naturalizes the paradoxes and contradictions of the human person, which is suspended between natural and positive law. The legal human person shares with business corporations the model of an incorporated self and provides cover for the very economic and cultural development projects that engage in the violation of human rights in the name of human rights.

9. The following passage from *Fanon* underscores the tension between narrative control for the author and its elusive hero: "Your fate, your destiny, your portion not something you can wait for or beg or borrow. No one can grant you freedom. If you're in charge, you never wait. You prepare. Gather the threads in your hands, connect them, braid them, take the next step you must take. That next step the only truth, all truth. But isn't truth, Fanon reminds himself, also true if you don't take charge. Your fate's your fate, whatever steps you take or don't take. No way out. And this reversible truth a kind of bittersweet comfort or a good laugh at himself squeezed out of the worst times when he lies awake, beyond the possibility of sleep, empty-handed, famished, waiting for something or someone he couldn't say what the fuck it might be, trying like a prisoner in a cell to remember in the middle of the night what he had believed was worth the risk of winding up in prison" (152).

10. Fontanier, *Les figures du discours* 404 ff., quoted in Riffaterre 107.

11. Deloughrey, "Heavy Waters" 710.

12. Dayan, *White Dog* 22. De jure statelessness is defined as an absolute lack of recognized legal identity; the 1954 United Nations Convention Relating to the Status of Stateless Persons, for example, defines the stateless person as "a person who is not considered as a national by any State under the operation of its law." See Mayer for an account of how many prisoners at Guantánamo—and presumably in other, more secret prisons around the world—were effectively sold to the U.S. military, which compensated Pakistani authorities and the Northern Alliance members, and many have been the victims of local rivalries, misunderstanding, and rumors. For an account of detention in the U.S. media that features the experiences of people who suffered extraordinary rendition before being released, see "Habeas Schmabeas." Judith Butler, following activists and human rights lawyers, points out that "these prisoners are not considered 'prisoners' and receive no protection from international law.... [A]s a result, the humans who are imprisoned in Guantanamo [detention camp] do not count as human; they are not subjects protected by international law. They are not subjects in any legal or normative sense" (*Precarious Life* xv).

13. Nonhuman Rights Project, "The Capacity to Have a Legal Right."

14. Mississippi Amendment Initiative #26, official state informational pamphlet.

15. The Mississippi Amendment Initiative #26 sought to define legal personhood to "include every human being from the moment of fertilization, cloning or the functional equivalent thereof." The full language of the initiative is the following: "Be it Enacted by the People of the State of Mississippi: SECTION 1. Article III of the constitution of the state of Mississippi is [hereby] amended BY THE ADDITION OF A NEW SECTION TO READ: SECTION 33. Person defined. As used in this Article III of the state constitution, 'The term 'person' or 'persons' shall include every human being from the moment of fertilization, cloning or the functional equivalent thereof.'"

16. Personhood USA.

17. The *Harvard Law Review* explains, "In *Commonwealth v. Cass*, the Massachusetts Supreme Judicial Court held that a fetus was a "person" within the meaning of the state vehicular homicide statute. Emphasizing that statutory terms should be construed in light of their ordinary meaning, the court argued that "[a]n offspring of human parents cannot reasonably be considered to be other than a human being, and therefore a person, first within, and then in normal course outside, the womb." The statute's ordinary meaning, and the failure of the legislature to provide any "hint of a contemplated distinction between pre-born and born human beings," effectively created a presumption that fetuses count as persons."

18. According to the ACLU, "As with forced c-sections, the pregnant women most likely to be reported and prosecuted for drug use are, like Jennifer Johnson, women of color and low-income women. In a 1990 study in the *New England Journal of Medicine*, researchers found that about 15 percent of both white and African-American women used drugs during pregnancy. The African-American women, however, were 10 times as likely as the white women to be reported to the authorities. Poor women were more likely to be reported than middle-class women. The ACLU's own tracking of prosecutions of pregnant women confirms this disparity." Such a disparity has been discussed in the context of the war on drugs; see Alexander.

19. Officials at John Peter Smith Hospital invoked the Texas Advance Directives Act to justify its decision to keep the dead woman on life support. In court the lawyer representing the hospital invoked "a section of the Texas Penal Code that states a person may commit criminal homicide by causing the death of a fetus," arguing that the law, as the lawyer put it, "must convey legislative intent to protect the unborn child, otherwise the Legislature would have simply allowed a pregnant patient to decide to let her life, and the life of her unborn child, end." A judge eventually ruled on the case in favor of the family, arguing that the hospital misinterpreted the law and ordering the hospital to remove her from life support. See McLean; Fernandez.

20. Of Amanda Kimbrough, a woman facing ten years' imprisonment for using meth while pregnant and ultimately delivering a premature baby who lived for only nineteen minutes, Angela Hulsey, an assistant district attorney on the case, said, "She caused the death of another person," "a person that will never have the chance to go to school, go to the prom, get married, have children of their own. You're dealing with the most innocent of victims." Calhoun, "Criminalization of Bad Mothers."

21. ACLU.

22. *Stallman v. Youngquist.*

23. Ibid.

24. See ACLU.

25. *Whitner v South Carolina Fact Sheet.* As the National Advocates for Pregnant Women points out, these prosecutions are aimed almost exclusively at African American women using illegal drugs, despite medical evidence that illegal drugs do no more harm than smoking or lack of prenatal care and despite the evidence that most cases of risks to the fetus in South Carolina are a result of legal alcohol use by white women.

One woman, Regina McKnight, was convicted for fetal homicide after authorities learned of her cocaine addiction. She has spent nearly eight years in prison, despite all evidence showing that she wanted the pregnancy and that cocaine addiction has not been linked to stillbirths and is no greater risk factor to a fetus than alcohol or lack of prenatal care. Her case was eventually overturned by the state supreme court on the grounds that she had an unfair trial due to factual error in the presentation of a causal link between her addiction and the stillbirth. See National Advocates for Pregnant Women, "Regina McKnight—Victory at Long Last."

26. Calhoun reports, "Originally created to protect children from potentially explosive meth labs, Alabama's chemical-endangerment law prohibits a "responsible person" from "exposing a child to an environment in which he or she . . . knowingly, recklessly or intentionally causes or permits a child to be exposed to, to ingest or inhale, or to have contact with a controlled substance, chemical substance or drug paraphernalia. . . . In 2006, Tiffany Hitson was charged with chemical endangerment the day after she gave birth to a baby girl who tested positive for cocaine and marijuana

but was otherwise healthy. When that prosecution was successful (Hitson was incarcerated for a year), other counties followed suit, making Alabama the national capital for prosecuting women on behalf of their newborn children."

27. National Advocates for Pregnant Women, "Punishment of Pregnant Women."

28 Prenatal Murder bill.

29. See HR 374, "Life at Conception Act."

30. Bassett.

31. Paltrow.

32. "Outcry in America."

33. Hyde 165.

34. For a brief reading of Hobbes's definition of the person, and of the person as a counter to impersonality, see Cameron viii.

35. Adopting the language and spirit of rights as protections from harm, animal rights have borrowed the language of international human rights discourse. For instance, the Great Apes Project (GAP) has campaigned for UN Recognition of a Declaration on Great Primates that accords them three basic rights: the right to life, the right to a protection of their individual freedom, and the right to be protected from torture.

36. PETA.

37. While PETA folds animal species into the same categories of difference as "gender, race, or religion," the Nonhuman Rights Project, which describes itself as "the only organization working toward actual LEGAL rights for members of species other than our own," makes an explicit bid to change the common law status of some nonhuman animals "from mere 'things,' which lack the capacity to possess any legal right, to 'persons,' who possess such fundamental rights as bodily integrity and bodily liberty, and those other legal rights to which evolving standards of morality, scientific discovery, and human experience entitle them." One blogger for the Nonhuman Rights Project relates the freedom suit of James Somerset: "In Western law, every nonhuman animal has always been regarded as a legal 'thing.' We can buy, sell, eat, hunt, ride, trap, vivisect, and kill them almost at whim. The reason is that legal things don't exist in law for their own sakes. They exist for the sakes of legal 'persons,' which we humans are. . . . The common law transformation of a nonhuman animal from 'legal thing' to 'legal person' is a primary objective of the Nonhuman Rights Project. Its main purpose is, through litigation and education, to persuade an American state high court to transform a nonhuman animal the way Lord Mansfield transformed James Somerset: by declaring that she is a legal person capable of possessing legal rights."

38. Fischer, "History and Catastrophe" 163.

WORKS CITED

Abu-Lughod, Janet. *Before European Hegemony: The World System, A.D. 1250–1350.* New York: Oxford University Press, 1989.

Ackermann, Hans-W., and Jeanine Gauthier. "The Ways and Nature of the Zombi." *Journal of American Folklore* 104.414 (Autumn 1991): 466–94.

"An African American Homecoming." African Burial Ground. www.african-burialground.gov/ABG_AnAfricanAmericanHomecoming.htm.

Agamben, Giorgio. "Beyond Human Rights." In *Means without End: Notes on Politics.* Translated by Vincenzo Binetti and Cesare Casarino. Minneapolis: University of Minnesota Press, 2007. 15–26.

———. *Homo Sacer: Sovereign Power and Bare Life.* Translated by Daniel Heller-Roazen. Meridian: Crossing Aesthetics. Stanford, CA: Stanford University Press, 1998.

Alexander, Michelle. *The New Jim Crow: Mass Incarceration in the Age of Color-blindness.* New York: New Press, 2010.

American Civil Liberties Union (ACLU). "Coercive and Punitive Governmental Responses to Women's Conduct During Pregnancy." September 30, 1997. www.aclu.org/reproductive-freedom/coercive-and-punitive-governmental-responses-womens-conduct-during-pregnancy.

Anderson, Carol. *Eyes Off the Prize: The United Nations and the African-American Struggle for Human Rights, 1944–1955.* Cambridge: Cambridge University Press, 2003.

Ardouin, Beaubrun. *Etudes sur l'histoire d'Haïti, suivies de la vie du Général J.-M. Borgella.* Vol. 1, 1853–1860. 2nd ed. Port-au-Prince: Chez l'éditeur François Dalencour, 1958.

Arendt, Hannah. *The Origins of Totalitarianism.* New York: Harcourt, Brace & Co., 1951.

Austin, Dan, and Sean Doerr. *Lost Detroit: Stories behind the Motor City's Majestic Ruins*. Charleston: History Press, 2010.

Austin, J. L. *How to Do Things with Words*. Cambridge, MA: Harvard University Press, 1962.

Ayala, César J. *American Sugar Kingdom: The Plantation Economy of the Spanish Caribbean, 1898–1934*. Chapel Hill: University of North Carolina Press, 1999.

Bales, Kevin. *Disposable People: New Slavery in the Global Economy*. Updated with a new preface. Berkeley: University of California Press, 2012.

——. *Understanding Global Slavery: A Reader*. Berkeley: University of California Press, 2005.

Banff Center. Interview with Melinda Hunt. www.banffcentre.info/inspired/2011/02/summoning-the-dead-melinda-hunt-commemorates-new-york%E2%80%99s-forgotten/.

Barrett, Tom. "Government of the Devil, by the Devil, and for the Devil." *American Daily*, March 11, 2004. July 30, 2010. americandaily.com/article/95.

Barringer, Felicity. "The World: 'Repatriation' Is the Trend for Refugees Worldwide." *New York Times*, November 17, 1991, Sunday Final Ed., S4, p. 4.

Barry, Dan, Campbell Robertson, and Robbie Brown. "When Cold Cases Stay Cold." *New York Times*, March 16, 2013. www.nytimes.com/2013/03/17/us/souths-coldcases-reopened-but-still-unresolved.html?smid=pl-share.

Bassett, Laura. "Personhood USA Blames Planned Parenthood for Loss in Mississippi." *Huffington Post*, November 9, 2011.

Batchelor, Carol. UNHCR, Department of International Protection, "The 1954 Convention relating to the Status of Stateless Persons: Implementation within the European Union Member States and Recommendations for Harmonisation." *Refuge* 22.2 (Summer 2004): 1–46.

Baucom, Ian. *Specters of the Atlantic: Finance Capital, Slavery, and the Philosophy of History*. Durham, NC: Duke University Press, 2005.

Bauman, Zygmunt. *Wasted Lives: Modernity and Its Outcasts*. Cambridge: Polity Press, 2004.

BBC News. "Full Text: Rice Defends U.S. Policy." December 5, 2005. news.bbc.co.uk/1/hi/world/americas/4500630.stm.

Behdad, Ali. *Forgetful Nation*. Durham, NC: Duke University Press, 2005.

——. "On Globalization, Again!" In *Postcolonial Studies and Beyond*. Edited by Ania Loomba et al. Durham, NC: Duke University Press, 2005. 62–79.

——. "Une practique sauvage: Postcolonial Belatedness and Cultural Politics." In *The Pre-Occupation of Postcolonial Studies*. Edited by Fawzia Afzal-Khan and Kalpana Seshadri-Crooks. Durham, NC: Duke University Press, 2000.

Bennett, Herman L. "'Sons of Adam': Text, Context, and the Early Modern African Subject." Special issue: Redress. *Representations* 92.1 (Fall 2005): 16–41.

Berger, John. "Twelve Theses on the Economy of the Dead." In *Hold Everything Dear: Dispatches on Survival and Resistance*. New York: Pantheon, 2007. 3–6.

Bergevin, Gerald W. "'Traveling Here Below': John Edgar Wideman's *The*

Island: Martinique and the Strategy of Melancholy." In *Critical Essays on John Edgar Wideman.* Edited by Bonnie TuSmith and Keith E. Byerman. Knoxville: University of Tennessee Press, 2006. 71–89.

Berlant, Lauren. "The Subject of True Feeling." In *Cultural Pluralism, Identity Politics, and the Law.* Edited by Austin Sarat and Thomas R. Kearns. Ann Arbor: University of Michigan Press, 1999. 49–84.

———. *The Queen of America Goes to Washington City: Essays on Sex and Citizenship.* Durham, NC: Duke University Press, 1997.

Best, Stephen M. *The Fugitive's Properties: Law and the Poetics of Possession.* Chicago: University of Chicago Press, 2004.

———. "Neither Lost nor Found: Slavery and the Visual Archive." Special issue: New World Slavery and the Matter of the Visual. *Representations* 113.1 (Winter 2011): 150–63.

Best, Stephen M., and Saidiya Hartman. "Fugitive Justice." Special issue: Redress. *Representations* 92.1 (Fall 2005): 1–15.

Blackmon, Douglas A. *Slavery by Another Name: The Reenslavement of Black Americans from the Civil War to World War II.* New York: Doubleday, 2008.

Blockson, Charles L. *The Underground Railroad.* New York: Prentice Hall, 1987.

"Boat People and Compassion Fatigue." Editorial. *New York Times,* July 14, 1988, A28.

Brady, Mary Pat. *Extinct Lands, Temporal Geographies: Chicana Literature and the Urgency of Space.* Durham, NC: Duke University Press, 2002.

Bramen, Carrie Tirado. "Speaking in Typeface: Characterizing Stereotypes in Gayl Jones's *Mosquito.*" *MFS Modern Fiction Studies* 49.1 (2003): 124–54.

Brathwaite, Kamau. "Caribbean Man in Space and Time." *Savacou* 11–12 (1975): 1–11.

———. *Contradictory Omens: Cultural Diversity and Integration in the Caribbean.* Mona, Kingston, Jamaica: Savacao Publications, 1974.

Braziel, Jana Evans. "Re-Membering Défilée: Dédée Brazile as Revolutionary *Lieu de Mémoire.*" *Small Axe* 18 (2005): 57–85.

Briggs, Laura. *Reproducing Empire: Race, Sex, Science, and U.S. Imperialism in Puerto Rico.* Berkeley: University of California Press, 2002.

British Museum. Egyptian holdings. www.thebritishmuseum.ac.uk.

Brown, Vincent. "Social Death and Political Life in the Study of Slavery." *American Historical Review* (December 2009): 1231–49.

Brown, Wendy. *Walled States, Waning Sovereignty.* New York: Zone Books, 2010.

Browning, John, and Spencer Reiss. *Encyclopedia of the New Economy: A Complete Reference Guide for Business in a Networked Economy.* San Francisco: Wired, 1998. www.wired.com/.

Burnett, Christina Duffy. "The Edges of Empire and the Limits of Sovereignty: American Guano Islands." Special issue: Legal Borderlands: Law and the Construction of American Borders. *American Quarterly* 57.3 (September 2005): 779–803.

Burnett, Christina Duffy, and Burke Marshall, eds. *Foreign in a Domestic Sense: Puerto Rico, American Expansion, and the Constitution.* Durham, NC: Duke University Press, 2001.

Bush, George H. W. "Address before Joint Session of the Congress on the State of the Union." Washington, DC, January 28, 1992.

Bush, Jonathan A. "'Take This Job and Shove It': The Rise of Free Labor" (review of *The Invention of Free Labor,* by Robert J. Steinfeld). *Michigan Law Review* 91.6 (May 1993): 1382–1413.

Butler, Judith. *Precarious Life: The Powers of Mourning and Violence.* New York: Verso, 2004.

Caistor, Nick. "Voodoo's Spell over Haiti." *BBC News Service,* August 4, 2003. news.bbc.co.uk/2/hi/americas/3122303.stm.

Calhoun, Ada. "The Criminalization of Bad Mothers." *New York Times,* April 25, 2012. www.nytimes.com/2012/04/29/magazine/the-criminalization-of-bad-mothers.html?pagewanted=all&_r=0.

Camacho, Alicia Schmidt. *Migrant Imaginaries: Latino Cultural Politics in the U.S.-Mexico Borderlands.* New York: New York University Press, 2008.

Cameron, Sharon. *Impersonality: Seven Essays.* Chicago: University of Chicago Press, 2007.

Carlisle, Rodney. "The 'American Century' Implemented: Stettinius and the Liberian Flag of Convenience." *Business History Review* 54.2 (Summer 1980): 175–91.

Caroit, Jean-Michel. "Protestants Gain as Catholic Split Threatens Haiti's Stability." *Manchester Guardian Weekly,* September 13, 1987, 13.

Carter, William M., Jr. "Race, Rights, and the Thirteenth Amendment: Defining the Badges and Incidents of Slavery." *UC Davis Law Review* 40.4 (April 2007): 1311–79.

de Carvalho, Aline Vieira. "Archeological Perspectives of Palmares: A Maroon Settlement in 17th Century Brazil." *Diaspora Archaeology Network,* March 2007 Newsletter. www.diaspora.uiuc.edu/news0307/news0307.html.

Castor, Suzy. "The American Occupation of Haiti (1915–1934) and the Dominican Republic (1916–1924)." Translated by Lynn Garafola. Special issue: Caliban. *Massachusetts Review* 15.1–2 (1974): 253–75.

Castronovo, Russ. *Necro Citizenship: Death, Eroticism, and the Public Sphere in the Nineteenth-Century United States.* New Americanists. Durham, NC: Duke University Press, 2001.

Césaire, Aimé. "Notebook of a Return to the Native Land." In *Aimé Césaire: The Collected Poetry.* Translated with introduction and notes by Clayton Eshleman and Annette Smith. Berkeley: University of California Press, 1983. 32–85.

Chambers, Ross. *Room for Maneuver: Reading (the) Oppositional (in) Narrative.* Chicago: University of Chicago Press, 1991.

Chamoiseau, Patrick. *Texaco.* New York: Vintage, 1998.

Chancy, Myriam J. A. "Floating Islands: Spectatorship and the Body Politic in the Traveling Subjectivities of John Edgar Wideman and Edwidge Danticat." *Small Axe* 36 (2011): 22–38.

Chandra, Sarika. "Interruptions: Tradition, Borders, and Narrative in Gayl Jones's *Mosquito*." In *After the Pain*. New York: Peter Lang, 2006. 137–55.

Chapman, Paul. *Trouble on Board: The Plight of International Seafarers*. Ithaca, NY: ILR Press, 1992.

Cheng, Anne Anlin. "The Melancholy of Race." *Kenyon Review*, n.s., 19.1 (Winter 1997): 49–61.

Christian, Barbara. "The Race for Theory." *Cultural Critique* 6 (Spring 1987): 51–63.

Christianity Today Magazine. "Christians See Official Recognition of Voodoo as Ominous: They Fear Aristide Plans to Renew 200-Year National Pact with the Devil." October 1, 2003. www.christianitytoday.com/ct/2003/october/18.28.html.

Clabough, Casey. "Afrocentric Recolonizations: Gayl Jones's 1990s Fiction." *Contemporary Literature* 46.2 (2005): 243–74.

Cliff, Michelle. "Caliban's Daughter: The Tempest and the Teapot." *Frontiers: A Journal of Women Studies* 12.2 (1991): 36–51.

———. *No Telephone to Heaven*. New York: Plume, 1996.

Clifford, James. "The Others: Beyond the 'Salvage' Paradigm." *Third Text* 3.6 (1989): 73–77.

Cloutier, Jean-Pierre. "HASCO Closes Its Doors." *Haiti Times*, May 1987. July 22, 2010.

Cole, Dorothy, and Kelle Schillaci. "Speed Reader." *Weekly Wire*, February 1, 1999. www.weeklywire.com/ww/02-01-99/alibi_speeder.html.

Coleman, James W. *Writing Blackness: John Edgar Wideman's Art and Experimentation*. Baton Rouge: Louisiana State University Press, 2010.

Collier, George A., with Elizabeth Lowery Quaratiello. *Basta!: Land and the Zapatista Rebellion in Chiapas*. 3rd ed. Foreword by Peter Rosset. Oakland: Food First Books, 2005.

Collins, Patricia Hill. *Black Feminist Thought: Knowledge, Consciousness, and the Politics of Empowerment*. 2nd ed. New York: Routledge, 1999.

———. "Learning from the Outsider Within: The Sociological Significance of Black Feminist Thought." In *The Feminist Standpoint Theory Reader: Intellectual and Political Controversies*. Edited by Sandra Harding. New York: Routledge, 2004. 103–26.

Comaroff, Jean, and John Comaroff. "Alien-Nation: Zombies, Immigrants, and Millenial Capitalism." *South Atlantic Quarterly* 101.4 (Fall 2002): 779–805.

Constitution of 1801. Signed by Toussaint Louverture. Translator unknown. Toussaint Louverture Historical Society. toussaintlouverturehs.org/Constitution1801.htm.

Constitution of 1805: Imperial Constitution of Haiti. In *Modernity Disavowed*, Appendix A. Constitution translated by Sibylle Fischer. Durham, NC: Duke University Press, 2004. 275–85.

Cooper, Frederick. *Colonialism in Question: Theory, Knowledge, History.* Berkeley: University of California Press, 2005.

Cooper, Frederick, and Ann Laura Stoler. "Introduction. Tensions of Empire: Colonial Control and Visions of Rule." Special issue: Tensions of Empire. *American Ethnologist* 16 (November 1989): 609–21.

Coser, Stelamaris. *Bridging the Americas: The Literature of Paule Marshall, Toni Morrison, and Gayl Jones.* Philadelphia: Temple University Press, 1994.

Crenshaw, Kimberlé. "Mapping the Margins: Intersectionality, Identity Politics, and Violence against Women of Color." In *Critical Race Theory.* Edited by Kimberlé Crenshaw, Neil Gotanda, Gary Peller, and Kendall Thomas. New York: New Press, 1995. 357–83.

Crittenden, Ann. *Sanctuary: A Story of American Conscience and the Law in Collision.* New York: Weidenfeld & Nicolson, 1988.

Crossette, Barbara. "The World; Citizenship Is a Malleable Concept." *New York Times,* August 18, 1996, S4, p. 3.

Croucher, Rowland, et. al. "Haiti: Boukman, Aristide, Voodoo and Church." *John Mark Ministries,* August 28, 2003. August 15, 2010. jmm.aaa.net.au/articles/11197.htm.

Cunningham, Hilary. *God and Caesar at the Rio Grande: Sanctuary and the Politics of Religion.* Minneapolis: University of Minnesota Press, 1995.

Dalmas, Antoine. *Histoire de la revolution de Saint-Domingue.* Paris: Mame Freres, 1814.

Danticat, Edwidge. "Between the Pool and the Gardenias." In *Krik? Krak!,* New York: Random House, 1996. 89–100.

———. *Create Dangerously: The Immigrant Artist at Work.* Princeton: Princeton University Press, 2010.

———. *Farming of Bones.* New York: Penguin, 1999.

———. "Thomas Jefferson: The Private War: Ignoring the Revolution Next Door." *Time Magazine,* July 5, 2004. content.time.com/time/magazine/article/0,9171,994563,00.html.

———. "A Wall of Fire Rising." In *Krik? Krak!,* New York: Random House, 1996. 51–80.

Davis, Angela. *Are Prisons Obsolete?* New York: Seven Stories Press, 2003.

———. *Women, Race, and Class.* New York: Random House, 1981.

Davis, Emily S. *Rethinking the Romance Genre: Global Intimacies in Contemporary Literary and Visual Culture.* New York: Palgrave Macmillan, 2013.

Dayan, Colin (Joan). *Haiti, History, and the Gods.* Berkeley: University of California Press, 1995.

———. *The Law Is a White Dog.* Princeton: Princeton University Press, 2011.

———. "Legal Slaves and Civil Bodies." *Nepantla: Views from South* 2.1 (2001): 3–39.

DeLombard, Jeannine Marie. "Salvaging Legal Personhood: Melville's *Benito Cereno.*" *American Literature* 81.1 (March 2009): 35–64.

Deloughrey, Elizabeth. "Heavy Waters: Waste and Atlantic Modernity." *PMLA* 125.3 (2010): 703–12.

———. *Routes and Roots: Navigating Caribbean and Pacific Island Literatures.* Honolulu: University of Hawai'i Press, 2007.

Denning, Michael. "Wageless Life." *New Left Review* 66 (November–December 2010): 79–97.

Dennis, Philip A. "The Costenos and the Revolution in Nicaragua." *Journal of Interamerican Studies and World Affairs* 23.3 (August 1981): 271–96.

Derrida, Jacques. *Archive Fever.* Translated by Eric Prenowitz. Chicago: University of Chicago Press, 1998.

———. *Memoires for Paul de Man.* New York: Columbia University Press, 1989.

———. *Of Hospitality.* Invitation to respond by Anne Dufourmantelle. Translated by Rachel Bowlby. Stanford, CA: Stanford University Press, 2000.

———. *Specters of Marx: The State of the Debt, The Work of Mourning and the New International.* Routledge Classics. New York: Routledge, 2006.

DeSombre, Elizabeth R. *Flagging Standards: Globalization and Environmental, Safety, and Labor Regulations at Sea.* Cambridge, MA: MIT Press, 2006.

Deutsche Presse-Agentur. "Protestant Pastor Slams Plans to Improve Voodoo's Status in Haiti." August 25, 1995. www.lexis-nexis.com/.

Dietrich, Laura J. "Political Asylum: Who Is Eligible and Who Is Not." Editorial. *New York Times,* October 2, 1985.

Dred Scott v. Sandford. 60 U.S. 393 (1857).

Dubey, Madhu. *Black Women Novelists and the Nationalist Aesthetic.* Bloomington: Indiana University Press, 1994.

———. "Gayl Jones and the Matrilineal Metaphor of Tradition." *Signs* 20.2 (Winter 1995): 245–67.

———. *Signs and Cities: Black Literary Postmodernism.* Chicago: University of Chicago Press, 2003.

Dubin, Steven. *Displays of Power: Memory and Amnesia in the American Museum.* New York: New York University Press, 1999.

Dubois, Laurent. *Avengers of the New World: The Story of the Haitian Revolution.* Cambridge, MA: Belknap Press, 2004.

Du Bois, W. E. B. *W. E. B. Du Bois on Asia: Crossing the World Color Line.* Edited by Bill V. Mullen and Cathryn Watson. Jackson: University Press of Mississippi, 2005.

Dudziak, Mary L. and Leti Volpp. "Introduction." Special issue: Legal Borderlands: Law and the Construction of American Borders. *American Quarterly* 57.3 (September 2005): 593–610.

Dussel, Enrique. *Ethics and the Theology of Liberation.* Maryknoll, NY: Orbis, 1978.

———. "Europe, Modernity, and Eurocentrism." *Nepantla: Views from South* 1.3 (2000): 465–78.

Ehrenreich, Nancy, ed. *The Reproductive Rights Reader: Law, Medicine, and the*

Construction of Motherhood. Critical America. New York: New York University Press, 2008.

Emmett Till Unsolved Civil Rights Crime Act of 2007. HR 923, 110th Congress. Pub.L. 110-344, 122 Stat. 3934 (2008).

Eng, L., and Shinhee Han. "A Dialogue on Racial Melancholia." *Psychoanalytic Dialogues* 10.4 (2000): 667–700.

Escobar, Arturo. "Imagining a Post-Development Era? Critical Thought, Development and Social Movements." Third World and Post-Colonial Issues. *Social Text*, no. 31–32 (1992): 20–56.

Fanon, Frantz. *Black Skin, White Masks.* Translated by Charles Lam Markmann. New York: Grove Press, 1967.

———. *The Wretched of the Earth.* Translated by Constance Farrington. New York: Grove Press, 1963.

Farmer, Paul. *The Uses of Haiti.* Monroe, ME: Common Courage Press, 1994.

———. "Who Removed Aristide?" *London Review of Books* 26.8 (2004): 28–31. www.lrb.co.uk/v26/n08/paul-farmer/who-removed-aristide.

Faulkner, William. *Requiem for a Nun.* New York: Routledge, 1987.

Fehskens, Erin M. "Accounts Unpaid, Accounts Untold: M. NourbeSe Philip's *Zong!* and the Catalogue." *Callaloo* 35.2 (Spring 2012): 407–24.

Fernandez, Manny. "Texas Woman Is Taken off Life Support after Order." *New York Times,* January 26, 2014. www.nytimes.com/2014/01/27/us/texas-hospital-to-end-life-support-for-pregnant-brain-dead-woman.html.

Ferré, Rosario. *Maldito Amor.* Río Piedras, PR: Ediciones Huracán, 1994.

———. *Sweet Diamond Dust.* New York: Plume, 1996.

Fick, Carolyn. *The Making of Haiti: The Saint-Domingue Revolution from Below.* Knoxville: University of Tennessee Press, 1991.

Findlay, Eileen J. Suárez. *Imposing Decency: The Politics of Sexuality and Race in Puerto Rico, 1870–1920.* Durham, NC: Duke University Press, 1999.

Fischer, Bryan. *Focal Point. American Family Association Blog.* August 2, 2010. www.afa.net/Blogs/BlogPost.aspx?id=2147491158.

Fischer, Sibylle. "Haiti: Fantasies of Bare Life." *Small Axe* 23 11.2 (June 2007): 1–15.

———. "History and Catastrophe." *Small Axe* 33 (November 2010): 163–72.

———. *Modernity Disavowed: Haiti and the Cultures of Slavery in the Age of Revolution.* Durham, NC: Duke University Press, 2004.

Fontanier, Pierre. *Les figures du discours.* Ed. Gerard Genette. Paris: Flammarion, 1968.

Foucault, Michel. *The Archaeology of Knowledge.* Translated by A. M. Sheridan Smith. New York: Pantheon, 1972.

———. "Different Spaces." In *Aesthetics, Method, and Epistemology.* Edited by James D. Faubion. Translated by Robert Hurley et al. New York: New Press, 1998. 175–85.

———. *The Foucault Effect: Studies in Governmentality: With Two Lectures by and an Interview with Michel Foucault*. Edited by Graham Burchell, Colin Gordon, and Peter Miller. London: Harvester Wheatsheaf, 1991.

———. "Nietzsche, Genealogy, History." In *Language, Counter-Memory, Practice: Selected Essays and Interviews*. Edited by D. F. Bouchard. Ithaca, NY: Cornell University Press, 1977. 139–64.

———. "Society Must Be Defended." In *Biopolitics: A Reader*. Edited by Timothy Campbell and Adam Sitze. Durham, NC: Duke University Press, 2013.

———. "The Subject and Power." In *Michel Foucault: Beyond Structuralism and Hermeneutics*. Edited by H. L. Dreyfus and P. Rabinow. Chicago: University of Chicago Press, 1983.

Francis, Donette. *Fictions of Feminine Citizenship: Sexuality and the Nation in Contemporary Caribbean Literature*. New York: Palgrave Macmillan, 2010.

Franco, Jean. *Cruel Modernity*. Durham, NC: Duke University Press, 2013.

Franklin, Bobby. Georgia State Assembly House Bill 1. 11 LC 21 0916.

Franklin, H. Bruce, ed. *Prison Writing in 20th-Century America*. New York: Penguin, 1998.

Fuchs, Barbara. *Romance*. New York: Routledge, 2004.

Fuss, Diana. "Interior Colonies: Frantz Fanon and the Politics of Identification." *Diacritics* 24.2–3 (1994): 19–42.

García, María Cristina. *Seeking Refuge: Central American Migration to Mexico, the United States, and Canada*. Berkeley: University of California Press, 2006.

Gates, Henry Louis, Jr. "The 'Blackness of Blackness': A Critique of the Sign and the Signifying Monkey." *Critical Inquiry* 9.4 (June 1983): 685–723.

———. "Critical Fanonism." *Critical Inquiry* 17.3 (Spring 1991): 457–70.

———. "Sanctuary." *New York Times Book Review*, November 14, 1999.

———. *The Signifying Monkey: A Theory of African-American Literary Criticism*. New York: Oxford University Press, 1988.

Geggus, David Patrick. *Haitian Revolutionary Studies*. Bloomington: Indiana University Press, 2002.

Gelin, Jean R. "God, Satan, and the Birth of Haiti: Part One." *Black and Christian*, October 2005. July 30, 2010. www.blackandchristian.com/articles/academy/gelin-10-05.shtml.

Gilroy, Paul. *The Black Atlantic: Modernity and Double Consciousness*. Cambridge, MA: Harvard University Press, 1993.

Glissant, Édouard. *Poetics of Relation*. Translated by Betsy Wing. Ann Arbor: University of Michigan Press, 1997.

Golden, Renny, and Michael McConnell. *Sanctuary: The New Underground Railroad*. Maryknoll, NY: Orbis Books, 1986.

Goldman, Francisco. *The Ordinary Seaman*. New York: Grove Press, 1998.

Gollnick, Brian. "History on Edge: Josefina Saldaña's *Revolutionary Imagination*." *A Contracorriente* (2004): 107–21.

Gonzalez, Juan. *Harvest of Empire: A History of Latinos in America*. New York: Penguin, 2001.

González Mendoza, Juan R. "Puerto Rico's Creole Patriots and the Slave Trade after the Haitian Revolution." In *The Impact of the Haitian Revolution in the Atlantic World*. Edited by David Patrick Geggus. Columbia: University of South Carolina Press, 2001. 58–71.

Gordon, Avery. *Ghostly Matters: Haunting and the Sociological Imagination.* Minneapolis: University of Minnesota Press, 1997.

Grandin, Greg. *The Last Colonial Massacre: Latin America in the Cold War.* Chicago: University of Chicago Press, 2004.

Gruesz, Kirsten Silva. "Utopía Latina: *The Ordinary Seaman* in Extraordinary Times." *MFS Modern Fiction Studies* 49.1 (2003): 54–83.

Gulick, Anne W. "We Are Not the People: The 1805 Haitian Constitution's Challenge to Political Legibility in the Age of Revolution." *American Literature* 78.4 (December 2006): 799–820.

Gutierrez-Jones, Carl. "Injury by Design." Special issue: The Futures of American Studies. *Cultural Critique* 40 (Autumn 1998): 73–102.

"Habeas Schmabeas." *This American Life*, National Public Radio, WBEZ Radio, Chicago, March 10, 2006.

"Haiti: Different Coup, Same Paramilitary Leaders." *Democracy Now! The War and Peace Report,* February 26, 2004. www.democracynow.org/2004/2/26/haiti_different_coup_same_paramilitary_leaders.

"Haiti 1804–2004: Tens of Thousands Mark Bicentennial of Haitian Revolution." *Democracy Now! The War and Peace Report,* January 2, 2004. www.democracynow.org/2004/1/2/haiti_1804_2004_tens_of_thousands.

Haiti Progres. "Exorcizing Boukman." August 11, 1998. www.hartford-hwp.com/archives/43a/520.html.

Handley, George B. *Postslavery Literatures in the Americas: Family Portraits in Black and White.* Charlottesville: University of Virginia Press, 2000.

Haney López, Ian. *White by Law: The Legal Construction of Race.* New York: New York University Press, 1997.

Hansen, Joyce, and Gary McGowan. *Breaking Ground, Breaking Silence: The Story of New York's African Burial Ground.* New York: Henry Holt & Co., 1998.

Harrington, Spencer P. M. "Bones and Bureaucrats: New York's Great Cemetery Imbrogolio." *Archaeology Magazine* (March–April 1993).

Hartman, Saidiya V. *Lose Your Mother: A Journey along the Atlantic Slave Route.* New York: Farrar, Straus and Giroux, 2008.

———. *Scenes of Subjection: Terror, Slavery, and Self-Making in Nineteenth-Century America.* New York: Oxford University Press, 1997.

———. "Seduction and the Ruses of Power." *Callaloo* 19.2 (1996): 537–60.

———. "Venus in Two Acts." *Small Axe* 26 (June 2008): 1–14.

Harvard Law Review. "What We Talk about When We Talk about Persons: The Language of a Legal Fiction." *Harvard Law Review* 114.6 (April 2001): 1745–68.

Harvey, David. *A Brief History of Neoliberalism.* New York: Oxford University Press, 2007.

———. *The Condition of Postmodernity: An Enquiry into the Origins of Cultural Change*. Oxford: Blackwell, 1989. 201–308.

Helms, Mary W. "Miskito Slaving and Culture Contact: Ethnicity and Opportunity in an Expanding Population." *Journal of Anthropological Research* 39.2 (Summer 1983): 179–97.

Henderson, Mae Gwendolyn. "Speaking in Tongues: Dialogics, Dialectics, and the Black Woman Writer's Literary Tradition." In *African American Literary Theory: A Reader*. Edited by Winston Napier. New York: New York University Press, 2000. 348–68.

Hernández, Ramona. "On the Age against the Poor: Dominican Migration to the United States." *Journal of Immigrant & Refugee Services* 2.1–2 (2004): 87–107.

Holland, Sharon Patricia. *Raising the Dead: Readings of Death and (Black) Subjectivity*. New Americanists. Durham, NC: Duke University Press, 2000.

Hsu, Stephanie. "Ethnicity and the Biopolitics of Intersex in Jeffrey Eugenides's *Middlesex*." *MELUS: Multi-Ethnic Literature of the U.S.* 36.3 (2011): 87–110.

Hunt, Melinda. *The Hart Island Project*. hartisland.net/wwwebs/Home/History/tabid/64/Default.aspx.

———. "Potter's Field." *New York Times*, January 24, 2011. www.nytimes.com/2011/01/24/opinion/l24burial.html?_r=2.

Huntington, Samuel. "The Clash of Civilizations." *Foreign Affairs* 72.3 (Summer 1993): 22–49.

Hurbon, Laénnec. "Current Evolution of Relations between Religion and Politics in Haiti." In *Nation Dance: Religion, Identity, and Cultural Difference in the Caribbean*. Edited by Patrick Taylor. Bloomington: Indiana University Press, 2001. 118–28.

Hurston, Zora Neale. "Characteristics of Negro Expression." In *African American Literary Theory: A Reader*. Edited by Winston A. Napier. New York: New York University Press, 2000. 32.

Hyde, Alan. *Bodies of Law*. Princeton, NJ: Princeton University Press, 1997.

International Commission on Shipping. "Ships, Slaves, and Competition." Report. Charlestown, NSW, Australia, 2000.

Irisarri, Pedro. "Informe dado por el alcalde don Pedro Yrisarri al Ayuntamiento de la Capital. 1809." In *Ramón Power y Giralt Diputado puertorriqueño a las Cortes Generales y Extraordinarias de España 1810–1812 (Compilación de documentos)*. Edited by Aida Caro de Delgado. San Juan: Municipio de San Juan, PR, 1969. 45–69.

Jackson, Maurice. "'Friends of the Negro! Fly with Me. The Path Is Open to the Sea': Remembering the Haitian Revolution in the History, Music, and Culture of the African American People." *Early American Studies* 6.1 (2008): 59–103.

James, C. L. R. *The Black Jacobins: Toussaint L'Ouverture and the San Domingo Revolution*. 2nd ed. New York: Random House, 1989.

———. *Mariners, Renegades, and Castaways: The Story of Herman Melville and the World We Live In*. Introduction by Donald E. Pease. New York: Privately printed, 1953; Detroit: Bewick, 1978; Hanover, NH: University Press of New England, 2001.

JanMohamed, Abdul R. *The Death-Bound-Subject: Richard Wright's Archaeology of Death.* Durham, NC: Duke University Press, 2005.

Johnson, Paul Christopher. "Secretism and the Apotheosis of Duvalier." *Journal of the American Academy of Religion* 74.2 (2006): 420–45.

Jones Act of 1917. Pub.L. 64–368, 39 Stat. 951 (1917).

Jones Act of 1920. 46 U.S.C. § 688 (1920).

Jones, Gayl. *Corregidora.* Boston: Beacon Press, 1975.

———. "From *The Quest for Wholeness*: Re-Imagining the African-American Novel: An Essay on Third World Aesthetics." *Callaloo* 17 (1994): 507–18.

———. "Gayl Jones: An Interview." By Michael Harper. *Massachusetts Review* 18 (1977): 692–715.

———. "An Interview with Gayl Jones." By Charles Rowell. *Callaloo* 16 (1982): 32–53.

———. *Liberating Voices: Oral Tradition in African American Literature.* Cambridge, MA: Harvard University Press, 1991.

———. *Mosquito.* Boston: Beacon Press, 1999.

———. "Palmares." Unpublished manuscript. Gayl Jones collection. Howard Gotlieb Archival Research Center, Boston University, Boston, MA.

———. *Song for Anninho.* Boston: Beacon Press, 1981.

Julien, Isaac, and Mark Nash. "Fanon as Film." *Nka Journal of Contemporary African Art* 11–12 (2000): 12–17.

Kaplan, Amy. *The Anarchy of Empire in the Making of U.S. Culture.* Cambridge, MA: Harvard University Press, 2005.

———. "Where Is Guantánamo?" *American Quarterly* 57.3 (September 2005): 831–58.

Kapoor, Ilan. "Hyper-Self-Reflexive Development? Spivak on Representing the Third World 'Other.'" *Third World Quarterly* 25.4 (2004): 627–47.

Katz, Sarah R. "Redesigning Civic Memory: The African Burial Ground in Lower Manhattan." Master's thesis, University of Pennsylvania, 2006.

Kaufman, Edward, ed. *Reclaiming Our Past, Honoring Our Ancestors.* New York: African Burial Ground Competition Coalition, 1994.

Kauanui, J. Kēhaulani. *Hawaiian Blood: Colonialism and the Politics of Sovereignty and Indigeneity.* Durham, NC: Duke University Press, 2008.

Keizer, Arlene R. *Black Subjects: Identity Formation in the Contemporary Narrative of Slavery.* Ithaca, NY: Cornell University Press, 2004.

Kelley, Robin D. G. "'But a Local Phase of a World Problem': Black History's Global Vision, 1883–1950." Special issue: The Nation and Beyond: Transnational Perspectives on United States History. *Journal of American History* 86.3 (December 1999): 1045–77.

———. *Yo' Mama's Disfunktional! Fighting the Culture Wars in Urban America.* Boston: Beacon Press, 1998.

Kelsen, Hans. *General Theory of Law and State*. Cambridge, MA: Harvard University Press, 1949.

Kent, R. K. "Palmares: An African State in Brazil." *Journal of African History* 6.2 (1965): 161–75.

Kerber, Linda K. "The Meanings of Citizenship." *Journal of American History* 84.3 (December 1997): 833–54.

———. "The Stateless as the Citizen's Other: A View from the United States." Presidential Address. *American Historical Review* 112.1 (February 2007): xvi + 1–34.

———. "Toward a History of Statelessness in America." *American Quarterly* 57.3 (September 2005): 727–49.

Khanna, Ranjana. "Frames, Contexts, Community, Justice." *Diacritics* 33.2 (2005): 11–41.

Kincaid, Jamaica. *A Small Place*. New York: Farrar, Straus, and Giroux, 1988.

King, Lovalerie. "Resistance, Reappropriation, and Reconciliation: The Blues and Flying Africans in Gayl Jones's 'Song for Anninho.'" *Callaloo* 27.3 (Summer 2004): 755–67.

King, Martin Luther, Jr. "Where Do We Go From Here?" Speech delivered at the Tenth Anniversary Convention of the SCLC, Atlanta, August 16, 1967. Martin Luther King, Jr., Research and Education Institute. mlk-kpp01.stanford.edu/index.php/kingpapers/article/where_do_we_go_from_here/.

Lanso, Peter. "Chronicle of a Tragedy Foretold." *New York Times*, July 19, 1998.

Laroche, Maximilien. "The Founding Myths of the Haitian Nation." Translated by Martin Munro. *Small Axe* 18 (2005): 1–15.

———. "The Myth of the Zombi." In *Exile and Tradition: Studies in African and Caribbean Literature*, ed. Rowland Smith. London: Longman, 1976. 44–61.

Lauro, Sarah. *The Transatlantic Zombie: Slavery, Rebellion, and Living Death*. New Brunswick, NJ: Rutgers University Press, 2015.

"Law of Salvage." Cornell Legal Information Institute. www.law.cornell.edu/background/amistad/legal_issues1.html.

Lazzarato, Maurizio. "Immaterial Labor." In *Radical Thought in Italy: A Potential Politics*. Edited by Michael Hardt and Paolo Virno. Minneapolis: University of Minnesota Press, 1996. 133–47.

Leary, John Patrick. "Detroitism." *Guernica*, January 15, 2011.

Lewis, David L. *W. E. B. Du Bois: The Fight for Equality and the American Century, 1919–1963*. New York: Macmillan, 2000.

Library of Congress. "The Abolition of Slavery in Puerto Rico." www.loc.gov/rr/hispanic/1898/slaves.html.

Lichtenstein, Alexander. *Twice the Work of Free Labor: The Political Economy of Convict Labor in the New South*. New York: Verso, 1996.

Life at Conception Act. H.R. 374. 112th Congress, 1st session. (2011–12).

Linebaugh, Peter, and Marcus Rediker. *The Many-Headed Hydra: Sailors,*

Slaves, Commoners, and the Hidden History of the Revolutionary Atlantic. Boston: Beacon Press, 2000.

Liptak, Adam, and John H. Cushman Jr. "Supreme Court Rejects Part of Arizona Immigration Law." June 25, 2012. www.nytimes.com/2012/06/26/us/supreme-court-rejects-part-of-arizona-immigration-law.html?_r=1&hp.

Locke, John. *An Essay Concerning Human Understanding* (1689). Edited by Peter H. Nidditch. New York: Oxford University Press, 1975.

———. *Fundamental Constitutions for the Government of Carolina* (1669). Avalon Project at Yale Law School. avalon.law.yale.edu/17th_century/nc05.asp.

———. *Two Treatises of Government* (1690). Edited by Peter Laslett. Cambridge: Cambridge University Press, 1988.

Lorde, Audre. "The Master's Tools Will Never Dismantle the Master's House" (1984). In *Sister Outsider: Essays and Speeches.* Berkeley, CA: Crossing Press, 1996. 110–14.

Louverture, Toussaint. Forced Labor Decree of 12 October 1800. In *Toussaint L'Ouverture.* Edited and translated by George F. Tyson. New York: Prentice-Hall, 1973. 51–55.

Loveman, Mara. "The U.S. Census and the Contested Rules of Racial Classification in Early Twentieth-Century Puerto Rico." Special issue: Puerto Rico between Empires: Population and Society. *Caribbean Studies* 35.2 (July–December 2007): 78–113.

Lowe, Lisa. *Immigrant Acts: On Asian American Cultural Politics.* Durham, NC: Duke Unversity Press, 1996.

———. "The International within the National: American Studies and Asian American Critique." *Cultural Critique* 40 (Autumn 1998): 29–47.

Lugones, María. "Heterosexualism and the Colonial/Modern Gender System." *Hypatia* 22.1 (2007): 186–209.

Lydon, Christopher. "Speaking of Race: John Edgar Wideman's Fanon." *Radio OpenSource,* 2008. www.radioopensource.org/speaking-of-race-john-edgar-widemans-fanon/

Macey, David. *Frantz Fanon: A Life.* London: Granta Books, 2000.

Madiou, Thomas. *Histoire d'Haïti (1492–1846).* Port-au-Prince: Editions Henri Deschamps, 1989.

Malavet, Pedro A. *America's Colony: The Political and Cultural Conflict between the United States and Puerto Rico.* New York: New York University Press, 2004.

Malkki, Liisa H. "Refugees and Exile: From 'Refugee Studies' to the National Order of Things." *Annual Review of Anthropology* 24 (1995): 495–523.

Marchand, Yves, and Romain Meffre. *The Ruins of Detroit.* Göttingen: Steidl, 2011.

Marston, Sallie. "The Social Construction of Scale." *Progress in Human Geography* 24.2 (2000): 219–42.

Marx, Karl. *Capital: A Critical Analysis of Capitalist Production.* Vol. 1, sec. 4. Translated from the 3rd German ed. by Samuel Moore and Edward Aveling.

Edited by Frederick Engels. Electronic Text Center, University of Virginia Library. etext.virginia.edu/toc/modeng/public/MarCapi.html.

———. *Grundrisse.* Translated by Martin Nicolaus. New York: Pelican Books, 1973.

Mary Bateman Clark Project. "Supreme Court Case." www.marybatemanclark. org/items/show/8.

Mary Clark a woman of Color v. G W Johnston, or The Case of Mary Clark, a Woman of Color. 1 Blackf. 122 (Ind. 1821).

Massey, Doreen. *Space, Place, and Gender.* Minneapolis: University of Minnesota Press, 1994.

Mayer, Jane. "Outsourcing Torture." *New Yorker,* February 14, 2005. www. newyorker.com/fact/content/?050214fa_fact.

Mbembe, Achille. "Necropolitics." Translated by Libby Meintjes. *Public Culture* 15.1 (2003): 11–40.

McAlister, Elizabeth. "From Slave Revolt to a Blood Pact with Satan: The Evangelical Rewriting of Haitian History." Unpublished MS. Wesleyan University, Middletown, CT.

McAlister, Melani. *Epic Encounters: Culture, Media, and U.S. Interests in the Middle East, 1945–2000.* Berkeley: University of California Press, 2001.

McCarran-Walter Immigration and Nationality Act, Pub. L. No. 82–414 (1952).

McClintock, Anne. "The Angel of Progress: Pitfalls of the Term 'Postcolonialism.'" *Social Text* 31–32 (1992): 84–98.

McDowell, Deborah. "The Whole Story." *Women's Review of Books* 16.6 (March 1999): 9–10.

McGraw, Bill. "Life in the Ruins of Detroit." *History Workshop Journal* 63 (Spring 2007): 288–302.

McLean, Paul C. "Texas Is Keeping a Dead Woman on Life Support Despite Her Family's Wishes." *Guardian.* January 10, 2014. www.theguardian.com/ commentisfree/2014/jan/10/texas-life-support-ethics-marlise-munoz.

Mehlman, Jeffrey. *Genealogies of the Text: Literature, Psychoanalysis, and Politics in Modern France.* Cambridge: Cambridge University Press, 1995.

Meirs, Suzanne. *Slavery in the Twentieth Century: The Evolution of a Global Problem.* Walnut Creek, CA: AltaMira Press, 2003.

Melas, Natalie. *All the Difference in the World: Postcoloniality and the Ends of Comparison.* Stanford, CA: Stanford University Press, 2007.

Melville, Herman. "Benito Cereno." In *Billy Budd and Other Stories.* New York: Penguin Books, 1986. 85-160.

Metress, Christopher. 2003. "'No Justice, No Peace': The Figure of Emmett Till in African-American Literature." *MELUS* 28.1 (Spring): 87–103.

Mignolo, Walter D. *Local Histories/Global Designs: Coloniality, Subaltern Knowledges, and Border Thinking.* Princeton, NJ: Princeton University Press, 2000.

Miller, J. Hillis. "Ariadne's Thread: Repetition and the Narrative Line." *Critical Inquiry* 3.1 (Autumn 1976): 57–77.

Miller, Jake C. *The Plight of Haitian Refugees*. New York: Praeger, 1984.

Miller, Joseph C. "Nzinga of Matamba in a New Perspective." *Journal of African History* 16.2 (1975): 201–16.

Mills, Fiona. "Telling the Untold Tale: Afro-Latino/a Identifications in the Work of Gayl Jones." In *After the Pain: Critical Essays on Gayl Jones*. Edited by Fiona Mills and Keith B. Mitchell. New York: Peter Lang, 2006. 91–116.

Mills, Fiona, and Keith B. Mitchell, eds. *After the Pain: Critical Essays on Gayl Jones*. New York: Peter Lang, 2006.

Mintz, Sidney W. Introduction to *Voodoo in Haiti*. By Alfred Métraux. New York: Pantheon Books, 1989. 1–14.

———. *Sweetness and Power: The Place of Sugar in Modern History*. New York: Penguin Books, 1986.

———. "Whitewashing Haiti's History." *Boston Review*, January 22, 2010. bostonreview.net/BR35.1/mintz.php.

Mississippi Amendment Initiative #26. "Definition of Person." Pamphlet issued by Delbert Hosemann. Jackson: Mississippi Secretary of State, in accordance with Miss. Code § 23-17-45 (2011).

Montag, Warren. "Necro-economics: Adam Smith and Death in the Life of the Universal." In *Biopolitics: A Reader,* edited by Timothy Campbell and Adam Sitze. Durham, NC: Duke University Press, 2013.

Moore, Andrew, and Philip Levine. *Andrew Moore: Detroit Disassembled*. Bologna and Akron: Damiani Editore and Akron Art Museum, 2010.

Moreno, Marisel C. *Family Matters: Puerto Rican Women Authors on the Island and the Mainland*. Charlottesville: University of Virginia Press, 2012.

Morrison, Toni. *Beloved*. New York: Penguin, 2000.

———. *Playing in the Dark: Whiteness and the Literary Imagination*. New York: Vintage, 1993.

———. "The Site of Memory." In *Inventing the Truth: The Art and Craft of Memoir*. Edited by W. Zinsser. Boston: Houghton Mifflin, 1987. 101–24.

Moten, Fred. "Blackness and Nothingness (Mysticism in the Flesh)." *South Atlantic Quarterly* 112.4 (Fall 2013): 737–80.

Moynihan, Daniel Patrick. "The Negro Family: The Case for National Action Office of Policy Planning and Research." United States Department of Labor, March 1965. www.dol.gov/oasam/programs/history/webid-meynihan.htm.

Mullen, Harryette. "African Signs and Spirit Writing." In *African American Literary Theory: A Reader,* edited by Winston Napier. New York: New York University Press, 2000. 623–43.

Munro, Martin. "Interdependence and Intertextuality in Lyonel Trouillot's *Bicentenaire*." *Small Axe* 27 (2008): 42–52.

Myers, Steven Lee. "Politics of Present Snags Remembrance of Past; Plan for Potter's Field Memorial Near African Burial Ground Stalls in Emotional Debate." *New York Times,* July 20, 1993.

Nash, Mark, and Isaac Julien. *Frantz Fanon: Black Skin, White Mask*. Directed by Isaac Julien, Produced by Mark Nash. San Francisco, CA: California Newsreel, 1996.

National Advocates for Pregnant Women. "Punishment of Pregnant Women." n.d. www.advocatesforpregnantwomen.org/issues/punishment_of_pregnant_women/.

———. "Regina McKnight: Victory at Long Last." Blog post. May 12, 2008. advocatesforpregnantwomen.org/blog/2008/05/regina_mcknight_victory_at_lon.php.

———. *Whitner v. South Carolina* Fact Sheet. Charleston, SC office. n.d. www.advocatesforpregnantwomen.org/issues/whitner.htm.

National Park Service. "Ellis Island, National Monument." www.nps.gov/elis/index.htm.

Neuman, Gerald L. "Anomalous Zones." *Stanford Law Review* 48.5 (May 1996): 1197–1234.

Ngai, Mae M. *Impossible Subjects: Illegal Aliens and the Making of Modern America.* Princeton, NJ: Princeton University Press, 2003.

Nixon, Rob. *Slow Violence and the Environmentalism of the Poor.* Cambridge, MA: Harvard University Press, 2011.

Nonhuman Rights Project. www.nonhumanrightsproject.org/the-capacity-to-have-a-legal-right/.

Noonan, John T., Jr. *Persons and Masks of the Law: Cardozo, Holmes, Jefferson, and Wythe as Makers of the Masks.* New York: Farrar, Straus and Giroux, 1976.

Norris, Andrew. "Giorgio Agamben and the Politics of the Living Dead." *Diacritics* 30.4 (Winter 2000): 38–58.

Nwankwo, Ifeoma C. K. "The Promises and Perils of US African-American Hemispherism: Latin America in Martin Delany's *Blake* and Gayl Jones's *Mosquito.*" *American Literary History* 18.3 (2006): 579–99.

Oikkonen,Venla. "Mutations of Romance: Evolution, Infidelity, and Narrative." *MFS Modern Fiction Studies* 56.3 (2010): 592–613.

Ong, Aihwa. *Buddha Is Hiding: Refugees, Citizenship, the New America.* Berkeley: University of California Press, 2003.

Ortega, Julio. *Reapropiaciones: Cultura y nueva escritura en Puerto Rico.* San Juan, PR: University of Puerto Rico Press, 1991.

"Outcry in America as Pregnant Women Who Lose Babies Face Murder Charges." By Ed Pilkington. *The Guardian.* www.guardian.co.uk/world/2011/jun/24/america-pregnant-women-murder-charges/print.

Paltrow, Lynn M. "Personhood USA: Promoting a Radical, Fetal-Separatist Agenda." *Huffington Post,* July 11, 2012. www.huffingtonpost.com/lynn-m-paltrow/personhoodusa-promoting-a_b_773572.html.

Palumbo-Liu, Alan, ed. *The Ethnic Canon: History, Institutions, Interventions.* Minneapolis: University of Minnesota Press, 1995.

Patterson, Orlando. "A Poverty of the Mind." *New York Times,* March 26, 2006. www.nytimes.com/2006/03/26/opinion/26patterson.html?pagewanted=all&_r=0.

———. *Slavery and Social Death: A Comparative Study.* Cambridge, MA: Harvard University Press, 1982.

Pear, Robert. "Citizenship Proposal Faces Obstacle in the Constitution." *New York Times,* August 7, 1996, A13.

Pease, Donald E. "Author." In *Critical Terms for Literary Studies.* Edited by Frank Lentricchia and Thomas McLaughlin. Chicago: University of Chicago Press, 1990. 105–17.

Peck, Jamie. *Constructions of Neoliberal Reason.* Oxford: Oxford University Press, 2010.

Pérez, Emma. *The Decolonial Imaginary: Writing Chicanas into History.* Bloomington: Indiana University Press, 1999.

Perez v. Brownell. 356 U.S. 44, 235 F.2d 364 (1958).

Perry, Imani. *More Beautiful and More Terrible: The Embrace and Transcendence of Racial Inequality in the U.S.* New York: New York University Press, 2011.

PersonhoodUSA.www.personhoodusa.com/blog/personhood-updates-nationwide.

PETA. "PETA Sues Seaworld for Violating Orcas' Constitutional Rights." Official blog post. www.peta.org/b/thepetafiles/archive/2011/10/25/peta-sues-seaworld-for-violating-orcas-constitutional-rights.aspx.

Philip, M. NourbeSe. *Zong!* Middletown, CT: Wesleyan University Press, 2008.

Prenatal Murder Bill. Act to Amend the Official Code of Georgia Annotated. H.B. 1, LC 21 0916 (GA 2011–2012). www1.legis.ga.gov/legis/2011_12/fulltext/hb1.htm.

Priest, Myisha. "'The Nightmare Is Not Cured': Emmett Till and American Healing." *American Quarterly* 62.1 (2010): 1–24.

Quijano, Anibal. "Coloniality of Power, Eurocentrism, and Latin America." *Nepantla: Voices from the South* 1.3 (2000): 533–80.

Radović, Stanka. "The Birthplace of Relation: Édouard Glissant's *Poétique de la relation.*" *Callaloo* 30.2 (Spring 2007): 475–81.

Rafaël, Lucas. "The Aesthetics of Degradation in Haitian Literature." Translated by R. H. Mitsch. Special issue: Haiti, 1804–2004: Literature, Culture, and Art. *Research in African Literatures* 35.2 (Summer 2004): 54–74.

Ramsey, Kate. "Without One Ritual Note: Folklore Performance and the Haitian State, 1935–1946." *Radical History Review* 84 (2002): 7–42.

Rediker, Marcus. *Between the Devil and the Deep Blue Sea: Merchant Seamen, Pirates, and the Anglo-American Maritime World, 1700–1750.* Cambridge: Cambridge University Press, 1989.

———. *Villains of All Nations: Atlantic Pirates in the Golden Age.* Boston: Beacon Press, 2004.

Renan, Ernst. "What Is a Nation?" In *Nation and Narration.* Edited by Homi K. Bhabha. London: Routledge, 1990. 8–22.

Renda, Mary. *Taking Haiti: Military Occupation and the Culture of U.S. Imperialism, 1915–1940.* Chapel Hill: University of North Carolina Press, 2001.

"Report on Colonizing the Free People of Color of the United States, of the House of Representatives." Dated February 1, 1817. Published in *Niles'*

Weekly Register vol. XIL, no. 7, Baltimore, Saturday, April 12, 1817. Digitized. Last accessed February 1, 2012.

Riffaterre, Michael. 1985. "Prosopopoeia." *Yale French Studies* 69: 107–23.

Robertson v. Baldwin. 165 U.S. 275, 280 (1897).

Rodríguez, Ana Patricia. "Refugees of the South: Central Americans in the U.S. Latino Imaginary." *American Literature: A Journal of Literary History, Criticism, and Bibliography* 73.2 (2001): 387–412.

Rodriguez, Denise. 2006. "Homewood's 'Music of Invisibility': John Edgar Wideman's 'Sent for You Yesterday' and the Black Urban Tradition." In *Critical Essays on John Edgar Wideman*. Edited by Bonnie TuSmith and Keith E. Byerman. Knoxville: University of Tennessee Press. 127–44.

Rosaldo, Renato. "Imperialist Nostalgia." *Representations* 26 (Spring 1989).

Rosenthal, A. M. "On My Mind; Dred Scott in San Diego." Editorial. *New York Times,* August 9, 1996, A27.

Roslan, Chris. "Statement Regarding Pat Robertson's Comments on Haiti." *Christian Broadcasting Network,* January 13, 2010. www.cbn.com/about/ pressrelease_patrobertson_haiti.aspx.

Rucker, Philip. "Mitt Romney Says 'Corporations Are People' at Iowa State Fair." *Washington Post,* August 11, 2011. www.washingtonpost.com/politics/mitt-romney-says-corporations-are-people/2011/08/11/gIQABwZ38I_story.html.

Ruffin v. The Commonwealth. 62 Va. 790, 796; 21 Gratt, 790, 796 (1871).

Rushdy, Ashraf H. A. *Neo-Slave Narratives: Studies in the Social Logic of a Literary Form.* New York: Oxford University Press, 1999.

———. "'Relate Sexual to Historical': Race, Resistance, and Desire in Gayl Jones's *Corregidora*." *African American Review* 34.2 (2000): 273–97.

Russ, Elizabeth Christine. *The Plantation in the Postslavery Imagination.* New York: Oxford University Press, 2009.

Russell, Margaret M. 2005. "Reopening the Emmett Till Case: Lessons and Challenges for Critical Race Practice." *Fordham Law Review* 73: 2101–32.

Said, Edward. *Covering Islam: How the Media and the Experts Determine How We See the Rest of the World.* New York: Pantheon Books, 1981.

Sailors' Union of the Pacific. *History of the Sailors' Union of the Pacific.* By Stephen Schwartz, under commission by the Union. 1985. www.sailors.org/ history.php.

Saldaña-Portillo, Maria Josefina. "Reading a Silence: The 'Indian' in the Era of Zapatismo." *Nepantla: Views from the South* 3.2 (2002): 287–314.

———. *The Revolutionary Imagination in the Americas and the Age of Development.* Durham, NC: Duke University Press, 2003.

Salgado, Sebastião. *Workers: An Archaeology of the Industrial Age.* New York: Aperture, 1993.

Sandoval, Chela. *Methodology of the Oppressed.* Foreword Angela Y. Davis. Minneapolis: University of Minnesota Press, 2000.

———. "U.S. Third World Feminism: The Theory and Method of Oppositional Consciousness in the Postmodern World." *Genders* 10 (1991): 1–24.

Santa Clara County v. Southern Pacific Railroad Company. 118 U.S. 394 (1886).

Sassen, Saskia. *Globalization and Its Discontents: Selected Essays, 1984–1998*. New York: New Press, 1998.

Scarano, Francisco A. *Sugar and Slavery in Puerto Rico: The Plantation Economy of Ponce, 1800–1850*. Madison: University of Wisconsin Press, 1984.

Schlund-Vials, Cathy. *Modeling Citizenship: Jewish and Asian American Writing*. Washington, DC: Temple University Press, 2011.

Schneider, Martin L. "Gilded Sugar." *New York Archives* Magazine 11.4 (Spring 2012). 24-27. www.archives.nysed.gov/apt/magazine/archivesmag_spring2012_gildedsugar.pdf.

Schwartzman, Myron. *Romare Bearden: His Life and Art*. Foreword August Wilson. New York: Harry N. Abrams, 1990.

Scott, David. *Conscripts of Modernity: The Tragedy of Colonial Enlightenment*. Durham, NC: Duke University Press. 2004.

———. Interview by Stuart Hall. *Bomb Magazine* 90 (2005): n.p. bombsite.com/issues/90/articles/2711.

Seamen's Act of 1915. Act to Promote the Welfare of American Seamen in the Merchant Marine of the United States. Ch. 153, 38 Stat. 1164 (1915).

Seckler-Hudson, Catheryn. *Statelessness: With Special Reference to the United States. A Study in Nationality and Conflict of Laws*. Washington, DC: Digest Press, 1934.

Sekula, Allan. "Between the Net and the Deep Blue Sea (Rethinking the Traffic in Photographs)." *October* 102 (Autumn, 2002): 3–34.

Sexton, Jared. "Ante-Anti-Blackness: Afterthoughts." *Lateral* 1 (Spring 2012): n.p. lateral.culturalstudiesassociation.org/issue1/content/sexton.html.

Sharpe, Jenny. *Allegories of Empire: The Figure of Woman in the Colonial Text*. Minneapolis: University of Minnesota Press, 1993.

Shaughnessy v. Mezei. 345 U.S. 206 (1953).

Shemak, April. *Asylum Speakers: Caribbean Refugees and Testimonial Discourse*. New York: Fordham University Press, 2011.

Shockley, Evie. "Going Overboard: African American Poetic Innovation and the Middle Passage." *Contemporary Literature* 52.4 (2011): 791–817.

Shuman, Amy, and Carol Bohmer. "Representing Trauma: Political Asylum Narrative." *Journal of American Folklore* 117.466 (2004): 405–6.

Slaughter, Joseph R. *Human Rights, Inc.: The World Novel, Narrative Form, and International Law*. New York: Fordham University Press, 2007.

Smith, Caleb. *The Prison and the American Imagination*. New Haven, CT: Yale University Press, 2009.

Smith, Neil. "Contours of a Spatialized Politics: Homeless Vehicles and the Production of Geographical Scale." *Social Text* 33 (1992): 76.

"Solving Europe's Refugee Crisis." Editorial. *New York Times*, July 27, 1992, A16.

Sommer, Doris. *Foundational Fictions: The National Romances of Latin America*. Berkeley: University of California Press, 1991.

Sourieau, Marie-Agnes. "Dessalines in Historic Drama and Haitian Contemporary Reality." *Small Axe* 18 (2005): 24–39.

Spectator Magazine. "Margaret Thatcher in Quotes." *Spectator* news blog. blogs. spectator.co.uk/coffeehouse/2013/04/margaret-thatcher-in-quotes/.

Spillers, Hortense J. *Black, White, and in Color: Essays on American Literature and Culture.* Chicago: University of Chicago Press, 2003.

———. "Mama's Baby, Papa's Maybe: An American Grammar Book." *Diacritics* 17.2 (Summer 1987).

Spivak, Gayatri Chakravorty. *Critique of Postcolonial Reason.* Cambridge, MA: Harvard University Press, 1999.

———. "Three Women's Texts and a Critique of Imperialism." In *"Race," Writing, and Difference.* Edited by Henry Louis Gates Jr. Chicago: University of Chicago Press, 1986. 262–88.

Stallabrass, Julian. "Sebastião Salgado and Fine Art Photojournalism." *New Left Review* I-223 (May–June 1997): 131–60.

Stallman v. Youngquist. 125 Ill. 2d 267, 531 N.E.2d 355 (1988).

Steinfeld, Robert J. *The Invention of Free Labor: The Employment Relation in English and American Law and Culture, 1350–1870.* Chapel Hill: University of North Carolina Press, 1991.

Stoler, Ann Laura, ed. *Imperial Debris: On Ruins and Ruination.* Durham, NC: Duke University Press, 2013.

Stringer, Scott M., and Andrew Friedman. "Unfair to Immigrants, Costly for Taxpayers." *New York Times,* April 4, 2011. www.nytimes.com/2011/04/05/opinion/05Stringer.html?_r=0#.

Subcomandante Marcos. *Our Word Is Our Weapon: Selected Writings.* New York: Seven Stories Press, 2001.

Sugrue, Thomas J. *The Origins of the Urban Crisis: Race and Inequality in Postwar Detroit.* Princeton Studies in American Politics. Princeton, NJ: Princeton University Press, 1996.

Sundquist, Eric. *To Wake the Nations; Race in the Making of American Literature.* Cambridge, MA: Belknap Press, 1993.

Tanner, Henry Ossawa. *Nicodemus Visiting Jesus.* 1899. *Nineteenth Century Art Worldwide.* www.19thcartworldwide.org/autumn_04/articles/brad.shtml.

Tarleton, John. "Seeking Dignity at Potter's Field." *The Indypendent,* no. 74 (August 11–31, 2005): 2. nyc.indymedia.org/media/2005/08/55392.pdf.

Tarr, Michael. "Haiti's Latest Hex: A Voodoo Dispute. Believers Say Voodoo Helped the Island's Slaves Win Independence in the 19th Century. Protestants, on the Other Hand, Contend Its Spirits Have Cast a Curse on the Country." *Globe and Mail,* August 29, 1991. www.lexis-nexis.com/.

Tate, Greg. "Going Underground." *Village Voice Literary Supplement,* February 1999. www.villagevoice.com/vls/160/tate.shtml.

Terry, Jill. "'reads kinda like jazz in they rhythm': Gayl Jones's Recent Jazz Conversations." In *After the Pain: Critical Essays on Gayl Jones.* Edited by Fiona Mills and Keith B. Mitchell. New York: Peter Lang, 2006. 117–36.

Thornton, John K. "Legitimacy and Political Power: Queen Njinga, 1624–1663." *Journal of African History* 32.1 (1991): 25–40.

Tillet, Salamishah. *Sites of Slavery: Citizenship and Racial Democracy in the Post–Civil Rights Imagination*. Durham, NC: Duke University Press, 2012.

Torres Rivas, Edelberto. "Notes on Terror, Violence, Fear, and Democracy." Epilogue to *Societies of Fear: The Legacy of Civil War, Violence and Terror in Latin America*. Edited by Kees Koonings and Dirk Kruijt. New York: Zed Books, 1999. 285–300.

The Trial of Captain John Kimber for the Murder of Two Female Negro Slaves, on Board the Recovery, African Slave Ship (1792). Internet Archive, Boston Public Library. archive.org/details/trialofcaptainjoookimb.

Trouillot, Michel-Rolph. *Haiti, State against Nation: The Origins and Legacy of Duvalierism*. New York: Monthly Review Press, 1990.

———. *Silencing the Past: Power and the Production of History*. Boston: Beacon Press, 1995.

Turner, J. M. W. *The Slave Ship*, or *Slavers Throwing Overboard the Dead and Dying—Typhoon Coming On*. 1840. Oil on canvas, 35 3/4 x 48 1/4 in. Museum of Fine Arts, Boston.

TuSmith, Bonnie. 2006. "Optical Tricksterism: Dissolving and Shapeshifting in the Works of John Edgar Wideman." In *Critical Essays on John Edgar Wideman*. Edited by Bonnie TuSmith and Keith E. Byerman. Knoxville: University of Tennessee Press. 243–58.

UNHCR. "Refugees by Numbers 2006 Edition." www.unhcr.org/basics/BASICS/3b028097c.html.

UNHCR. "The World's Stateless People: Questions and Answers." September 1, 2006. www.unhcr.org/basics/BASICS/452611862.pdf.

United Nations. "Background." Millennium Development Goals: A Gateway to the UN System's Work on the MDGs. 2013. www.un.org/millenniumgoals/gender.shtml

———. "Convention on the Reduction of Statelessness, Adopted on 30 August 1961, by a Conference of Plenipotentiaries which met in 1959 and reconvened in 1961 in pursuance of General Assembly resolution 896 (IX) of 4 December 1954. Entry into force: 13 December 1975, in accordance with article 18." www2.ohchr.org/english/law/statelessness.htm.

———. "Convention relating to the Status of Stateless Persons, Adopted on September 28, 1954, by a Conference of Plenipotentiaries convened by Economic and Social Council Resolution 526 A [XVII] of April 26, 1954." www.ohchr.org/english/law/statelessness.htm.

———. Universal Declaration of Human Rights. 1948. www.un.org/en/documents/udhr/index.shtml.

———. Ad Hoc Committee on Refugees and Stateless Persons. *A Study of Statelessness, United Nations, August 1949, Lake Success - New York*, 1 August 1949, E/1112; E/1112/Add.1. www.refworld.org/docid/3ae68c2do.html.

U.S. Department of State. "Advice about Possible Loss of U.S. Citizenship and

Dual Nationality." http://travel.state.gov/law/citizenship/citizenship_778. html.

Vergès, Françoise. "Creole Skin, Black Mask: Fanon and Disavowal." *Critical Inquiry* 23 (Spring 1997): 578–95.

———. *Monsters and Revolutionaries: Colonial Family Romance and* Métissage. Durham, NC: Duke University Press, 1999.

Wacquant, Loïc. "Decivilizing and Demonizing: The Remaking of the Black American Ghetto." In *The Sociology of Norbert Elias.* Edited by Steven Loyal and Stephen Quilley. Cambridge: Cambridge University Press, 2004. 95–121.

Wagner, Bryan. *Disturbing the Peace: Black Culture and the Police Power after Slavery.* Cambridge, MA: Harvard University Press, 2009.

Walcott, Derek. "The Antilles: Fragments of Epic Memory." Nobel Lecture, December 7, 1992. www.nobelprize.org/nobel_prizes/literature/laureates/1992/walcott-lecture.html.

———. *Collected Poems: 1948–1984.* New York: Farrar, Straus and Giroux, 1986.

Wald, Priscilla. *Constituting Americans: Cultural Anxiety and Narrative Form.* Durham, NC: Duke University Press, 1995.

Waligora-Davis, Nicole A. "Phantom Limbs." *Mississippi Quarterly* 56.4 (Fall 2003): 657–75.

———. *Sanctuary: African Americans and Empire.* New York: Oxford University Press, 2011.

Walker, Kara. Art21 Exclusive. "A Subtlety, or the Marvelous Sugar Baby." Episode 204. Produced by Ian Forster. Published on Youtube, May 23, 2014. www.youtube.com/watch?v=sRkP5rcXtys.

———. *At the behest of Creative Time Kara E. Walker has confected: A Subtlety, or the Marvelous Sugar Baby, an Homage to the unpaid and overworked Artisans who have refined our Sweet tastes from the cane fields to the Kitchens of the New World on the Occasion of the demolition of the Domino Sugar Refining Plant.* May 10–July 6, 2014. Site-specific public art installation. Polysterene blocks, sugar, molasses, cast resin. Domino Sugar Factory, South 1st Street at Kent Ave., Williamsburg, Brooklyn. May 10–July 6, 2014.

———. *Gone: An Historical Romance of a Civil War as It Occurred b'tween the Dusky Thighs of One Young Negress and Her Heart.* 1994. Paper installation, Overall 13 x 50 ft. Museum of Modern Art, New York City.

———. "Kara Walker Decodes Her New World Sphinx at Domino Sugar Factory." Interview by Antwaun Sargent. *Complex* Magazine, May 13, 2014.

———. "A Sonorous Subtlety: Kara Walker with Kara Rooney." Interview by Kara Rooney. *The Brooklyn Rail,* May 6, 2014.

———. "The whole reason for refining sugar is to make it white." Interview by Paul Laster. *Timeout,* May 6, 2014.

Wall, Cheryl, ed. *Changing Our Own Words: Essays on Criticism, Theory and Writing by Black Women.* New Brunswick, NJ: Rutgers University Press, 1989.

———. "Extending the Line: From *Sula* to *Mama Day.*" *Callaloo* 23.4 (Fall 2000): 1449–63.

Walvin, James. *The Zong: A Massacre, the Law, and the End of Slavery*. New Haven, CT: Yale University Press, 2011.

Weissbrodt, David S., and Clay Collins. "The Human Rights of Stateless Persons." *Human Rights Quarterly* 28.1 (February 2006): 245–76.

White, Hayden V. *Metahistory: The Historical Imagination in Nineteenth-Century Europe*. Baltimore: Johns Hopkins University Press, 1973.

Whitner v. State of South Carolina. 492 S.E.2d 777 (S.C. 1997).

Wideman, John Edgar. *Brothers and Keepers*. New York: Mariner, 2005.

———. *Fanon*. Boston: Houghton Mifflin, 2008.

———. "Interview: John Edgar Wideman." By Caryl Phillips. *Bomb* 49, 1994. bombsite.com/issues/49/articles/1815. Last accessed April 18, 2012.

———. *The Island: Martinique*. Washington, DC: National Geographic, 2003.

———. "Looking at Emmett Till." In *In Fact: The Best of Creative Nonfiction*. Edited by Lee Gutkind. New York: Norton, 2005. 24–48.

———. *Philadelphia Fire*. New York: Mariner, 2005.

———. *Sent for you Yesterday*. New York: Avon Books, 1983.

Wiegman, Robyn. *American Anatomies: Theorizing Race and Gender*. Durham, NC: Duke University Press, 1995.

Williams, Eric. *Capitalism and Slavery*. Chapel Hill: University of North Carolina Press, 1994.

Williams, Patricia J. "Slow Motion." *The Nation*, June 14, 2004. www.thenation.com/article/slow-motion.

Williams, Randall. *The Divided World: Human Rights and Its Violence*. Minneapolis: University of Minnesota Press, 2010.

Wong, Edlie L. *Neither Fugitive nor Free: Atlantic Slavery, Freedom Suits, and the Legal Culture of Travel*. New York: New York University Press, 2009.

Yaeger, Patricia. "Circum-Atlantic Superabundance: Milk as World-Making in Alice Randall and Kara Walker." *American Literature* 78.4 (December 2006): 769–98.

Zamora, Lois Parkinson. *The Usable Past: The Imagination of History in Recent Fiction of the Americas*. New York: Cambridge University Press, 1997.

Index

abolition movements and legislation, 4, 11, 24, 25, 33, 38, 221*n*21
aesthetics of salvage: in Jones's works, 141–82; and legal personhood, 8, 10, 18, 23; in Wideman's works, 183–204
African Burial Ground (New York City), 40, 51, 83–90, 224*n*52
Afro-pessimism, 7, 246*n*4
afterlife of property, 12
Agamben, Giorgio, 27, 28, 29, 30, 31, 41, 142, 147, 166, 228*n*114, 228*n*117
Algeria, 187
alienation, 33, 163, 170–71
American Sugar Refining Company, 92
Amistad slave revolt (1839), 58
Anderson, Benedict, 129
animal rights movement, 21, 216–17
anticolonial narratives, 8, 9, 92–137, 111
antiprostitution campaigns, 19, 23, 97, 123, 124
antiromance, 98, 99
archival absence, 2–3, 6
archival memory: as auditory memory, 146, 157, 171, 175; and the Black Atlantic, 2–7; in relation to law, 173–74
Ardouin, Beaubrun, 240*n*26
Arendt, Hannah, 29, 41, 142, 187, 228*n*109
Aristide, Jean-Bertrand, 102, 105, 241*n*32, 242*n*35
Austin, J. L., 54
Ayala, César J., 239*n*15

Bakhtin, Mikhail, 172
Bales, Kevin, 224*n*52
bare life, 18, 30–31, 142, 147, 210, 224*n*53, 228*n*114
Barthes, Roland, 253*n*85
Batallón de Lucha Irregular (BLI, Nicaragua), 50
bateys, 9, 114
The Battle of Algiers (film), 192
Baucom, Ian, 221*n*16
Bauman, Zygmunt, 16
Bearden, Romare, 186, 197–98, 201
Benito Cereno (Melville), 9, 56, 58, 73
Benjamin, Walter, 228*n*108
Bennett, Herman, 229*n*129
Best, Stephen, 2, 6–7, 220*n*6, 222*n*26
"Beyond Human Rights" (Agamben), 27
Bhabha, Homi, 254*n*10
bildungsroman, 8, 183–204, 208, 257*n*6
biopolitics, 21, 22, 28, 31, 32, 81, 142, 189, 214
The Black Jacobins (James), 106, 129
Blackmon, Douglas A., 230*n*130
Black Skin, White Masks (Fanon), 190, 193, 195, 196, 207
Blockson, Charles L., 167–68, 250*n*64
Bois Caïman ceremony, 100–104, 240*n*26, 242*n*32, 242*n*35, 243*n*48
Boukman, 101, 118, 240*n*24, 241*n*29, 243*n*48
Brady, Mary Pat, 54, 162

Bramen, Carrie Tirado, 165, 248*n*40
Brand, Dionne, 92
Brathwaite, Kamau, 4, 15, 17
Brazil, 14, 40, 144, 147–54
Briggs, Laura, 124
Brown, Danny, 223*n*36
Brown, Sterling, 250*n*61
Brown, Vincent, 229*n*127
Brown, Wendy, 203
Bush, Jonathan A., 64
Butler, Judith, 192–93, 258*n*12

Cahier d'un retour au pays natal (Césaire), 12
Calhoun, Ada, 259*n*26
Cameron, Sharon, 23
Campos, Morel, 135–36
Carder, Angela, 213
Carmichael, Stokely, 187
Case of Mary Clark, A Woman of Color (1821), 61
Castor, Suzy, 244*n*62
Césaire, Aimé, 12
Chamoiseau, Patrick, 13
Chapman, Paul, 237*n*68
Cheah, Pheng, 74
Christianity, 101, 172–73, 241*n*28, 242*n*32
citizenship, 26, 28, 36, 122, 159, 160, 170
civic estrangement, 22, 35
civil death, 35, 63, 142, 224*n*53
Cleaver, Eldridge, 187
Cliff, Michelle, 13, 15–16, 223*n*39, 226*n*90
code-switching, 251*n*66
collage, 189, 196, 197, 198, 201, 202, 204
commodification, 12, 97
common law doctrine, 63–64
Constitution (Haiti), 37, 38, 231*n*147
Constitution (U.S.), 19, 38
Contras (Nicaragua), 52
Convention Relating to the Status of Refugees (UN), 54
Convention Relating to the Status of Stateless Persons (UN), 258*n*12
Cooper, Frederick, 123, 233*n*10
corporate persons, 14–15, 24, 39, 51, 66
corporeality, 66, 148, 152, 212, 216
Corregidora (Jones), 145
counterinsurgency operations, 50
creative *marronage*, 15–16, 41, 144
Creative Time (organization), 94
Crittenden, Ann, 159, 160, 250*n*65
Cuba's sugarcane industry, 93, 95
cultural bilingualism, 152, 157

cultural nationalism, 130, 135
Cunningham, Hilary, 158, 160
Customs and Border Patrol (U.S.), 41

Dalmas, Antoine, 240*n*26
"Damned Love" (Campos), 135–36
Danticat, Edwidge, 9, 40, 92–137, 209
Darbonne Sugar, 244*n*62
Davis, Angela, 153
Davis, Emily S., 240*n*17
Dayan, Colin, 1, 2, 33, 34, 35, 36, 41, 63, 87, 142, 205, 219*n*2, 229*n*129, 230*n*138, 235*n*33, 241*n*31
death-bound paradigms, 25, 26–43, 40, 41, 142, 143, 203, 210
Declaration of Human Rights (UN), 65–66, 194
decolonization, 15–16, 99, 106, 174–75, 177, 182, 204
Delano, Amasa, 58, 73
DeLombard, Jeannine, 9, 57
Deloughrey, Elizabeth, 17, 225*n*69
Denning, Michael, 225*n*73
Derrida, Jacques, 2, 161, 173–74
desaparecidos. See disappeared people
Dessalines, Jean-Jacques, 37, 102, 105, 118, 244*n*68
detritus, 12, 13, 15–18
developmentalism, 193–94
Dinkins, David N., 86, 87
disappeared people (*desaparecidos*), 14, 80, 82, 90
Dominican Republic, 9, 21, 38, 93, 95, 97, 114
Domino Sugar Factory, 92, 93, 238*n*2
Dred Scott v. Sandford (1857), 66, 122
drone killings, 211
drowned captives, 3–4
Dubey, Madhu, 151, 248*n*44
Dubois, Laurent, 116–17
Du Bois, W. E. B., 182, 254*n*7
Dussel, Enrique, 236*n*55
Duvalier, François, 102, 114, 244*n*61
Duvalier, Jean-Claude, 114, 225*n*66

Ejército Zapatista de Liberación Nacional (EZLN), 177. *See also* Zapatista movement
Ellis Island, 40, 51, 86, 87, 238*nn*80–81
El Salvador, 14, 52
Emmett Till Unsolved Civil Rights Crime Act (2007), 256*n*19
Equiano, Olaudah, 221*n*18

Eva's Man (Jones), 145
exceptional personhood, 50, 51, 64, 141
existence, etymology of, 11, 223*n*43
extramarital sex, 120, 125, 126
extraordinary rendition, 210–11, 258*n*12
EZLN (Ejército Zapatista de Liberación
  Nacional), 177. *See also* Zapatista
  movement

Fanon, Frantz, 24, 26, 39, 183–204, 205,
  206–7, 256*n*31, 257*n*2
Fanon (Wideman), 25, 40, 183–204, 217
Farmer, Paul, 242*n*35
feminist responses to romance genre, 9, 99,
  121, 239*n*7
Ferré, Rosario, 9, 40, 92–137, 152
fetal personhood movement, 21, 212–16
Findlay, Eileen J. Suárez, 92, 122–23
Fischer, Sibylle, 18, 37, 103, 106, 217, 219*n*2,
  231*n*142
flag-of-convenience system, 59, 69–71, 72
FLN (National Liberation Front, Algeria),
  187, 194
Flying Africans Myth, 116
Foucault, Michel, 2, 29–30, 31, 41, 67,
  173, 222*n*26, 223*n*43, 226*n*84, 227*n*96,
  253*n*85
foundational fictions, 95, 100
Fourteenth Amendment, 66
Francis, Donette, 98, 99
Franco, Jean, 14
Franklin, H. Bruce, 229*n*130
Frantz Fanon: Black Skin, White Mask
  (film), 187, 254*n*11
Freud, Sigmund, 173
"From *The Quest for Wholeness*: Re-
  Imagining the African American
  Novel" (Jones), 174
Frye, Northrup, 95, 106–7
Fuchs, Barbara, 95
Fugitive Slave Act (1850), 58, 146, 250*n*64
fugitivity, 40, 141–82. *See also* marronage
Fuss, Diana, 195

Ganga-Zumba (military leader), 149,
  247*n*24
García Márquez, Gabriel, 47
Gates, Henry Louis, Jr., 155–56, 187,
  248*n*40, 249*n*45, 252*n*81, 254*n*10
genealogy, 99, 121, 132, 137, 227*n*96,
  232*n*158
General Services Administration (GSA),
  83, 85, 89, 90

Geneva Convention on the High Seas
  (1958), 236*n*57
gentrification, 239*n*3
Gilroy, Paul, 67
Glissant, Édouard, 4, 15, 119, 141, 144,
  222*n*23
globalization, 1, 49, 204, 209, 233*n*10
Global Mariner, 74–75, 76
Godard, Jean-Luc, 217
Golden, Renny, 167
Goldman, Francisco, 13–14, 40, 47–91, 113
*Gone: An Historical Romance of a Civil
  War...*(Walker), 96
Gone With the Wind (Mitchell), 96
Gordon, Avery, 224*n*53, 239*n*6
governmentality, 41
Great Apes Project (GAP), 260*n*35
Gregson v. Gilbert (The *Zong* Case, 1783),
  4, 5, 10
Gruesz, Kirsten Silva, 50
GSA. *See* General Services Administration
Guantánamo detainees, 17, 192–93, 258*n*12
Guatemala, 14, 52
guerrilla personality, 166, 179, 250*n*62
Gutierrez-Jones, Carl, 227*n*90
Guyton, Tyree, 223*n*36

habeas corpus, 192, 234*n*27
Habermas, Jürgen, 172
Haiti: abolition of slavery in, 36–37;
  demonic possession narrative of, 101;
  forced disappearances in, 14; legal
  personhood in, 98; *marronage* in,
  144; nation-building narratives in,
  97; postcolonial history in, 112–15;
  refugees from, 17; revolution in, 58,
  100–101, 104; sugarcane industry in,
  9, 40, 112–15; U.S. occupation and
  peacekeeping missions in, 105, 114;
  zombie figures in, 36, 230*n*138
Haitian American Sugar Company
  (HASCO), 114, 244*n*62
Handley, George P., 99, 240*n*16
Harlan, John Marshall, 61, 63, 64, 234*n*24
Harlow, Barbara, 257*n*7
Hart Island potter's field, 40, 51, 76, 80,
  81, 90
Hart Island Project, 82
Hartman, Saidiya, 1, 2–3, 10–12, 35, 142,
  205, 206, 220*n*7, 220*n*12
Harvey, David, 233*n*8
Havemeyer family, 238*n*2
The Healing (Jones), 145

Hegel, Georg Wilhelm Friedrich, 228*n*100, 243*n*51
Heidelberg Project (Guyton), 223*n*36
Henderson, Mae Gwendolyn, 172
heterotopia, 67
historical error, 222*n*24
Holland, Sharon Patricia, 142
Homo Sacer (Agamben), 30, 147, 229*n*120
Honduras, ship registry system in, 69, 73
humanism, 194
human rights discourse, 170, 185, 211. *See also* international human rights law
human trafficking, 19, 55
Hunt, Melinda, 82, 89, 238*n*84
Hurricane Katrina (2005), 28
Hyde, Alan, 216

imagined community, 129
immigration, 28, 49, 141, 160, 163. *See also* refugees
Immigration and Naturalization Service (INS), 88, 238*nn*80–81
imperialist nostalgia, 48, 50, 232*n*5
impersonality, 23
impressment, 18, 60
imprisonment, 22–23, 33–36, 80–82, 162–63, 188–89
indentured servants, 18, 55, 61, 62
inheritance, 120, 126, 132
institutional sanctuaries, 169
Insular Cases (1901–1905), 122
internally displaced persons, 16–17
international human rights law, 17, 26, 65–66, 185, 208, 255*n*19
International Registries, Inc., 73
International Transport Workers Federation (ITF), 74, 76
Irisarri, Don Pedro, 119
The Island: Martinique (Wideman), 184, 254*n*5
Isnel, Destimare Pierre (Louko), 217–18

Jamaica, *marronage* in, 144
James, C. L. R., 58, 88, 100, 106, 107, 238*nn*80–81
James, Henry, 174
JanMohamed, Abdul, 142
Jeune, Joel, 241*n*32
Jim Crow laws, 192
Johnson, James Weldon, 252*n*78
Johnson, Jennifer, 259*n*18
Johnson-Reed Act (1924), 28
Jones, Gayl, 16, 23, 25, 40, 41, 141–82

Jones Act (1920), 73, 122, 236*n*59
Jorde, Peggy King, 89, 90
Julien, Isaac, 187, 254*n*11
Just Outside the City (Hunt & Lovejoy), 89

Kauanui, J. Kēhaulani, 21
Kelsen, Hans, 226*n*82
Kennedy, Anthony M., 252*n*71
Kent, R. K., 149, 247*n*23
Kimber, John, 220*n*12
Kincaid, Jamaica, 13, 224*n*51
Kristeva, Julia, 253*n*85

Lanzmann, Claude, 255*n*13
Laroche, Maximilien, 102
Latina/o culture, 156
Law of the Sea, 17
legal debris, 8, 18, 20, 26
Legal Information Institute, 234*n*19
legal personhood, 26–43. *See also* personhood
legal precedence, 63
Liberia, ship registry system in, 69–71, 73
Liberian International Ship and Corporate Registry (LISCR), 73
Linebaugh, Peter, 67
living dead, 142. *See also* zombies
Locke, John, 219*n*2
Long, Edward, 219*n*2
Longworth, Bryan, 215–16
"Looking at Emmett Till" (Wideman), 191
Louko (Destimare Pierre Isnel), 217–18
Louverture, Toussaint, 37, 102, 105, 106, 107, 113, 242*n*35
Lovejoy, Margot, 89

Macey, David, 187, 206–7
Madiou, Thomas, 240*n*26
Malavet, Pedro A., 122
"Maldito Amor" ("Damned Love") (Campos), 135–36
Mansfield, Lord, 4–5
marginalized populations, 18
maritime law, 4–6, 234*n*19
Maroon communities, 40, 147–54
marronage, 16, 41, 144, 206
Marshall, John, 224*n*54
Marshall Islands, ship registry system in, 73
Martinique, 144, 183, 186–96, 206, 257*n*2
"Marvelous Sugar Baby" (Walker), 95
Marx, Karl, 225*n*73
masks of personhood, 19–26

Massey, Doreen, 233*n*8
Mbembe, Achille, 6, 31–32, 142, 227*n*100, 246*n*4
McAlister, Elizabeth, 240*n*27, 241*n*30
McCarran-Walter Act (1952), 238*n*80
McConnell, Michael, 167
McDowell, Deborah, 155, 158, 181
McKnight, Regina, 259*n*25
Meillassoux, Claude, 33
Melville, Herman, 9, 56, 57, 68, 234*n*24
memoirs, 188
Merchant Marine Act (1920), 73, 122, 236*n*59
Merchant Marine (U.S.), 73
Metress, Christopher, 191
Military Commissions Act (2006), 192
Mintz, Sidney, 114, 239*n*14
mirror trope, 195–96
Mitchell, Margaret, 96
Modernity Disavowed (Fischer), 231*n*142
Montag, Warren, 32
Moore, Christopher, 90
Moreno, Marisel C., 130, 246*n*88
Morrison, Toni, 24, 223*n*39, 249*n*45
mortuary apartheid, 84
Mosquito (Jones), 16, 25, 40, 41, 141–82
Moten, Fred, 7
mother-daughter relationships, 180
Moynihan Report (1965), 255*n*12
Mullen, Harryette, 175, 252*n*81
Muñoz, Marlise, 213
Myth of the Flying Africans, 116

NAFTA (North American Free Trade Agreement), 177, 253*n*82
narrative failure, 1–13
narthex, 249*n*50
Nascimento, Abdias do, 150
natal alienation, 33
National Advocates for Pregnant Women, 216, 259*n*25
national identity, 26, 33, 128
National Liberation Front (FLN, Algeria), 187, 194
natural persons, 19
necro citizenship, 142
necro-economics, 32, 210
necropolitics, 32, 142, 210
negative personhood, 36, 210
Negroes Burial Ground, 83, 84. *See also* African Burial Ground
neoliberalism, 25, 38–39, 49, 50, 193, 204, 209, 255*n*12

Ngai, Mae, 28
Nicaragua, counterinsurgency in, 50, 52
Nixon, Rob, 17, 223*n*32
nonhuman animal rights movement, 21, 216–17
Nonhuman Rights Project, 211–12, 217, 260*n*37
Noonan, John T., 20, 226*n*77
norms, 11
Northup, Solomon, 147
No Telephone to Heaven (Cliff), 16, 226*n*90
Nwankwo, Ifeoma, 165

O'Brien, John, 250*n*61
Ogé, Vincent, 242*n*38
The Ordinary Seaman (Goldman), 13–14, 40, 47–91, 113
Our Music (film), 217

Palmares, Brazil, 148–54, 247*n*24, 248*n*29
Paltrow, Lynn, 216
Pan-African movement, 150
Panama, 52, 69, 73
paternalism, 159
patriarchy, 97, 131
Patterson, Orlando, 32–33, 142
performative speech, 54
persona, 20, 185
personhood: collage for construction of, 202; exceptional, 50, 51, 64, 141; and fugitivity, 146; legal fiction of, 1–2, 19–21; masks of, 183–204, 196, 197–204; models of, 146, 156; negative, 36, 210; scavenging of, 23
Personhood USA, 212, 215
PETA, 216–17, 260*n*37
Philip, M. NourbeSe, 10
Picture the Homeless (organization), 90
pirates, 9, 57
plantation economy, 15, 37–38, 133
poetics of relation, 4, 15
political refugees, 160. *See also* refugees
political rights, 19, 27, 28–29
Pontecorvo, Gillo, 192
positive law, 20
Priest, Myisha, 191
Prince, Mary, 223*n*39
privatized violence, 192
property rights, 39, 216
prosopopoeia, 185–86, 197–204, 205, 254*n*11
prostitution, 120–21. *See also* antiprostitution campaigns

public sphere, 169–70
Puerto Rico: antiprostitution campaigns in, 97; demographics of, 120; legal personhood in, 26–27, 98, 121–22; nation-building narratives in, 97; slavery in, 245n72; sugarcane industry in, 93, 98, 119–37

racial melancholia, 12, 22
racial vulnerability, 147
recycling, 79
Rediker, Marcus, 60, 67
refugees, 9, 16–17, 19, 27, 28, 54, 151, 160
rehearsal, 98, 102–3, 104, 105, 110, 111–12, 175
Renan, Ernst, 6, 222n24
rendition, 210–11, 258n12
Rice, Condoleezza, 210–11
Riker's Island, 80, 81–82
Riley, Solomon, 81
ritual practice, 175
Robert, Georges, 200
Robertson, Pat, 242n32
Robertson v. Baldwin (1897), 35, 40, 50, 56, 58–61, 62, 64, 113
Rodríguez, Ana Patricia, 50, 236n56
Roe v. Wade (1973), 213, 215
romance genre, 8, 9, 92–137, 107
Rosaldo, Renato, 232n5
Ruffin v. The Commonwealth (1871), 34–35, 230nn133–34

Said, Edward, 254n10
Sailors' Union of the Pacific, 62
Saint Domingue slave revolt (1791), 100–101, 104. See also Haiti
Salgado, Sebastião, 47, 48, 49, 91, 237n70
Salmon, Colin, 187, 255n11
salvage, 9, 13–19. See also aesthetics of salvage
salvage archaeologists, 83, 85
"Salvages" (Brathwaite), 17, 209
salvation, 11
sanctuary, 40, 143, 145, 154–82
Sanctuary movement, 145, 157, 159–61, 165–70, 178
Sandinistas (Nicaragua), 50, 233n12, 234n12
Santa Clara v. Southern Pacific (1886), 24
Schneider, Martin L., 239n2
Scott, David, 17, 103, 104, 106, 132, 243n51
Seamen's Act (1915), 73, 236n59
Sekula, Allan, 74–76, 233n9
semicolonial world, 182

Sexton, Jared, 246n4
sexual agency, 153
sexual citizenship, 98, 124
Sharp, Granville, 5, 221n18
Sharpe, Jenny, 10
Shemak, April, 50, 54, 232n159
Sherman Anti-Trust Act (1890), 239n2
ship-breaking industry, 47
ship registries. See flag-of-convenience system
Slaughter, Joseph R., 19, 65, 170, 203, 208, 254n6, 254n8, 257n6, 257n8
slave codes, 35
slavery: archival violence of, 11–12; in Benito Cereno, 9; and biopolitics, 32; and legal personhood, 2, 7–8; mask of, 24–25; sites of, 6, 13, 22; and slave trade, 3–4; and sugar industry, 97
Slavery and Social Death (Patterson), 32
slow violence, 7, 17
Smith, Adam, 32
Smith, Caleb, 7, 34
social death, 32–33, 142, 229n127
Somerset, James, 260n37
Sommer, Doris, 95, 106, 129, 132
Somoza Debayle, Anastacio, 233n12
Song for Anninho (Jones), 16, 25, 40, 41, 141–82
sovereignty, 11, 26–27, 31, 32, 33, 72
sovereign violence, 41, 142, 203
spatial marginalization, 88
spectral nationality, 74
Spillers, Hortense, 148
Spiral Group, 186, 198
Stallabrass, Julian, 48
Stallman v. Youngquist (1988), 214
stateless persons, 16–17, 141
Statue of Liberty, 86
Steinfeld, Robert J., 61–62, 63–64
Stettinius, Edward, Jr., 70
Stettinius Associates-Liberia, Inc., 73
Stoler, Ann Laura, 7, 8, 99, 123, 222n29
structural violence, 189
subjectivity, 194, 195, 236n55
A Subtlety (Walker), 9, 93–95
sugarcane industry, 9, 92–137
Sundquist, Eric, 57
Supreme Court (U.S.), 26, 56, 59, 122, 213. See also specific cases
Sweet Diamond Dust (Ferré), 98, 99, 106, 119–37, 152

talking book trope, 145

Tate, Greg, 156, 249*n*47
Taylor, Charles, 71
Texas Advance Directives Act, 259*n*19
Thatcher, Margaret, 39
Thiong'o, Ngugi wa, 182
Third World aesthetics, 158, 174
Thirteenth Amendment, 33, 34, 59, 61, 63
threshold paradigm, 30–31, 41–42, 166
Till, Emmett, 40, 191, 192, 255*n*19
Tillet, Salamishah, 6, 22, 96
tragedy narrative, 107, 108–10
Trouble on Board: The Plight of International Seafarers (Chapman), 237*n*68
Trouillot, Michel-Rolph, 103, 104, 220*n*6, 243*n*53, 244*n*61
Tryal slave revolt (1805), 58
Twelve Years a Slave (Northup), 147

unauthorized refugees, 28. *See also* refugees
Underground Railroad, 16, 40, 165, 166, 250*n*64
undocumented migrants, 49, 141, 163
United Fruit Company, 69
United Nations: Convention Relating to the Status of Refugees, 54; Convention Relating to the Status of Stateless Persons, 258*n*12; Declaration of Human Rights, 65–66, 194; High Commission on Refugees, 160
Universal Declaration for Human Rights (UDHR), 19, 254*n*6, 257*n*7

Velho, Domingos Jorge, 150
"Venus in Two Acts" (Hartman), 2, 206
Vergès, Françoise, 195, 196, 254*n*10, 256*n*31

Vicente, Rafael Guillen, 253*n*82
visionary literacy, 177
Vodou, 101–2, 103, 240*n*26, 241*n*28, 241*n*31

Walcott, Derek, 15
Wald, Priscilla, 26, 227*n*97
Waligora-Davis, Nicole, 9, 27, 28, 41, 57, 58, 143, 158, 177, 181, 231*n*140, 234*n*24, 249*n*50
Walker, Alice, 250*n*61
Walker, Kara, 1, 9, 92, 93–96, 103
"A Wall of Fire Rising" (Danticat), 98, 100–119
Walvin, James, 221*n*15
war on drugs, 52
war on terrorism, 25, 192, 210–11
Wealth of Nations (Smith), 32
White, Hayden, 95, 106
Whitner v. South Carolina (1997), 214
Wideman, John Edgar, 13, 23, 25, 40, 43, 183–204, 187, 205, 208, 217
Wilderson, Frank B., III, 246*n*4
Williams, Patricia J., 192, 256*n*21, 256*n*26
Williams, Randall, 185, 254*n*7
Wired magazine, 48–49, 233*n*8
Workers: An Archaeology of the Industrial Age (Salgado), 47, 48, 91
The Wretched of the Earth (Fanon), 187, 189, 194, 199

Zapatista movement, 40, 145, 177–78, 253*n*82
zombies, 36, 230*n*138
Zong (slave ship), 4, 5, 10, 221*n*15. *See also Gregson v. Gilbert*
Zong! (Philip), 10
Zumbi (military leader), 149, 150